UNDERSTANDING COGNITIVE DEVELOPMENT

SAGE
50
YEARS

UNDERSTANDING COGNITIVE DEVELOPMENT

Maggie McGonigle-Chalmers

Los Angeles | London | New Delhi
Singapore | Washington DC

Los Angeles | London | New Delhi
Singapore | Washington DC

SAGE Publications Ltd
1 Oliver's Yard
55 City Road
London EC1Y 1SP

SAGE Publications Inc.
2455 Teller Road
Thousand Oaks, California 91320

SAGE Publications India Pvt Ltd
B 1/I 1 Mohan Cooperative Industrial Area
Mathura Road
New Delhi 110 044

SAGE Publications Asia-Pacific Pte Ltd
3 Church Street
#10-04 Samsung Hub
Singapore 049483

Editor: Luke Block
Assistant editor: Keri Dickens
Production editor: Imogen Roome
Copyeditor: David Hemsley
Indexer: Adam Pozner
Marketing manager: Michael Ainsley
Cover design: Wendy Scott
Typeset by: C&M Digitals (P) Ltd, Chennai, India
Printed and bound in Great Britain by
Ashford Colour Press Ltd, Gosport, Hants

First published 2015

Library of Congress Control Number: 2014946290

British Library Cataloguing in Publication data

A catalogue record for this book is available from the British Library

ISBN 978-1-4129-2880-9
ISBN 978-1-4129-2881-6 (pbk)

For Brendan

CONTENTS

ABOUT THE AUTHOR

Margaret McGonigle (aka Maggie McGonigle and Maggie McGonigle-Chalmers) is a Faculty Fellow at the University of Edinburgh, having retired from her post as Senior Lecturer in the Psychology Department in 2012. She has published research articles and book chapters on comparative and developmental cognition, and more recently on cognitive functioning in children with Autism Spectrum Disorders, ranging from perceptuo-motor skills to language dysfunction. She is co-editor (and author) of *The Complex Mind: An Interdisciplinary Perspective* (Palgrave-Macmillan, 2012). Other publications are listed at http://www.psy.ed.ac.uk/affiliated_faculty/maggie_mcGonigle.php.

PREFACE: HOW TO READ THIS BOOK

This book has been constructed with both student and lecturer in mind. The inset panels provide PowerPoint-type bullet points and contain all the illustrative material, much of which can be cut and pasted into teaching slides. This textbook may therefore correspond in whole or in part to lecture courses. The panel plus text structure of the book means that it can be read at two distinct levels: one at a glossing/revision level; the other providing the linking narrative and the fine details of the cited studies.

Chapter 1 is an important introduction that should help you, the student, understand why there have been several broad theoretical approaches to cognitive development, what their differences are, and how they have influenced the experimental investigations of children's minds. It is important to read this first. Thereafter the textbook focuses on empirical findings from perception in infancy to the thinking and reasoning of children up to about 10 years old.

Each chapter is divided into two or three parts and each part is divided into numbered sections that correspond exactly to the summary panels. For a quick overview of the chapter contents, look at the boxes labelled 'Learning Landmarks' in which these sections are listed and where a brief description is provided for each one. These are included as a guide to the chapter contents but also as a summary of the key revision points that may be needed for an exam or essay. A comprehensive list of all the studies cited is provided in the References at the end of the book. Important keywords are highlighted in bold in the text and in italics in the panels.

You will sometimes find links in the panels to videos on the Web that give very good examples of some of the behaviours listed. A full index of these is given on page xiv. These are usually on YouTube, courtesy of devoted parents and their obliging children!

Powerpoint slides of the panels in the book can be found on the companion website at study.sagepub.com/mcgoniglechalmers

Maggie McGonigle-Chalmers
July, 2014

ACKNOWLEDGEMENTS

I would sincerely like to thank the following people in connection with the preparation of this book. Acknowledgements are due to Louisa Miller for line drawings, and to Shutterstock for the many of the cartoon and photographic images, which are listed separately on pages xi to xiii. Other photographs were obtained with the help and support of UniTots nursery at Edinburgh University, Dalkeith Road and Little Monkeys Day Nurseries in Edinburgh, as well as Little Treasures Nursery in Jedburgh. Thanks are due also to Alexia Sawyer for some of the videotaping of nursery children. I would also like to thank Mette Svennevig for agreeing to appear in the 'Thatcher Illusion' and Elsie Steele (1 year old) for appearing as herself.

Many of the authors who gave permission for me to depict their studies also offered invaluable corrective and editorial advice and I thank them all. I would also like to offer sincere thanks for the sustained help, support and endless patience of Edinburgh (IT) University User Support group; in particular Toby Morris and Crystal Webster. Sincere thanks are also due to Edinburgh (Philosophy and Psychology) University librarian, Karen Fleet for her generous help throughout. I would also like to express gratitude to Apple Inc. for their excellent user support services and to Thomson Reuters for their prompt help with EndNote Bibliographic software.

I would very much like to thank all my family and friends for their unwavering trust that the book would be finished 'someday'. Finally I have to thank two Irish Water Spaniels – Fergal and Woodruff – for reasons I don't need to explain.

IMAGES FROM SHUTTERSTOCK, INC.

Chapter 2

Panel number	**Image**	**Creator**
2.1	Foot-fanning in newborn	Juriah Mosin
2.4	Imaging	Alex Kh

Chapter 3

Panel number	**Image**	**Creator**
3.1	Infant head turn	Artpose/Adam Borkowski
3.3	Bell	Christos Georghiou
	Drum	Sashkin
3.6	Penguin	schmaelterphoto
	Rabbit	staras

Chapter 5

Panel number	**Image**	**Creator**
5.3	Tongue protrusion	Samuel Borges Photography
	Strongarm men	lineartestpilot
5.6	Crying newborn	MitarArt
	Talking boy	Hannamariah
5.7	Mother and baby	MJTH

Chapter 6

Panel number	**Image**	**Creator**
6.3	Mother and baby	leolintang
6.4	Mother talking to baby	Tom Wang
6.6	Mother reading book to baby	Oksana Kuzmina
6.7	Boy with fish	Photo Africa

Chapter 7

Panel number	**Image**	**Creator**
7.1	Mother pointing to picture	Monkey Business Images
7.3	Cartoon dolls	alexokokok
7.5	Boy with spinning top	StockLite
7.7	Pointing boy	Velazquez77

Chapter 8

Panel number	Image	Creator
8.4	Baseball man	R. Gino Santa Maria

Chapter 9

Panel number	Image	Creator
9.7	Bozo the clown	OneSmallSquare
	Donald Duck	PAISAN HOMHUAN

Chapter 10

Panel number	Image	Creator
10.3	Face profile	Lo-Random
10.5	Traffic	Brian A Jackson

Chapter 13

Panel number	Image	Creator
13.1	Marmoset	Karel Gallas
	Owl	Bildagentur Zoonar GmbH
	Monkey	Kjersti Joergensen
	Nest	Oldrich
	Orangutan	Kitch Bain
13.5	Soap	oksana2010
	Dispenser	Denis Semenchenko
	Towels	33333

Chapter 14

Panel number	Image	Creator
14.4	Cartoon girls	olillia
14.8	Mouse	Budi Susanto
	Santa	Sebastian Kaulitzki
	Soldier	TroyDesign

Chapter 15

Panel number	Image	Creator
15.1	Chocolate bar	Mike Elliott
	Cartoon boy	Matthew Cole
	Cartoon woman	Technomatix
	Smarties	Jon Le-Bon
	Furniture	Matthew Cole
15.5	House	mayamaya
	Church	artshock
	Fountain	artshock
	Boy with ice cream	OkPic
	Running girl	xtt008
	Ice cream van	koya979
15.8	Boy and girl	Klara Viskova

Chapter 16

Panel number	**Image**	**Creator**
16.3	Boy with crutches	Sarawut Padungkwan
	Shelves	3drenderings
	Cartoon girl	Matthew Cole
16.4	Genie	Klara Viskova
	Rolled carpet	lineartestpilot

INDEX OF VIDEO CLIPS

Chapter 2
Panel 2.1
www.youtube.com/watch?v=PTz-iVI2mf4&feature=related
www.youtube.com/watch?v=S0dfbyyVSRU&feature=related
www.youtube.com/watch?v=xneStHZ0Kho&NR=1
www.youtube.com/watch?v=CkGjOwPXsvo

Chapter 5
Panel 5.6
www.youtube.com/watch?v=kVubueQpgAM
www.youtube.com/watch?v=WCJj-E-8e3E
Panel 5.7
www.youtube.com/watch?v=RSrEgP7hMW0
Panel 5.8
www.youtube.com/user/cindyhilger

Chapter 6
McGurk effect
www.youtube.com/watch?v=G-lN8vWm3m0).
www.youtube.com/watch?v=aFPtc8BVdJk
Panel 6.5
www.youtube.com/watch?v=PI42LSbwc8E&feature=related
Panel 6.7
www.youtube.com/watch?v=PI42LSbwc8E&feature=related
Panel 6.9
www.youtube.com/watch?v=9D7jcHex_jQ

CHAPTER 1

INTRODUCTION: STUDYING HOW THE MIND GROWS

It is often said that the human brain is the most complex object in the universe. This refers to the billions of neural connections and their extraordinary organisational structure. But what gives us even more pause for thought is what seems to be contained within that relatively small organ. For not only does it enable superb feats of motor dexterity and incredible adaptations to the demands of a challenging physical world, it *contains* that world in the form of conscious knowledge. If we include that which we have accumulated through scientific advance, it is not an exaggeration to say that in this tiny little speck of cosmic matter, we have in effect internalised the cosmos itself – to its furthest known reaches in space and time.

This is because we have minds, not just brains. We have the ability to represent the space in which we live: to perceive, predict, remember, talk and reason about it. This book concerns the first decade of life, at the end of which all of these abilities will be approaching adult levels. To follow the journey the child takes from helpless infancy to mastery of its own particular universe, we will be considering the main driving forces of this growth and how they interact. We will start with elementary perceptual and motor abilities and how these combine to give the child increasing control over its personal and interpersonal space. We will trace the way in which a natural desire to interact, share and communicate with others becomes grafted onto the tools for making this possible – speech and language. Perception, memory and language all grow and combine to let the child make predictions about time, space, objects and people, eventually leading to logical reasoning and the ability to think beyond the self and into a more objective reality.

How do we know all this? As you may be aware, there have been various theories of cognitive development, each leaving its mark in terms of experimental discoveries and its methods of investigation. The methodologies you will encounter in this book range from simply charting the natural patterns of skill acquisition to more contrived experimental situations aimed at narrowing down the important factors involved in acquiring a particular ability. You will also sometimes come across attempts to specifically train children on certain skills. This book tells the narrative of what has been uncovered about the growing mind of the child – whatever the methods and general approach motivating the discoveries. You will see that, despite the many and sometimes disparate theoretical leanings behind all this research, a remarkable cohesion emerges as the story progresses. In some ways to understand cognitive development you simply have to know and consider what develops, when and how. It tells its own story.

Before we start, however, it is important for you, the student, to be aware of some of the broader 'theories' of development, to know at least a little about those who have tried to impose an over-arching theory on the development of cognition, and the methodologies that emerged from them. In this brief introduction, we will consider some of these.

PIAGET: HIS IMPORTANCE AND HIS CRITICS

You may have heard of Piaget, the Swiss psychologist and philosopher (1896–1980), and may even be familiar with his phases and stages of development, but do you know why he has been such a hugely influential figure in psychology? You could refer to his prolific output in terms of detailed research monographs covering topics ranging from children's understanding of time and space (Piaget & Inhelder, 1967; Piaget, 1969) to their comprehension of the nature of life (Piaget, 1973). But the main reason Piaget was so exceptional is because of the *question he asked*, which was 'where does knowledge come from?' By this he did not usually mean knowledge gained directly through our senses or passed on by repute (such as 'Italy is a country in the Mediterranean'). He centrally and enduringly wanted to know about the kind of knowledge we would call logical or mathematical. For example, how do we come to know that it is necessarily true that if $A = B$ and $B = C$ that $A = C$, or that $2 + 2 = 4$ necessarily implies its inverse: $4 - 2 = 2$? Of course it is true that logical and mathematical truths have been 'discovered' by logicians, and mathematicians such as Plato, Aristotle and Euclid. But many philosophers, even today, would consider these as truths that somehow exist independently of us and 'in the world'. Piaget's audacious idea was that they are constructs of the human mind.

This is why Piaget turned his attention to child development. Aware that mathematics and logic are constantly evolving disciplines, he believed that each new discovery or system of logic is the product of a private intellectual achievement that we are all capable of. So if logic is not a 'given', how are we to discover how it is 'constructed' from personal experience? This is what Piaget says:

> In contemporary man, an enormous number of structures have already been formed, and we don't know their history. It's a concept that has been collectively elaborated over an enormous number of generations. You don't grasp the mode of construction in these cases, you get the products. Products aren't enough for me! Thus reconstructing history – it can be done as far back as the Greeks, but even then ... *What is wonderful about the child is that you have an individual starting from scratch, and you can see how all this occurs.* (Bringuier, 1980: 20)

This quotation tells you why Piaget studied children. It is also why his approach is called **genetic epistemology** (the growth of knowledge). Also notice the word 'structures'. If you have studied Philosophy, you will know that **Structuralism** was a general theoretical movement that influenced many disciplines from Linguistics to Sociology. In line with this movement, Piaget thought of the mind as the instrument by which logical structure is created. Influenced by contemporary French and Swiss mathematicians, he conceptualised logic in terms of a connected system of **operations.** These were called the INRC group, meaning Identity, Negation, Reciprocity and Correlation. You can think of three of these as ways of making a simple logical change (Identity means no change). Let's take Negation; an example would be converting +3 to –3, and what was important for Piaget is that this operation is reversible such that by negating –3 you get back to +3. An example of a reciprocal operation would be to turn the proposition A is bigger than B (A > B), into B is smaller than A (B < A) – another reversible operation. Correlation refers to using negation and reciprocity together, so here we might say when A > B is negated into A < B, then by correlation B > A. The main idea to get from this is the fact that the operations work as a system or a structure.

A biologist by training, Piaget's second adventurous idea was that there is a kind of 'biology of knowledge' (Piaget, 1971) in which logical structures represent a way of keeping the psychological world in a balanced state or **equilibrium** in much the same way that hunger, thirst and thermo-regulation operate. Piaget thus adopted words that normally apply to biological functioning like **assimilation** (similar to e.g. eating) and **accommodation** (this might be adjusting the muscles in relation to external pressure). By a constant cycle of feedback from taking in and adapting to the external world, Piaget thought the child would learn to predict it in ways that are evident in **action schemas** (or sometimes, **schemata**). These are repeatable stable behaviours that work for the time being, until the child's system is ready and open to take in a bit more information – to reach a new structural level if you like. A simple example is a baby throwing its toy over the edge of the pram repeatedly, and then suddenly elaborating this schema to now include the behaviour of visually tracking its disappearance by looking over the edge. This is the beginning of what is known as the **object concept** and we will be picking up on this in Chapter 4. The gradual expansion of these behavioural schemas is what is known as the **Sensorimotor Phase** of development that Piaget thought to last until about 18 months. If you now put this idea together with the structural one, you may understand why so many of Piaget's tasks were about the transformational structure of physical situations.

Piaget's third big audacious idea is perhaps the hardest to grasp, but it is the key to why he famously argued that development should be divided into four main phases. He believed that these sensorimotor adaptations to the physical world are actually an expression of the logical operations mentioned above. Operations, in other words, start out as the transformations that are carried out at the level of actual behaviour. These can produce reversible consequences like moving an object from place A to B and back again. He believed that the origin of logic is actually *in* the actions carried out on the world. Thus at the very heart of Piaget's theory is the idea that mental development is due to the **interiorisation of action**. Thus, his proposed second main developmental phase – **Pre-operational** – refers to the fact that, with the growth of symbolisation, such as play and imitation, and through their language, children become able to mentally represent these transformations. However, he argued that the pre-operational phase (as its name implies) is characterised by children's thoughts failing to achieve the mental equilibrium that is the hallmark of a true operational structure. They can, in other words, internalise and represent certain transformations but not their logical interconnections. This is perhaps most famously illustrated by his **conservation tasks**, such as the conservation of liquid and numeric amounts as depicted in Panel 1.1. Young children cannot represent the reversibility in these physical transformations of state as illustrated by the two four year olds here. Piaget used a method of detailed verbal questioning with children to try to understand their mental processes during the gradual emergence of operational thought. When they *start* to think in terms of logical structures (the **Concrete Operational Phase**) their answers show that they can now grasp that the relations 'taller than' and 'wider than' must be correlated – an increase in width is compensated for by a decrease in height, and vice versa – and they will refer to this in some way when justifying their answers. How does this new insight come about? According to Piaget, it is through specific concrete experiences with physical changes such as these that children learn the elements of logical rules, and how to co-ordinate them within a system. The start of the **Formal Operational Phase** marks the point when these rules are themselves represented. So from around the age of 11 or so, the child can now (he argued) represent an in-principle logical relationship in the absence of a concrete example, such as 'A is bigger than B: B is bigger than C; therefore A is bigger than C'. One of the operations involved here is the transformation of 'A is bigger than B' to 'B is smaller than A', allowing the formation of the logical series A > B > C, where B is the middle term, and the conclusion that A must be bigger than C. This is called a **hypothetico-deductive** inference and we shall be returning to it in Chapter 16.

If you are interested in following Piaget's ideas further, you should try to read the work by the man himself (in translation). One short and relatively easy summary of his position is his book *The Child and Reality* (Piaget, 1972).

So why is Piagetian theory now part of psychology's history rather than its present? Why do we not still talk about operations and INRC groups and so on? The fundamental reason was that the logical model was too restricted and too rigid to have general applicability. It curiously both under-estimated children's logical abilities as well as overestimating them. As for the first, the **Neo-Piagetian** approach refers to research by the many independent developmentalists who studied Piaget's tasks (including conservation) and found that children could solve them earlier than Piaget claimed. This was, however, only if certain changes were made. These drew attention, for example, to the salient bits of the task (McGarrigle & Donaldson, 1974), changing the wording to reduce confusion (Rose & Blank, 1974), or to make the point of the task more obvious (McGarrigle et al., 1978). Sometimes simple training was used to achieve improved performance (e.g. Pasnak et al., 1987). These were all important bits of research – maybe less because of the (sometimes a bit repetitive) claim that Piaget had got the 'age' of reasoning wrong, but rather because they drew attention to the fact that logic is not grasped as a totality, but is gradual and piecemeal and very dependent on numerous psychological factors.

Panel 1.1 The influence of Jean Piaget (1896–1980)

The profound and provocative theory of the Swiss developmental psychologist, Jean Piaget, was based on a search for the origins and growth of logical thought. His massive output covered sensorimotor development in infancy through to adolescent reasoning skills. Believing logical thought to derive from the gradual internalisation and mental co-ordination of actions performed in the real world, Piaget's task typically involved physical transformations in space.

For example, his very famous conservation tasks demonstrated that young children may understand physical relationships without being able to connect them within a logical system. Pre-operational children (below the age of around 6 years old) would typically fail to co-ordinate the width of a vessel with its height or the spacing (density) of a row of counters with its extent. They would therefore not understand that transforming two visually identical amounts by pouring liquid from a small wide glass into a taller, narrower glass, or by spreading out one of two rows of counters does not affect their equivalence (see figure below). One of the most famous 'wrong' answers in developmental psychology is 'this one has more'.

Four year olds performing conservation tasks

Piaget's tasks have been successfully replicated over subsequent decades but his findings have been considerably re-interpreted in the light of changes to the tasks and new approaches that do not view cognitive development within the very restricted context of logical thought.

Piaget was nevertheless regarded as one of the great thinkers of the twentieth century and he remains, to this day, the greatest influence on how to study the growth of mind.

In fact, as researchers became progressively detached from trying either confirm or disconfirm Piaget's claims, an alternative picture of logical development started to emerge. This essentially showed that the psychological factors such as language understanding, memory and world knowledge are the very basis on which reasoning and inference grow and this remains true into adulthood. Psychological research was increasingly indicating that Piaget's emphasis on logical structure did not really capture the essence of human cognitive development. We shall be considering examples of these more psychological interpretations of children's reasoning in Chapters 13, 14 and 15. In short, Piaget's logicomathematical model failed to be applicable to everyday reasoning skills, because cognitive development is not centrally about the grasp of logical structure. However, children do become capable of relatively abstract reasoning as we shall see in the final chapter. Likewise mathematics does of course feature as part of the child's learning. In the last chapter we shall consider the cognitive demands this makes on children as they start to reconcile their 'natural' modes of thinking with the more formal structural properties of the number system that most children will acquire at school.

NEO-NATIVISM

One of the more dramatic reactions to Piaget was with regard to his account of the slow emergence of skills during the sensorimotor phase, and his argument that this complex cycle of schema development arose very gradually from a few simple reflexes. He strongly believed in biological maturation as well as the role of practical experience, but his position (called **interactionist** or **constructivist**) was based neither on pure learning nor genetic pre-programming. Given the rise in interest in genetics during the 1970s, there was a something of an outcry that Piaget accorded the infant with so little by the way of ready-made skills. Equipped with new methodologies, the **neo-nativists** were researchers that re-considered and re-investigated very early infancy. Amongst these were Tom Bower at Edinburgh University, Liz Spelke at Harvard and Renee Baillargeon at the University of Illinois. In the main, this movement resulted in rather strong claims about the capabilities of very young babies that have been somewhat modified since by improved knowledge of what the infant brain is (and isn't) capable of. This wave of research has nevertheless introduced a vast new body of work on early perceptual sills, and we will be reviewing what has been learned from it in Chapters 2 to 4.

Strong claims about 'innateness' are also associated with very pronounced and somewhat controversial views on the nature of human language, spawned by the work of linguist Noam Chomsky, in his ground-breaking book *Syntactic Structures* (1957), arguing for the innateness and thus universality of grammar. This was not based on a criticism of Piaget, but rather the Behaviourist movement with its focus on learning from experience, but it helped to bolster the general nativist trend. It also served as a reminder that Piaget had been rather quiet on the important subject of language acquisition and communication. What we know now about this topic – partly as a result of the 'Chomsky' debate – has more than made up for Piaget's shortcomings and we shall be covering this topic in Chapters 5 to 9.

DOMAIN-SPECIFICITY AND R-R THEORY

Another overt criticism of Piaget was with regard to his one-size-fits-all concept of operationality, which became known as a **domain-general** approach. Around the time that the famous cognitive psychologist and linguist, Jerry Fodor, published a book describing the mind as made up of 'modules' each designed to carry out its own special function (Fodor, 1983), similar arguments were applied to developmental psychology (see Hirschfeld & Gelman, 1994 for a review). Annette Karmiloff-Smith, amongst others, promoted a new approach emphasising the **domain-specific** ways in which perceptual, linguistic, numerical and other skills emerge, but each from their own different innate blueprints and therefore not necessarily all at the same rate (Karmiloff-Smith, 1992). In this way, she was able to endorse a nativist approach whilst also maintaining Piaget's constructivist ideas about how knowledge grows within those domains. Her resolution of the Piagetian domain-generality problem was therefore to posit a common mechanism that could drive cognitive change but in different ways depending on the domain. This she called **representational redescription** (R-R). This resonated with other theories of cognitive development drawing specific attention to increasing levels of conscious awareness and 'abstraction' of knowledge as children get older (e.g. Werner, 1948; Kendler, 1995). Karmiloff-Smith specifically proposed that 'implicit' knowledge during early development becomes accessible in increasingly explicit formats.

Here is an example. As you will learn in Chapter 7, children learn very early that the little word 'a' (the indefinite article) performs a different function from the word 'the' in which one and only one of a set of things is being identified. However, in French the indefinite article ('une') can also refer to 'one'. Karmiloff-Smith (1979) identified a backwards progression in French-speaking children where they started to use the French version of 'une' as if it meant one and only object rather than one of many and she argued that the understanding that the article can perform two different functions – une meaning 'one' and une meaning 'a' – was becoming *explicit* knowledge in the child's mind and interfering with what they carried out at an *implicit* level earlier. Karmiloff-Smith (1992) gives other examples from different domains of knowledge such as physics, mathematics and so on, and R-R theory has continued to be successfully applied to accounts of spelling, grammar and drawing, amongst other things (Cheung & Wong, 2011; Critten et al., 2013). It has even been found useful in considering the nature of consciousness itself (Timmermans et al., 2010).

However, there is still some debate as to how implicit knowledge becomes 'accessible' (Lin & Zhou, 2005) and indeed there are cogent arguments that some highly explicit understanding underwriting skills such as driving a car, actually become automatic with practice and much *less* accessible to conscious awareness (Shiffrin & Schneider, 1977). This argument has even been applied to the early development of infants in terms of how they quickly learn to negotiate movements in physical space (Diamond, 2006).

But whilst a great deal of cognition either becomes or remains inaccessible to conscious awareness, it does seem to be conscious explicit knowledge that is subject to most developmental change after infancy and it therefore represents a large part of the content of this book. We shall be returning to the implicit/explicit distinction in Chapter 11.

SOCIO-CULTURALISM

An entirely different reaction to Piaget's views came from the observation that he paid very little attention to the influence of adult culture on the child's development. This does not mean he was insensitive to its importance or to the effects of cultural variation across different countries and even across different historical epochs – he often noted that formal structures are 'linked' to their cultural evolution. But Piaget's account is essentially about the universal child interacting alone and 'privately' with his or her physical environment. An extraordinary antidote to this rather skewed view came from the work of Soviet psychologist, Lev Semenovich Vygotsky (1896–1934). Born in the same year as Piaget, Vygotsky only carried out about 10 years of research with children until his early death. So why the massive impact of this still very famous and much-cited psychologist? In fact, the impact wasn't felt in the West until the mid 1960s after the publication of a translation of collected works by Vygostky (Vygotsky, 1962) and promoted strongly by a very influential and articulate American psychologist called Jerome Bruner. Vygotsky's views supported the Marxist–Leninist position predominant in the Soviet Union at his time of writing, which emphasised the role of society in shaping individual behaviour through language in particular. So, for example, mental concepts, such as 'flower' or 'dog' were thought to be acquired by a process of shaping whereby the language of the adult gradually 'guides' the child towards the precise attributes that belong exclusively to that class. This process of social tuition through language was argued by Vygotsky to produce an internalisation of language into something he called **inner speech**, which starts to have an enabling role in thinking and problem solving. Although there was a famous disagreement between Piaget and Vygotsky over this (by letter – they never met), they ended up with a reconciliation and high mutual regard. We will be considering the development of classification in Chapter 13 and you will see how both Piaget and Vygotsky were indeed both correct – it is the external forces of language and adult tuition working alongside some universal cognitive constraints on understanding that let the child acquire 'adult-like' concepts. Vygotsky's emphasis on the role of adult culture on the child's development did much to redress the balance towards considering the social and linguistic factors involved in cognitive development, and it is not surprising that Vygotsky had, and continues to have, a major impact on educational theory. The role of inner speech, or talking to oneself, has always been notoriously difficult to measure, but has again become a topic of considerable interest since the development of brain imaging technology opened up new possibilities of determining more precisely how it may be related to other cognitive processes (see Alderson-Day & Fernyhough, 2015, for a review).

INFORMATION PROCESSING APPROACHES

When trying to understand cognitive development, it is important to distinguish between characterising how it progresses and accounts trying to explain *why* it progresses. For Piaget, the main causal driving force is a kind of adaptation similar to the environmental adaptations that cause new species to emerge through evolution. The maturing brain, he argued, is itself affected by these adaptations (an idea very much in line with contemporary views of brain development). And all accounts that put some emphasis on learning through experience (such as the R-R theory) are similar in that regard. Some, however, place a greater emphasis on biological maturation as a cause in itself, and for them cognitive growth might seem to progress almost autonomously because of an increase in brain power – rather like having your computer regularly upgraded for a more powerful one. Explanations of cognitive development using this computing metaphor often go under the name of **information processing** theories. These have been used to explain developmental changes on problem-solving tasks, including Piagetian ones, as well as on standard memory tasks. These approaches are particularly associated with researchers (based in Canada, the USA and Australia) such as Juan Pascual-Leone, Robbie Case and Graeme Halford. As the name implies, the emphasis is on how much information a child at a given age can process, and it draws on concepts deriving from classical memory research, such as short- and long-term memory, storage capacity, speed of processing and attentional mechanisms. By measuring such things during cognitive tasks, this type of approach has yielded valuable information on how speed and efficiency of processing information increases with age (Kail, 1991). However, memory 'processes' are not independent of familiarity and knowledge of the material to be remembered (Chi, 1978), and, as you will see, there is only limited predictability of developmental change arising from pure processing concepts alone. The content of a child's knowledge (and the basis for their reasoning) is founded primarily on things like the 'who', 'what', 'where' and 'when' of people, objects and events in their lives, and we shall be considering memory process in specific relation to these things in Chapters 10, 11 and 12.

The computer metaphor is not just about memory and speed; it is also about how information is used, and progress in artificial intelligence during the 1970s saw a burgeoning number of computer simulations of human problem solving that were sometimes applied to the solving of classic Piagetian tasks (Halford, 1993). A particularly pertinent approach was called Production Systems as it described rules that could be modified in line with changes of state brought about by a given action (Young, 1976). These early and perhaps rather brittle metaphors gradually gave way to more 'probabilistic' explanations of problem solving based on something more like the human mind. These were the **neural net**, or **connectionist** models, which could take account of the fact that mental processing can have many elements working in parallel. As models of learning mechanisms, they remain a valuable adjunct to empirical research in developmental psychology (Yermolayeva & Rakison, 2014).

EXECUTIVE FUNCTIONING

The recognition that there are many 'domains' of cognitive development is very much in tune with our rapidly advancing knowledge of brain function, which increasingly points both to the *multiplicity* of brain mechanisms and their complex functional *interconnectivity*. Although understanding the workings of the brain is still regarded as science's greatest challenge, the evidence from children's development is increasingly interpretable in these terms, and many contemporary explanations of developmental change make a direct appeal to neuroanatomical development. A central concept in this is **executive functioning** (EF). This is a powerful concept, with widespread applicability to cognitive development, and we shall be returning to it frequently throughout the book. It has a very sound grounding in our understanding of a part of the brain called the **prefrontal cortex** and deals with the neural pathways that connect sensory information with other parts of the brain, including those involved in memory, decision-making and the planning of action. The prefrontal cortex is likened to a command centre that is involved in co-ordinating these connections. EF links behaviour with the brain by encapsulating the complex interplay between information gained through the senses, memory and attentional mechanisms in order to explain how plans are formulated and behavioural goals are achieved, and even what kind of mental processing is involved. A key element in EF is the ability to flexibly adjust to changes in the environment, affording greater individual control at the level of both thought and action. Whilst the EF approach points up the massive interconnectivity across domains of cognition, psychology's history – its own 'narrative' – has been very much concerned with the isolation of different aspects of cognition, such as perception, action, memory, language, thinking and reasoning, and so this book, like most, will chart the story of development in these terms, as the chapter titles make evident. But as the structure of the book also reflects, the interdependence of cognitive skills is a cumulative process; reasoning is based on what the child knows, and this on what is remembered, what is remembered on what has been encoded perceptually, and what is encoded perceptually on how the child moves and behaves in the world.

This brings us, at the end of this short introduction, to the most salient fact about understanding cognitive development: it is not about how 'the' mind grows by itself, it is about how the mind in a body grows in a world. Where Piaget was perhaps at his most prescient was in trying to understand cognitive development from the viewpoint of the child in a world with which he or she interacts both mentally and physically. So we shall now accompany the child, mind and body, on its voyage of discovery, starting with its first few minutes of life.

CHAPTER 2

SENSORY DEVELOPMENT AND VISUAL PERCEPTION DURING EARLY INFANCY

What does a newborn infant need to know about the world into which it has entered? It will need to understand the new space in which it finds itself and know where and how to find sustenance and warmth. The infant will also need to quickly learn that the world is an airy three-dimensional space occupied by hard objects. From its very first cry, the newborn – or **neonate** – will itself be the source of new happenings in its world, from the sounds it makes to visual transformations caused by movement of its own head and body. Move your head around and consider the changes in visual information that produces. Bang your arm against a table and contemplate that feeling. The reason you are not disturbed by queasy changes in visual information when you move, and why you don't normally hurt yourself by bumping into objects, is that you have strong sense of **agency**. Your body and brain can interpret the difference between yourself acting on the world and the world acting on you. This lets you safely navigate the landscape beyond your body, providing a sense of being 'you' within that landscape. In this chapter we will explore that growing awareness from simple reflexes through to knowledge and awareness of people and things.

FROM REFLEXES TO LEARNED VOLUNTARY BEHAVIOURS

LEARNING LANDMARKS

2.1 Reflexes. By the end of this section, you should be able to name and describe some of the simple reflexes made by very young infants.

2.2 Voluntary movements and instrumental learning. You should know the difference between reflexive behaviour and voluntary behaviour. You should understand what instrumental conditioning is and be able to cite an example of its use with babies.

2.3 Primitive discoveries about space. You should know what motion parallax is and understand why it is important in depth perception. You should be able to describe at least one study demonstrating depth perception in very young infants.

2.1 REFLEXES

An elementary requirement for the newborn is to be able to distinguish self-produced sensory effects from those that are externally produced, such as the visual changes caused by being passively carried and lifted. How, when and to what extent do babies make these distinctions, and how, what and when do they learn from them?

One built-in opportunity to learn about the self in relation to the impinging world is through the **reflex**. It has long been observed that very young infants are already prepared to respond to various sorts of stimulation with no apparent learning. Charles Darwin listed 'sneezing, hickuping, yawning, stretching and of course sucking and screaming' by his own son within the first seven days of life (Wallace et al., 1994). The essence of a simple reflex is that it is not under voluntary control, and Darwin notes the typical characteristics of the jerk reflex when 'on the seventh day, I touched the naked sole of his foot with a bit of paper and he jerked it away, curling at the same time his toes, like a much older child when tickled'. What purpose do such reflexes serve? Clearly when the child has minimal voluntary control, reflexes can protect from possible sources of pain, and they also provide a repertoire of adaptive motor responses to help the child connect with its mother and the world. Some of these are listed in Panel 2.1.

Most reflexes persist only for the first 4 or 5 months of life; absence or unusual prolongation can denote neurological abnormalities. Reflexes are not learned in the course of the individual's life, rather they have evolved for adaptive reasons and are thus often described as **hard-wired**. Certainly, many reflexes can be found in a primitive form before birth, such as the rooting reflex, which has been found in 8-week-old foetuses. Some reflexes such as the blink reflex remain throughout life.

Reflexes come 'ready-made' and don't need any sense of agency on the part of the baby. But although reflexes are not themselves learned, they can create opportunities for learning and a platform for how to separate self from world. These behaviours may give the child a primary source of **contingency** between what it does to the world and how the world responds back. Similarly, when a baby makes an involuntary movement such as extending or flexing a limb, it is likely to discover something new, e.g. that the wall is hard, or, when turning towards a source of stimulation, that a sound gets louder or a light gets brighter. Neither 'hard-wired' nor intentional in the first instance, this set of involuntary behaviours is very important as it puts the infant in the position of being able to adjust or change the

Panel 2.1 Reflexes

- Reflexes are involuntary actions with head and limbs provoked by certain types of stimulation that typically occur only in the first few months of life
- Some well-known reflexes and what provokes them:
  - Babinski reflex – a toe fanning response to foot stroking
  - Blinking at a sudden sight or sound
  - Moro reflex – an extending of arms and legs when (apparently) falling backward
  - Palmar grasp reflex – birth to 5 months – curling and clinging with fingers
  - Rooting – a feeding reaction of turning head towards a stimulus placed near the mouth
  - Stepping reflex – a walking type reaction seen in neonates
  - Sucking when an object is placed in the mouth
  - Tonic neck reflex – when the head is turned to one side, the arm and leg on that side will extend, whilst the other arm and leg flex
- Reflexes probably have an adaptive evolutionary purpose and, like involuntary behaviours, are an important platform for making discoveries about the world

motor response to make it better tuned to the environment. Some psychologists, including Piaget, have argued that even simple reflexes evolve into more voluntary exploratory behaviour through elementary learning. And whether through a new learning mechanism, or through a maturation of the involuntary system itself, it is certainly the case that changes occur in the complexity of the motor reactive system that in turn help to make the contact between child and world a more sustained and more coherent experience. By 7 or 8 weeks, infants will respond to the sound of their mother's voice not just by reflexive head turning but by looking at her eyes, and by 10/11 weeks will co-ordinate the actions of looking at her face, listening and smiling at her (Dawson & Fischer, 1994). These developments remind us of something very important: for contingencies to be used to control behaviour, there must be a motive to learn. The appearance of smiling and even laughter in very early infancy tells us that babies find their new world to be an endless source of interest and fun. So when can we say that babies acquire *voluntary* behaviours because they have learned that they are rewarding? We review this next.

2.2 VOLUNTARY MOVEMENTS AND INSTRUMENTAL LEARNING

Some very early voluntary movements of infants seem to have an adaptive purpose, as they appear to be selectively tuned to the sorts of stimulation that are either important for survival or particularly relevant to human development. For example, newborns are more likely to orient towards the sound of a rattle than a pure tone (Clarkson & Clifton, 1991) or to a cloth pad carrying the odour of their mother rather than that of another woman (MacFarlane, 1975). However, because they appear so early it is hard to know if they are innate and acquired by evolutionary design (like reflexes) or through very rapid learning. Learned behaviours that are deliberately repeated to produce a rewarding outcome are called **instrumental**. Psychologists have invented a means for studying such behaviours in animals and this has also been used with human infants – and it tells us when such behaviours can be acquired through learning. The technique is called **instrumental conditioning** and was developed in particular by B. F. Skinner, a famous Harvard psychologist from the Behaviourist tradition of the mid-twentieth century. The core idea is to harness a naturally occurring exploratory behaviour and then attempt to modify it through selective reinforcement. A rat that learns to press a lever to obtain a food reward is a classic example (see Panel 2.2). The rat in the Skinner box learns an arbitrary connection between a natural action (pressing with its foot) and a specific consequence (getting a food pellet).

So when does the human infant learn to profit from such contingency detection? Using instrumental conditioning, experimenters selected naturally occurring behaviours such as kicking or head turning to see if that aspect could then be specifically selected by the baby to produce a rewarding outcome (such as sucking on a nipple). For example, Einar Siqueland conditioned babies who were only days old to turn their heads to one side when a bell was sounded and the other when a buzzer went off (Siqueland & Lipsitt, 1966).

In another study (Siqueland & DeLucia, 1969), he found that babies could learn to suck at a particular amplitude to observe a picture of a face or hear a human voice. Famously, Anthony DeCasper and Wiliam Fifer (1980) conditioned newborn babies to suck at a particular rate to hear their mother's voice rather than that of a stranger – a famous example because it also showed a natural preference for orienting towards the mother in babies who were only a few days old. By 3 months old, babies will learn to make a kicking movement in order to activate a mobile attached to the child's leg with a ribbon (Rovee-Collier & Capatides, 1979). This is known as the **mobile conjugate reinforcement paradigm** and it is depicted in Panel 2.2.

Panel 2.2 Voluntary movements and instrumental learning

- Voluntary behaviours are self-produced and lead to growing discoveries about the world
- Behaviours will be repeated if they produce a desirable outcome
- B. F. Skinner invented an apparatus for inducing this sort of learned behaviour
    - A rat learns that he will be rewarded with food whenever he presses a lever
    - This is called *instrumental conditioning*
- The *mobile conjugate reinforcement* paradigm is a similar technique designed for infants
    - A baby of 3 months old can learn to turn a mobile by kicking its leg attached to a ribbon

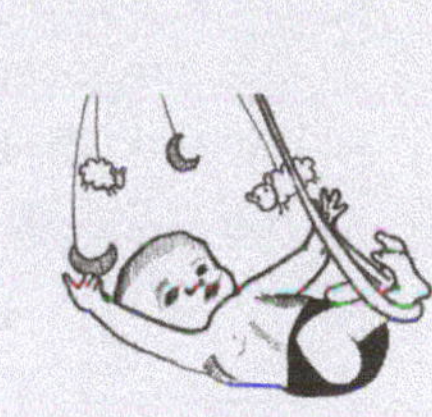

Drawings by Miller

2.3 PRIMITIVE DISCOVERIES ABOUT SPACE

Quite literally, the 'biggest' discovery an exploring infant will make is that it is enveloped within a vast world extending from its own self – the epicentre of this space. By far the most important source of this information comes from moving its head. Move your head very slightly, and become aware of the way in which the visual space suddenly assorts into moving planes sliding over one another at different rates. The biggest swings come from things close to you; the smallest from those at the greatest distance. If you were driving through the Arizona desert, nearby cactus plants would speed past, distant rocks would barely move at all and wherever you are driving, the moon stands still! This is one of the most powerful naturally occurring contingencies between voluntary behaviour and a perceived outcome.

Panel 2.3 Primitive discoveries about space

- A powerful cue for depth is *optical expansion*
  - Babies of 1 week old respond to the appearance of an object looming towards them
  - This has been demonstrated by shadow caster experiments comparing 'virtual' approaching objects on a 'hit' versus a 'miss' trajectory

One-week-old babies make a defensive reaction to a virtual object on an apparent 'hit' path (After Bower, Broughton and Moore, 1970)

- *Motion parallax* is the most powerful cue for perceiving depth
  - It is produced by even the slightest movement of the head, assorting objects of different distances into planes moving at different speeds
  - The same effect occurs when travelling in a moving vehicle such as a train

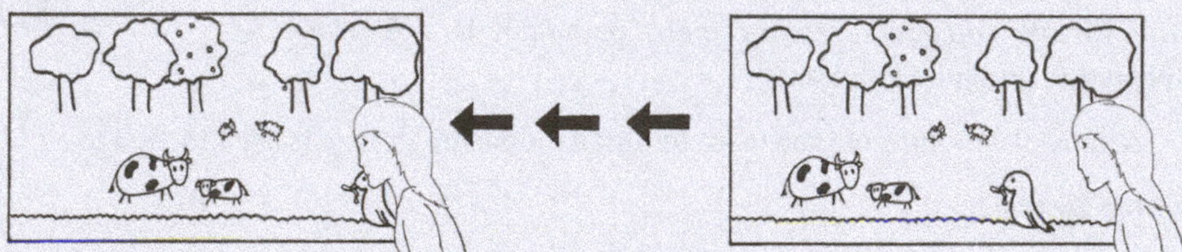

- Babies seem to respond the apparent nearness of the object, not just the retinal size
  - They show a defensive reaction to a near object and not to a larger one that has the same retinal size but stops farther away
- This suggests they have used motion parallax to interpret the expansion

Drawings by Miller

This effect is called **motion parallax** and it is such a powerful cue for depth that it will over-ride any other cue such as **texture gradient** (the changing density of visual texture with distance) or **interposition** (visual overlapping of one object by another). For a baby, this is a powerful, yet simple way to start considering its own self as a fixed point within an enveloping space. Similarly, head movements backwards and forwards quickly identify objects near to you, as their **retinal size** (the area projects onto the back of the eye) will expand more rapidly than farther objects. We cannot be certain that a neonate uses the cues produced by head movements in this way, but there is strong circumstantial evidence that it is highly likely. This was the conclusion drawn by Tom Bower in the 1970s following an ingenious set of experiments carried out at Edinburgh University (Bower, 1974). In one study, he presented babies of only 1 week old with a visual display that created the illusion of an object approaching them on a collision path. This effect was created by using a shadow caster; a screen behind which an object was moved towards a light source, casting an expanding image on it, as depicted in Panel 2.3. He found that babies of only 1 week old would respond defensively to the looming image as indexed by eyes widening, head retraction and moving their arms in front of their face. Bower went on to investigate whether this could be interpreted as a genuine perception of an object moving through space, by comparing the apparent approach of a large object that 'stopped' at some distance from the baby and that of a smaller object coming much closer but stopping at the point where it produced the same retinal size as the larger object. Finding that only the second of these produced a defensive reaction, Bower concluded that there was more to the baby's visual perception of space than images of varying retinal size, and that the 'depth' perceived by the baby in the shadow caster experiment was based on having had a true experience of three-dimensional space supported by **kinetic** (or movement-based) information.

Even though young infants may be able to differentiate themselves from the world through gross cues such as motion parallax, it would wrong to imagine that they perceive the world around them in exactly the same sense that we do. The infant has yet to undergo a complex cycle of interaction between voluntary behaviours and their sensory consequences for its actions to become more purposeful and its perceptions of the world more fine-tuned. However, the sensory and motor systems themselves need to mature and grow. Before we proceed further with this story, we shall take a look at early brain growth, so that we can make some inferences about the child's neural capability of dealing with sensory information.

BRAIN GROWTH DURING INFANCY

There is certainly much that we need to be aware of in terms of developments of brain functioning in the first year of life. There are rapid changes in brain growth during early infancy and these are often described as **spurts** – sudden advances that seem to occur at around 3–4, 7–8, 10–11 and 15–18 weeks. Slowing down after that, there are spurts again at 8, 12 and 20 months. During these, new neural connections are formed and others are 'pruned back' and the overall outcome is both towards better *specificity* of function as well as better *generality* (Fischer & Rose, 1994). Specificity means a particular sort of neural organisation or **architecture** and even particular kinds of electrochemical activity for performing a particular function, such taking in visual versus auditory or **olfactory** (smell-based) information. Generality means that the brain works as a system – different areas need to work in tandem – what you taste is partly determined by what you see on your fork, for example. Also, brain areas are not necessarily dedicated to any one type of activity. For example, some left hemisphere areas used for processing language can also be involved in the control of motor activities such as controlling hand movements. We shall now consider basic aspects of brain anatomy starting with a review the techniques used to assess the developing functioning of these different parts of the brain.

LEARNING LANDMARKS

2.4 Measuring brain changes during infancy. This section refers to some well-known techniques that have been used to chart neuroanatomical changes in the infant brain. You should know what each acronym stands for.

2.5 The development of the cortex in infancy. You should know what the cortex is, the main parts of a nerve cell, and what is meant by synaptogenesis. You should be able to name the four main lobes of the cerebral cortex and their functions. You should know what is meant by synaptic pruning.

2.6 Differential cortical growth. You should know what this means and be able to describe the different roles of the dorsal and ventral pathways for processing visual information.

2.4 MEASURING BRAIN CHANGES DURING INFANCY

There are numerous elements to the complex process of brain growth, but it can be thought of in terms of two key aspects. One is the increasing role of the upper **cortical** layers of the brain associated with regions for processing different types of stimuli. The other is the establishment of major neural pathways for performing different sorts of function and their interconnections. These developments in the neuroanatomy of the brain can be identified through various means to assess brain electrical activity. Some of these are listed in Panel 2.4.

2.5 THE DEVELOPMENT OF THE CORTEX IN INFANCY

The part of the brain that becomes functionally established during the first few months of life is the newest part of the brain in evolutionary terms, and is referred to as the **cerebral cortex** or **neocortex** (some deeper bits of the brain also have the name 'cortex' attached, such as the cingulate cortex, but appear to have an earlier evolutionary history). The neocortex is the large convoluted surface of the brain and, at birth, is about only one third the size of an adult's. Most cerebral growth occurs during the first year of life, but in what sense is the baby's brain 'growing'? By birth, most of the nerve cells or **neurons** will be in place, even in the neocortex. A neuron consists of an **axon** (the long arm of the nerve cell that transmits messages through chemical conductors), **dendrites**

Panel 2.4 Measuring brain changes during infancy

- Devices for measuring brain activity in adults can also be used with very young infants. These are based on:
  - Recording from electrodes attached to the scalp using a special cap
    - (a) *Electroencephalograms* (EEGs) measure voltage changes at different parts of the brain
    - (b) *Evoked reaction potentials* (ERPs) measure increased electrical activity as a consequence of specific stimulation

Drawing by Miller

- Scanning the structure and function of the entire brain
  - (a) *Magnetic resonance imaging* (MRI) measures anatomical structures using the effects of magnets on hydrogen atoms in the body
  - (b) *Functional magnetic resonance imaging* (fMRI) measures blood flow to and from different parts of the brain during different sorts of activity
  - (c) *Positron emission tomography* (PET) measures both structure and functioning of the brain by using radioactive tracers in the blood that can be converted into 3D images

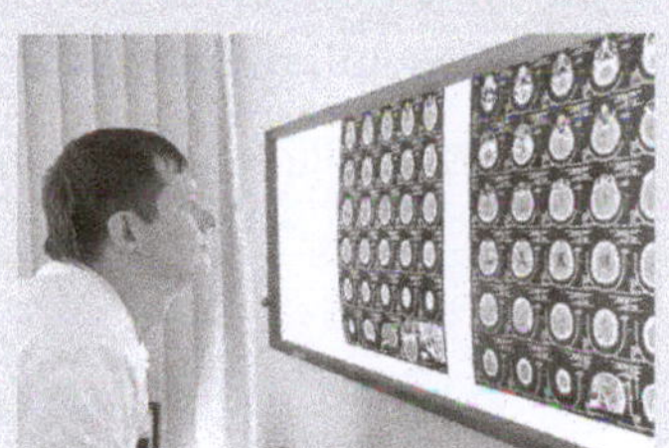

(the receptive ends of the nerve) and **synapses** (the site for chemical messages to be passed via **neurotransmitters**). Cortical development can be thought of as tree-like, with nerve fibres gradually extending upward and outward. The growth in brain mass after birth is caused mainly by a large increase in the connections made by the dendrites. This is why early brain growth is usually described as an increase in **synaptic density** or **synaptogenesis**. This actually adds fibre mass to the brain, as does the growth of **myelin** – a fatty insulating sheath around the axon. Huttenlocher (1994) has found that most synaptogenesis occurs in the first six months, increasing by a factor of ten during that time.

The four lobes of the neocortex

The cerebral cortex is characterised both by having specialised areas of functioning as well as by high levels of connectivity between and amongst these areas. The specialisation of function is represented neuroanatomically by horizontal layers of different sorts of nerve cell assemblies, but also vertically by organised columns of nerve cells that cut through the layers, and

Panel 2.5 The development of the cortex in infancy

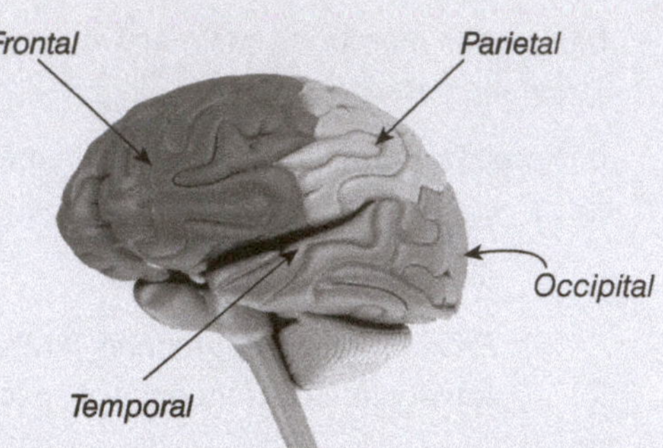

- The *cerebral cortex* is the convoluted outer surface of the brain
- Its vertical organisation is roughly into four main functional parts:
  - Visual information: *occipital lobe*
  - Auditory and olfactory information: *temporal lobe*
  - Tactile information: *parietal lobe*
  - Movement control and planning: the *frontal lobe*
- Its horizontal layers grow in a tree-like fashion during the first year of life as more and more neural connections are made
  - This is called *synaptogenesis*

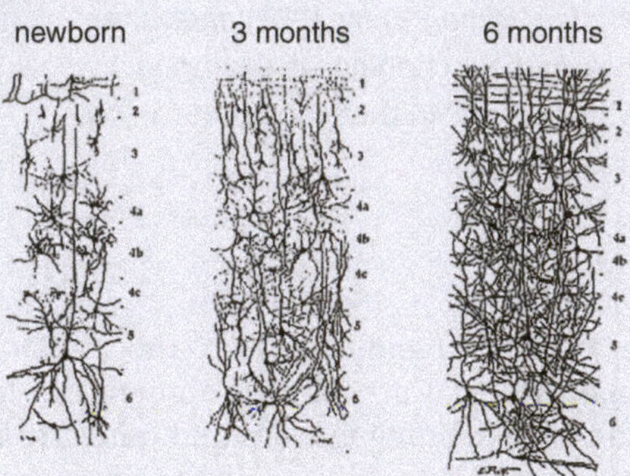

Dendritic growth in the visual cortex during the first six months (Reproduced from Johnson, 1997, with permission)

- Brain activity in the first four weeks is mainly *sub-cortical*
  - The maturing of the cortex after that is rather like bringing new areas of sensory awareness 'on-line'
- Cortical growth through synaptogenesis in the first year is also characterised by *synaptic pruning*
  - Some earlier connections disappear and it is thought that this gives the brain its plasticity

most obviously by four main **lobes** or portions of the cortex, three of which have been shown to be specialised for three main types of sensory input, and the fourth for planned action and movement. These are shown in Panel 2.5. The two halves of the brain, connected by the **corpus callosum**, also have their specialisations and we shall come to these in Chapter 4.

Positron emission tomography (PET) scans in infants have shown that most of the brain activity of the neonate is **sub-cortical** but thereafter (at about 4 weeks or so), there is increasing activity in the cortical regions of the brain. Some have described early brain maturation as bringing some of the main sensory systems of the neocortex 'on-line', i.e. having them capable of tuning in to the full set of sensory experiences. However, during synaptogenesis, there is also a process of neural elimination. That is, some synapses (connections across neurons) disappear if they have not proved necessary. There may be a pre-programmed 'cell death' element to this, but it is thought that much of it is a kind of **synaptic pruning**, i.e. making a wide variety of neural connections available during the critical process of cortical growth. This means that the brain is designed to respond flexibly at certain **critical periods** to specific experiences such as learning to discriminate the acoustic signals associated with the particular language(s) most often heard by the infant in its first few months of life. Synaptic pruning can go on in different ways right throughout childhood to support (and reflect) 'spurts' in more advanced aspects of cognition (Thatcher, 1992) and it seems likely that the initial over-production has evolved to make the system more **plastic**, meaning that the brain is capable of responding to injury by allowing other areas to take over from damaged ones.

2.6 DIFFERENTIAL CORTICAL GROWTH

The functional development of the sensory system can be illustrated by changes in elementary orienting behaviours in young babies. For the first two months or so, they are more likely to gaze at peripheral stimuli than those in the central or nasal field, and seem to need a high-contrast frame around the stimulus. Their visual tracking is **saccadic** (based on discrete fixations) at this age. At about the age of 3 months, they show the onset of smooth tracking of an object and visual anticipation of its continued trajectory, and this has been surmised to reflect the maturation of new and more 'outward' layers of the visual cortex (Johnson, 1997). Around this age, they also become sensitive to the more detailed interior properties of visual stimuli. This is now thought to be due to the slightly later and separate development of a type of visual processing that is more about *what* an object is rather than *where* it is.

Two visual pathways

The visual system is thought to have two quite distinct pathways for dealing with different kinds of information. Goodale and Milner (Goodale et al., 1991; Goodale & Milner, 1992) were first to propose that there are two different streams of visual processing in the human brain similar to that first found in macaque monkeys. It is known that information from the retina of the human is passed through the optic nerve to an area of the brain known as the **lateral geniculate nucleus** (LGN) and after that to the primary visual cortex. However, it appears that this information is then transmitted for further processing either through the **dorsal** stream or, almost literally, over the back of the brain to the **posterior parietal cortex** or through the ventral stream meaning 'under' to the **inferotemporal cortex** of the brain (see Panel 2.6). The cells in the LGN that form these streams are roughly divided into layers known as **magnocellular** (dorsal) and **parvocellular** (ventral). It is now widely recognised that these projections are differentiated according to what the visual information is needed *for*. The dorsal stream seems to be involved in processing information about the location, orientation and size of an object in the visual field, i.e. information that would be important for acting in relation to the object, such as reaching for it. Goodale and Milner consider that the control of this type of information is fast and unconscious, whilst the ventral stream appears to process information relevant to the identity of the object for more conscious recognition and remembering of its visual properties. It has been proposed by Atkinson (1998) that the dorsal system has an earlier onset than the stream for processing 'what' information, but that the ultimate development is the *integration* of information from these different areas of brain activation, as we normally need to register both the location and the identity of what we are looking at. One of the last parts of the cortex to mature is the **prefrontal** part, which is involved in conscious action planning, and we shall return to this in Chapter 4.

Panel 2.6 Differential cortical growth

- Different functions of the brain can mature at different rates – even within the same modality
  - The looking behaviour of babies suggests that they do not attend to the internal detail of objects in the first month or so
- This is consistent with the fact that there are two main visual pathways:
  - The *dorsal stream* – processes the location of visual input
  - The *ventral stream* – processes object identity information
- The dorsal stream develops first consistent with the basic need to know where objects are located in space

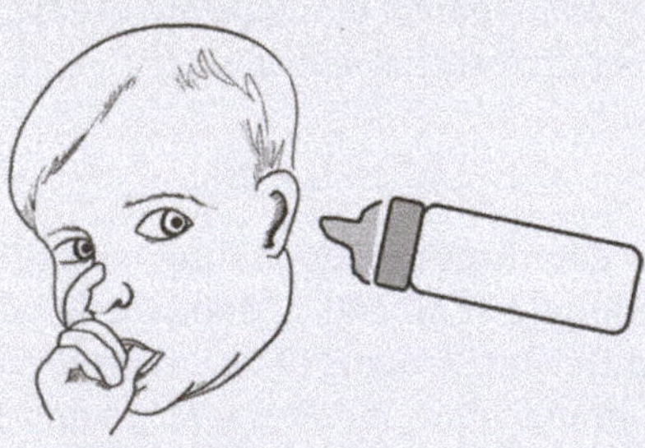

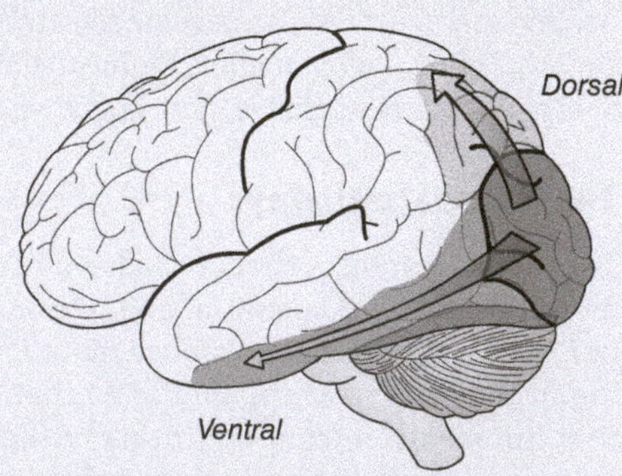

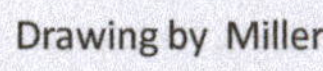
Drawing by Miller

(Image by Selket; Wikimedia Commons)

THE VISUAL PERCEPTION OF OBJECTS

Knowing how the brain's sensory areas develop is hugely important but it doesn't tell us what a child is actually experiencing or specifically learning about the world. For a start, sensory input does not directly translate into subjective experience. If perception was simply about registering myriad visual, auditory, tactile and olfactory sensations coming from the outside world, we would very quickly overload the brain's storage capacity. Look at the scene around you and try to regard each bounded space as a separate entity with a unique character. The world is split into patches of shape and colour with no coherence or meaning. Viewed in this way, any one scene taken from a static perspective is already a pattern of challenging complexity. Move a little within this space and it could quickly become a mosaic of kaleidoscopic confusion. But it doesn't. The world sorts itself into things and spaces that behave in an orderly way. And that is not all – the bounded spaces mean things to us; they are 'seen' as objects, people, etc. We manage this explosive information by sorting the visual world into different things and into types of thing. As the famous psychologist Jerome Bruner once remarked: 'Every act of perception is an act of categorisation'. This act of categorisation is based on learning; it has ramifications for how we store, remember and recall the world, how we talk about it, and even how we reason about it. But these perceptions are essentially private and invisible to the observer. So how can we discover the extent to which they can be experienced by a small infant who cannot tell us what he or she sees, hears or understands about the world? We need techniques that use the child's behaviour to make inferences about what they perceive. These are reviewed in Section 2.7 below, and what we have learned from them is summarised in the sections that follow.

LEARNING LANDMARKS

2.7 Behavioural methods for studying elementary perception. You should be able to describe at least four behaviour-based techniques for measuring the infant's awareness of the world.

2.8 Solidity and wholeness. You should be able to describe a study showing that babies appear to perceive whole objects even when they are partly obscured.

2.9 Size and shape constancy. You should know what this means, and be able to cite studies demonstrating the infant's perception of both.

2.10 Perceptual classification. You should know how classification of objects is tested in babies. You should know in what sense classification has developed by the age of 12 months.

2.7 BEHAVIOURAL METHODS FOR STUDYING ELEMENTARY PERCEPTION

There are many behavioural 'instruments' for studying perceptual development in the very young infant. We have already seen that Bower used a defensive reaction to measure the perception of approach. Here are some others:

- **Preferential looking**. The infant's vision is not stereoscopic until about 3 months, as integration from the two eyes occurs at cortical rather than sub-cortical levels. However, even though their acuity is very poor at the neonatal stage, babies can use foveal vision from birth in order to detect at least some features of objects. (This means that they will direct their eyes such that the fovea is centred on an object of interest.) Used since the 1960s, the preferential looking method is based simply on presenting two contrasting stimuli to see whether the infant will spend significantly more time looking to one than another. This can be used to assess both what an infant *can* discriminate as well as what she or he prefers to watch.

- **Visual habituation**. From the very first, infants will show a normal human tendency to stop looking at something that initially captured their interest. This is known as **habituation**. If the object changes in some way or is replaced by another and the looking time is significantly increased, then this would be recorded as **dishabituation**. This is adaptively useful as it allows the perceiver to be in a state of readiness for new and potentially important information. There are different ways of measuring this, but one common example is to measure the mean looking time over three successive fixations until it drops to less than half the original. A test stimulus is then substituted for the original and if there is no change in looking time it suggests that the infant did not register a difference. A return to original looking time levels shows dishabituation and permits the inference that the baby had detected a difference across the two stimulus conditions.

- **Auditory habituation: non-nutritive sucking**. A similar effect occurs for unchanging auditory stimuli, which will become relegated to background noise until a change is detected. But although the baby will look towards a sound source at its onset, it will not necessarily sustain its gaze – nor would such a behaviour be a clear indication of what it can hear or discriminate at the auditory level. So how can change detection be measured? A solution is to use high-amplitude sucking, based on the observation that when babies are interested in something going on in their surroundings, they will rapidly suck on an artificial nipple (with no milk delivery!). Bursts of sucking are measured until they reach a stable rate; recovery of the bursts indicates renewal of interest and can thus determine what sorts of sounds can be discriminated.

- **Conditioned head turning**. Another behaviour, and one that has arguably a more intentional element to it than visual or auditory dishabituation, is head turning. We have already seen how instrumental conditioning

Panel 2.7 Behavioural methods for studying elementary perception

- The length of time an infant stares at an object can be used to infer what s/he can understand about the world
  - o *Preferential looking* is based on presenting two images to an infant and seeing if one attracts significantly more interest
    - This tells us what the baby can discriminate as well as what s/he likes to look at
- The way an infant is attracted to a novel visual or auditory event tells us about what they can perceptually differentiate
  - o *Visual habituation* systematically measures the interest a baby shows in a new object using number and length of gazes at the object
    - When this measure drops and stabilises, the baby has habituated to the object
    - If it shows a significant increase when a new object is presented, then the baby has dis-habituated and has demonstrated that it can discriminate between the two objects
  - o *Auditory habituation* uses sucking behaviour to measure interest in a new sound – increased sucking rate denotes that the baby is alert to the new sound
    - When sucking stabilises and returns to its normal rate, it indicates that the infant is now treating the sound as not particularly novel
    - If sucking amplitude increases when a new sound is presented, then the baby has dis-habituated and has demonstrated that it can discriminate between the two sounds
- Voluntary conditioned behaviours can also tell us about discrimination and preference
  - o *Conditioned head turning* presents a stimulus that is always paired with a particular voluntary behaviour such as a right head-turn
    - If this is reinforced by a rewarding event like a Jack-in-the-box, then the baby will learn to make that behaviour every time the stimulus is presented
    - Varying the stimulus and looking at its effect on the behaviour tells us what the baby regards as the same as the original
    - Varying the reward can tell us what things the baby likes to experience
  - o *Conditioned sucking* pairs a particular auditory stimulus with a spontaneous increase in sucking rate
    - An increase in the extent to which the baby chooses to suck at that rate can tell us if he likes to hear that particular sound.

(the mobile conjugate paradigm) has been used to discover when infants are capable of modifying a voluntary behaviour to obtain a reinforcing sight or sound. Suppose you now wish to know if a baby can perceive the difference between two objects. A technique is to instrumentally condition the baby to turn its head only when preceded by a particular visual or auditory stimulus. So, for example, when the baby makes a voluntary head turn to the right on any occasion on which a particular stimulus has just been presented, that behaviour is reinforced by sight of an interesting toy or maybe a peek-a-boo from Mum. This continues to the point where the stimulus would reliably elicit the head turn. Changing the stimulus and observing the learned head turning then allows the experimenter to determine whether or not the baby considers the new stimulus to be the same or different from the original one – another measure of discrimination.

- **Conditioned sucking**. As well as passively registering interest in a stimulus through sucking amplitude, sucking, like head turning, can be used to see what an infant will actively choose to see or hear. The technique is to first establish the base rate of non-nutritive sucking, but when an infant spontaneously deviates from the base rate, i.e. sucks for either a longer or shorter inter-burst interval, a specific stimulus is consistently paired with this particular sucking rate. Following this exposure, we can then see whether the infant will start to preferentially suck at the rate that 'brings on' a particular sound or sight.

What have these methods added to our understanding of what a young and relatively non-mobile infant can perceive about the world? The answer to this is 'a great deal'. Using these special instruments to peer into those unstored and forgotten experiences of the first few months, developmental psychologists have gone to considerable lengths to elaborate on this relatively short period in human development. In the next sections we shall review some of the remarkable discoveries made.

2.8 SOLIDITY AND WHOLENESS

A first requisite of object perception is to identify which parts of the mosaic of visual patterns presented to the eye can be assorted into bounded spaces denoting objects. We have already seen that neonates are prepared already to look at contours of shapes, but this in itself will not create a percept of a whole object. For one thing the contour is likely to be interrupted by something that occludes a part of it. Look around you: how many 'things' that you see around you are displayed in their entirety?

From what we now know about the spurt in synaptic density in the visual cortex at about 2 months, it seems likely that it is around this age that more fleeting sensations supported by sub-cortical activity start to become more enduring and coherent percepts of objects. Habituation methods have indeed indicated that it is around this age that infants appear to 'see' whole objects, despite the fact they are partly occluded. In a pioneering study, Kellman and Spelke (1983) habituated 4-month-old infants to a display in which a rod moved horizontally behind a block that occluded its midsection (see Panel 2.8). The test displays consisted either of the original rod without the occluder (making a different visual pattern from the original) or the two sections moving in synchrony (making the same visual pattern as before). An adult would of course perceive the original display as a whole rod behind an occluder. This is such a powerful tendency that a group of early twentieth century German psychologists (Max Wertheimer, Wolfgang Kohler and Kurt Koffka) called it the perception of 'Gestalt', meaning a whole unified form. Now with new methods we can test just how early the perception of wholeness appears in the human infant. From Kellman and Spelke's experiment it appeared to be present even in the 4-month-old infant, as babies of this age dishabituated only to the rod segments, and not to the whole rod. Subsequent experiments were carried out to discover the age of onset of this perception of wholeness, and to be careful that the contrast conditions were optimal, as infants in the first two months look particularly at areas of high contrast. From these studies it appears that, under the right conditions, this type of perception occurs at 2 months; at earlier ages the infants appear to have a more fractured percept (Johnson & Aslin, 1995).

Panel 2.8 Solidity and wholeness

- The perception of a whole object – or *Gestalt* – from fractured parts is a powerful effect in human perception
  - It allows us to 'see' whole objects that are partly occluded
- Babies appear to have a similar percept
  - When habituated to a rod moving behind an occluder, babies of 4 months dishabituate only to the separate parts, not to the presentation of the whole rod

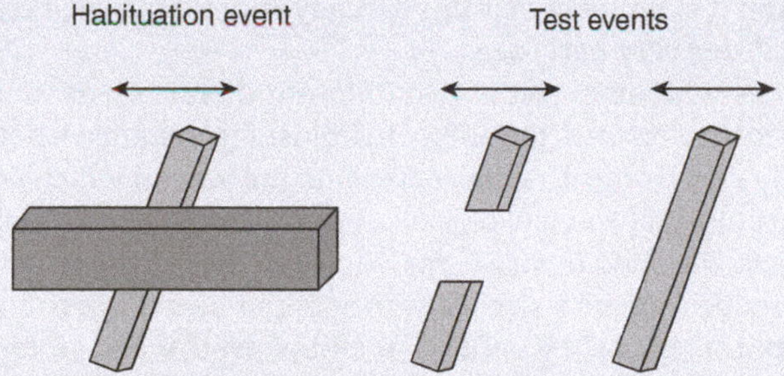

Young infants regard the whole moving test rod as similar to the original partly occluded one

(After Kellman & Spelke, 1983)

2.9 SIZE AND SHAPE CONSTANCY

Another visual skill that you probably take for granted is size constancy. Size constancy refers to the fact that that when a single object is located at a different distances from the viewer, the corresponding retinal changes don't denote a change in the object. You don't actually see a distant car as small, but rather as a normal sized car at a distance. Clearly this is a skill that will develop as the ability to perceptually classify develops. If something that looks just like a real living elephant crosses your visual field but appears to be very small, you will assume that it is at a safe distance! If you can't actually classify an object but can merely perceive its outline shape, there are other and more primary cues for assessing its size. The cues for distance themselves, such as motion parallax, help to place even unfamiliar objects at their correct distance from the observer and to help specify their actual size. So, at an age where knowledge of the world is fairly restricted in terms of objects that it can classify, when can a baby use basic visual distance cues to decide whether or not an object, such as a toy placed at different distances, is the same toy – whatever its apparent size variation?

A pioneering study on size constancy was carried out in the 1960s by Tom Bower, using the conditioned head turning technique described in Section 2.7. Bower used a cube of a certain size (30 cm^3) and at a certain distance (1 metre) as the conditioned stimulus, as shown in Figure A, Panel 2.9. When replaced by a larger cube that would present the same retinal pattern (90 cm^3 at 3 metres), infants of 2 months showed fewer than 25% of the original head turns and also less than half the number elicited by the *same* cube when presented three times further away than before (at 3 metres). The babies had learned to respond to a particular size of cube irrespective of distance – something that suggests they could perceive size in relation to distance. Since then, others have suggested that size constancy may be present at birth, as similar results can be obtained by simply habituating the baby to a particular size at a particular distance as in Bower's study. When they are then presented with a test stimulus that is larger but further away they dishabituate to this stimulus as if they see it as different despite it having the same retinal size (Slater et al., 1990). However, taking all the combined evidence of neonatal perception together, it is unlikely that this actually represents the recognition of a constant solid object at this very early age.

Presenting babies with an object at two different distances, as in the above studies, may tell us whether they possess the ability to adjust for distance – but it is unlikely that this experimentally contrived situation represents the way in which this skill is actually acquired. It is more normal to view objects under a continuous transformation where they move relative to the child or vice versa, such as a drinking cup being brought to the child's mouth. It can be seen why size constancy might be a fairly primitive discovery as changes in the apparent size often occur in 'well-behaved' ways – looming and receding in space, bounded by continuity in time as well as its own continuous contours.

Suppose, however, an object is twisted around whilst being moved back and forth. Now the contour as well the area of the object will vary dramatically as it projects onto the retina. Another basic 'constancy' that can be picked up if an object is viewed under continuous transformation is that it remains the same shape. Yonas and colleagues (Yonas et al., 1987) found that babies of 4 months old were indeed sensitive to kinetic

Panel 2.9 Size and shape constancy

- *Size constancy* is the perception that something has the same size (is the same object) despite changes in retinal size due to distance from the observer
- Babies show size constancy within the first two months
  - A *conditioned head-turning* technique showed that 2-month-old babies continue to treat an object to which they have been conditioned as the same size even when it is moved further away

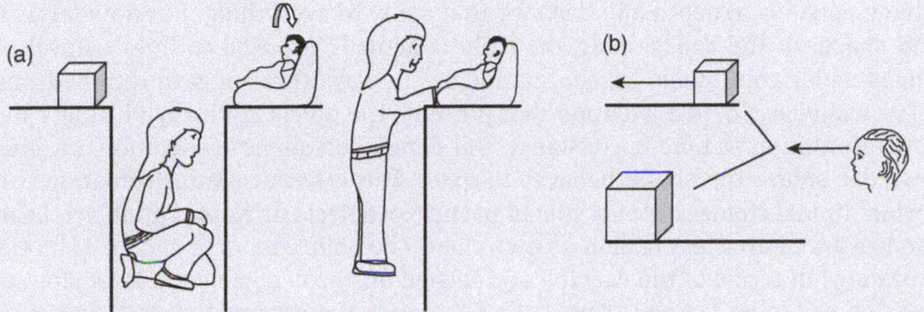

A The baby's right head turn is rewarded by peek-a-boo every time the cube is present (a). The conditioned stimulus (top) is moved farther way *or* replaced by a larger test stimulus (bottom) placed so that it has the same retinal size as the original (b). It is still the original stimulus that elicits most head turns (After Bower, 1966)

Drawing by Miller

- *Shape constancy* depends on picking up how an object is transformed through movement
  - A flat 2D triangle and a 3D tetrahedron look the same from the front until they are rotated
- Babies detect this difference at 4 months

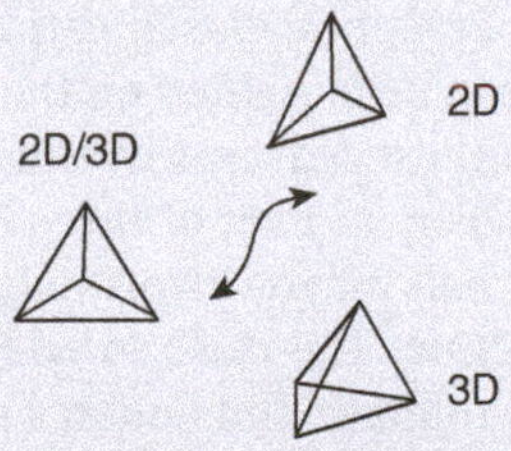

B Babies are habituated to projection of a rotating tetrahedron. They dishabituate to a flat triangular shape based on rotating a flat bisected triangle but not to a flat triangular shape representing a still from the tetrahedron (After Yonas et al., 1987)

information provided by an object rotating in space and could use this to distinguish two very similar shapes. These experimenters used a shadow caster to mimic the effects of an object rotating in real space, rather like the way Bower used it to mimic approach. Two similar objects were used – a flat triangle with intersecting lines or a 3D tetrahedron – see Figure B, Panel 2.9. Babies at 4 months old were habituated to one of these only and in tests could detect when a presented transformation was familiar or novel as measured by dishabituation.

There is an important difference between size and shape constancy. Although it would be improved by object knowledge (as in the elephant example above), size constancy does not depend on it. All objects undergo the same retinal transformations as they recede from the observer; a totally unfamiliar object can be judged in terms of the unchanging rules of depth and distance that apply to everything. But now let us think about shape. In the Yonas study, the child is actually exposed to how a novel object changes under continuous transformation, i.e. in ways that apply to tetrahedrons but not flat triangles. So, in a situation that presents the object statically at time 1 then in a new orientation at time 2, constancy will depend on shape recognition, i.e. *previous* knowledge of how this shape 'behaves' in space. This is because transformations caused by orientational changes are specific to particular objects or classes of object. Learning these is a very important skill in its own right. The ability to see a cup as a cup (in any orientation) in terms of the way it – and indeed all cups – change under spatial transformation has to be learned. This is the beginning of perceptual **classification** and in some senses the beginnings of object *knowledge*. So as babies become equipped with the ability to see solid objects, and to correct for how far away they are, what objects do they come to classify and thus know about? And how well can they achieve these first, and we might argue – truly cognitive – acts?

2.10 PERCEPTUAL CLASSIFICATION

There are two sorts of things we need to study in relation to perceiving and knowing objects during infancy. One is to study the mechanisms of classification; the other is to study what infants may already have classified. And this is exactly what investigators have done. In this section, we deal with the first.

In a pioneering study, Barbara Younger and Leslie Cohen at Purdue University set up a situation that could provoke perceptual classification. In the normal visual environment, there are few things that can be classified on the basis of a single feature, such as red, shiny or round. Individually these features would include everything from a drawing pin to the planet Mars, but taken as a set of three correlated features, the choice is smaller – an apple, tomato or a ball maybe? Normally, it is the correlation amongst a subset of visual features that defines the class to which the object belongs. Although they were simple line drawings, Younger and Cohen's stimuli (Younger & Cohen, 1983) were composed of three attributes that were correlated, e.g. animals who had giraffe-like neck and ears, fluffy tails and club-shaped feet or cow-shaped bodies, feathered tails and webbed feet (see Panel 2.10). In real life, objects in a class will also vary amongst themselves in irrelevant ways: tomatoes may be attached to a vine; balls may be made of plastic, rubber or cloth, for example. Accordingly, in Younger and Cohen's study, their pictures objects varied also amongst themselves in irrelevant ways such as having antlers or ears, or two visible legs versus four.

Panel 2.10 Perceptual classification

- The processes of perceptual classification can be studied using artificial stimuli such as invented animal drawings
- Babies are habituated to artificial animal stimuli composed of different values on a set of attributes such as shape, neck length, type of tail and type of feet
- They can be habituated to items where a number of attributes go together to define a category whilst others are irrelevant (e.g. ears versus antlers)
- By the age of 7 months babies will treat a novel exemplar as belonging to a class if it has the same key correlations amongst relevant features

Cartoon animals allow measurement of when one animal type can be classified according to a set of relevant features and also to correlations amongst features, such as (here) giraffe-like neck and ears, fluffy tail and club feet

(Adapted from Younger & Cohen, 1983, with permission)

These investigators found that by the age of 7 months the infants would dishabituate to examples of these animals when some of the original features of the original stimuli were re-presented but in novel combinations, such as a giraffe body with feathered tail and webbed feet. This shows that the features had somehow been used *collectively* during the habituation stimuli to form perceptual classes. A single feature was not enough to define the class. After many further studies along these lines over the last decade or so, Younger and her colleagues have arrived at the conclusion that this ability develops between 4 and 10 months of age. A key aspect of this development is the ability to **parse** (sort) categories into the set of variations that unites some things but excludes others. For example, when exposed to photographs of cats and horses, 10-month-old babies, unlike 4- and 7-month-old babies, treated these as distinct categories so that when shown a novel horse (old category) versus a dog (new category), they looked longer at the dog as if it did indeed represent a new type of category and not just another example of a type of thing they had already seen (Younger & Fearing, 1999). Categories are established through sets of features that tend to be correlated such as four legs, barking and waggy tails. Younger and Cohen (1986) found that babies at 4 months responded on the basis of total similarity across the features rather than *patterns* of correlations across features. Seven-month-old babies, however, showed the beginnings of sensitivity to the holistic properties of the category, and would treat novel stimuli with the same pattern of correlation as similar to the test stimuli – but only if *all* the features were correlated. It is as if crude classes can be formed at this age, provided all the defining features behave together in clearly distinct ways.

These studies and others like them tell us how babies learn to classify. But we need to turn away now from the basic mechanisms of perception and consider the growing subjective experiences of our infants. What we need to know is *what* they learn to classify. In other words, what correlated features of real-world objects are they likely to attend to naturally? No prizes for guessing that one of the most important object classes for an infant is the human face. We consider this in the next section.

THE VISUAL PERCEPTION OF PEOPLE

LEARNING LANDMARKS

2.11 Neonatal preference for face-like stimuli. You should be able to cite a study showing a preference for face-like stimuli in newborns and know what visual information this preference is based on.

2.12 Face recognition in neonates. You should be able to cite a study showing limited face recognition in newborns and very young infants and the memory limitations on this skill.

2.13 Face and emotion recognition by 6 months. You should know the extent to which detailed face and emotional expression processing is in place by 6 months and be able to cite one relevant study.

2.11 NEONATAL PREFERENCE FOR FACE-LIKE STIMULI

Let's go back to the newborn and the next two months or so of its development. Remember that visual processing at this is age is sub-cortical rather than cortical, and based on fleeting impressions of a somewhat indistinct world. As yet it simply does not have the neural mechanisms to perceive a face in the way that it will do from 2 months onwards. Nevertheless, evidence accumulated since the 1970s shows that the neonate does indeed have a preference for crude face-like patterns and will have its gaze 'captured' by stimuli that have some key face-like features. In a pioneering study, Goren et al. (1975) found that infants only 10 minutes old will track a card with face features, eyes, nose and mouth farther than one with those same features scrambled or with no features at all. Several studies have replicated this finding (Maurer & Young, 1983; Johnson et al., 1991), but it seems that this preference disappears within about 30 days. Morton and Johnson (1991) concluded that the sub-cortical response to faces is different from the way faces are subsequently learned and recognised.

Panel 2.11 Neonatal preference for face-like stimuli

- Newborns prefer to 'track' moving stimuli that look like faces than ones with the same features scrambled
- We now know that in the first month this is based on a preference for vertical asymmetry in pattern arrangement where the features are grouped in the upper half of the face

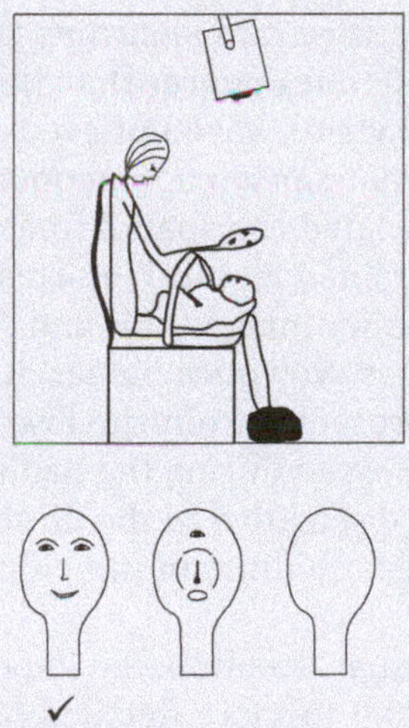

A Newborn babies are more likely to have their gaze captured by a card with a 2D face like pattern moving across their visual field than by one with the same features scrambled

(Johnson et al., 1991; figure reproduced with permission)

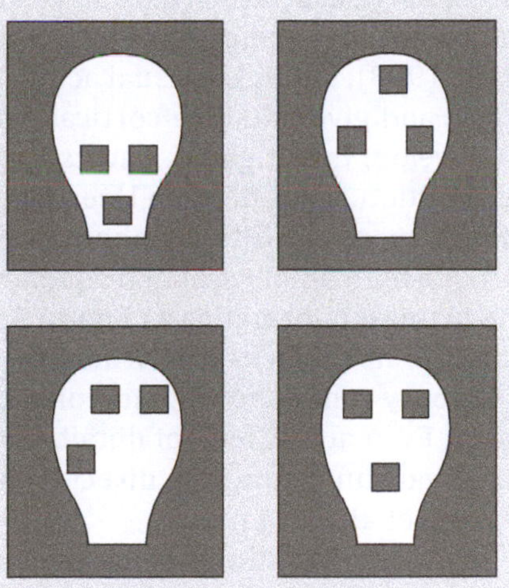

B Newborns prefer to look at patterns with more features in the top half of the visual field even if they are not face-like (top right) and show no particular preference for a face versus a non-face when this vertical asymmetry is present (bottom)

(Turati et al., 2002; stimuli reproduced with permission)

So how can we best understand the very early and apparently innate 'recognition' of a face? More recent research with young babies has shown that the human system seems pre-disposed to attend to gross **configural** (sometimes called **configurational**) properties of a face, possibly because this provides an adaptive bias for the child to look towards a care-providing source. An important configural property is up–down asymmetry. Chiara Turati from the University of Padua and her colleagues (Turati et al., 2002) found that newborns prefer stimuli where there are more blobs in the upper portion of the 'face' than in the lower. In fact, provided there is an asymmetry favouring the denser pattern at the top half of the stimulus, then there is no particular preference for a face-like arrangement as shown in Panel 2.11. This was interpreted by the authors as possibly due to the fact that a sub-cortical structure for visual processing – the **superior colliculus** – is known to be involved in visual exploration of the top half of the visual field. Certainly, such up–down asymmetry would indeed be a simple alert to a possible face in the visual field, although more recent research has suggested that very early face preference may arise as simple by-product from very basic brain mechanisms involved in newborns having to integrate information from both eyes (Wilkinson et al., 2014).

2.12 FACE RECOGNITION IN NEONATES

Having a preference for face-like stimuli is one thing, but can neonates actually *recognise* a particular face? There have been several claims of individual face recognition in newborns (Field et al., 1984), which may be based on very rapid learning (Walton et al., 1998). But as the visual acuity of the newborn is 40 times poorer than that of an adult, and given that the cortical pathways for detailed vision have not even started to develop, investigators have sought to discover in what sense such neonatal face recognition is possible. de Heering et al. (2008) manipulated the spatial frequencies of face images by filtering photographs so that they contained featural information at either a high or low spatial frequency. Low spatial frequency images blur and coarsen the featural information as Figure A, Panel 2.12 illustrates. Newborn babies dishabituated to novel faces only when the information was present within the low spatial frequency range showing that only coarse cues are processed during the habituation stage. Even at this level of detail, however, newborns are sensitive to the direction of gaze and can distinguish direct from averted gaze at least within an individual face (Rigato et al., 2011).

With face-like stimuli being the focus of newborn's visual attention, the importance of the face for the infant will continue to help it to attend to more detailed face-like information as its vision matures. Maurer and Salapatek (1976) found that infants at 2 months old start to fixate on the internal features of a face-like stimulus rather than simply on high contrast areas such as its boundaries, which suggests the beginnings of more fine-tuned face perception – consistent with findings from later studies on the development of the visual cortex.

If newborns can distinguish between a face to which they have just been exposed and a novel one (at least under certain circumstances), when can they be said to actually recognise a familiar face in the way that an adult can? At an advanced level, a face seen once only can be picked out subsequently from an identity parade. This is a sophisticated skill that takes a surprisingly long time develop, as we shall see in Chapter 11. However, if infants can distinguish crude face-like configurations from birth, then for how long can a particular configuration such as a mother's face be retained in memory and 'recognised' on a subsequent occasion? Ian Bushnell from Glasgow University has argued that this ability in infants should be related to how much time they actually spend awake and looking at their mother (Bushnell, 2003). He recorded the sample patterns of behaviour from 29 infants in their first three days of life to work out how much time they spent asleep or awake and looking in their mother's direction. After three days, they were taken from the maternity ward to a special viewing room where the baby could see the mother's face or that of a volunteer female stranger. Twenty seconds of fixation to either or both faces was recorded from the moment the baby first fixated on either face. Other visual and olfactory cues were masked, and the mother and stranger swapped positions halfway through. Bushnell found that the length of time spent looking at the mother's face was strongly correlated with the length of time spent looking at her in the previous three days. This does not mean that the baby has a long-term memory for the mother, however. Bushnell found that although recognition could still occur after 15 minutes, there was a suggestion that it was beginning to decay in some of the infants.

Panel 2.12 Face recognition in neonates

- Babies under 2 months perceive the contours of a face only at low spatial frequencies (upper row)
    - This affects their recognition abilities as measured by dishabituation
- They may be able to distinguish gaze direction at birth even with this level of information
- Individual face recognition (e.g. of the mother) by neonates is possible, but fleeting
    - Recognition of the mother's face starts to decay around 15 minutes after the last exposure to her

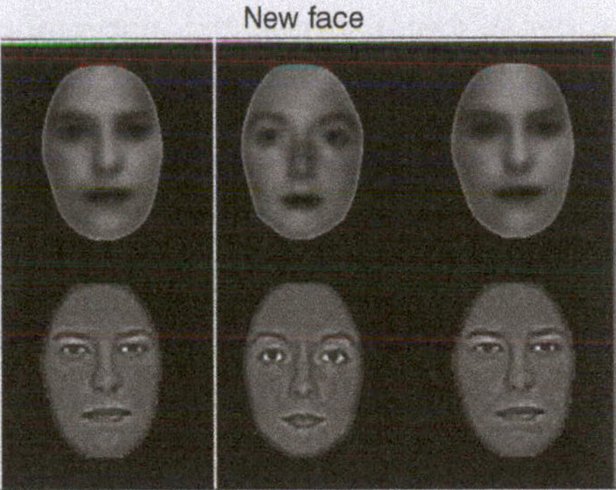

Babies can recognise that a face is 'new' following habituation to the left-hand face but only in terms of coarse visual information (top)

(de Heering et al, 2008; stimuli reproduced with permission)

2.13 FACE AND EMOTION RECOGNITION BY 6 MONTHS

We have seen that a face percept starts to become more detailed from about 2 months and it also starts to become more enduring in memory. By 6 months, it appears that babies have a sufficiently long-term memory of their mother's face to recognise her even under the conditions of a controlled memory test. When viewing video recordings of their mother from neck up and with no distinctive clothing visible, **evoked reaction potential** (ERP) recordings from infants of this age showed different patterns of activity than when viewing a stranger's face under the same conditions (de Haan & Nelson, 1997). The pattern of neural activity was somewhat different, however, when the stranger's face was similar to the mother and greater attention to their differences was required. Indeed ERP recordings for familiar and unfamiliar faces continue to change in various ways over the next four years (Carver et al., 2002) according to the complex interplay of factors such as preference for mother's face, interest in strangers' faces and improvements in attention.

Later developments notwithstanding, another important element for social interaction is to know what that face is signalling by way of emotion. Happiness, sadness, fear and anger are key emotions which are expressible by re-configuring the face through muscular contractions such opening and narrowing of eyes, tensing and relaxing jaw and mouth, etc. When do babies distinguish amongst these different expressions of emotional state? Using the visual habituation method, Bornstein and Arterberry (2003) carried out a systematic study of 35 5-month-old infants to answer this question. One of the methodological problems in such a study is that two different things have to be measured. First, not all smiling expressions - even from the same person - are all the same. They vary in intensity and, when particularly intense, a smile will become 'toothy', altering the face quite dramatically. So, just as children have to learn to classify shapes under different sorts of transformation, so they also have to learn to classify an emotional expression independently of variations in intensity. To measure this, Bornstein and Arteberry exposed babies to real-life faces expressing happiness or fear in static,

Panel 2.13 Face and emotion recognition by 6 months

- Face perception becomes more detailed and recognition memory more enduring after 2 months
- By 6 months, babies recognise videos of their mother as measured by neural activity
- Different emotional expressions can be distinguished by 5 months as measured by habituation

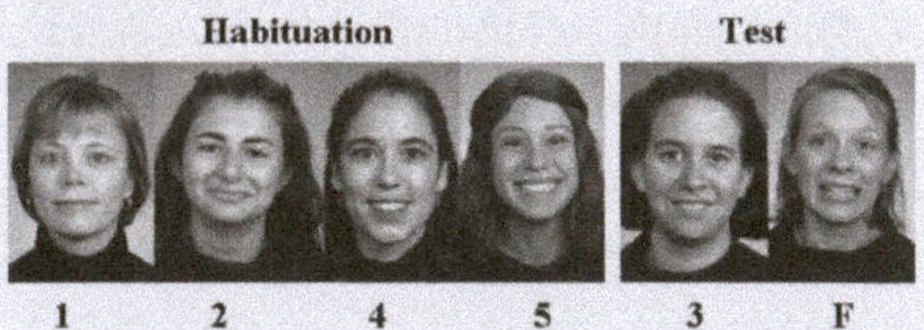

Babies are habituated to a smile across a range of faces and will dishabituate only to a novel face with a different expression (fear)

(Bornstein & Arterberry, 2003; figure reproduced with permission)

videotaped shots. In one condition, the infants were habituated to the same person smiling across an even range of intensity from mild to extreme (toothy). In the test phase, the babies were shown the same face but expressing a novel mid-point within that range, or the same person showing a mid-point within a new range of fearful expressions. They looked longer at the new expression than at the novel smile, showing that they could treat smiles and fear within a single face as belonging to different categories. But does this mean that this can also be applied across faces? Bornstein and Arteberry also habituated infants to a set of different faces showing a range of smiles (see Panel 2.13) and found that at 5 months they could detect the universal properties of a smile and distinguish it from a fearful expression, over and above individual variation such as hair length and shape and configuration of the face.

CHAPTER SUMMARY

Newborns have reflexes and elementary voluntary behaviours that give way to learned behaviours based on detecting the contingency between an action and a rewarding outcome. Visual perception is fragmentary and fleeting for the first two months but affords space and depth perception, and crude face recognition. Rapid cortical development between the ages of 2 and 10 months leads to considerable changes in object classification and facial perception.

LOOKING AHEAD TO CHAPTER 3

Vision is a very immediate way of learning about the world but it is certainly not the only one. The smell, feel and sounds of objects and other humans are all things that enrich the baby's experience. In the next chapter, we take a look at what habituation studies have revealed regarding these other sources of 'knowing the world'.

CHAPTER 3

PERCEPTUAL DEVELOPMENT DURING THE FIRST YEAR: THE MULTISENSORY INFANT

Vision is a predominant means for humans to know their world, but the other main senses contribute to this knowledge in no small part. This enriches the baby's experience of its new world, but also demands that these senses cohere, each making 'sense' of the other. For this reason, studies on non-visual senses are usually about their integration with vision and/or other senses (e.g. touch and smell). During its first year the infant will learn how the world behaves through a variety of sensory channels, which then build up of expectations of how it *should* behave.

SOMATOSENSORY, OLFACTORY AND VISUAL INTEGRATION

LEARNING LANDMARKS

3.1 Touch and smell. You should be able to describe a study that has established that newborns can associate the smell of their mothers with their touch.

3.2 Touch and vision. You should be able to describe an experiment on cross modal matching between touch and vision.

3.1 TOUCH AND SMELL

Touch and smell rarely exist in isolation as cues to an object's identity. The sight of an object may not be accompanied by the opportunity to smell or touch it, but the reverse is less likely. Therefore much of the research on **somatosensory** (touch-based) and **olfactory** (smell-based) perception is concerned with how these sources of information work in conjunction with one another (as well as with sight) . For example, does a newborn baby treat the smell of its mother as independent from her touch or as part of an integrated experience of her presence? **Classical conditioning** has been used to answer this question. The technique is to use naturally occurring behaviours (as in instrumental conditioning described in Chapter 2) and then look to see if a connection can be formed between this behaviour – the **unconditioned response** (or UCR) and a preceding 'cue' which is called the **unconditioned stimulus** (UCS). If the connection is formed, then the cue alone will start to produce the behaviour. This is called the conditioned response (CR). The most famous example is Pavlov's dog,

Panel 3.1 Touch and smell

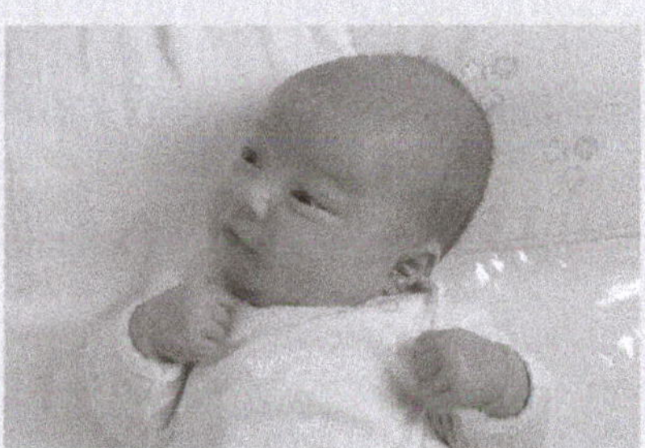

- *Somatosensory* (touch) and *olfactory* (smell) senses are very important in helping a baby bond with its mother
- Newborns have the ability to connect the smell of their own mothers with the feel of her touch
  - *Classical conditioning* can be used to show this
- The *unconditioned stimulus* is the mother's touch
  - This elicits a head turn to mother
- The *conditioned stimulus* is a scent presented just before the touch
  - This 'prepares' the child for the feel of the mother's stroking
- Subsequently the baby turns its head to be stroked on smelling the scent alone
- This shows a natural and adaptive propensity to associate smell and touch

where the smell of food (UCS) elicited the UCR (salivation), but when it was immediately preceded by a tone (conditioned stimulus, or CS) for a while, the tone alone then produced the salivation (CR). Classical conditioning only works when the CS precedes the UCS – it works as a cue or predictor. In one such study with 1-day-old infants (Sullivan et al., 1991), the baby's natural response to tactile stimulation was the unconditioned response. This was gentle stroking of the baby's face and limbs, which produced general activity and some turning towards the source of the stroking (this could be the rooting reflex you learned about in Chapter 2). In one condition, the stroking was preceded by the presentation of a cotton swab of a citrus odour; in a second, the swab was presented after the stroking (a control condition). The next day, the investigators presented the test stimulus, which was the odour on its own. General activity and head turning towards the odour was only found for babies in the condition where the odour preceded the touching, showing that they could be classically conditioned to respond to an odour stimulus cue. This can be taken at two levels. First it shows that a psychological and physiological connection can be formed between a smell and a tactile sensation. Second it could imply that this is the way in which neonates normally associate the smell of a carer with their touch, as smell in the real world is often a cue for what is about to be experienced through other senses.

3.2 TOUCH AND VISION

When connections are formed across different sensory modalities such that an object identified by one sense can be identified through another, it is often described as **cross-modal matching**. One of the earliest studies on cross-modal matching in young infants explored sight and touch. Meltzoff and Borton (1979) placed spherical shapes attached to dummies in the mouths of 1-month-old infants for over a minute without letting them see them first. Some were given a smooth sphere to explore with their mouth; others were given knobbly ones. When similar objects were given to them immediately afterwards, 24 out of 32 infants looked at the matching shape significantly more often than

Panel 3.2 Touch and vision

- Infants of 1 month old can recognise a 'knobbly' dummy that they have sucked on but not seen
  - This is called *cross-modal matching*
- Slightly older infants have shown similar matching abilities through dishabituation
- They are presented with an object to explore in either the visual or the tactile modality
- When this is presented in the other modality later they spend less time exploring it than with a novel object
- This shows transfer of familiarisation from one modality to the other

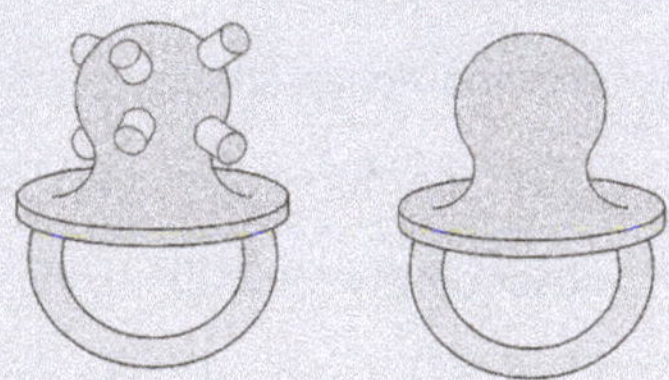

Infants suck on either a smooth or a knobbly dummy and will subsequently stare longer at the one that was in their mouth

(After Meltzoff & Borton, 1979)

expected by chance (71% of the time) – a finding replicated by others since. Using a slightly different method, Rose et al. (1983) let 6-month-old infants either feel an object they could not see, or look at it without touching. When it was presented in the other modality afterwards, along with a novel object, they played more with the new one, showing habituation to the original even though they were familiarised with it through a different modality. (See Meltzoff & Borton, 1979 for an explanation of why they expected a preference for, rather than habituation to, the original stimulus in their study.)

Most of the subsequent work on cross-modal matching, however, has been carried out with regard to the very important area of sight and sound. So let us start by thinking now about the development of auditory perception.

AUDITORY PERCEPTION AND AUDITORY-VISUAL INTEGRATION

LEARNING LANDMARKS

3.3 Locating sound sources. You should know when sound perception comes under cortical control and how that affects expectations about sound sources. You should know why the core ability to learn sight/sound pairings seems to be innate.

3.4 The perception of elementary speech sounds. You should know when babies seem sensitive to speech sounds, when they can differentiate syllables and when they have the ability to discriminate speech sounds specific to their native language.

3.5 Integrating speech perception with vision. You should know when infants can link perceived mouth movements with the sound of speech. You should be able to describe a study showing that babies link vowel sounds with lip movements.

3.3 LOCATING SOUND SOURCES

Responding to sound is part of the reflexive repertoire of the infant. Just a few minutes after birth, a newborn will orient its head towards a rhythmic rattle sound presented to one side of the baby's head (Wertheimer, 1961; Muir & Field, 1979). However, consistently with what we now know about brain development, the infant's response to sound comes under cortical control and is also better co-ordinated with visual tracking at around 4 months or so. These developments result in behaviours showing that the baby can perceive sound as coming from a visible source, i.e. as 'belonging' to an object.

One strand in the evidence that auditory perception changes from sub-cortical to cortically based at this age is the fact that sound localisation (shown by head turning) suddenly becomes more rapid and more accurate at 4 months. At this age, infants also display a phenomenon known in adults as the **precedence effect**. If identical sounds are played through two loudspeakers but separated by a delay of several milliseconds, an adult will hear this as a single sound coming from the first loudspeaker; an integration known to be produced by the auditory cortex. Darwin Muir and colleagues (Muir et al., 1989) found that before 4/5 months of age infants turn their heads towards one or other of these sound sources rather than towards one only, suggesting that their locational processing of sound is still at an immature level.

As for connecting the sound to a visible source, it has to be noted that the development of the size and shape of the visual field during the first four months is different from the size and shape of the effective auditory field. For vision, the field expands from the midline outward, reaching an effective 'adult-like' stereoscopic range by about 4 months, whilst the auditory field becomes better differentiated from a crude separation of 'to the front' or 'to the side' (0 or 90 degrees from midline) to more fine-tuned localisation (e.g. 45 degrees from midline) during that period. Not surprisingly then, 4 months, the age at which the visual and auditory fields are in some harmony, is the age identified by researchers as the point at which sound and sight seem to be correlated by the infant at least in terms of location information. It is around this age that the infant 'expects' a sound to come from a visible source, as shown by onset of reaching towards an invisible sound source played in the dark (Hillier et al., 1992). It seems also to be the age at which there is an expectation that different (unseen) noises probably mean different objects. Wilcox et al. (2006) found that infants aged 4½ months expected two objects to be behind a screen when they heard two distinct rattle sounds separated by a time gap; they were surprised when the screen was lowered and only one rattle was present.

But the world is full of objects making noises – it is one thing to look towards a sound source, such as a noisy radiator, it is quite another to expect the radiator to make a particular sort of noise. You may expect it to make a clunking sound but you wouldn't expect it to start singing. The nature of auditory-visual correlations is complex and depends on how objects are becoming classified. Early findings in this area of research showed that, at 4 months, there is already a crude classification of type and pattern of sound made by an animate versus inanimate source. For example, Spelke (1976) showed 4-month-old infants a film of a baton hitting a block at one side of the visual field and of a woman playing peek-a-boo at the other, whilst a speaker placed centrally played a soundtrack corresponding to either one or the other. The infants preferred to look at the appropriate film. It has been discovered since then that the basic ability to *learn* a pairing between sight and sound seems to be present from birth. Morongellio et al. (1998) habituated newborns to a toy making a particular sound and found no dishabituation when its location was altered, but they did find dishabituation if the sound was paired with a different toy. Remember that the 'knowledge' of that particular toy is likely to be fleeting and not yet part of a stable memory of the world. But the apparently innate ability to pair sight and sound with regard to an object's identity is the key basis on which the child will then start to form the more stable cross-modal perceptions of objects that emerge at a few months old. We also now know that another general property of sounding objects learned at an early age is the temporal and spatial synchrony that usually accompanies objects in a dynamic situation, i.e. that a sound moves in the direction of a moving object. An expectation that this should occur was shown in 2-month-old infants. Bremner et al. (2011) habituated babies to a moving ball on a video display and used a setup with two speakers that created a sound in synchrony with the direction of movement of the ball. They then found that babies dishabituated during dislocation of the apparent movement of the sound (i.e. such that the sound seemed to move in the opposite direction from the ball).

Taken together, these studies show that the brain's ability to create an intersensory percept of an object is present from very early on, and allows for learning about the general properties of sounding objects.

Panel 3.3 Locating sound sources

- Sight/sound co-ordinations seem to stem from an innate ability to learn pairings between objects and the sounds they make
    - Newborns who are habituated to a toy/sound pairing will dishabituate if the sound is switched to a different toy
- It is thought that hearing becomes under cortical rather than sub-cortical control at around 4 months
- This is accompanied by *intersensory co-ordination* of sound and sight which causes a baby to expect:
    - a sound to come from a visible source at the location of the sound
    - the type of sound made to be consistent with the properties of the visible source

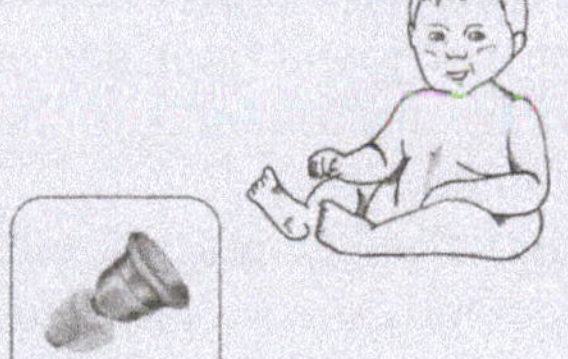

Drawing of baby by Miller

One of the most prevalent sounding objects in a baby's life is the human face, and so one of the first *specific* intersensory correlations we might expect it to learn is the sight of moving lips and the sound of a human voice. We explore this in the next section.

3.4 THE PERCEPTION OF ELEMENTARY SPEECH SOUNDS

There has been a natural interest in the sound source that is of paramount importance to our species – the human voice. A natural question therefore is whether speech is heard by an infant as a special sound coming from another human. This seems to be the case. In fact the origins of speech perception go right back to the child's experience **in utero** (in the womb). A 5–7-month-old foetus can hear the intrauterine sounds of blood flow. However, the sounds of the female voice are distinctively different in both frequency and decibels levels from these background noises. In a study by Lecanuet et al. (1989), the speech sound 'babi' or 'biba' were played through loudspeakers close to the abdomens of expectant mothers in the last three months of pregnancy. On hearing a sound the foetus' heart rate slowed down initially before returning to normal. In the majority of cases studied, the heart rate slowed down again when the sound was changed from either from 'babi' to 'biba' or vice versa, which implies discrimination. DeCasper et al. (1994) found similar effects when the sound was a rhyme recited by the mother on a daily basis for four weeks during late gestation. Heart rate dropped below normal when a tape recording of the recitation was played as compared to a control recording.

You may be wondering if the babies were sensitive not only to a particular rhyme but also to their own mother's voice and, if so, do they remember this sound after they are born? Research using the non-nutritive sucking method described in Section 2.7 has suggested that this is indeed the case. DeCasper and Fifer reported a seminal study in *Science* showing that newborns prefer the sound of their own mother's voice reading a story to that of another female (DeCasper & Fifer, 1980). Other work by DeCasper and colleagues has elaborated on these findings and has shown that the process of learning sounds continues rapidly and immediately after birth. By 2 days old infants already prefer to hear sounds in their native language (Moon et al., 1993) and can distinguish syllables that are associated with the onset of their mother's voice from others that are not (Moon & Fifer, 1990).

What is actually being acquired during the development of early speech perception? Before speech sounds come to have actual meanings, they have to be **segmented** into the units that will later become words or parts of words – syllables. Conditioned sucking was used by Eimas and colleagues to produce the rather dramatic finding that infants as young as 1 month old can distinguish **phonemes** 'ba' and 'pa' (Eimas et al., 1971). Adults can distinguish these sounds using an acoustic characteristic called the **Voice Onset Time (VOT)**, which refers to the lag between the burst of air expelled and the movement of the larynx that converts it to sound. At a certain VOT value along a continuum, adults either hear the 'voiced' consonant 'b' or the unvoiced consonant 'p'. The infants in the Eimas study were conditioned to suck at a high rate every time an auditory stimulus was played. Once the sucking rate had declined to a base level using either the 'ba' or 'pa' sound, infants dishabituated to sounds with a different VOT. Importantly, most recovery of interest was found when this interval crossed the categorical boundary perceived by adults, i.e. between the sound 'ba' and the sound 'pa'. This finding, published in *Science*, kick-started an avalanche of research on infants' sensitivity to the syllable structure of their native as well as foreign languages. Moon et al.

(1992) found syllable differentiation in 2-day-old infants. It soon emerged that very young infants seem to have an ability to distinguish phonemes in non-native languages as well as in their own, but that this ability starts to disappear after about 8 months (Werker & Tees, 2002). This is now known to be related to cortical development and the process of synaptic pruning you read about earlier.

Panel 3.4 The perception of elementary speech sounds

- Unborn babies seem to be sensitive to the sound of a human voice as measured by changes in heart-rate when speech syllables are played close to the pregnant mother's abdomen
  - They prefer to listen to their mother's voice rather than that of a stranger after they are born, as measured by increased sucking rate
- Infants can discriminate syllables almost from birth as measured by sucking rate using the habituation paradigm
- They continue to show that they can differentiate speech sounds until about 8 months
  - After this, their sensitivity to speech sounds becomes specific to their native language
- This is thought to be the result of synaptic pruning

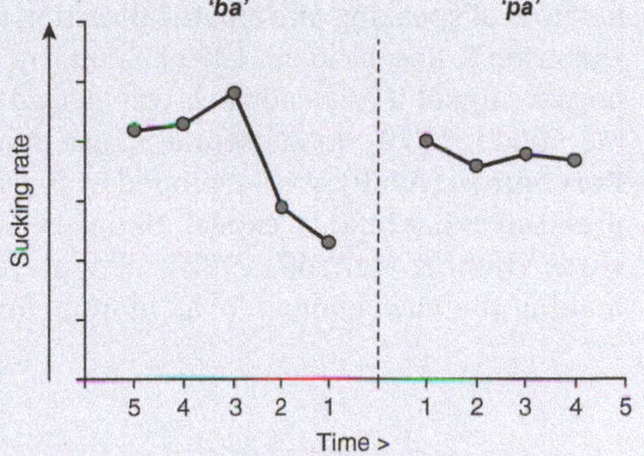

Newborns detect the boundary between 'ba' and 'pa'

(Adapted from Eimas et al., 1971)

Stress, intonation, the duration of vowels, amplitude, pitch and pauses all combine to produce a rhythmical pattern called **prosody**. For example, English usually has a multi-syllable rhythmical pattern that puts a stronger stress on the first syllable (DOGgie, BOW-wow, BUMPS-a-daisy). The infant's detection of prosody was studied by Peter Jusczyk at Johns Hopkins University in Baltimore, who established that infants under 1 year old will listen longer to passages with prosodic breaks at clauses or phrases than to passages with interruptions (artificially) inserted elsewhere in the speech stream. Because immersion in a particular language starts to dominate the development of speech perception, the basis for such auditory segmentation varies across languages.

Different languages not only have different syllabic stress patterns, they also vary in terms of which of the prosodic features need to be attended to and Jusczyk found that specific sensitivity to the stress patterns in the native language becomes evident during the second half of the first year of life (Jusczyk, 1999). In short, it seems that the early learning of speech is about acquiring the rhythms of your native language.

3.5 INTEGRATING SPEECH PERCEPTION WITH VISION

This rapid early learning of the importance of speech sounds sets in train a lengthy process that will result in the baby generally smiling when spoken to by 2 months, being able to discriminate different emotional intonations between 3 and 7 months, and then actually responding to specific words between 8 and 12 months. So a key question is, when does a baby connect the characteristics of the speech sounds it hears with the visual properties of a 'talking head'? Some early studies showed that babies at 2 months old would be upset by a setup causing a separation between the location of speaking face and the direction from which the sound was apparently coming (Aronson & Rosenbloom, 1971). Similarly, infants between 10 and 16 weeks old would become upset if a soundtrack was played out of synch with a film of a person speaking (Dodd, 1979). In subsequent research, a method called **Auditory-Visual Speech Perception** (AVSP) was developed by Patricia Kuhl and Andy Meltzoff to discover more precisely what infants 'expect' to hear when they see someone speak. In a pioneering study (Kuhl & Meltzoff, 1982), they played filmed side-by-side images of a speaker making the vowel sound 'o' as in 'pop' or 'ee' as in 'peep' with a loudspeaker placed

Panel 3.5 Integrating speech perception with vision

- Babies expect speech to come from a 'talking head' from at least 4 months old
    - This can be demonstrated by playing sound tracks of a mother's voice that appear to come from a different location from the mother
        - This will cause distress to the infant
- The *Auditory-Visual Speech Perception* (AVSP) technique used preferential looking to establish that babies could link specific lip movement with the vowel sounds 'oo' and 'ee' between 4 and 5 months

Drawing by Miller

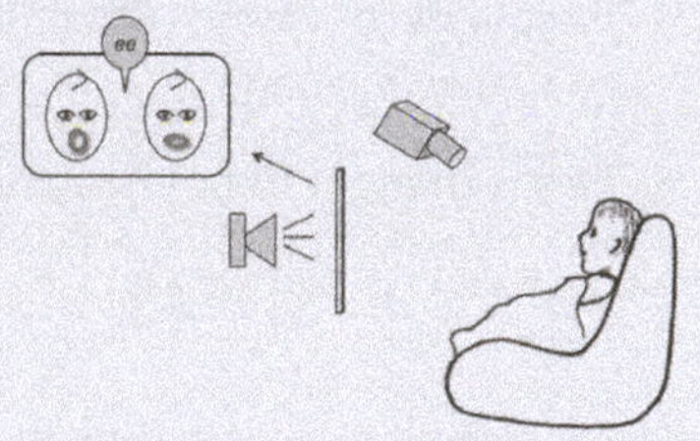

Babies are shown videos of a face making an 'oo' or 'ee' sound with one of those sounds located midway between the two faces. They look longer at the face that is mouthing the heard sound

(After Kuhl & Meltzoff, 1982)

between the two images making one or other of those two sounds. They found that 24 out of 32 infants between 4 and 5 months looked significantly longer at the face corresponding to the soundtrack. Recent research has found evidence that the linking of perceived lip movements and voice can be found at 2 months (Patterson & Werker, 2003) and even at a few hours old (Aldridge et al., 1999). These findings point to a (possibly innate) binding between phonetic and visual information at a very primitive level. Having said that, it cannot be automatically assumed that synchronised audio-visual input from a face is necessarily beneficial for infant face perception, as there is some evidence that it can actually interfere with the ability to discriminate faces in the first two months (Bahrick et al., 2013).

Not only does speech perception soon become dependent on the particular linguistic environment of the child, extensive research by Kuhl has indicated that the full integration of visual and acoustic information in speech perception crucially involves the child's own ability to articulate speech sounds (Kuhl, 1985). This also concerns the child's motor and imitative development, and we shall pick up the theme of the development of speech perception again in Chapter 5.

LEARNED EXPECTATIONS ABOUT THE PHYSICAL WORLD

A world populated by things and people is not a static picture but a constantly moving mosaic of things, people and background. The dynamics of this world are of course governed partly by the laws of physics; some events in space are possible, such as an object being stopped in its tracks by an obstacle, or a glass shattering when it falls to the floor; others are not – such as the object moving through the obstacle or the glass re-assembling itself. Using its many senses to learn how the world usually behaves is important in allowing a child to predict what happens when he or she acts on the world or when objects in the world act on one another. This is sometimes called 'naïve physics' and we consider this now.

LEARNING LANDMARKS

3.6 The Violation of Expectation (VoE) method. You should know what this means and what is inferred from it. You should be able to explain how it differs from preferential looking.

3.7 Occlusion events. You should know at what age babies seem to understand that a moving object re-appears after being temporarily occluded. You should know

(Continued)

(Continued)

at what age expectations about occlusion take account of the relative height of the object and the occluder.

3.8 Invisible blocking. You should be familiar with a famous drawbridge experiment and know how and why it seemed to overturn one of Piaget's claims about the perception of object occlusion.

3.9 Containment. You should be able to cite a study showing the difference between a baby's expectations about occlusion versus their expectations about containment and also how using transparent occluders and containers alters these.

3.10 Support. You should know how babies' surprise at the impossible suspension of objects becomes gradually more sophisticated during the first year of life.

3.6 THE VIOLATION OF EXPECTATION (VOE) METHOD

Most of the research regarding the infant's growing knowledge of the physical world has been based on studying looking behaviours, and in a large part through an extensive series of studies conducted by Renee Baillargeon and her colleagues at the University of Illinois commencing from the 1980s. Using the length of time an infant stares at an event in the world, Baillargeon has built up a picture of what the infant comes to expect when, for example, one object collides with, disappears behind, or is balanced on another. As we have already seen, the way an infant looks at something is a means of measuring the content of its perceived world – what it already seems to 'know' about and can discriminate accordingly. In Baillargeon's studies, looking behaviour is used as a measure of what the child finds surprising. As she puts it, 'infants look reliably longer at events that violate as opposed to confirm their physical expectations'. In her studies, different events are presented to the child and, essentially, Baillargeon is assuming that if these events appear 'normal' to the infant, then they are already part of the world to which the child has become habituated. They will thus attract less interest in the first place than events that seem impossible or bizarre. She calls this technique the Violation of Expectation (VoE) method.

Sometimes it is observed that this argument seems contradictory to the one used in connection with preferential looking, which assumes that babies look longer at something that is actually 'expected' or 'normal' – such as orienting towards speech sounds coming from where the speaking head is located. The difference is this: in preferential looking, the baby's choice of what to engage with *in the first place* is measured, and the assumption is that babies don't choose to look first at something that is either disturbing or uninteresting; whilst in VoE studies, they are usually already familiarised with a 'normal' event until it is no longer of any particular interest – as in habituation studies. So what is measured here is whether they look longer at a *subsequent* event that presents an impossibility versus one that doesn't. If they do look longer at the impossible event, the assumption is that they can tell the difference between the two types of event, and that they look longer at it because it is surprising.

A further concern is that what we are really measuring (in both cases) here is simply the relative excitability of the nervous system in response to a change in stimulation. This can be subject to a whole variety of influences that can predict some of the outcomes without having to infer anything at all about the infant's actual understanding of the world. But there is one argument that invites us to accept Baillargeon's account, and that is that there is a certain logic to the gradual unfolding of sensitivity to increasingly complex types of information. If we accept her own interpretation of the VoE results, Baillargeon has apparently shown how the infant expects the world of objects to behave at different ages and stages of infancy.

Panel 3.6 The VoE method

- A variation of the habituation method that is used to study how the child expects the world to behave is the *Violation of Expectation* (VoE) technique
- This is based on habituating the infant to aspects of the physical world and then measuring their looking time (dishabituation) when a deliberate violation of a physical law is introduced
    - This can be related to:
        - How things move in space
        - How things are occluded
        - How things are supported
- If the baby stares longer at the impossible event than at a possible one, then it suggests that the baby knows how objects in the physical world should behave
- This is different from preferential looking, which measures what a baby will *choose* to look at; the baby has no choice in VoE and longer looking indicates surprise at what they see
- The VoE method is sometimes criticised as it assumes that a heightened interest in the impossible event is necessarily a 'surprise' reaction
    - But it could be that the impossible event is just particularly different from the familiar event and causes increased arousal

3.7 OCCLUSION EVENTS

From around 3 months, infants show **smooth pursuit tracking** and can even start to anticipate the location of a moving object (Johnson, 2002). When an object disappears behind another under these conditions, its contours become systematically 'wiped' by the occluding object; it doesn't just disappear as if the lights were turned off. From studies done first by Bower, we know that infants of around 5 months expect an object in a moving trajectory to emerge from behind an occluder at a time consistent with their velocity before disappearing. Disruption of eye tracking occurs only if the object appears too quickly.

Baillargeon's work has elaborated further on the many ways in which an object can be occluded; an object can be covered or obscured by another moving object, or it can disappear behind another whilst in motion or by being placed inside another object. Infants have to learn the dynamics of these different occlusion events and it appears they do so in gradual stages throughout their first year. This learning occurs in tandem with what they are learning about the shape and size of objects, by sight, touch or hearing. So in the young infant looking at, listening to, and exploring objects manually helps to create different sorts of categories of physical event related to objects disappearing. Whilst it is impossible to specify the precise steps in this learning, it is possible to take a 'litmus' test of what the child seems to have learned at different ages about these events. Let us take one specific example, based on the scene shown in Panel 3.7. Luo and Baillargeon (2005) found that infants of 2½ months were not surprised when

Panel 3.7 Occlusion events

- Babies at 2½ months expect to see a rolling ball re-emerge behind the screens in (a) but not in (b), suggesting they have a basic concept of occlusion but no concept of an occluder with a 'gap'
- At 3½ months babies expect a tall object to partly re-appear behind a short screen but are not surprised when a short object fails to re-appear
- They do not show this at the age of 3 months

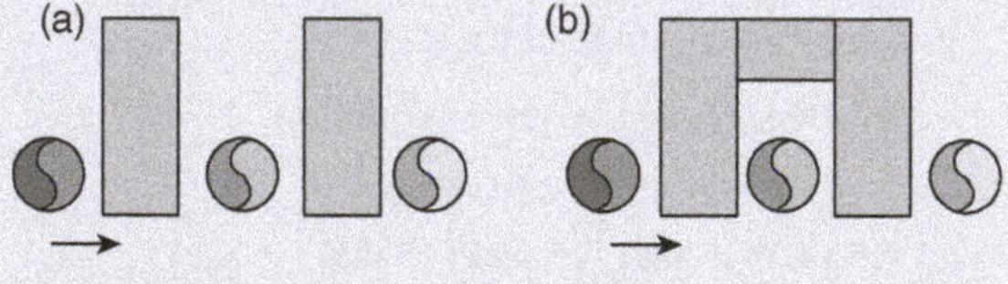

(After Luo & Baillargeon, 2005, with permission)

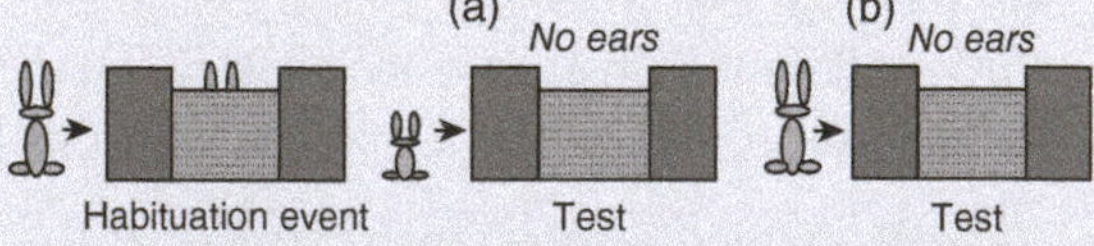

At 3½ months babies are not surprised when a short object fails to re-appear behind a short screen (a) but expect a tall object to partly re-appear and are surprised by event (b). (After Baillargeon & Graber, 1987, with permission)

the cylinder moving in a left-to-right trajectory reappeared after passing behind each of the screens in (a). However, they showed surprise at the object's re-appearance mid-trajectory, when the screens were connected at the top as illustrated in (b), suggesting that they did not see the cut-away mid-portion as a gap but rather perceived the whole screen as a single occluding object.

Whilst this effect disappeared by about 3 months, it is another few weeks before they appear to have learned another aspect of occlusion, and that is the consequences of having a moving object that is either taller or shorter than the occluding object. Before this, they fail to register selective surprise when a tall (as opposed to a small) object does not partly show when moving behind an occluder that is lower in height as depicted in Panel 3.7.

3.8 INVISIBLE BLOCKING

Baillargeon's most famous example of an occlusion event has a strong bearing on an issue we return to in detail in Chapter 4. For now, you need only know that Piaget claimed that infants younger than 8 months behave as if objects cease to exist when they are fully occluded behind a cloth or screen. Already you can see from tracking studies that this cannot be entirely true. However, there is an arguable difference between situations that invite the baby to track with head and eyes – providing a sort of motor momentum – and invisible 'blocking' situations where the baby is looking straight ahead at something static that is then covered over (as in Piaget's studies). In her 'drawbridge' experiment,

Panel 3.8 Invisible blocking

- Piaget found that babies would not reach behind a screen for a fully occluded object until they were aged around 8 months
- If the VoE method is used, however, it can be demonstrated that they understand 'object permanence' well before this age
- In the drawbridge experiment, infants of 4 months old show surprise when a screen continues in a full arc, showing that they expect it to be blocked in its path by the 'invisible' object

Drawing by Miller

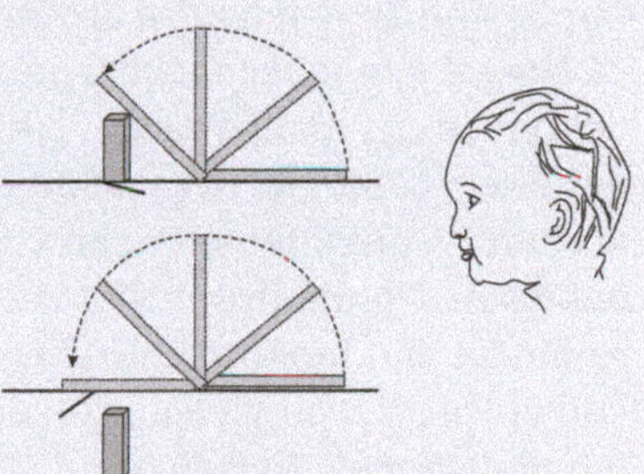

An infant of 4 months will stare longer at an impossible event (created using a trapdoor) where a recently occluded object should block the path of a screen being lowered backwards

(After Baillargeon, 1987, with permission)

Baillargeon (1987) presented babies with the scene depicted in Panel 3.8. The motion of the flat occluder (the drawbridge) as it is moved in a vertical arc will be arrested at about 120 degrees when it comes to rest on the upright object. That object will therefore have been invisible during the time the drawbridge was in the upright position. Does that invisibility mean that the baby now 'forgets' that there is an obstacle in the way? If so, it should not be surprised when the occluder continues to move through 180 degrees, until it comes to rest on its back. This 'impossible' scenario was contrived through sleight of hand by letting the obstacle fall through a trap door as depicted in Panel 3.8. Babies as young as 4 months displayed the VoE effect in this situation. Baillargeon provided a clear demonstration not only that young babies appear to understand that static objects continue to exist when occluded, but also that one object can invisibly block the movement of another. We shall return to why Piaget did not find evidence of this kind of object 'permanence' in Chapter 4.

3.9 CONTAINMENT

In the first few months, infants will have more opportunities to see occlusion events than to explore objects manually. So it makes some sense that occlusion events requiring understanding of 'inside' rather than simply 'obscured' take somewhat longer to appear. In a study by Hespos and Baillargeon (2001), infants were presented with events depicted in Panel 3.9. In scene (a) a tall or short object is dropped behind a cylindrical container with its back cut away in a possible (upper) or impossible (lower) manner; in (b) exactly the same scenes are witnessed, but, as the container is complete, this is containment rather than occlusion. The awareness that a tall object *should* remain partly visible in the (lower) scenes was in evidence in (a), as before, by around 4/5 months – and they registered surprise when a tall object disappeared completely behind a short occluder. But at this age, the infants showed *no* surprise when tall objects disappeared *into* short containers (b) and only looked longer at this impossibility when aged around 7½ months.

Now try to make an informed guess. In a variation of this study, Luo and Baillargeon, described in Baillargeon (2002), compared occlusion and containment when the occluder/container was made of transparent Plexiglass. An object and the transparent occluder/container were shown side by side. A screen was placed in front of both, and the baby saw a hand drop the object down towards the occluder/container. The screen was removed and looking time was measured for a 'possible' event in which the object was still visible but now behind/inside the occluder/container and an 'impossible' one where it had disappeared from view. What do you think they found? One mark for guessing that *both* situations failed to elicit a surprise reaction in babies until they were considerably older than those who showed surprise in the standard opaque occluder/container situation. Transparency is a property of only some time types of object and is likely to require some extensive experience with materials such as glass and plastic. A second mark if you reckoned, however, that there would still be an advantage of occlusion over containment; the former elicited surprise in the impossible condition at around 8½ months; the latter only at 10 months. Three marks if you reasoned that, actually, transparency is *more* likely to be encountered in containment situations through bottles, drinking glasses, etc. as this shows you are really thinking! However, this is not what was found, and Baillargeon's own reasoning was that the child is actually learning first and foremost about different types of *event*, rather than different types of *thing* – and that containment and occlusion are very different events. Which, of course, they are.

Panel 3.9 Containment

- Babies at 4½ months old are surprised when tall objects disappear completely behind short occluders (a) but are 7½ months old before they show the same reaction when an object is dropped into a container (b)
- It is argued that this shows that infants learn about the different types of ways in which an object can disappear
- Transparency is an unusual version of an object being occluded or contained and this develops some two months after understanding in regard to opaque materials

Drawing by Miller

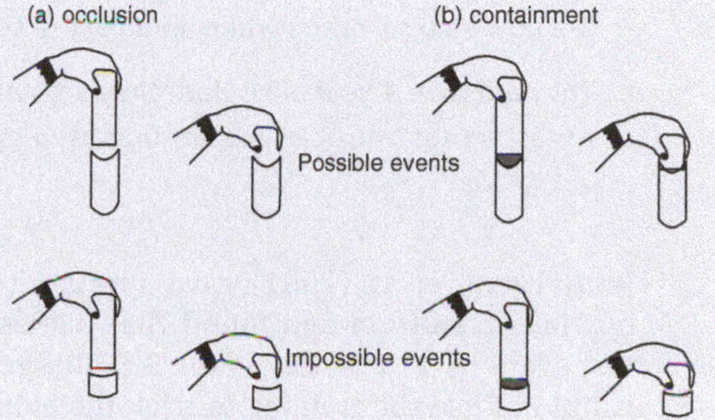

Babies show surprise when objects completely disappear behind occluders or containers that are smaller than the object (bottom two pictures)

(After Hespos & Baillargeon, 2001, with permission)

3.10 SUPPORT

Statics and dynamics are another everyday aspect of the physical world. Move an object too close to the edge of the table and it will fall off. Baillargeon used her technique of measuring looking time to see if infants express surprise about the suspension and support of objects that would seem impossible to us. As a broad category of experience, the child seems to learn the rules of support gradually and in line with the complexity of the rule being acquired. At 3 months, babies register surprise if an object appears to be suspended in mid-air above another but not when supported by another object. By 6½ months, they will distinguish 'possible' events from 'impossible' ones – where the bulk of the object (and its centre of gravity) is not resting on the support object. And it is not until after the child's first birthday that he or she will take into account the weight distribution of the object as depicted in Panel 3.10. In line with the view that this is actually learned through experience,

Panel 3.10 Support

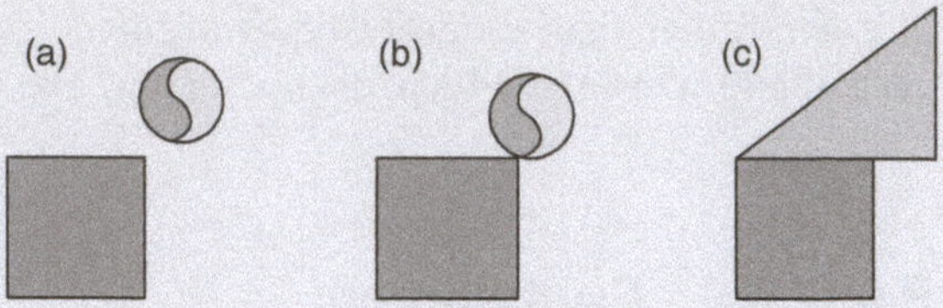

- Babies show surprise at 3 months old when they see one object apparently suspended in mid-air with support (a)
- By 6½ months old, their expectations are more sophisticated and they are now also surprised when an object is 'supported' in an impossible manner (b)
- They are over 1 year old before they are naturally sensitive to the distribution of weights necessary for one object to be supported by another (c)

(a) (b) (c)

Baillargeon et al. (2001) gave specific 'teaching' on a normal box-stays versus a box-falls condition and found that babies could show surprise at an 'impossible' test event by 11 months (Wang & Baillargeon, 2008). Reassuringly, the investigators could not use the training to trick the babies into thinking that inadequate support would *not* lead to the box falling. Clearly their world knowledge was strong enough to resist any such 'teaching'.

Finally, you may have noticed that these developments are largely to do with object behaviour rather than object properties such as shape. Is it possible for the rules about object dynamics to be in place without necessarily having strong expectations about the continued visual *identity* of objects under different sorts of relocation? The ability to represent an object in space without apparently representing or remembering its defining features is an unusual concept for us, but it is precisely what has been found for 6-month-old babies by Kibbe and Leslie (2011) and is fully consistent with what you are about to learn about the 'object concept'.

CHAPTER SUMMARY

Information becomes correlated across the senses in the first few months: touch and vision from around 1 month; sight with sound by 4 months. Elementary speech sounds are detected at birth and become progressively correlated with the properties of a 'talking head'. Techniques based on looking time show progressive tuning to the physical properties of the world such as movement, occlusion and support. By 10 months, babies have a fully integrated perception of the physical world and expect it to obey simple physical laws.

LOOKING AHEAD TO CHAPTER 4

As you can now see from the last two chapters, a considerable amount of what *we* have learned about the child's growing awareness has been gleaned from the visual modality, i.e. looking behaviours. But looking alone will not have been the child's only route to that knowledge. By the ages at which these skills are emerging, the child will *also* have reached out for objects, touched them, turned them around and (later) even crawled amongst them, providing opportunities for sensory integration in a rich three-dimensional world. One of the most important elements within a dynamic world therefore is the child's own behaviour, enabling a cycle of feedback between action, expectation, outcome and next action. So far, we have touched very little on the contribution made by the child's own activity. However, in the next chapter, we shall move on to consider the contribution to cognitive development made by more bodily means of exploring the world.

CHAPTER 4

SENSORIMOTOR DEVELOPMENT IN INFANCY: GAINING CONTROL IN A PHYSICAL ENVIRONMENT

As you have seen, the infant's knowledge may be *measured* without him or her doing much other than look or suck, but this chapter will remind you that knowledge about the world is unlikely to be *acquired* without considerable input from the baby's movements in the world. There are numerous ways in which the baby's explorations with limbs and body continue to develop an awareness and understanding of the world of space and objects during the second year of life, through the cycle of feedback between new motor skills and their outcomes. This is critically related to the functional development of the brain as you will see.

GOAL-DIRECTED BEHAVIOUR AND THE FRONTAL CORTEX

LEARNING LANDMARKS

4.1 The frontal cortex and executive functions. You should know where this is located in the brain and be aware of its role in complex actions. You should know what executive functioning refers to.

4.2 The frontal cortex, action sequencing and the object concept. You should understand why complex actions involve action sequencing and impulse inhibition, and be able to relate this to an important stage of the 'object concept'.

4.3 The A-not-B task and motor inhibition. You should know what this task is, and why it is a test of motor inhibition in infants.

4.1 THE FRONTAL CORTEX AND EXECUTIVE FUNCTIONS

What is a goal-directed behaviour? What are executive functions? Broadly speaking, these are the same thing and can be any thing from making a cup of tea to playing the piano. In the context of infant development, it is often about deliberate actions towards objects. Even an apparently simple act of taking a toy from a toy box will call on the brain's command centre for this sort of goal-oriented behaviour. This area of the brain is the frontal cortex. At the top is a part that is heavily connected to the motor cortex called the **supplementary motor area** (SMA) (see Panel 4.1) – an area that shows increased electrical activity towards the end of the first year of life. This is thought to be involved in the sequencing of actions – a fundamental element of goal-directed behaviour as you will see in the next section. But executive functioning (often shortened to EF) is also thought to depend on an area of the brain called the **prefrontal cortex** (or PFC). Located at the front of the frontal lobes, the PFC represents about one third of the human brain. It is the last brain region to mature, with changes in its functioning continuing into adolescence. It is also the best 'connected' part of the brain with neural pathways extending into most other brain regions. It is itself composed of separate regions: the **dorsolateral** region which has strong connections with all the sensory cortices (visual, auditory and somatosensory) and the **orbitofrontal** region which, amongst other things, is thought to have a strong role in inhibiting sensory information when necessary – see e.g. O'Hearn et al. (2008). For several decades now, it has been clearly established that it is the prefrontal area of the cortex that performs the complex task of allowing a motor plan to be executed until a goal has been achieved. This is because it serves a number of key functions that are relevant to the goal, but also because it integrates all the sources of information that are required to plan what to do next. The main components of executive functioning (EF) are commonly split into:

- Performing a particular *sequence* of actions to obtain a goal
- *Monitoring* relevant sensory input and making choices
- *Inhibiting* sensory input and behavioural impulses that are not relevant to the goal

- Keeping *working memory* active and updated with sensory input until the goal has been achieved
- *Planning* the next action in the sequence of behaviours required to obtain the goal

Panel 4.1 The frontal cortex and executive functions

- The frontal cortex is a highly connected area of the brain
  - It is involved in planned *goal-directed behaviour*
- This is also known as *executive functioning* (EF)
  - Many elements of EF seem to depend on the part of the frontal lobes known as the prefrontal cortex (PFC)
- Executive functions usually entail:
- Actions to be executed in a sequence
  - This is controlled by the *supplementary motor area* (SMA) of the frontal cortex
- Monitoring relevant sensory input and making choices
  - This is heavily dependent on the *dorsolateral region* of the PFC
- Inhibiting irrelevant responses
  - This is controlled by the *orbitofrontal region* of the PFC

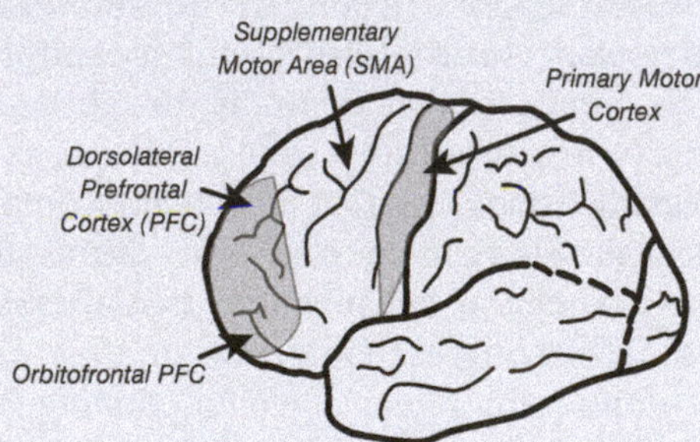

- Updating working memory
  - This involves connections between the PFC and sensory cortices as well as deep parts of the brain such as the *hippocampus*
- Planning the action sequence
  - This involves connections between the PFC and the SMA

Drawing by Miller

Some of this we know from lesion studies with animals and from patients with damaged frontal lobes, but the increasing research using **fMRI** (functional magnetic resonance imaging) is also helping to indicate areas within the PFC that seem particularly implicated in the different elements of EF. For example, sensory monitoring and decision making seems to particularly involve the dorsolateral prefrontal cortex, whilst the inhibitory functions seem to implicate the orbitofrontal prefrontal cortex. To update working memory, connections are needed between the PFC and the sensory cortices that are relevant to the goal. If the action plan requires spatial navigation, it will also implicate connections between the PFC and the deep memory centre of the brain that seems specialised for spatial information known as the **hippocampus**. The frontal cortex is not only highly connected to other structures in the brain, it also has complex internal structures that are only now being unravelled. For example, action planning has been shown to be based on connections between the orbitofrontal PFC and the supplementary motor area (Rempel-Clower, 2007). Let is now return to thinking about the development of the infant's goal-directed behaviour and consider it in these terms.

4.2 THE FRONTAL CORTEX, ACTION SEQUENCING AND THE OBJECT CONCEPT

As they approach their first birthday infants become more obviously goal-directed in their behaviour. For example, one of the major achievements of the second half of an infant's first year, as famously documented by Piaget, is to succeed on the first of two crucial stages of acquiring what is sometimes called the **object concept** or a test of **object permanence**. There are many preliminary stages and sub-stages of the object concept but two in particular demonstrate new goal-directed activities. One (Stage 4) is the ability at around the age of 6/7 months to remove a cloth or occluder in order to reach for a toy hidden underneath or behind it. Before then, the baby fails to do this even if the object makes a sound or is causing a distinct bulge in the cloth. Why do the cortical connections that already exist between vision and movement not allow successful retrieval? We know from Baillargeon's studies using looking time (see Chapter 3, Section 3.6) that babies seem to 'know' that an object is behind an occluder at 4/5 months old. We also know that babies can reach for a visible object at this age. So what special demands does this particular reaching-for-an-occluded-object task make on the baby's brain? We can now answer this in terms of the development of executive control.

Adele Diamond at the University of Pennsylvania argued that the Piaget's Stage 4 test of object permanence is a **means–ends** task; requiring two actions to be executed to secure a goal, such as reach and lift cloth, then reach for object. Diamond argued that even a simple act of reaching into an open box to grasp an object may require an action sequence: moving the hand out toward the centre of the box (action 1) and then back towards the front wall of the box (action 2) to locate the toy (see Panel 4.2). Based on findings from studies with monkeys and clinical research with humans, Diamond argues that the ability to execute two actions in a sequence requires the SMA part of the cortex to be fully functional. Tested over a variety of different conditions (Diamond & Gilbert, 1989), it became clear that the two-directional reach was indeed the source of difficulty for babies under 7 months old.

Panel 4.2 The frontal cortex, action sequencing and the object concept

- Goal-directed behaviour often requires actions to be executed in sequence such as combining two movements in order to reach an object

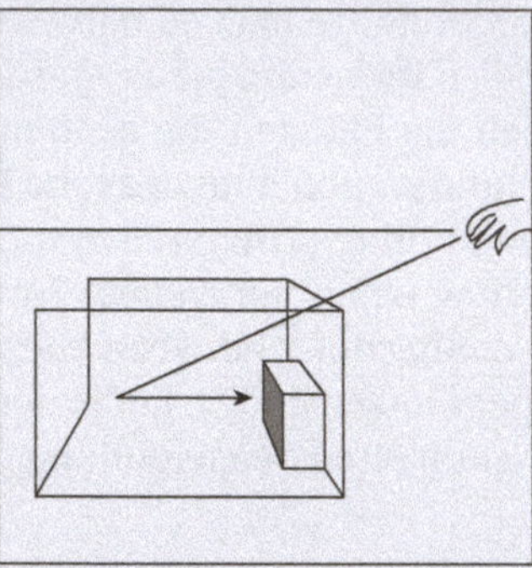

(From Diamond & Gilbert, 1989, with permission)

- The development of elementary reaching behaviours in the second half of the first year of an infant's life is related to the functional maturing of the supplementary motor area
- It also often involves inhibiting other behaviours
- Initially this might be competing reflexive tendencies
    - Such as reflex withdrawal when an obstacle is touched
- *Motor inhibition* is known from clinical studies to be performed by the prefrontal cortex (PFC)
- *Action sequencing* often requires inhibiting one goal directed behaviour in order to switch to another action to complete the task
- The ability to perform goal-directed sequences is related to success on Piaget's Stage 4 of the object concept

- This is a first indication of action sequencing and the involvement of the PFC

But sequencing is not all. Diamond also pointed out that young infants may have to inhibit a **predominate response tendency** such as the grasping reflex, which would normally terminate the behaviour after the hand touched a solid object. It was indeed apparent that one of the problems with younger infants was the tendency to reflexively grasp the side of the box should the hand touch it by mistake, after which they would withdraw the hand and start again. Diamond argued that another key development at around 7 months was to be able to *inhibit* a reflexive behaviour that was getting in the way of the final goal. This not only seems to explain the emergence of motor sequences but also the disappearance of some earlier reflexive behaviour, such as the grasp reflex, which gradually disappears between 5 and 8 months of age.

Even after reflex behaviours are suppressed, the child still has to be able to *switch* from one action segment to another, and in that sense inhibit the first goal-directed behaviour in order to be able to engage in the second. This is known to involve the PFC. It has been well established from the 1960s that damage to the frontal cortex in human patients results in all sorts of inhibitory failure, a clinical presentation that is sometimes described as **perseverative** behaviour. This refers to the fact that a 'frontal' patient will respond to an object simply because it is there, like drinking from an empty cup or putting on someone else's jacket. These patients have difficulties carrying out psychological tasks that require them to ignore a **prepotent response** and choose something different. The development of action sequencing required by the object concept suggests to Diamond that the frontal cortex is beginning to exert normal inhibitory control in infancy. But it is still not fully functional in children under 1 year old. Let us return to the object permanence task to see why.

4.3 THE A-NOT-B TASK AND MOTOR INHIBITION

If you remember, Piaget's Stage 4 of the object concept is characterised by the fact that babies are finally able to remove a cloth occluder at about 8 months old, i.e. combining *knowledge* (demonstrated by the drawbridge experiment) with a goal-directed *action*. Now imagine that the object under the cloth is re-positioned in full view of the child. This was called a **visible displacement** by Piaget. Although many may dispute Piaget's interpretation of what happens next, the fact that it happens has rarely been challenged and constitutes Stage 5 of the object concept. At first, the infant will continue to reach to the original location even though the cloth is in the new position and again may have a highly visible bulge! Overcoming this error takes a few months and success on Stage 5 would normally occur at around 1 year of age. This transition during infant development has been the source of considerable research by (amongst others) British psychologists, George Butterworth, Gavin Bremner, Peter Willats and Paul Harris.

During this more recent research, Piaget's Stage 5 task of visible displacement has been converted into a simpler form, called the A-not-B task. A toy is hidden a few times in one of two 'wells' embedded in a tabletop and the two wells are covered simultaneously. After the child has found the object at position A a few times, the position is switched to B. When success is achieved on the A-not-B task, it appears that one cause of the success is the acquisition of the ability to inhibit the prepotent response of reaching to the first position. Indeed Diamond (1985) seemed to find that when making reaching errors, babies at around 7 months sometimes *look* at B whilst reaching for the cloth at A. Although this disconnect between looking and reaching has not been reliably replicated, when looking

Panel 4.3 The A-not-B task and motor inhibition

- Another important stage in the development of the object concept is the ability to switch from retrieving a hidden object at a familiar hiding place to a novel location
- Here the object is retrieved a few times from location A and then quite visibly hidden under a cloth in location B
    - The classic error at this stage is to continue reaching at location A
- This is called the Stage 5 or *Place Error* and occurs between 8 and 12 months
- Sometimes the baby may even look to the new hiding place (B) but can't inhibit the motor response of removing the cloth at the usual location

Location A

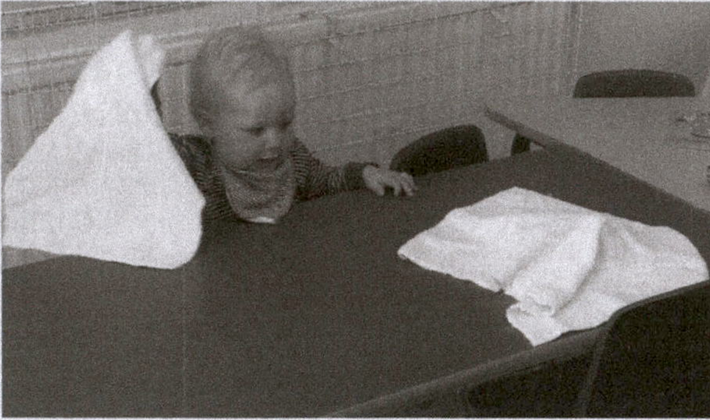

Location B

- The co-ordination of looking and reaching in this task is an executive skill requiring inhibition of a prepotent motor response

and reaching are measured separately, it does seem to be the case that correct looking behaviour precedes correct reaching until about 10 months (Cuevas & Bell, 2010). This is consistent with the idea that the motor control in making a reach is more complex at a neuropsychological level than simply looking at a remembered location in space.

Inhibiting a reaching response in order to establish a new one is one important aspect of this complexity. However, neither Diamond nor any of the other researchers suggest that the development of motor control at this stage is *just* about inhibition. Even in the A-not-B task, the baby is not just 'learning to inhibit'; he or she is establishing a new and specific complex behaviour of which motor inhibition is only a part. The baby is learning to retrieve a hidden object. There are several more senses in which this is an executive task and also in which it is a significant cognitive achievement. For this reason it has been subject to considerable research effort as you will see next.

OBJECT RETRIEVAL

LEARNING LANDMARKS

4.4 The A-not-B task and working memory. You should know why working memory is relevant to success on this task, but why it is not really accurate to say that the child has 'forgotten' where an object is 'hiding'.

4.5 The A-not-B task and spatial memory. You should understand what this task reveals about spatial memory, and be able to cite a study showing how visual information can help the baby to locate objects relative to its own position.

4.6 The A-not-B task and memory for occlusion. You should understand the psychological difference between reaching to the location in which an object has been occluded versus comprehending that an object has been occluded.

4.7 Object retrieval and planning. You should know that planning is an important aspect of goal-directed behaviour, and be able to describe a study showing planning in relation to object retrieval.

4.4 THE A-NOT-B TASK AND WORKING MEMORY

Any complex act that requires co-ordination of different components is going to make some demands on memory. Think about making a morning cup of tea. You may do it when you are sleepy and not really 'thinking', but your system will nevertheless have a short-term memory of what stage you are in the process as you go through it. Such **on-line monitoring** of behaviour is necessary for control of the physical environment and the memory it requires is known as **working memory** (WM), as it supports ongoing behaviour. If you had left the tea bags on the draining board whilst you washed your cup, it would be important to keep their new location in WM until you needed them. In the A-not-B task, the monitoring of where the object was last seen may be fragile if WM is weak, especially as there may be **proactive interference** built up from repeated experience with the previous location. The build-up of this form of interference is certainly suggested by the reliable finding that the more the hiding trials at A, the more the perseverative errors at B (Marcovitch & Zelazo, 2003).

If working memory is a significant factor in the A-not-B task, then increasing the delay between hiding the object at the new location, B, and the opportunity for retrieving it should be a sensitive index of difficulty. It is. Diamond (1985) has documented a clear systematic relationship between the length of the delay and success on this task as illustrated in Panel 4.4. Significantly, the tolerance for delay increases as the child gets older. If these achievements do imply increasing involvement of the frontal lobes, then we may expect them to be correlated with some neurophysiological changes. Bell and Fox (1992) recorded scalp EEGs in babies between 7 and 12 months of age and found that the babies who could tolerate long delays between the hiding and retrieval at the B location on the A-not-B task had greater power values recorded from the frontal brain regions, i.e. electrical activity with more 'mature' wavelength characteristics.

Measuring correlates of working memory doesn't quite tell us, however, *what* is changing in regard to the child's conception of the world. The classic problem with reconstructing the infant mind is in trying to imagine what a more primitive conception of the world would be like. Consider this. As Butterworth (1977) was one of the first to observe – the A-not-B

Panel 4.4 A-not-B task and working memory

- The A-not-B task sets up considerable *proactive interference* with laying down a memory trace for the new location
    - o The delay between seeing the object being hidden and being able to retrieve it has been found to be an age-related factor

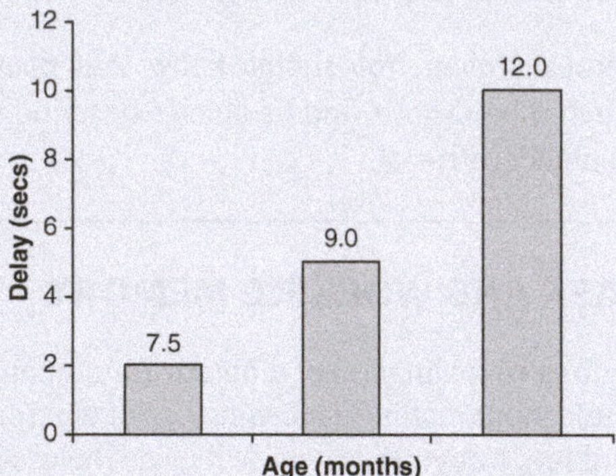

Working memory affects the A-not-B task as measured by tolerance for a delay between hiding and retrieval. It is also highly age-related (Data from Diamond, 1985)

- The fact that the error can occur even when the object is visible under a transparent cup (right picture) suggests that the memory is for where the object can be reached rather than where it is 'hidden'

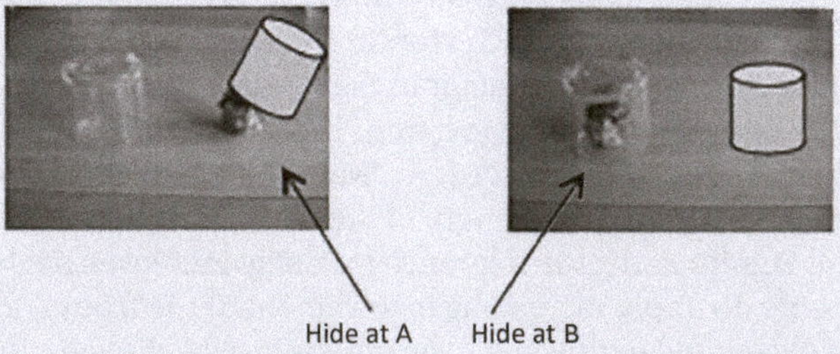

reaching error still (curiously) occurs in some 9 month olds when the cover at B is transparent *and the object is fully visible underneath*. In other words, it is not really accurate to say that the infant at this age has 'forgotten' that the hiding place has switched to B, because the encoding of the occlusion event does not yet seem based on a perception of 'hidden' in the sense of object-under-cover. Whilst a reduction in this error was found by Yates and Bemner (1988) when the babies were familiarised with the transparent cover first, it is nevertheless clear that we cannot presume that infants spontaneously encode a hiding event in the way we do as adults. We have already seen from the VoE studies that 'hiding' does not have all the connotations for an infant as it does for an adult; hiding in, behind and under are all quite different in terms of how one object behaves in relation to another, and the baby under 1 year of age does not respond to these in a single uniform way. In short, the 'memory' or 'concept' of a hidden object has yet to be established. So how does the infant conceive of the hidden object *before* adult-like knowledge has been fully acquired?

4.5 THE A-NOT-B TASK AND SPATIAL MEMORY

A very fundamental way in which the baby might represent the goal in the A-not-B task is to simply remember where things can be found in local space. Making the cover transparent has no effect on the younger infant because, Butterworth argued, the primary encoding at this age is in terms of its place in space rather than in terms of its 'objectness'. This makes sense from an evolutionary point of view, as spatial location is of fundamental importance in 'remembering' a food source or nest site, for example. Comparative psychology is rich with examples where animals behave like children in the A-not-B task.

Butterworth (1975) speculated further that an object's spatial identity might be encoded by an infant by its position relative to its own self rather than to the 'objective' space in which it was situated. In a study by Bremner and Bryant (1977), 10-month-old infants were moved to the opposite side of a table after the hiding trials. The position of B was therefore in the same position relative to the infant as it was in the original retrieval trials, and this now produced successful searching. Hiding the object in the original position (now different relative to the infant), however, produced the usual errors, as the graph in Panel 4.5 illustrates. This shows that the baby was using an **egocentric** (body-relative) spatial frame of reference for determining where to look for the object. Sometimes egocentric cues are described as **intrinsic** cues and they remain an important part of motor control throughout life.

As the only way of encoding the world, however, egocentric encoding is rather risky. If spatial position itself can be better remembered in **extrinsic** terms, this would help the infant solve the A-not-B tasks. In the tea-making example, extrinsic cues for your memory could be spatial location relative to other things (near the window), the general property of the space in which it is found (on top of blue work-top) or something specific to the object itself (look for something white and rectangular). The fact that babies make the place error shows they are not using extrinsic spatial co-ordinates such as location relative to other things. In their first study, Bremner and Bryant found that fixing the hiding location by always having it on the black half of a table did not over-rule the effect of egocentric reaching as illustrated in the graph in Panel 4.5, suggesting that that the general properties of the hiding place didn't help either.

Panel 4.5 The A-not-B task and spatial memory

- The kind of memory involved in the A-not-B task seems to be spatial in nature
- A rotating table experiment demonstrates that the spatial information is encoded in terms of a body-relative movement

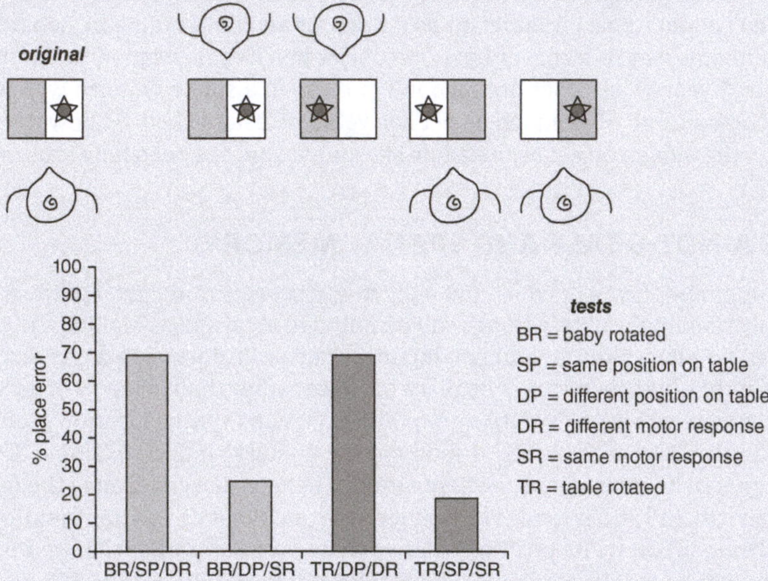

The place error is found (1st bar) when the spatial position is conserved from hiding to finding trials but the baby is moved. It is reduced (2nd bar) when its actual position is not conserved but the new hiding place is in the same position relative to the child's body. When the table is rotated so that the background colour of the hiding position is conserved, the baby still makes the place error (3rd bar), but not when body-relative position is conserved and background colour altered (4th bar). (Adapted from Bremner & Bryant, 1977, with permission)

- This is sometimes described as the use of *egocentric* or *intrinsic* cues
    - Rather than allocentric or extrinsic, such as spatial location relative to other things

But the visual properties of the object's hiding place do gradually get incorporated into the searching scenario. We have already seen that babies can learn about transparent covers. In a subsequent study by Bremner, covers of different colours were used to occlude the objects in the wells – and this did dramatically reduce the classic error. Uzgiris and Lucas (1978) found that increasing the separation between the two locations also has a large effect. These studies show that using some extrinsic visual cues is an important part of the acquisition of how to find things in a space that is still largely egocentrically defined.

4.6 THE A-NOT-B TASK AND MEMORY FOR OCCLUSION

These developments tell us about reaching to a remembered point in space but do they really tell us about learning to find a hidden object? To what extent can we say that the baby's *goal* in the A-not-B task is '*retrieve hidden object* at location x'. There is a world of difference between a goal defined in terms of *reaching* to a spatial location (because that reach has proved rewarding), versus a goal defined in terms of *retrieve a hidden object* from that location. Think of taking the lid off the tea caddy to get at the tea bags. To actively search for a hidden object, the fact that you want it, that it is behind, in or under something else, and the means of recovering it have all become an explicit part of the memory system in most of our adult search behaviours. But we cannot assume this for the infant. Importantly then, some investigators have pointed out that errors observed in the A-not-B task do not necessarily mean that the baby has been building up a representation of '*object-hidden-at-A*' at all, so much as a motor memory of '*reach-to-A*' – because it is rewarding. This may not be the repetition of a simple motor habit, however, so much as a more subtle case of 'the infant trying out the hypothesis that this is the place where appropriate action will reveal objects' (Bremner, 1994: 154).

If this is true, then earlier researchers have perhaps over-interpreted the A-not-B task as having anything at all to do with the concept of occlusion. Subsequent experiments by Smith et al. (1999) appeared to confirm this. In one of their tasks, babies are cued simply to pick up a lid – rather than find an object – at the A location and then pick up a lid at the B location – as indicated by the experimenter waving the appropriate lid (see Panel 4.6). The authors found that the same perseveration to location A occurs under these conditions, showing that the place error is not specific to hiding tasks, implying that the 'hiding' tasks may not necessarily be about 'hiding' as far as the infant is concerned.

So when does a baby incorporate specific expectations about the nature of occlusion into its goal-directed behaviour towards a hidden object? And how can we distinguish this understanding from simply knowing where to reach in space? In a recent study, Andy Bremner and Peter Bryant at Oxford University cleverly resolved this by distinguishing between the use of visual cues to indicate a location from using them to indicate where something is hidden. Think about picking up a cup versus picking up the tea caddy lid; one signals to you 'cup' – the other signals 'tea under this'. Now suppose you have a green cup and a blue cup, but also a green tea caddy lid and a blue coffee jar lid. The differentiation of green versus blue lids will be far more useful in directing you to your 'get some tea' goal than differently coloured cups when you just want a cup. Indeed,

Panel 4.6 The A-not-B task and memory for occlusion

- The place error occurs even when the object is not actually occluded. Picking up a lid (only) at place A will also produce perseveration errors
  - This was discovered using differently coloured lids
- By 10 months hiding objects at place A and place B under differently coloured lids reduces the place error, but it remains the same for 'lids only'

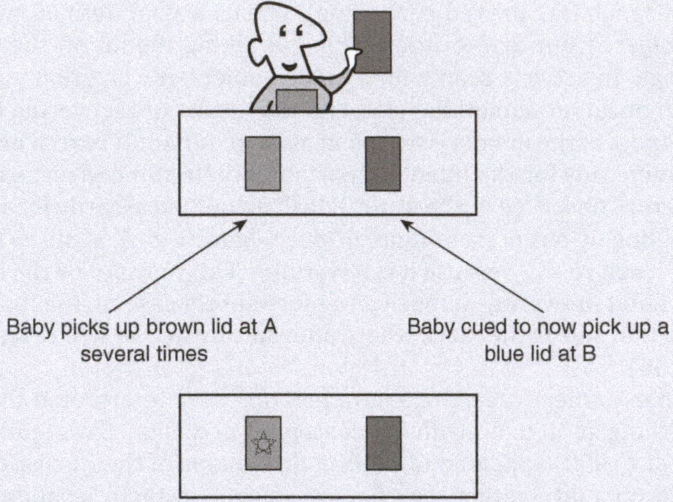

At 10 months, differentiating occluders does not diminish perseveration in a pick-up-occluder-only condition (top), but it does reduce the place error when the occluder is hiding an object (bottom). This suggests the notion of occlusion/hiding (as opposed to reach and retrieve) is becoming incorporated into the baby's repertoire (After Bremner & Bryant, 2001, with permission)

- This implies that the visual differentiation is helping to specify the notion of an object hiding under another – a single goal (retrieve an object) is being aided by visual differentiation
  - In the lids task there are really two goals – pick up this and pick up that

in the latter case, it may confuse you to have a choice! This is precisely the distinction that Bremner and Bryant (2001) brought to the 'lids only' versus the 'lids over hidden object' versions of the A-not-B task with infants at around 10 months old. The lids were differentiated by strong visual cues (shape and colour) and it was found that, whilst this helped to reduce errors for the hidden object condition, it enhanced the errors for the lids only condition. This selectivity suggests that by 10 months of age there *is* a difference between a hiding and a non-hiding condition and that the infant can be enabled to retrieve an object from under a cover – if it is denoted by a strong visual cue. Indeed noise-based cues also can enable correct searching in infants of 10 (but not 8) months old (Moore & Meltzoff, 2008). These results show that there can be an awareness of a genuine hiding scenario by 10 months of age. The differentiated lids only condition is something quite different: lift this lid here and then lift another lid there. This may be harder because there are two sorts of lid, i.e. two goals rather than a single goal. Solving this is not a less important skill – it is simply a less revealing one in terms of requiring flexibility and updating – the key role of the prefrontal cortex. Many years after Piaget's first extraordinary discoveries, then, it does indeed seem that the 1-year-old brain can cope with a genuine goal-directed behaviour towards an occluded object it regards as 'hidden' under some circumstances that we now more clearly understand.

So far, the behaviours that have been described have been elicited by hiding objects during play. The control of the action sequences were determined by the experimenter – e.g. hide object at A three times, then move it to B. The world is normally less passive than this, however, and to exert control over it, we usually have to consider an action sequence and its possible consequences in advance. This is called *planning* and we consider this next.

4.7 OBJECT RETRIEVAL AND PLANNING

It may seem that there has been a bit of overkill regarding the topic of the object concept, but remember that its behaviour towards something unseen offers a useful window on what the infant 'cognizes' about the world. A similar importance applies to the concept of planning. To have a plan, the child's conception of the world needs to contain mental representations of its own behaviours and outcomes. Action planning is a widely recognised role for the prefrontal cortex. Let's go back to tea making. When you move smoothly around the kitchen collecting kettle, mugs and milk, even if you are only half-awake, you have actually planned this sequence of actions in advance. This is why when you go to switch on the kettle you may also pick up the mugs, which happen to be near the kettle, even if your next action is 'get the tea bags' – because you will need the mugs later on in your sequence of tea-making actions. Planning is a major element in human intelligent activity and can be as complex as the moves required to win an international chess tournament. In the meantime, it appears as if the child at around 1 year has gained the necessary knowledge to plan some complex sequences of actions that will result in object retrieval.

Peter Willatts from Dundee University has provided some clear examples of planned behaviour in infants by giving them a motor problem to solve in order to reach a toy. In one such study, the experimental condition involves presenting the baby with a toy at some distance on a table, but the toy can be retrieved by pulling on a string to which it is attached (Willatts, 1999). The string, however, is also out of reach! *It* can be retrieved by pulling on a cloth on which the string is resting. The final obstacle to retrieving the toy is a barrier that has to be removed in order to pull on the cloth as shown in the photo in Panel 4.7. Any evidence that the baby spontaneously lifts the barrier to pull the cloth to reach the string and retrieve the toy would be a clear sign that at least some of this sequence has been planned. The behaviour of the babies on this condition was compared with one where the toy was visibly not attached to the string. In the experimental condition, the baby was more likely to approach and remove the barrier faster to get it out of the way, faster to contact the cloth and more likely to pull the string and gain the toy, suggesting a goal-directed behaviour that was at least partly planned in advance.

There is an issue of whether the ultimate goal (obtaining the toy) is really part of the initial action plan, however. Sommerville et al. (2005) explored this using a visual habituation technique in which babies observed actors pulling objects on cloths, and found that babies of 12 months (but not 10 months) treated a new final goal (same action/different toy) as a novel event, but not when the test event involved a different means (pulling on a different cloth to obtain the *same* toy). These authors concluded that the observed action was construed by the older babies as a hierarchically constructed plan in which specific behaviours are not simply understood as separate components in a sequence but are directed towards an over-arching goal (get that particular toy).

Where does this understanding come from? In a second study, the authors found that the ability to perceive the behaviour of an actor as goal-directed was directly related to the child's own ability to be planful in its cloth and object behaviours, as measured by looking attentively at the object prior to pulling on the cloth, maintaining attention and grasping as soon as it was within reach. The idea that the child needs to have constructed goal-directed behaviours itself before being able to identify them in the behaviour of others is a theme to which we shall return shortly.

Panel 4.7 Object retrieval and planning

- By around 12 months babies show that they can act on objects in an organised sequence directed to an ultimate goal
- If they are habituated to an observed goal-getting behaviour acted out by someone else, they will dishabituate if the goal is changed even if the goal-getting behaviour (such as pulling on a cloth) remains the same
- This ability is directly related to the degree to which they appear planful in their own goal-getting behaviours
    - This is measured by visual attention to the goal and swift retrieval when it comes within reach

A 12 month old removes a barrier to reach a cloth, pulls the cloth towards her to reach a string and pulls on the string to retrieve a toy (After Willatts & Rosie, 1989)

By the end of the first year of life, the baby is in considerable control of a world within which things may move around and disappear, and it can plan some of its actions accordingly. There is no end to this process of forward planning – even a skilled piano player continues to practise mastery over the keys. Some of the universal features of the playroom, however, such as bricks and containers, are likely to prompt new action plans to achieve new goals. Fitting shapes into the appropriate holes is one fairly universal game-based activity for example (and it is about 22 months before there is mastery of this over a range of shapes). Once children are on this path, the nature of the object relations they are dealing with become important factors in these motor skills. For example, stacking same-sized bricks in a tower is not the same as stacking differently sized bricks, which is different again from fitting nested cups together. Motor control, the perception of object relations and organising the behaviour into units that themselves can be organised into larger units (as in nesting cups) are all elements that will affect behavioural mastery in various ways. But what all these behaviours have in common is the combination of behavioural components into a planned sequence in order to achieve a goal – an executive skill.

THE LOCOMOTIVE INFANT

We have seen that there is a huge advance by the end of the first year in terms of an infant's cognitive understanding of the world as measured by the intentional goal-directed behaviours he can make using the upper body – head, arms, hands. Now consider the fact that these are not the only types of motor behaviours that develop in the first year of a child's life. He also gains uprightness and locomotor skills, usually first achieved by crawling, giving the child a freedom of self-motion that has to be re-acquired when standing upright. The entire body must also learn to adjust muscle control in relation to highly disparate sorts of external force. The changes that occur during the second half of the first year are not just motor developments in their own right; they are key contributors to cognitive development. Just as reaching out for objects creates opportunities for learning, so standing, crawling and walking add to the universe of changes and transformations that will lead to new knowledge about the world. In the next sections we shall retrace the child's development through the first year with a focus on how locomotion plays its part in cognitive development.

LEARNING LANDMARKS

4.8 Depth and distance. You should know how the perception of depth and distance is affected by being able to crawl and how this is measured in visual cliff experiments. You should know what proprioception is and how it contributes to the new awareness of depth.

4.9 Developments in attention. You should understand the significance of head-up crawling for improvements in attention and search.

(Continued)

(Continued)

4.10 The transition to bipedalism and postural control. You should know the approximate age at which a child is able to move to an upright bipedal posture. You should understand how this involves the vestibular system and visual proprioception.

4.11 Hands-free cognition and hemispheric specialisation. You should know what bi-manual co-ordination is and when it appears. You should know which hemisphere controls fine motor skills and what end-state comfort is.

4.8 DEPTH AND DISTANCE

In Chapter 2 you learned that very young infants can perceive spatial depth and distance. You might think that what needs to develop next is simply the ability to move through the space they can perceive. But on the view that action is itself the basis for acquiring new knowledge, then you would expect that depth perception would continue to develop as locomotor experience grows. This is precisely what has been found by research carried out by Joseph Campos and colleagues and the University of Berkeley.

One starting point for Campos' work was a classic study known as the **Visual Cliff** experiment devised by Eleanor Gibson and Richard Walk at Cornell University (Gibson & Walk, 1960). These authors designed an apparatus that would give a crawling infant an impression of coming to an edge of a cliff where the sudden change in the texture of the visual field would signal a deep drop. A plane of glass was placed over the entire surface, and the babies were placed on the 'shallow' side whilst their mothers called to them from the opposite 'deep' side of the apparatus as illustrated in the drawing in Panel 4.8. Infants as old as 6 months refused to crawl over the deep side, though they were happy to crawl to Mum when she was on the shallow side. The question for Campos and his colleagues was whether the activity of crawling was itself contributing to the developing perception of depth. In order to study this, a measure of depth perception was required that was not itself based on crawling, and so an increase in the baby's heart rate was used instead as a measure of 'fear'. Campos et al. (1970) found that children younger than crawling age showed no evidence of fear when they were placed at the deep side of the apparatus.

This group has since demonstrated that the onset of crawling promotes developments in **visual proprioception** – information about where you feel you are in space relative to the visual environment – and that this is responsible for the fear and avoidance reaction in the visual cliff. It had been noted that sensitivity to the peripherally detected **lamellar** flow – the particular flow that occurs at the sides of the visual field – develops between 7 and 9 months. This was measured using a device invented at Edinburgh University by David Lee and colleagues, called the swinging room. This was a fake moving room that gives the visual cues normally associated with forward motion of the self (and we shall consider it greater detail in Section 4.10).

Witherington, Campos and Kermoian (see Campos et al., 2000) studied the degree of postural compensation shown by 8-month-old infants in the swinging room as and in that way measured their sensitivity to lamellar flow. This was then compared with the level of reluctance to crawl to the deep side of a visual cliff. These measures were not only highly correlated with one another, but were also correlated with how much crawling experience the babies had. It is not just the picking up of peripheral visual cues by movement that is important, therefore, because that could be picked up by passive movements. Rather, the self-produced proprioceptive information of where the limbs are in relation to the visual changes becomes part of a powerful experience of moving forward in the frontal plane. This self-motion information learned from crawling on hands and knees then leads to a violation of expectation and a reluctance to crawl when the guiding visual cues from front and below change abruptly as in a cliff situation. In fact the idea that babies are actually fearful in this situation has now been replaced by the idea that their sensitivity to locomotor cues simply signals that descent is impossible (Adolph et al., 2014).

Panel 4.8 Depth and distance

- Learning to crawl alters the visual world for the infant in terms of the kind of self-produced feedback it can provide
  - This affects and enriches the perception of depth of distance
- A clear example is the change in behaviour on the classic '*visual cliff*' set-up
  - Babies show a fear response measured by increased heart-rate at around 6 months but *only if* they have learned to crawl

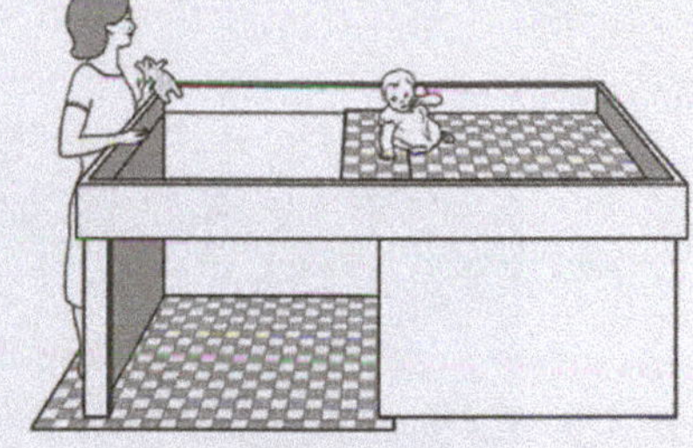

Eleanor Gibson and Richard Walk created a famous apparatus called the Visual Cliff that created the illusion of a sudden drop using a change in texture gradient. (Image from Adolph et al., 2014, with permission)

- The new information comes from feedback known as visual proprioception
  - This is the link between the feedback information about position of limbs in relation to the visual environment; in this case the textural 'flow' caused by the child's own movement

4.9 DEVELOPMENTS IN ATTENTION

Becoming locomotive means the baby is now quite literally in a better position to focus its attention on new problems to be solved. A baby who can only crawl on its tummy will still be using all its resources to develop this skill (Horobin & Acredelo, 1986). By contrast, a baby with effective hands and knees crawling will have developed the ability to look up with its head towards a guiding goal. Not only will this postural change give her more attentional resource to spare on other things, it will also help her detect new transformations of objects and space. For Campos and colleagues, this suggested that object-oriented tasks such as the A-not-B task would benefit from the development of locomotion even though, on the face of it, the tasks of locomoting and finding objects under covers do not appear to be particularly connected. Kermoian and Campos (1988) divided infants into different locomotor levels, i.e. assisted walking, hands and knees

Panel 4.9 Developments in attention

- The transition to head-up-crawling and then standing changes the focus of attention in various ways

- The child's attention becomes freed-up from having to use all its resources just to move forward
- It is also in a better position to monitor the movements of things in space
    - Belly crawlers are worse than head-up tummy crawlers on the A-not-B task
- Attention can be focussed on longer range targets
    - Finding objects in 'far' space is significantly improved after several weeks of head-up crawling
- The transition to walking improves attention again for all the same reasons

crawling, 'belly crawling', and no locomotion, and noted the length of time they had experienced any of these levels of independent motion. It is important to note that the babies were all around the same age; it was simply their level of locomotor experience that differed across the groups. Search success in the A-not-B task correlated positively and significantly with measures of independent locomotion. For example, tummy crawling infants were significantly worse than hands and knees crawlers, suggesting that the transition to effective head up crawling does indeed allow for attention to be deployed in new ways with consequences for learning.

Another way in which increased mobility expands the child's cognitive horizons is the distance that she can now traverse. Remote space will not just be something that the child can gaze into but a place that may be incorporated into new plans and goals. Research conducted at Campos lab by Freedman (1992) showed a distinct change in how infants looked into distance space after locomotor experience. The task was to manipulate a canister in order to activate a display. The canister and display was either within reach or out of reach. Only babies with hands and knees crawling or walking experience actually focussed on the objects in far space, showing changes to the attentional range caused by their new locomotor skills. As you might expect, this extends the infant's abilities to find objects in large spaces. Clearfield (2004) found that only infants with at least six weeks crawling or walking experience could learn to find a hidden object signalled by a visual cue in a large space.

4.10 THE TRANSITION TO BIPEDALISM AND POSTURAL CONTROL

The 'average' infant can sit leaning forward and stand supported by an adult at around 6 months; at around 8/9 months, he can crawl and stand by holding onto a support. These changes already promote cognitive growth, as we have seen from the above. But the most dramatic change occurs from about 10 months (on average) when the child can walk sideways whilst holding onto furniture (called 'cruising') and from about 1 year, stand alone, and walk independently (the timing and sequencing of these events can vary substantially across individuals). Not surprisingly, we tend to start changing the name for baby to 'toddler' from around the age of independent walking, to mark this important and exciting transition to the upright mobile biped that evolution has taken so many millennia to evolve. Considerable motor learning occurs during these transitions. Let us consider some of the key elements in this major change in the child's motor system

The vestibular system

Even if it is a matter of simply staying in one place, the body has to compensate for natural 'sway' to maintain balance under different conditions of posture. The neural mechanisms for maintaining balance involve co-ordinating information from head, eye and body movement in relation to gravity and are referred to as the **vestibular system** – thought to be located in the older primitive part of the brain known as the brainstem. From the presence of reflexes that produce, for example, compensatory eye movements when the body is tilted, it is thought that the vestibular system is fully functional at birth (Jouen, 1990).

Visual proprioception

The information from the head and eyes, however, is not just about their spatial position in relation to the body; it also gives optical information as a consequence of the movement. In order to 'see' the three-dimensional world assort itself into receding space, through motion parallax, the infant must correlate the visual changes with its own head movements. If these changes occur externally (e.g. by gently pushing eyeballs sideways), then a dizzying shift occurs completely disrupting the stable space that would normally be perceived. From the evidence on neonatal depth perception, it appears that a correlation between lateral head movement and optical change is established shortly after birth. However, proprioceptive information is not just for controlling the head – the nature of visual proprioception changes as the range of postures and bodily movements increase, as we see next.

Postural control and visual proprioception

David Lee and Eric Aronson at the University of Edinburgh were the first to document the use of visual proprioception to control upright posture in young infants who had just reached the standing stage. To do this they used the ingenious setup called a swinging room created by Lee and his colleague Roly Lishman (that we came across earlier). In a normal room with four walls, any forward motion of the body would produce an **optic flow** (see Panel 4.10). This is produced by the changing texture of a normal environment when you move through it. The flow directly in front as you move in a forwards direction with head and eyes looking forward is called **radial flow** – a pattern of expansion from a central point and projected onto the centre of the retina, whilst it takes more of a linear parallel form at the sides of your head. The lamellar flow mentioned in Section 4.8 is picked up by peripheral receptors in the retina. In the swinging room, a change to the normal correlation between the body motion and optic flow was effected by Lee and Lishman by making the walls move forward or back whilst the perceiver stood still on a stable floor facing forward (Lee & Lishman, 1975). The optic flow produced in the absence of an intentional motion would have to be interpreted by the brain as a loss of balance and it was found that adults made compensatory movements when the walls moved. They fell forward when the room moved forwards to compensate for what felt like falling backwards and backwards when it moved backwards as they felt as if they were falling forwards. The next question was when this form of postural control is established in children. In their study, Lee and Aronson (1974) found compensatory movements in standing infants aged between 13 and 16 months. Butterworth and Hicks (1977) subsequently found that optic flow caused compensatory sway in seated infants around 11 months old who had not yet learned to stand, suggesting an early role for the visual control of posture from information directly in front of the child. As you learned in Section 4.8, it is now known that compensatory sway is not only found in crawling infants but that it is correlated with measures of depth perception such as the visual cliff.

Panel 4.10 The transition to bipedalism and postural control

- The vestibular system controls balance and it is thought to be fully functional at birth
  - But the transition to standing upright means that the toddler may have to compensate by whole body movements if it starts to lose balance
- Visual proprioception is the learned link between visual information and the sense of where the limbs and body are in space
  - This is used to gain postural control
- The optic flow produced usually by forward motion can be simulated (without proprioception) in a swinging room to see when this connection has been learned

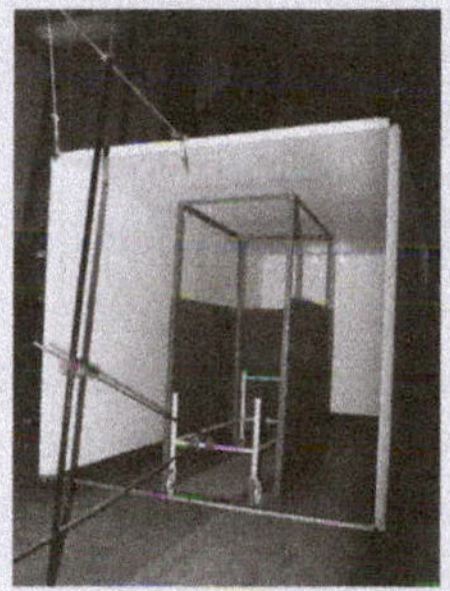

Lee and Lishman's Swinging Room: Walls and ceiling move forward: toddlers compensate for the impression that they have tilted backwards by falling over (Photo Courtesy of D. N. Lee)

- Seated infants (who can't stand) show the compensatory mechanism in the upper part of their body at 11 months
- The transition to standing and walking means that many more visual proprioceptive connections have to be learned
  - Standing toddlers will sway backwards or forwards to compensate for apparent motion from around 13–16 months

4.11 HANDS-FREE COGNITION AND HEMISPHERIC SPECIALISATION

The liberating effects of learning to crawl might be expected to be repeated in new ways when the child actually stands up and begins to walk. When this important transition took pace in evolution, it was thought to free up the forelimbs and hands for new activities and is widely regarded as the key step towards tool use in hominids, possibly appearing as early as 4.5 million years ago and certainly by tool-using hominids around 2 million years ago. Anatomical evidence from the first hominid, *Homo habilis*, suggests it could use its hand in a pincer grip, i.e. to hold an object firmly between forefinger and thumb, an action that suggests a specific holding role for one hand whilst the other is doing something else with the object. The evolutionary heritage of the child, therefore, is the ability not just to use its hands but also to use its hands co-operatively. But then, an expert sitter might be in a better position to practice manual co-ordination than a novice walker who may need both hands simply for balance and holding on! Corbetta and Bojczyk (2002) observed within a longitudinal study with nine infants that around the onset of walking at about 1 year there was indeed a return to two-handed reaching. Once balance control was established, however, the infants returned to the one-handed reaching they had achieved prior to walking onset.

The most obvious sign of co-operative hand use is asymmetry or handedness – a weakness in one hand denotes strength in the other for finer motor skills. Let's briefly review how the brain is involved in handedness and the emergence of related skills.

Hemispheric asymmetry

The two hemispheres in the human brain (and indeed in many animals) are not mirror images of one another. They are slightly different in size and shape at different regions and also in their biochemistry. It has long been observed that the left side of the brain seems to be associated with manual skill such that the right hand (controlled by the left hemisphere) is the predominant one in the human population for fine motor skills such as handwriting. (Working out exactly what visual information is recruited for these tasks by the left hemisphere is an area that is still being explored with adults.) When do children start to show such a bias? We know that at 1 year old they have the ability to hold small objects in their hands when sitting, and to place one object inside another or stack one on top of another. Initially these skills do not universally favour one hand over another, though from about 8 months old, infants will use both hands in free play more often than just one. However, the selective use of one hand over another can be seen in reaching for an object. Hand-use for reaching is initially determined mainly in relation to where an object is presented; i.e. usually (though not always) the left hand if the object is to the left of mid-line, and right hand if it is to the right. This is called **ipsilateral** reaching and will continue to predominate into adulthood. Using the nearer hand has the obvious overall advantage and reaching and grasping an object rarely requires fine motor control. Tasks that do require finer control such as grasping a small object in a pincer grip will only start to favour the right hand selectively from about 16 months (Provins, 1992).

When it does emerge, however, the dominant use of the right hand (for most people) still depends on the demands of the task given and it is no surprise that handedness for fine motor control continues to develop right through middle childhood as the child's repertoire of manual skills increases. An important element in this is the planning that you learned about earlier. Once hand dominance is established in relation to object manipulation the child still has to consider in advance the sequence of movements that will achieve its goal whilst avoiding an uncomfortable or impossible act. Take right-handed reaching to a spoon that is facing left-to-right. This will result in a failure of what is called **end-state comfort** (ESC). The more appropriate action plan is reach with left then transfer and place the spoon the right way up in the dominant right hand. Achieving ESC for a simple polarised object is an ability that improves dramatically over the preschool years (Weigelt & Schack, 2010) and continues right up to 10 years old across a variety of tool use situations.

Panel 4.11 Hands-free cognition and hemispheric specialisation

- The evolution of bipedalism seems to have heralded the use of *bi-manual co-operation*
    - A typical task would be holding an object with one hand whilst operating it on the other as in stone tool-making
- One-handed reaching is likely to favour the hand nearest the object from about 8 months old – and this tends to endure into adulthood
- Co-operative use of both hands in actually manipulating objects is seen after the first birthday – by about 16 months this will usually favour the right hand for fine motor control
- The right bias in humans is reflected in brain asymmetry in which the left hemisphere seems to control actions that require fine motor control
- Object manipulation also requires planning in terms of *end-state comfort* (ESC)

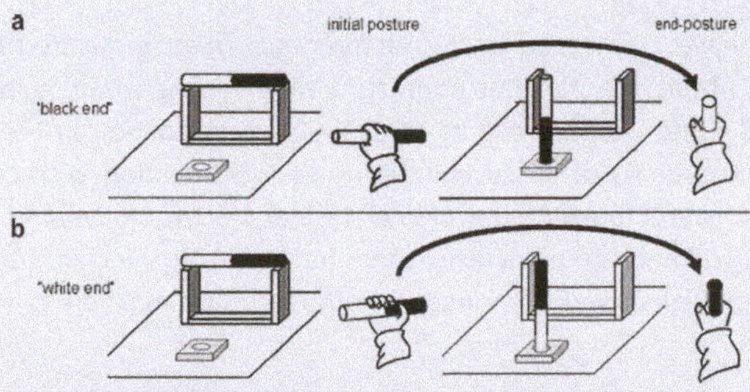

Placing the rod white side down (b) requires planning the movement as an underhand grip if it is to be achieved comfortably. (After Weigelt & Schack, 2010, used by permission ©2010 Hogrefe Publishing, www.hogrefe.com)

Despite its challenges, bi-manual co-ordination makes sense; what is less clear is why humans have a right bias for fine motor control. The evidence suggests that this bias is learned through a combination of factors. There is some evidence that handedness may be genetic in origin (Annett, 1985) and rather more evidence that it is the practices of parents and teachers that serves to cement the right-hand bias in the population. Provins (1997) suggests that one of these practices is the consistent placing of articles to be manipulated (such as spoons) in the right hand of the infant. In support of this Harkins and Michel (1988) had shown that it was only infants of left-handed mothers that showed a left-hand bias. Once children are at school there may be a pressure to use the right hand for writing in some cultures. What may be more universal, however, is the fact that once a bias is established, say, for feeding, then it would naturally transfer to other skills using the same muscle groups such as holding a pencil, or toothbrush. You may be wondering if left-handed children therefore have a different bias in their hemispheric function; research with right- and left-handed adults suffering from left-hemisphere damage suggest that this is not the case; the damage affects control of action in the same way for right- and left-handers.

CHAPTER SUMMARY

From around 1 year, behaviour becomes more goal-oriented due to the functional development of the frontal regions of the brain. Executive functioning involving planning, the control of inhibition, and working memory explains important developments in the 'object concept'. The transition from crawling to standing produces new perceptuomotor and cognitive skills.

LOOKING AHEAD TO CHAPTER 5

Everything we have considered in this chapter has been motivated by the child's interest in the physical world. But interest in other humans will also lead to new behaviours and these will increase its control and participation in the social world. These are developments of social imitation and reciprocation with other humans. Vocalisation also starts to exert control in ways that start to go beyond merely crying for attention. It will become the lynchpin that helps to knit the child's self-discoveries into a social world of shared experience and inter-communication as we shall see in the next chapter.

CHAPTER 5

SENSORIMOTOR DEVELOPMENT IN INFANCY: THE ELEMENTS OF SOCIAL INTERACTION

We have seen how children learn to exert control over an inanimate world. It is now time to remember that during infancy – more than at any other time (apart from incapacity brought on by illness or old age) – the human is under the control of others. Most of its locomotion will have been provided by carers, and its early attempts at self-locomotion will have been heavily stage-managed for safety. The social bond between infants and their parents, carers and family members is an integral part of this process. Interacting with other humans is, in many ways, the warp and woof of normal human development. It depends crucially upon the meshing of actions of both child and adult, from watching one another's gaze to active imitation of behaviours. Of all these skills, the one that will most enable the passage into the world of other humans is vocalisation and the beginnings of speech and communication. We will trace the emergence of these interactive skills in this chapter.

JOINT ATTENTION

LEARNING LANDMARKS

5.1 Point and gaze following. You should know what joint attention is, when babies start to follow the point or gaze of an adult and how this develops within the first two years.

5.2 Own pointing. You should know when a child will spontaneously point referentially and be able to cite a study showing when babies can refer by pointing to an absent object.

5.1 POINT AND GAZE FOLLOWING

One of the most eloquent gestures of human social interaction is pointing. Directing another's attention to a remote object or scene using an extended hand or arm can convey interest, a desire to share excitement with another, or simply a request for something out of reach. When does a child first exhibit any of these behaviours and first appear to understand the pointing behaviours of others?

Following the point or gaze of another is often referred to as **joint attention**. Research by Butterworth and others (Butterworth, 2004) suggests that elementary point following seems to begin at around 10 months. Before this age, the baby will look at the pointing finger or hand instead of the object. Morissette et al. (1995) found that there was a large change between 12 and 15 months in both the distance as well as the width of arc that could be used to encourage a baby to look towards the indicated target.

Grover (1988) found that pointing by an adult was more likely to produce joint attention in 1 year olds than the more subtle cues of head and eye orientation – gaze. These cues are also more subtle for the investigator, and require caution in their interpretation. For example, objects themselves can capture attention, and so an orienting response made by the baby when following, say, his mother's head turn can lead to his attention actually being captured by an object in the general direction of her body orientation rather than by specifically following her line of sight. Butterworth described the former ability as an **ecological** (environmentally produced) mechanism and the latter ability as being based on a **geometric** mechanism as it appears to require extrapolating directly from the mother's gaze to the target object. The geometric mechanism implies a greater awareness that the mother is looking at something. The crucial test of this is whether a baby can alight specifically on the target, ignoring other distractor objects in the general area of the gaze. Butterworth and Jarrett (1991) found that babies were able to do this by about 12 months old, provided the target was in the baby's current visual field, but by 18 months, their gaze could be directed to look outside their own visual field and even into the space behind them, provided there were no competing objects in their front visual field. As to why children would learn to follow the gaze of adults, recent research has found that gaze following in infants under 1 year old is likely to occur when their caregivers were looking at and handling objects, leading to the conclusion that babies learn to associate an adult's gaze with an interesting event (Deak et al., 2014).

To be sure of the extent to which gaze following is a truly social act, however, it would be important to know if the child is really attempting to share the interest shown by the adult. This is referred to as the distinction between the **predictive** versus the **referential** aspect of the gaze. In the first case, the gaze is a learned mechanical cue to where something interesting might be happening in the environment – try *not* looking up at the sky if you see someone else do it! But that person may not have the intention of signalling to you that you should look too. A contrasting case would be someone pointedly looking across towards a door in a room to signal the arrival of someone to another person (referential). To make this distinction in a gaze-following study,

Panel 5.1 Point and gaze following

- Babies will follow the direction of an adult's point from about 10 months
    - Later they will pick up the gaze direction of the adult
- Early gaze following may be *ecological*
    - The baby follows the general body orientation of the mother and alights on an object of interest
- By about 12 months gaze and point following is more geometric
    - The baby extrapolates the location of interest from a pointing finger

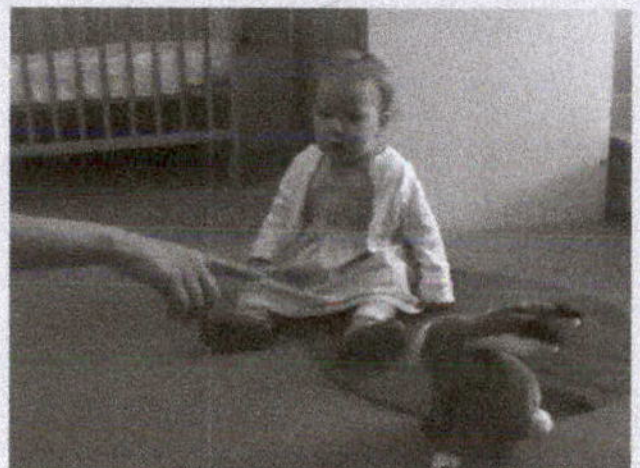

- Toddlers can locate objects outside their visual field from about 18 months by following the gaze direction of others
- A gaze can be interpreted as an act of social reference or simply cue the child to look in a certain direction
    - By obstructing the adult's view of an object (see below, right), it has been found that babies only interpret the gaze as referential (i.e. towards a seen object only) by about 18 months

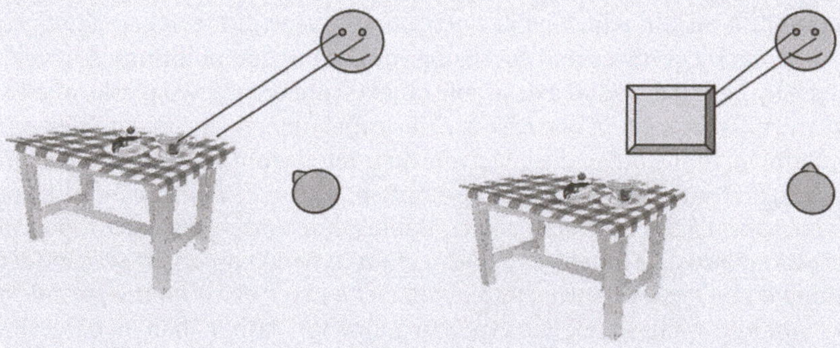

Butler et al. (2000) obstructed the adult's line of sight using a screen. This provided the predictive cue as to where to look, but not the referential one, as there could be no intention attaching to the adult's gaze. The authors reported that it was only by 18 months of age that infants would selectively ignore the screen condition, turning their own gaze towards the direction of the adult's only when it was unobstructed or when there was a window cut into the screen.

This does not mean that there is no social understanding of a more explicit referential *gesture* before 18 months. Caron et al. (2002) found that, when adults indicated a target by turning and pointing, 14-month-old infants could follow the gesture and were significantly less likely to follow the point in the window condition when the adult's eyes were closed, suggesting that following an explicit pointing gesture does have a referential element by this age.

5.2 OWN POINTING

Understanding referential pointing is likely to be connected with being capable of that action oneself. To demonstrate that infants can point referentially it would be important to show that it only occurs when there is a partner present; otherwise the gesture could be interpreted simply as a reach. Butterworth found that pointing by infants occurred under these conditions by about 14 months – the age at which Caron et al. (2002) found evidence of point comprehension. These pointing gestures were made with the index finger, and as Butterworth (2004) has pointed out (see his chapter for a review), this social gesture certainly appears to constitute the singling out of an object for joint attention. Franco and Butterworth (1996) recorded a marked increase from around 16 months in the extent to which such point gestures were accompanied by visual 'checking' behaviours towards a social partner during and after the point gesture.

A more nuanced aspect of pointing is to use it to indicate the existence of a virtual object rather than a gesture towards something real. Consider an estate agent walking around a building plot with an adult and pointing to an empty spot and saying, 'the loggia will be facing the sun as you can see'. So pointing in the absence of a visible referent could give us an idea of what the baby can represent that is not in the here and now. But how? An ingenious study carried out by Liszkowski and colleagues (Liszkowski et al., 2009) used a modelling task in which babies of around 1 year old watched adults requesting desirable objects by gestures and vocalising (but not actual pointing). A 'giver' followed the requests by giving the adult a desirable object from one of two platforms. Then it was the baby's turn to request; in one case the desirable object was now hidden by the giver under a platform, in the other the giver was distracted from hiding the object in the normal place and all that remained were the empty platforms – one of which had previously been the location of the desirable object. Babies, but not chimpanzees, pointed to this empty location almost as much as to the location in which an object was hidden.

Well done if you are wondering if this is in fact a place error on the part of the infants (which as you know can result in a reach to a location rather than an object). However, the babies in this study were rather too old for the place error and also they had not

Panel 5.2 Own pointing

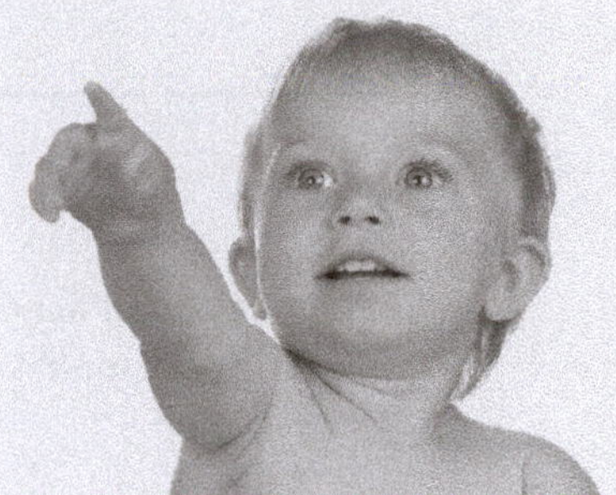

- Children can point with an index finger from about 14 months
- The fact that they do so only when another is present suggests that it is truly 'referential' at this stage
- Babies of 1 year old – but not chimpanzees – can request a desirable object by pointing to a location where an object has been seen to be placed before even if it is not currently visible
    - This is taken as a sign that the pointing is referential and not just cued by sight of the object

(a)

(b)

Baby now seated in adult's chair points to location of object (now absent)

The infant watches someone request an object by vocalising and gesturing; when it is the baby's turn, the object is shown to the child but then hidden elsewhere. Only human babies will point to the place where they had prior sight of the object. (From Liszkowski et al., 2009, with permission)

actually reached to the location before – the tests (either to object present or object absent) were one-off and so no previous motor pattern had been established. All in all, it looks as if using and understanding pointing as a true act of reference is an achievement of the first half of the second year of life.

IMITATION AND SELF-AWARENESS

LEARNING LANDMARKS

5.3 Imitation of actions. You should know that imitation can occur at different levels. You should know what mirror neurons are and what is meant by deferred imitation.

5.4 Imitation of goal-directed behaviours. You should be able to describe the difference between elementary imitation and goal-directed imitation and be able to say why imitating unusual actions are relevant to this.

5.5 Self-awareness. You should know what the MSR test stands for and what has been learned from it with regard to children and the great apes.

5.3 IMITATION OF ACTIONS

In reading the last section, you may have realised that the model did not actually point in order to avoid direct imitation by the child. So when does imitation appear and what level of control and initiative does it imply on the child's part? It has indeed been known for nearly a century that imitation of simple facial and mouthing gestures is present from the first few months and some, like tongue protrusion, from shortly after birth. However, the development of these is not entirely linear; some imitated behaviours disappear at around 6 months and re-appear later in a slightly different way – usually faster and more clear-cut. Also, facial gestures are not in themselves outcome-producing where the action has a clear consequence in the world. Imitation can take the form, therefore, of anything from an elementary (some would say reflexive) mechanism for social bonding to the explicit copying of an adult's goal-directed behaviour such as using a tool. We shall consider the development of these forms of imitation in the next section. First, however, we return once again to thinking about the brain and how it is involved in this important element of human cognition.

Mirror neurons. All imitation involves the copying and thus representation of actions. Rizzolatti and colleagues made an exciting discovery with macaque monkeys that is now widely regarded as having revealed significant neurological underpinnings for the primate ability to represent the actions of others (Rizzolatti et al., 2001). The region of the monkey's premotor cortex known as F5 has neurons that that fire when whole actions are performed, such as 'grasp with hand' or 'hold with a precision grip'.

What came as great surprise, however, was the discovery of other neurons in this region that also fired in this way towards different actions, but not when the monkey performed the action – only when it observed *another* monkey (or human) doing so.

Panel 5.3 Imitation of actions

- Children imitate simple gestures such as tongue protrusion almost from birth

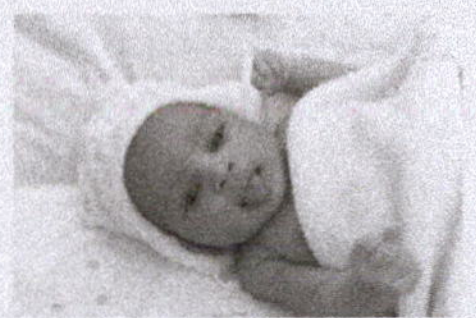

- It is thought that there are certain brain cells specialised for representing actions simply by watching others perform them
- These are called *mirror neurons*, and in the human they seem to be located in the left inferior frontal gyrus – near Broca's area – as well as near the premotor cortex

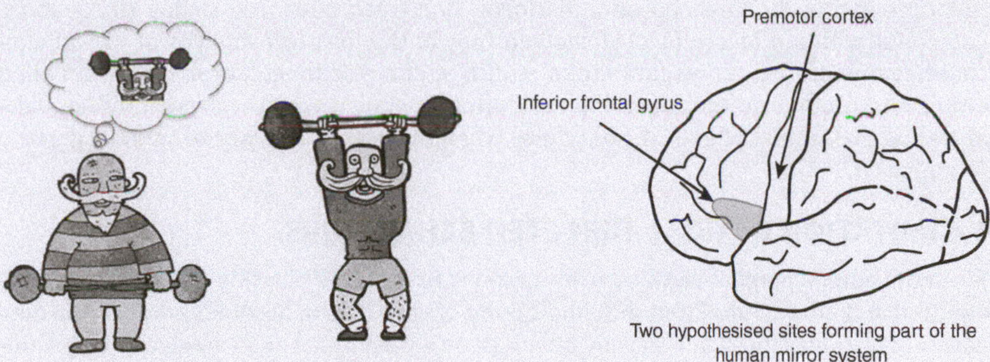

Two hypothesised sites forming part of the human mirror system

- Delayed copying of actions is called *deferred imitation*
  - Delayed copying of lip protrusion (by over a day) has been observed in 1-month-old babies, showing that it is not just reflexive
  - It is provoked by the sight of the adult who initiated the original action

The same 'mirror' neurons have not been identified in humans in quite the same way. However, some areas of the human brain have been found to be implicated in representing the observed actions of others. One of those areas is regarded as the one that maps most closely to F5 in the monkey brain and is called the left inferior frontal gyrus and is related to speech production – otherwise known as **Broca's area**. The special feature of activation in this area is that it only seems to occur when the observed action has a meaningful goal or outcome, such as cutting bread. When they know, however, that they have to reproduce an action (meaningful or not), humans also show activation in parts of the parietal cortex adjacent to the premotor cortex (Grezes & Decety, 2002). Rizzolatti has described this as **low-level resonance** *as* it implies a provoked correspondence between seeing an action and performing it without having any obvious goal or point to the action. Research into the mirroring system in humans is still ongoing (Mukamel et al., 2010; Cook et al., 2014).

So when can we say that these different levels of imitation are present in infancy? We know about neonatal imitation from a pioneering study reported in 1977 by Meltzoff and Moore, who showed that infants as young as 2 weeks old could imitate precise movements such as lip protrusion, and in 1983 these authors established the same capability in babies less than one hour old! Meltzoff and Moore (1977) dispelled a long-held belief that this kind of imitation is necessarily reflexive, however, by showing that newborn babies could withhold the imitation until a dummy (placed in their mouths at the time of the performed action) was removed. This is called **deferred imitation**. Meltzoff (1988) found that babies of 8 months could imitate a novel gesture (gently banging the forehead on a platform) one week after first seeing the gesture. Later Meltzoff and Moore (1994) showed that in the first few months of life, infants could even store the representation of mouth opening or tongue protrusion modelled either by a mother or a stranger and correctly associate it with the correct individual – imitating the gesture after a 24-hour delay when the person who performed the gesture reappeared.

5.4 IMITATION OF GOAL-DIRECTED BEHAVIOURS

From the adult's point of view, then, imitation is first of all a pleasing index of social recognition and interaction. From the child's point of view it soon becomes a way of learning useful behaviours through everyday interactions with parents and caregivers. For example, Braten (2008) records 11 month olds reciprocating familiar spoon-feeding actions by 'feeding Mum' and imitating the mouth opening whilst doing so. This is enabled, Braten argues, by the fact that the infant has already participated as the recipient of the action. But an important milestone in imitation is to be able to repeat new and unusual behaviours that are not already within its repertoire of goal-directed actions and this seems to occur from about 1 year old. Research carried out by Abravanel et al. (1976) suggests that deferred imitation of unusual actions with objects, such as putting a bead into a cup or patting a doll with an open hand, develops between 12 and 15 months.

There is nevertheless considerable variability in the novel goal-directed behaviours that children can represent and repeat later. Research carried out by Abravanel suggests that specific deferred imitative play with objects, such as joining two toys in a certain way or using a drumstick to push a toy out of a cylinder, develops between 12 and 15 months (Abravanel & Gingold, 1985). This study, however, revealed considerable variability in deferred imitation depending on the task. For example, the authors found an increase from 36% to 80% between the ages of 12 and 18 months in successful deferred imitation of a barrel-opening task (to reveal a smaller barrel), whilst the corresponding scores for a more complex action involving a screwtoy were 13% and 34% respectively. In general, the ability to remember the goal of an unusual complex action – in order to repeat it later – seems to take off in the first half of the second year of life.

Panel 5.4 Imitation of goal-directed behaviours

- Representing an action as a goal-oriented behaviour is an important milestone in imitation
    - Unusual actions provide a useful way of distinguishing between the imitation of new goal-directed behaviours as opposed to simply repeating a familiar action
    - This can be observed between 12 and 15 months (though the age depends on the complexity of the behaviour being modelled)

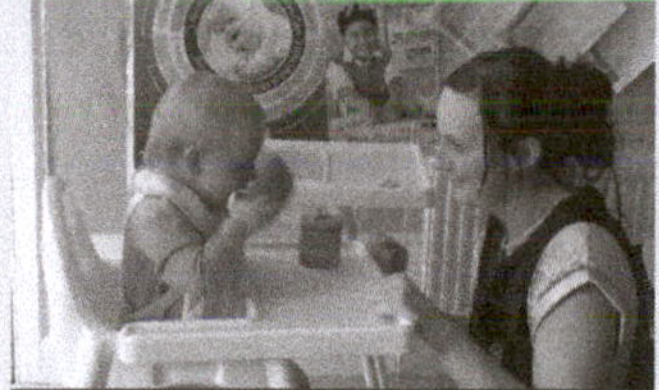

A 12-month-old girl imitates an unusual action with a bowl

- Another way is to see if the child imitates the apparent *intention* of the action, not just the action itself
    - By 18 months infants will complete an action such as pulling the end off a dumbbell – even though the adult modeller fails

- Imitation at this age is specific to watching a human – rather than a mechanical device – perform the action

Imitation often involves more than copying a behaviour; it also requires a perception of the other's *intention* to achieve a goal. At what point does the child understand the intended goal of the action such that they could even use other objects or movements to achieve the same end? One way to test this is to separate the *completion* of the goal from the intention to achieve it, by having an adult model a failed attempt to reach a goal. Will an infant simply copy the observed unsuccessful action or try to achieve the finished goal? Meltzoff tested this with infants aged around 18 months, by having them watch an adult female attempt to pull the end off a dumbbell, but fail to do because her hand kept slipping off (Meltzoff, 1995). However, when given the dumbbell to play with, 60% of infants successfully pulled it apart afterwards. When compared with a condition (that the infants found equally interesting) in which a mechanical device performed the same action as the human, only 10% completed the goal after watching the mechanical device. Meltzoff also noted that, in the first condition, if the child happened to fail at first, they persevered until they succeeded. In other words, the infants in the first condition appeared to be re-enacting a human's intended goal-directed behaviour.

This study shows that, by 18 months, observation of adults becomes an important way of acquiring new ways of exerting control over the world. The differentiation between self and other is central to this development and it could even be said that the child's concept of self is becoming emancipated through observation and imitation of others. Is this true, and how might we look more directly at the child's understanding of his or her own self?

5.5 SELF-AWARENESS

We all develop a concept of self that corresponds to a perceivable whole person acting on the world, despite the fact that none of us is normally in a position to see ourselves in this way. Many psychologists and philosophers have debated what it is to have this concept of self. Whatever, the answer, one indisputable *index* of that concept is self-recognition: recognising ourselves in a photo, film or reflecting surface. Mirror recognition therefore ought to be a good litmus test of how the child's self-concept develops in the second year of life.

Mirror recognition

Since Darwin noted that his baby could recognise himself in a mirror, there have been many informal observations along these lines. However, a more formal technique was published in *Science* in 1970 by Gordon Gallup, designed initially to test for self-concept in chimpanzees (Gallup, 1970). Since its publication, the test has been widely used with other species. It involves surreptitiously marking the animal with a coloured dye and then observing its reaction in a mirror. Indications that the animal perceives the reflected image as its own self include posturing in such a way as to get a better view of the mark, touching it, or trying to remove it.

Using rouge to mark part of a baby's face, the **mirror self-recognition** (MSR) test has been tried many times with human infants since. First tried by Amsterdam (1972), the results are usually the same. Before 1 year old, the infant behaves as if the mirror baby is a playmate. There follows a period of a few months when the baby will be withdrawn or upset when viewing the image and it is usually only after 18 months that there are signs of recognition: pointing to self, vocalising (says name), touching or attempting to remove the spot. In a rigorous study using robust criteria to establish self-recognition, such as looking at the mirror whilst touching the mark, Bard et al. (2006) found that children do not reliably pass the mark test until around 24 months of age. And even then, they may have to be prompted by the mother ('what's that?' etc.). Whilst the interpretations vary with regard to what sort of self-concept is implied by mirror self-recognition, most agree that that there must be some form of 'secondary' representation, i.e. that the mirror 'stands' for the self, and can thus be used to guide actions accordingly.

The self-aware primate

The mirror test brings us to a very close convergence with research on non-human primates and it is perhaps time to reflect a little on how the young 'universal' human at

Panel 5.5 Self-awareness

- Behaviour towards self when looking in a mirror has been used as a test of self-awareness in children
- *Mirror self-recognition* (MSR) is assessed using the Mark Test first designed for chimps
  - A removable mark is placed on the face or head to see if it will be removed by the child

- Children under 18 months interact with the 'child' in the mirror as if it were another person but pass the mark test at between 18 and 24 months
  - Chimps also pass the test at around this age

around 18 months compares overall with other primate species. Just how advanced in evolutionary terms are the core cognitive abilities shown by children by their second year of life?

Child development does not parallel evolutionary development; the forces for change are very different as are the adaptive purposes that guide those changes. Monkeys and apes are, at one and the same time, faster to achieve independence from their mothers, yet more bound to social and group dynamics in their adult behaviour. But there are many parallels when it comes to the basic requirements for getting a cognitive system 'off the ground' whatever the time scale. As we have seen in this and previous chapters, perceiving the 'means to an end' and knowing how to achieve it is a first indication of cognitive mastery over the environment. Primate cognition abounds in examples of this from very early discoveries of how apes can use sticks to retrieve food items (Kohler, 1925) to the more recent discovery that monkeys can use their minds alone to control a robot arm (Lebedev et al., 2005). And you have already learned that mirror neurons have been found in the brains of macaques. If these are the things that help to shape self-awareness in children, then do primates also show mirror self-recognition (MSR)? Bard et al. (2006) found that, like children, chimpanzees show MSR from about the age of 2. Other species of ape have also passed the mark test but when it comes to monkey species the issue is still being investigated. But whatever its shared cognitive abilities, the young human primate is bound on a very different path from its non-human cousins. One of the most obvious elements in this divergence is the astonishing human proficiency with language. We turn to this now.

EARLY VOCAL DEVELOPMENT AND TURN-TAKING

By now, you can see that a huge amount of social interaction can be acquired by simply acting in the world and looking at others. But of course, none of this happens in a silent world. From the very beginning, the child's journey is constantly accompanied by sounds from humans, and during its first year its own sounds will become part of the process of interchange with adults, and indeed part of its growing sense of 'self'. By the second year, speech-like vocalisation will help to bind child and adult in a shared world of meaning and intent. In the next sections we shall consider how this remarkable ability gets off the ground.

LEARNING LANDMARKS

5.6 Self-exploration with sound. By the end of this section, you should know the types of vocal sound a baby will learn to make in its first half-year. You should be aware of the articulatory control that is required to produce the sounds that give rise to babbling.

5.7 Auditory input from others. You should know what is meant by Infant Directed Speech (IDS), and the function it serves.

5.8 Facial and vocal imitation and conversational turn taking. You should know the sorts of early imitation that are important in sound articulation, and how babies pause or 'take turns' in their communications.

5.6 SELF-EXPLORATION WITH SOUND

In Chapter 3, you learned how speech forms a key element in the child's auditory world. So how does hearing the voice of an adult help the development of the child's own voicing? A first and essential ingredient is for the child to actually want to hear him- or herself. This requires an element of self-stimulation from the mere fact of vocalisation and, on the whole, it seems to be a desire to listen to the sounds of their own voice that gets infant speech off the ground. In this section we concentrate on those stages that lead towards word-like sounds through self-exploration of vocal control.

Crying

The first sound a baby will make will be an involuntary cry in response to the need to breathe in a new way. Thereafter discomfort from factors such as hunger, cold fatigue, etc. will ensure that crying to release negative emotions will be a feature of its vocalisations for some time. Other noises that a baby will make in the first two months are also part of its normal regulation of biological functions, such as coughing, sneezing and burping. Already, however, crying seems to be more than just a reflexive release of distress; babies seem to be aware of their own crying and prefer it to the crying sounds of other babies! Martin and Clark (1982) found that 16-hour-old infants responded differentially to tape recordings of their own versus other babies' cries, and were more likely to stop crying on hearing the former and to start crying on hearing the latter.

Cooing, laughing, and the elements of speech

At around 2 months, the vocalisations of the infant start to include sounds that are clearly different from distress crying, including laughter, chewing and sucking noises. These vocalisations will also include sounds that are perceptibly like speech. As Dore (1985) colourfully put it: 'Young infants cry squeal, coo, gurgle, grunt, moan fuss, fret, fulminate and otherwise vocally emote'. The 'cooing' or more accurately 'gooing' sound that appears between about 2 and 4 months is enabled by the growth of the head and neck area which produces a greater separation of nasal and oral cavities. This allows **consonant articulation** by different ways in which the lower and upper **articulators** (lips, teeth, tongue and roof of mouth) are brought into contact. **Stop consonants**, or **plosives**, are consonants made by stopping airflow at various parts of the mouth. For example, **nasal stops** – the sounds 'm', 'n' and 'ng' as in 'meat', 'neat' and 'sing' – are made when the **velum** (soft palette of the mouth) is raised and air escapes through the nose. The control of oral and nasal cavities also permits the production of vowel sounds. Vowels are produced by setting up a vibration of the two folds of connective tissue within the larynx called the **vocal fold**.

The earliest consonants and vowels produced by infants are those produced at the back of the mouth. **Velar stop consonants** – the sounds 'k' and 'g' as in 'lake' and 'good' – appear very early in development and are produced at the back of the mouth by the tongue touching the raised velum. Vowels such as 'a' as in 'rather', also heard in these early speech-like vocalisations of infants, are also produced at the back of the mouth. But for these sounds to be made, let alone become developed into syllables and words, it is essential that this activity is enjoyable and stimulating in its own right. As long ago as 1965, a pioneer in the study of children's language acquisition, Eric Lenneberg, and his colleagues tape-recorded the vocalisations of infants over the first three months of life. Ten of the infants were hearing children of hearing parents raised in a normal environment, but six comparison children had deaf parents, and one of these children was himself deaf. No differences were found across any of the infants in their levels of 'fussing' and 'cooing'. Since then, other studies have confirmed that babies with profound hearing impairment will vocalise as much as hearing infants even as late as 7 months old (Oller et al., 1985).

Vocal play

From 4 to 6 months, experimenting with sound increases and not always in the direction of perceptible speech. Babies will now use breath control to vary the loudness and quality of the sounds they make from whispers to yells and squeals to growls. Another non-speech sound that is discovered at this stage is the **bilabial trill** – the fun of making a 'raspberry' sound by blowing air through pursed lips. At this stage, closure of the vocal tract is produced by raising the soft palette to produce most consonant sounds, and these will start to show some rudimentary signs of alternation with the vowel sounds. This alternation forms the basis for the production of first syllables, which appear at the next stage – babbling.

Babbling

One way of thinking about this stage is to see it as part of a general expansion – not to say explosion – in the realm of motor control. Babbling precedes the advent of sitting, crawling and pulling to a standing position by just a few weeks. In that sense, the fine motor tuning that the baby practices at this stage is part of a general surge in motor abilities. From about 6/7 months, babies will start to make vocalisations composed of syllables. This occurs by controlling the jaw such that it alternates between a lift, enabling a consonant type of sound, and a drop, enabling a vowel. In conjunction along with the movements of lips and tongue described above, this regular and repeatable alternation of consonant with vowel produces clearly detectable syllables such as 'ma' or 'da'. Repetition of these sounds, called **reduplicated babbling**, makes elementary words such as 'mama' and 'dada'. Whilst these 'first words' have the delightful property of apparently naming the child's nearest and dearest, it is not likely that they are produced by a desire to name – and much more likely that they emerge naturally from the

Panel 5.6 Self-exploration with sound

- The earliest sound a baby makes is a cry

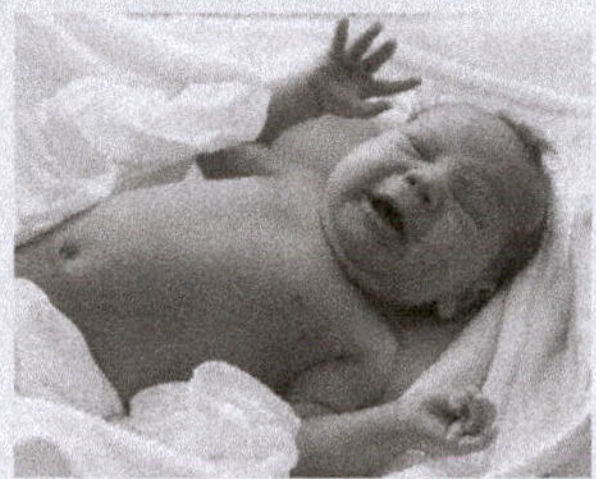

- From around 2 months babies will make 'gooing' along with laughter and other sounds that mark the beginning of sound control
- This develops into *vocal play* which even deaf babies indulge in. It is based on exploring the different sounds that can be made using the vocal tract, lips and teeth

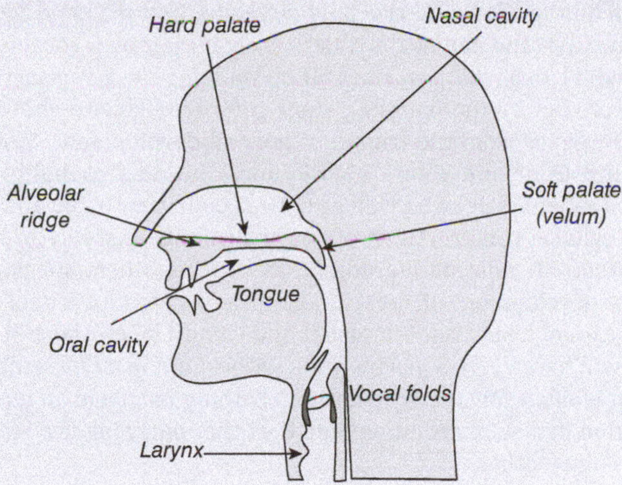

The vocal tract and articulators. By 6 months the baby will be able to make some basic vowel sounds through vibration of the vocal folds, consonant sounds by raising the tongue against the velum, as well as some trilling sounds by bringing the lips together

(Outline image by Tavin; Wikimedia Commons)

- From 6/7 months babies start to babble by controlling their jaws so that vowels can be alternated with consonants to make repeatable syllables – such as 'baba' and 'mama'
  - This is called *reduplicated babbling*

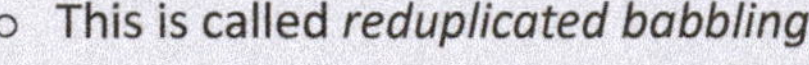

sounds that are easiest to make (Locke, 1993). In fact the elements in babbling are fairly universal across all languages (Deutscher, 2005).

A great deal of this progress is driven by the child's continuing desire to experiment with sound. During the three months or so after babbling starts, babies continue to show signs of self-exploration with sound, actually vocalising in this way more when they are alone than with others (Delack, 1976). And there is a great deal for them to discover. In addition to nasal and velar stops, they start to use other stop consonants: **bilabial stops** 'p' and 'b' (using upper and lower lips); **labiodental stops** 'f' and 'v' (teeth against lower lip); the **fricative** sound 's' (made like an alveolar stop but without actually making contact between tongue and ridge); **alveolar stops** 't' and 'd' (using the tongue against a ridge behind the top teeth). They will also start to use sounds called **glides**, 'w' and 'j', which are like vowels but with more constriction required of the vocal tract such as bringing the lips together ('w') or touching the palette of the mouth with the tongue ('j'). These types of sound are likely to be in the repertoire of babies by their first birthday (Locke, 1983).

5.7 AUDITORY INPUT FROM OTHERS

There is clearly an impetus for vocalisation from wanting to play with sounds, but the directions in which it develops are crucially dependent on the child being able to hear the sounds it is making (and babies react negatively if their own vocal feedback is artificially tampered with). Deaf children start off by showing the same sorts of vocalisation as hearing children, but by the babbling stage they are likely to show the beginnings of a dramatic divergence from the course of normal development. Stoel-Gammon and Otomo (1986) and Oller and Eilers (1988) have found that babbling in severely hearing-impaired infants is delayed well into the second year of life and also shows only a fraction of the syllable constructions of hearing infants. Inability to hear themselves is of course not the only missing ingredient, as hearing others speak is also a crucial component in the development of speech. The disadvantage for a deaf child, therefore, is not just that it cannot hear itself but also that it cannot hear others. A hearing child of hearing parents will have been experimenting with sound in an incredibly rich auditory environment that is often specifically geared to helping language on its way. Let us now switch our attention to that environment and the other party involved in bringing on the child's language – the mother.

The mother's input

In Chapter 3 it was pointed out that **phonology**, or the elements of speech, are not are not just built from syllables but also include pitch, stress and intonation, known as the **prosodic** features of speech. It is a fairly universal feature of caregivers' speech patterns to children to use higher pitch and exaggerated stress and intonation to their infants. This is referred to as **motherese**, **Infant Directed Speech** (IDS) or **Child Directed Speech** (CDS), along the lines of 'WHOOSE a lovely baby then? YES – OOO are a lovely baby, AREN'T ooo?', etc. Several studies have established empirically that mothers are more likely to use, for example, a higher pitch (Garnica, 1975), with lengthened final syllables in their speech to preverbal children than to their older siblings. This appears to reflect an intuition by adults as to what may make speech more vivid and easier to segment. Certainly conditioned head turning techniques suggest that babies prefer motherese to normal adult language (Fernald, 1985). However, there is some evidence that it is more likely to be the strong positive **affect** (emotional intonation) that accompanies such speech that babies are responding to. In a study by Singh et al. (2002), it was found that motherese without the positive affect that is usually introduced into this speech was actually less preferred by 6-month-old infants than 'adult' talk that retained the element of positive affect. This is consistent with findings that depressed mothers who use less motherese were less able to elicit a particular response from their babies than were strangers who talked to the babies with more positive affect (Kaplan et al., 2002).

The positive influence provided by Mum is not just about her tone of voice. In many ways, the mother or other primary caregiver is a kind of conductor. The baby comes to the dialogue with a desire to listen to and experiment with sounds. A willing new performer, he also likes to look at his mother, as well as listen to speech and her speech in particular. For her part, the mother is eagerly seeking the first signs of linguistic proficiency, and in fact Bloom and Lo (1990) found that when viewing videotapes of 3-month-old babies, adults actually liked those babies making the most speech-like sounds, rating them as 'cuddlier' or 'more fun'. The interactive chemistry between mother and baby is therefore complex; each seeking social and emotional reinforcement from the other. The mother has an additional agenda in her role as conductor, however, and that is to use the exchange to establish shared meaning. Golinkoff (1983) noticed that conversations between a mother and a babbling child are aimed at trying to find out what the baby wants when repeating a nonsense babble such as 'tis', offering him a drink or toy, etc. until the baby seems to have what it was 'asking' for (e.g. cheese). Thereafter the mother will respond to 'tis' according to the apparently intended meaning, but will replace it in her reply with the correct word ('is it the *cheese* you want?'). This will ensure the baby keeps hearing the correct word in that particular context. Snow (1977) provides another such an example from an exchange between a mother and a 12-month-old baby based on:

> Child: "Abaaabaa"
>
> Mother: "Baba – yes that's you, what you are"

Finally, it should be remembered that CDS is not just about words – it is about the function of words to communicate. Snow points out that mothers are trying to engage children in conversation and consequently there is a higher than average proportion of questions in their CDS (Snow, 1977). For reasons that may reflect their somewhat different social relationship with the child, fathers and siblings are less likely to pick up on an infant's utterance using CDS and are slightly more directive in the 'conversation' (Barton & Tomasello, 1994). And so, although there is a primary desire for babies to experiment with their voice on their own, the social reinforcement provided by adult listeners seems designed to inculcate the baby into using speech as a mode of social dialogue. This is crucial to the next stages of linguistic development and we shall explore the dynamics of this dialogue next, starting with facial imitation.

Panel 5.7 Auditory input from others

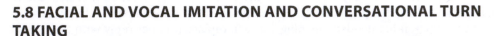

- Mothers encourage children's vocalisation by using exaggerated speech
  - This is called '*motherese*' or
  - *Infant Directed Speech* (IDS) or
  - *Child Directed Speech* (CDS) 
- Researchers think that IDS is an attempt by mothers to make a 'conversation' out of their baby's vocalisation
  - Mothers, in particular, ask their babies questions
- The *positive affect* associated with IDS is an important element
  - 6 month olds prefer adult talk to IDS if it retains a strong affective component

5.8 FACIAL AND VOCAL IMITATION AND CONVERSATIONAL TURN TAKING

Early facial imitation

In a dialogue between baby and adult, the adult alone knows the full score and it is primarily up to the adult to 'conduct' it. But to get this dialogue moving, the baby has to initiate the process somehow. One of the most powerful ways of attracting another's attention is to imitate their facial movements. If you remember, newborns will make reflexive imitations of elementary movements of the adult's face such as tongue protrusion. Tongue and mouth movements are not just simple ingredients in an imitative game; they are also the ingredients for articulation. Kuglumutzakis (1999) presented babies with an adult face making mouth opening, essential for vowel production, and tongue protrusion, requiring the same dexterity with the tongue that will later be required for consonant production. They did this for several periods of time up to 15 minutes duration. From as young as under one hour old up to about the third month of life, babies were found to imitate these movements, typically whilst watching the moving parts of the adult's face. So selective movements of the mouth and lips can be engendered by social imitation, suggesting that facial imitation is one important strand in the development of speech.

Early vocal imitation

It is through another sort of imitation, however, that vocalisation gets its main impetus for turning into speech – and that is **vocal imitation.** In the research by Kuglumutzakis, the babies were presented with adult models of basic speech sounds. The vocal models were rhythmical repetitions of the sounds 'a', m' and 'ang'. Interestingly, as the incidence of visual imitation decreased, the incidence of vocal imitation increased, and babies were significantly likely to imitate all three sounds between 2½ and roughly 4 months of age, the age at which reflexive facial imitation was declining. So vocal imitation helps to enrich and enhance the dialogue. It also clear that listening to others at this stage causes genuine phonological 'learning'. Babies don't just imitate immediately after a vocal stimulus – they also learn very quickly how to reproduce, at will, sounds that they have heard earlier, which you now know to be 'deferred imitation'. In a study by Kuhl and Meltzoff (1996) infants between 3 and 5 months were exposed to one of three vowel sounds ('a', 'i' or 'u') over three daily episodes of five minutes. They were more likely subsequently to make a vowel-like sound like the one played to them than either of the others. Exposure to the heard world of speech in fact drives the babbling stage forward to the extent that, by the age of 1, children seem to have acquired a phonetic signature that is characteristic of the ambient language around them. Benedict De Boysson-Bardies and colleagues at the Sorbonne studied infants reared in different linguistic environments, such as monolingual English, French, Arabic and Chinese, and found that the phonetic patterns that differentiated these groups in the adult native language were clearly apparent in the children's pre-speech at only 10 months (de Boysson-Bardies et al., 1984). This group also found that the intonation in long segments of pre-speech allowed adults to correctly identify infants from their own linguistic community.

Panel 5.8 Facial and vocal imitation and conversational turn-taking

- Early attempts at speech involve imitated mouth movements as well as imitated sounds
- Facial imitation gives way to *vocal imitation* and this in turn gives rise to learning how to make spontaneous sounds that have been previously imitated between 3 and 5 months
- By 10 months, children will have learned to imitate the intonation patterns of their native language
    - Their phonetic patterns even at this pre-speech phase allow adults to identify their native tongue
- Episodes of mutual vocal imitation by baby and mother have the 'turn-taking' properties of a conversation

'Conversational' turn taking

The child's own imitative actions clearly form the bedrock to provoke self-exploration of sound as well as a basis on which to learn by listening to those around them. It is important therefore that their time is shared between the two activities and they don't try to do both at the same time. Indeed, from the very beginning there is a 'first-me, then-you' aspect to an infant's dialogue with an adult, rather like two people trying to communicate on a Walkie-Talkie. In a study by Kuglumutzakis (1993) spontaneous vocal imitation in infants was observed at regular intervals between 15 days after birth and 6 months. The babies seemed to comply with the pattern of dialogue – only vocalising when the other was not, and with only a small percentage of the baby's vocalisation occurring when the adult was talking. This pattern is called **turn taking** and continues to be an important framework for language development well after the development of elementary speech.

CHAPTER SUMMARY

Social interaction is established through joint attention and the development of gaze and point following. It is also enabled by imitation, first of simple behaviours and later by copying meaningful goal-directed behaviours of adults. This heralds the start of self-awareness as measured by mirror self-recognition. Social interaction through the medium of speech starts with extensive self-exploration with sound, gradually turning into 'babbling' and heavily reinforced by the mother. By 12 months old, a baby will be able to engage in apparently 'conversational' exchanges with its caregivers.

LOOKING AHEAD TO CHAPTER 6

One of the most obvious characteristics of the human is the need to talk to others. Listen to the sounds in a theatre at the start and end of a lecture or performance. With the development of the mobile phone, the human urge to communicate has become even more obvious. We have seen how babies try to engage in this activity almost from the moment they can vocalise. But what they are about to do next is one of the most remarkable of all human achievements: they learn to communicate through words. We pursue the first stages of language learning in the next chapter.

CHAPTER 6

THE EMERGENCE OF SPEECH

We now know that infants rapidly progress to speech-like sounds in the second half of their first year. But to speak in words, the infant still needs to be able to connect the sounds it hears with the facial movements it sees when others are talking, and with the sounds it makes itself. We start by reviewing the neuroanatomical structures that make speech – and ultimately language – humanly possible.

THE BRAIN AS AN ORGAN FOR LANGUAGE

Let us consider for a moment what the baby has to master here. She began by making the appropriate mouthing movements to form the rudiments of consonants and vowels. But for these sounds to develop further, she has to connect the movements of mouth and vocal tract with the sounds she hears herself make, and also connect and compare these heard sounds with ones made by those talking to her. Before any of this is invested with adult meaning, the baby will start to build a personal 'lexicon' and know how to produce it at will. These are complex, intermodal and interpersonal connections that require the child's brain to be organised in a very particular way. Let us turn our attention to the anatomical architecture that permits this amazing skill.

LEARNING LANDMARKS

6.1 Brain centres for language: classic models. You should be familiar with the neuroanatomical foundations for language and classical models for how the brain is thought to be specialised for language.

6.2 Brain centres for language: newer models. You should be aware of some of the contemporary re-thinking with regard to the neuroanatomy of language. You should know why mirror neurons might be important in language learning.

6.1 BRAIN CENTRES FOR LANGUAGE: CLASSIC MODELS

It is still not well understood how the many aspects of language are dealt with by the human adult brain, let alone the brain of the developing child. Until quite recently, much of what was believed about the functional anatomy for language came from ideas put forward by nineteenth century clinicians; most notably the French physician, Paul Pierre Broca and the German neurologist, Carl Wernicke. Broca famously carried out a post-mortem study of a brain-damaged patient whose speech production was almost completely impaired apart from the ability to utter the word 'tan'. Broca located the damaged area in the front left hemisphere – a brain region known since as **Broca's area** (Panel 6.1) – and considered to be the area for the motor production of speech sounds in grammatical strings. **Broca's aphasia** is still used today as a clinical term for anyone who speaks effortfully in short phrases with very little grammatical structure. Wernicke, on the other hand, identified another sort of aphasia (meaning an impairment in the production or comprehension of language) in which patients could speak with an apparently normal grammatical pattern and rhythm but with no meaning attached to the speech stream and sometimes with no meaning attached to the words. This is now known as **receptive aphasia**, or **Wernicke's aphasia**, and was thought to be caused by damage to an area in the brain called the **superior temporal gyrus** (STG) that encircles the auditory cortex. Wernicke's area, as it became known, is located on the left STG along a part of the brain known as the **planum temporale**, itself located within the large fissure separating the parietal and temporal lobes, called the **Sylvian fissure** (see Panel 6.1). These two areas are connected via a fibre tract called the **arcuate fasiculus**. The broad conclusions are that **lexical access**, or word meaning, is localised at Wernicke's area and that motor commands to output meaning in sentences are created as motor plans in Broca's area.

In the middle of the last century, an American neurologist, Norman Geschwind, revived interest in these areas by discovering that the planum temporale was larger in the left than the right hemisphere in most patients. Geschwind popularised the idea that the human language centres are normally located in the left hemisphere of right-handed people (Geschwind & Levitsky, 1968). This idea of a left hemisphere specialised in humans for language has received some support from studies of infants. In a study by Locke et al. (1991), pre-babbling infants (4/5 months) and babbling infants (6–9 months) were given rattles placed in either the right or left hand (see Locke, 1993: 187). A significant increase in right-handed shaking of the rattles was observed in the babbling infants, leading Locke to conclude that the left hemisphere comes to control rhythmic manual movements through a common mechanism that also allows the increased control of the vocal tract.

6.2 BRAIN CENTRES FOR LANGUAGE: NEWER MODELS

New ideas and findings are beginning to modify the classic view of the language 'centres' in the brain. An altogether more complex picture is now emerging, as we gain more detailed information about the different sorts of speech disorder that can occur as a results of brain dysfunction, and as hypotheses about brain localisation become

Panel 6.1 Brain centres for language: classic models

- Language was thought to be processed in the left hemisphere because of certain cases of brain damage
- Two areas were classically identified with language processing
  - *Broca's area*
    - Damage to this area seem to affect the ability to produce speech
      - Broca's apahasia today refers to impairments of producing grammatical language
  - *Wernicke's area*
    - Damage to this area resulting in grammatical utterances that were devoid of meaning
      - Today this is known as Wernicke's aphasia or *receptive aphasia*

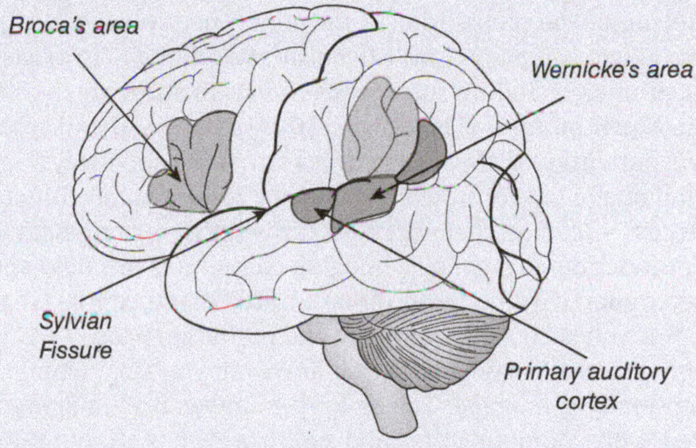

(Image by James.mcd.nz; Wikimedia Commons)

- It was thought that Wernicke's area controlled lexical access whilst Broca's area controlled motor output of meaning, but this is now thought to be an over-simplification
- There is still some support for the idea that rhythmic motor output is located in the left hemisphere and it is generally the case that the left hemisphere is dominant in language processing

specifically tested by functional imaging of normal healthy brains. The classic view of biologically localised 'areas' for grammar and for lexical information turns out to be based on a somewhat inaccurate model of how the brain is organised.

First of all, the very concept of left-hemisphere specificity for language has been challenged by striking evidence from patients who have had an entire brain hemisphere surgically removed (usually in order to control epileptic seizures). In a study of 48 child patients who had undergone this surgery (called **hemishperectomy**), Curtiss and de Bode (1999) found that they were actually twice as likely to be seriously language-impaired after removal of the *right* hemisphere than the left. More subtle impairments of language are certainly found in all adult patients undergoing this operation, whichever hemisphere is removed, and it does seem to be true that difficulties in the more complex aspects of grammar are more likely to occur after left-hemisphere removal. But it is also clear that from the fact that some left-hemispherectomised patients suffer no obvious language impairment, that the right hemisphere can sustain a considerable amount of language processing on its own. This is especially true of children, and, in particular, children who are pre-linguistic will make a near normal recovery after damage to the 'classic' left-hemisphere language centres (Bates et al., 2001).

Hemispheric specialisation apart, the idea of two clearly distinct locations for grammatical and lexical function has been challenged by a more complex and fine-grained analysis of language itself (Poeppel & Hickok, 2004). What is actually meant by 'lexical' (word-based) information, for example? It can be both phonological ('pa' versus 'ba') as well as connected to the recognition of meaning ('pad' versus 'bad'). As many are now reporting, moreover, some aphasias can occur after damage to areas outside the classic language-based ones including sub-cortical areas such the deep 'old' part of the brain known as the **basal ganglia** (Lieberman, 2002). And, as Dronkers and Larsen (2001) have reported, patients with damage to Broca's area are not always 'agrammatical', whilst patients with damage to Wernicke's area do not always suffer difficulties with meaning and lexical access – leading them to re-assess whether or not such specific attempts at localisation of function are realistic. Imaging techniques are now shedding light on the complex interconnectivity between different areas involved in language listening and language production such as the auditory and motor cortices.

In children who are learning to speak, however, you may wonder when these areas become functionally connected. This is hard to answer as imaging techniques are not normally used with young healthy children. However, a study by Redcay et al. (2008) compared fMRI activity in toddlers of around two years olds with that of speaking children about one year older during natural sleep, in the course of which they were exposed to speech played both forwards and backwards. The children showed diffuse activation to forwards speech involving frontal cerebellar and occipital regions, but only the older children also showed activation in the temporal areas associated with speech processing in adults (see Panel 6.2). Although this is a preliminary finding, it points to how different brain regions become recruited in language learning and how the brain has become functionally re-organised for speech perception by the age of three.

Returning to our young infant imitating and exploring speech sounds, the general phonetic structure of vocalisation is rapidly becoming like that of the adults, but lexical and motor access to real words is still a very long way off. Are there any brain mechanisms that help the child towards the speech it is hearing around him?

Panel 6.2 Brain centres for language: newer models

- There is growing evidence that the right hemisphere can play an important role in language processing
    - In brain-damaged patients (especially young children) it can take over the left hemisphere's function
- Modern imaging techniques have identified a greater role for the right hemisphere and have helped reveal the interconnections involved in different aspects of language use
- They also show how the brain starts to become functionally re-organised for language at around 3 years

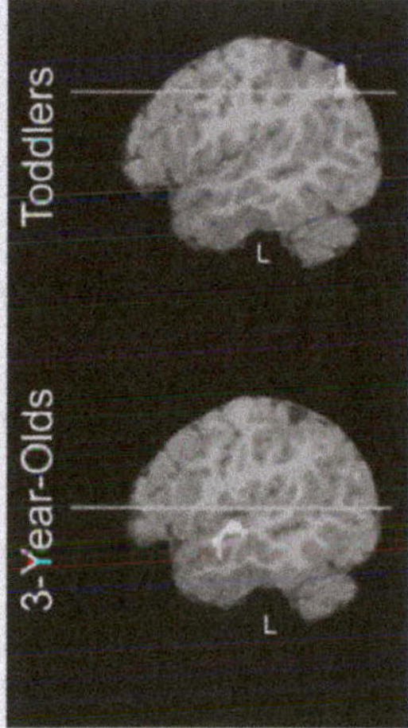

Three year olds show a significant shift toward increased activation in the superior temporal region of the brain when listening to forwards as opposed to backwards speech (Adapted from Redcay et al, 2008, with permission)

- Many issues still remain – such as whether there are auditory 'mirror neurons' that allow children to imitate sounds

Mirror neurons and speech

If you remember from Chapter 5, there is a hypothesised brain mechanism in humans that allows visually perceived behaviours to be imitated. This is the mirror system, in which certain motor regions of the brain fire when actions of others are passively observed. The idea that this may be related to language has been largely fuelled by the fact that one of the active regions that fires during different sorts of observed actions is one of the 'classic' language centres – Broca's area – provoking various theories suggesting that human language has evolved from an older centre in the primate brain for coding action. A reasonable speculation arising from this is that there may be a common neural substrate for coding the sound of another's voice and the motor movements that are required to make that sound oneself, just as there seems to be a common substrate for perceiving and carrying out an action with hand or limb. Are there 'auditory' mirror neurons that allow us to copy sounds? No one knows at present. And even if there are, they are unlikely to work in isolation, as speech perception – the foundation for speech production – is multimodal – depending on sight as well as sound. A connection has to be made between the heard sound and the (visible) motor act required to produce it. Even if there is a mirror system that supports this, anatomical readiness alone cannot propel the child forward. The brain has to learn this connection, and this has to be done not only in terms of connecting sight with sound but also by building on the auditory match and mismatch between what is produced and what is heard from others through active learning.

LEARNING MECHANISMS FOR SPEECH

LEARNING LANDMARKS

6.3 Learning from others. You should be aware of the multimodal nature of speech learning and know the extent to which direct reinforcement can help in early speech production.

6.4 Learning through self-regulation. You should understand why the main spur for making word-like sounds seems to be through the child's self-regulation of its own output.

6.3 LEARNING FROM OTHERS

There is growing behavioural evidence regarding how infants make connections between what they hear and what they see when watching someone talk. As you know, visual imitation based on lip and mouth occurs very early but this type of visual imitation seems to disappear after the first two months. Certainly, looking at someone's mouth is not an ideal way to start learning phonology, not least because many of the first uttered and copied sounds are made at the back of the mouth with very little observable effect on the lips. We also know that vocal imitation takes over from visual imitation from the second month. Recently, moreover, it has been recognised that visual attention seems to shift from the eyes back to the mouth between 4 and 8 months and then, at about 1 year, there is a shift of the infant's attention back to eyes when watching someone talk. This is only true if the adult is speaking in the child's native tongue, suggesting that they now have the attentional capacity to pick up social cues, if the phonology is familiar (Lewkowicz & Hansen-Tift, 2012). This is a more complex speech learning mechanism than one based on auditory imitation alone, and indeed looking at the mouth continues to be an important factor in adult speech perception. Adult humans can famously be influenced by what they see the mouth do when they watch someone speak, as demonstrated by the dramatic **McGurk effect.**

Learning from adult feedback

Despite their growing attention to the sight and sound of others, babies take a long time to make sounds an adult can recognise as a word. Does specific feedback from the speaking adult play a part? Adults do not punish or admonish babies for not being able to speak properly in the way that the same adult might scold a puppy for making a mess on the living-room carpet. But just as the adult will lavish praise on the puppy for appropriate toilet behaviour, so the adult provides a huge amount of positive reinforcement during their dialogue with the baby. But can we be sure that this produces specific learning of actual vocal content by the child? In an early study by Routh (1967), the vocalisations made by babies between 2 and 7 months old were recorded and then, over a period of days, the researchers selectively reinforced the baby's own particular consonant-like sounds or, conversely, its own particular vowel-like sounds. They did this by smiles, sounds and stroking when the baby made one or other of these vocalisations. This significantly enhanced the frequency of production of the particular sound type that had been reinforced. Equally, in a somewhat unethical experiment by Wahler (1969), a mother was asked not to reinforce her baby's vocalisations but to 'freeze' on hearing, e.g., cooing or babbling when these first appeared. This reduced the emission of these sounds by the baby, but fortunately, he recovered when her normal behaviour was restored.

The implication from these studies is that deliberate reinforcement by Mum increases the frequency of the sounds the child was experimenting with anyway. This has been supported by a study carried out by Uzgiris et al. (1989), in which it was found that the mother's imitation of her infant increased significantly at about 8 months. Although babies do not imitate their mothers as much as the other way around, there was nevertheless an increase observed in their sample of 80 mother–baby pairs at around 8 months in the extent to which the baby would repeat the vocalisation that had just been imitated by the mother. Social reinforcement clearly acts not just as a stimulus to self-exploration with sound but also as a stimulus for the baby to repeat particular sounds that the mother recognised as speech-like.

Panel 6.3 Learning from others

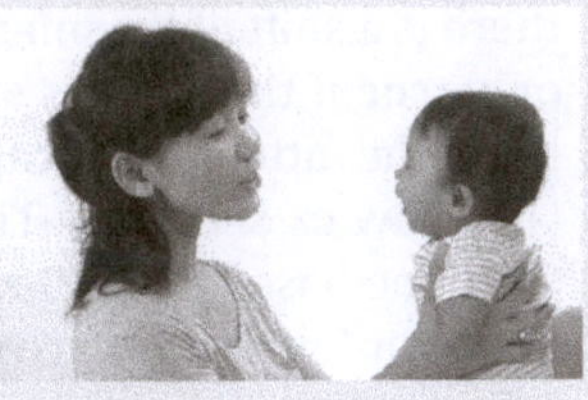

- Speech is learned by a complex imitative process that involves looking at the mouth and eyes of someone speaking
  - Very young babies tend to focus on the eyes
  - Between 4 and 8 months, they focus more on the mouth
  - By 12 months, they focus back on the eyes if the speaker is talking in their native language

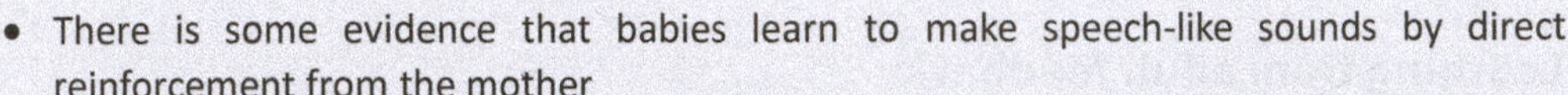

- There is some evidence that babies learn to make speech-like sounds by direct reinforcement from the mother
  - They can be conditioned in the lab to selectively repeat either consonant or vowel sounds if these are reinforced with smiles and tickles
- Imitation by the mother of the baby's vocalisation also acts as a reinforcer
  - This shows an increase at around the babbling stage
- In the main, most learning seems to derive from the mother imitating and reinforcing sounds that the baby was already experimenting with

6.4 LEARNING THROUGH SELF-REGULATION

Unlike dogs that can be (sometimes!) be trained to say 'sausages', language learning in children is no one-off learning achievement. The sheer number and precision of speech sounds that a child will learn in its first year suggests that the child's lexicon is constantly updated by an internal feedback mechanism – or as Gleason (2005: 79) puts it, 'a way of assessing his own performance'. But even this concept requires clarification. How do you assess your performance when trying out your French pronunciation on holiday in France? Is it only when corrected by the native French speakers you meet? Or are you guided at least as much in terms of your own criterion of failure, i.e. when what you hear yourself say doesn't come out the way you intended? In infants it appears that the latter type of experience is crucial. Whilst there is considerable evidence, as we have seen, that babies are led in certain directions through imitative exchanges with the mother, there is very little evidence that discoveries at the babbling stage are acquired by being directly 'corrected' by others. This is a little surprising is it not? For you now know that imitative acts by the mother contain expansions and embellishments of what the baby has just uttered, giving ample opportunity for the baby to learn directly from her 'corrective' input – just as you may adjust your French pronunciation by hearing your words corrected by a French speaker. Yet the numerous studies of language learning during the babbling period have found no evidence that this actually occurs. In fact, Locke (1993) cites at least 10 empirical studies from 1968 to 1990

Panel 6.4 Learning through self-regulation

- Mothers embellish and expand on the speech-like sounds of babies
- Whilst this suggests that babies might learn to adjust their speech by being directly corrected during imitative exchanges, there is no evidence for this
- The growth of the vocal tract, increased articulatory exploration and matching against perceived sound is the main promoter of coherent word production

showing that the developmental literature is actually 'replete with failures' (p. 167) to show how children actively learn from corrective feedback from adults, suggesting that the feedback that drives the learning must be largely internally monitored.

This has been supported by measurements of how the growth of the vocal tract between 4 and 7 months together with increased exploration of sounds can by itself give rise to advanced babbling. Serkhane et al. (2007) constructed a detailed model showing how articulatory development through the growth of the vocal tract is tightly related to acoustic output between 4 and 7 months. It is highly likely that this same process will continue to help the babbling turn into recognisable 'words'. In fact, the relationship between the fine tuning of speech motor control in relation to auditory feedback continues on into adulthood (Shiller & Rochon, 2014).

In the early stages of word production, therefore, the baby really needs to learn about his own voice and how he can modify it in relation to what he hears. Although it is socially reinforced, it seems this is a largely self-propelled voyage of discovery. But its ultimate purpose is to communicate meaning and be understood. The communicative elements of language become increasingly evident in the second half of the first year as we see next.

SPEECH AS COMMUNICATION

LEARNING LANDMARKS

6.5 The beginnings of intentional communication. You should know what is meant by conversational or variegated babbling.

6.6 Joint attention and linguistic reference by the adult. You should know what deictic pointing refers to, and what is meant by dyadic interaction. You should be able to cite at least one study correlating dyadic interaction with language onset.

6.5 THE BEGINNINGS OF INTENTIONAL COMMUNICATION

In the realm of direct perception, meaning is a 'given', whether it is about a looming object or a disappearing toy. Human speech is curiously different in that it starts off without meaning and, as we have seen, can advance in pre-speech form for nearly a year without it. What it does need, however, is a communicative purpose if it is ever to be used as a way of expressing and sharing meaning with another. The foundations for this desire to share and interact are in place well before speech begins and they form the platform from which it will finally emerge.

Conveying meaning non-vocally

When expressing meaning in face-to-face adult dialogue, we very rarely rely completely on sound. How many of us are able to talk without waving our arms in the air and making signs and gestures with our hands? There is considerable debate amongst evolutionary biologists as to whether language has evolved directly from such signing – especially

Panel 6.5 The beginnings of intentional communication

- The stage between babbling and meaningful speech shows the intention to convey meaning with sound
- By 12 months, the baby will have more vowels and consonants in its repertoire and be capable of re-duplicated babbling using strings of syllables with varied pitch and intonation. This is called:
  - *variegated babbling* or
  - *conversational babbling*
- It is accompanied by eye-contact and gestures that indicate that the baby intends to refer to something

(Image Ava O'Hara; copyright Kevin O'Hara)

given the possibility that there is an action mirroring system in Broca's area. And whilst it is usually fully a year before the child makes a sound that is definitely a meaningful word, the ability and desire to convey and share meaning are evident in the child's gestural behaviour much earlier. In fact, a key landmark phase in the development of vocalisation is called **conversational babble** – vocalisations that are accompanied by clear non-vocal attempts to communicate, using gestures.

Conversational babble

This is an important transition stage between standard or canonical babble and true speech. Also referred to as jargon or **modulated** or **variegated babble**, it starts at about 10 months and overlaps with the appearance of first words. By this stage, babbling has taken on a more complex character with strings of syllables uttered with stress and intonation that sounds very like speech. Variegated babbles are syllables strings, but with varying rather than repeated consonants and vowels such as 'daba' and 'bagidabu'. Variegated babbling predominates over reduplicated babbling after 12 months and overlaps with the production of the first true words.

The qualifying criterion for conversational babble is that it occurs along with eye contact with the listener and/or gestural behaviours such as the newly acquired skills of pointing and looking towards a desired object. In other words, it is as if the baby now knows that these sounds should help make his intentions clearer. This is a crucial development, for it is through eye contact and mutual gaze that the mother can start to establish a shared meaning for the sounds the baby makes. In this coming together of communication, gesture and sound, then, the central discovery an infant makes is that certain sounds *have* meaning, a crucial precondition for learning what those meanings are.

6.6 JOINT ATTENTION AND LINGUISTIC REFERENCE BY THE ADULT

In Chapter 5, you saw how children can start to use pointing and eye gaze by about 14 months to single out an object for joint attention. These pointing behaviours are called **deictic** (from the noun **deixis**). That is, the point has a meaning that can be understood by the broader context in which it appears. Confusingly, they are likely to occur in a situation often referred to as **dyadic** – a pairwise interaction between two people. Deixis brings a particular common context into this interaction; for example, a child extending a finger towards an object whilst looking from the object to the mother and back again. Pointing at this stage is likely to be accompanied not just by glances to the mother but also by vocalisation (Leung & Rheingold, 1981). This gives the mother a valuable clue about what interests the baby, and she can use this to help build the use of naming. Murphy (1978) reported that mothers would name an object that the baby pointed out during storybook reading significantly more often than chance, and Masur (1982a) reported a similar finding for objects in the general visual field pointed at by the baby. Of course the mother doesn't simply name the item, but normally engages in what Bruner (1983) has described as **naming rituals**. She will say for example 'look – what's that's – it's a teddy'. Whilst the baby will not understand the actual words 'look' 'what's that?', etc., Bruner argued that phrases such as these, uttered in the context of joint attention, make the baby aware that a naming event is going on and that the baby understands the naming process as part and parcel of a 'conversation' about a thing. Baldwin and Markman (1989) found that such naming by mother then increased subsequent attention to the named item. This implies that it is more effective for the mother to pick up on the child's natural interest than to try to direct his attention. Tomasello and Farrar (1986) found higher levels of name comprehension by 17-month-old children following four short training sessions in which objects were named *after* the child had already indicated interest rather than at the time when their interest was being directed by the adult.

But how do we know for certain that children really intend to share meaning with an adult? After all, pointing is quite an ambiguous gesture – it can denote an interest for self as much as a desire to share interest. Tomasello and colleagues at the Max Planck Institute in Leipzig have investigated this by disrupting the normal exchange between a child and adult, such that instead of a child's point and vocalisation being followed by a typical elaboration by (usually) the mother ('yes that's a nice green ball isn't it?'), the mother departs from her normal behaviour. Instead of looking to the object, for example, she goes on looking at her book or directly at the infant. They found that if the mother is looking at the child but refuses to look where he or she is pointing (i.e. the mother's attention is 'available'), then the child is twice as likely to repeat the point than in the case of a normal interaction where the mother looks immediately to the source of interest. Such repeat points are less likely, however, when the mother's attention is unavailable – e.g. reading a book (Liszkowski et al., 2008).

Whilst results such as these are open to more than one interpretation of what the child understands about his mother's mental state (Gomez, 2007), there is no doubt that the active involvement of the child in an act of referral helps the mother to latch onto the child's intended meaning, and there is considerable evidence that dyadic interactions (involving deixis) do contribute substantially to early language acquisition. Masur (1982b) found that children with larger vocabularies had been exposed to more frequent object-of-interest naming by their mothers. Tomasello and Todd (1983) found a positive correlation between degree of social interaction at 12 months, measured by length of joint attention episodes, and vocabulary size at 18 months. The degree of deictic pointing by the child was found by Bates (1979) to be correlated with first word onset.

Whilst we might expect the word learning process to be child-led in this way, it would be very maladaptive if children only absorbed meaning in connection with their own ongoing interest. Part of the dynamics of conversation is for the listener to be attuned to the fact that it is the speaker's object of interest that determines the meaning of the words being spoken. Indeed young infants are not immune to the attempts by the mother to direct their attention to something new. Baldwin (1991) found that 16-month-old children showed comprehension of object names that were labelled by the experimenter despite the fact that the child was actually showing interest in another object, confirming Bruner's contention that there

Panel 6.6 Joint attention and linguistic reference by the adult

- Pointing and looking to an object to direct the attention of another starts at around 13 months and is known as *deictic pointing*

- This is increasingly used by the mother to start building on the child's interests in her conversations with her baby
    - These are called *dyadic interactions*
- It is more effective for language learning for the mother to build on the child's interest (by naming an object they have pointed to) than to try to direct attention to something herself
- However, children of 1 year old can also learn by being asked to point out the referent on hearing the word

- The extent and quality of deictic exchanges involving naming around 12 months predicts vocabulary size at 18 months

is some genuine mutuality in the interaction between child and adult at this stage. Bannard and Tomasello (2012) have confirmed this recently by showing that new words are acquired by 1 year olds during a learning context in which they have to point out the referent to the experimenter.

From all of this we can see that from around the child's first birthday, joint attention is not only setting up the conditions both for comprehending new words but also setting up the conditions for the child to do the naming himself.

THE ACQUISITION OF FIRST WORDS

With communicative and articulatory mechanisms in place, the infant now progresses to true speech. It is important to note at this point that the timing and duration of this phase varies considerably across individual children. For example, some children may have a 'silent' phase between babbling and speech; for some babbling may co-exist for some time with speech, and the age of onset of speech itself can be highly variable. However, in what follows, you will learn about what is generally true of the emergence of real speech during (usually) the second year of life.

LEARNING LANDMARKS

6.7 Protowords and word pronunciation. You should know what protowords are, and some of the pronunciation constraints that children encounter.

6.8 The vocabulary spurt. You should know what this refers to and the rough age at which it happens.

6.9 Word learning in deaf children. You should know the similarities and differences between hearing and non-hearing children in this phase of early language acquisition.

6.7 PROTOWORDS AND WORD PRONUNCIATION

Protowords

When children start to consistently refer to an object or event with a particular sound, this is the start of naming. Initially, however, the child's attempt to name may be so far from any known word that it has to be described as a **protoword**. It qualifies as word-like in that it will be used recurrently in a context appropriate way. A common example is the name given to a favourite toy or comforter, perhaps 'wa-wa' or 'mooly', recognised by parents, caregivers and family members ('he wants his mooly') but not by a visiting stranger.

Word pronunciation

Sounds acquired during the babbling stage eventually have to conform to precise phonological rules, and this simply takes time to practice. In a way, this is the child's first real brush with cultural constraints. They may choose for themselves what sounds they like to play with during babbling, but now they have to contend with specific voicing and stop rules – and many of them. To deal with this, children seem to impose certain phonological constraints on their own pronunciation; in other words, they will conform to some rules but systematically ignore or alter others. This makes the learning more manageable but it can also make progress seem quite bizarre and bumpy. Here are some of the typical constraints that occur in children's first attempts at speech.

Constraints against consonant clusters

In babbling, children will have used consonants to start a sound. To start many words, however, consonants often have to be run together, whist voiced separately: 'bread', 'cross', 'drink', 'flag', 'green', 'play', 'stick', 'try', for example. Worse still, sometimes, three consonants will start a word: 'scratch', 'scream', 'splash', etc. One simplifying rule employed by many children when dealing with these is to simply omit the first sound, especially when it is the relatively late-appearing fricative sound 's', producing 'tick' for stick or 'cool' for school, for example. However, when the first consonant is the easier labial sound 'b', another common rule is to omit the second consonant (e.g. 'bed' for bread; 'coss' for cross, 'dink' for drink) or to replace it with the bilabial glide 'w' which requires less vocal tract constriction than the liquid consonant 'r' and unlike 'r' does not require the tongue to touch the palette. This produces words such as 'bwed' for bread, 'cwoss' for cross and

Panel 6.7 Protowords and word pronunciation

- A child's first words may be his own invention, such as 'mooly' for a favourite toy
  - These are called *protowords*
- Real words can be hard if they use consonants that require fine-tuned motor control, such as the 'r' sound where the tongue must touch the palette
- Words are even harder if consonants have to be run together, such as 'bread'
  - Here children will omit or replace the difficult consonants, producing 'bed' or 'bwed'
- Omissions will also occur when the child tries to pronounce a multi-syllable word, such as umbrella or elephant
  - Here it is often the unstressed syllable that is left out, producing 'bwella' or 'efant'
- Pronunciation difficulties do not imply that the child has mis-heard or mis-remembered a word
  - The child may say 'fis' for 'fish' but reject that mis-pronunciation from an adult

'dwink' for drink – so common in child language that in the stories of William Brown by Richmal Crompton, William's younger acquaintance, Violet Elizabeth, famously taunted him with her threat to 'scweam and scweam until I'm thick'!

Constraints against multisyllable words

It is difficult enough for children to get their tongues round single syllable words; worse still when the words are made up of different syllables. Most words have what is known as a stress pattern – some syllables are stressed, others unstressed. In English, it is very common to stress the first syllable, *Eng*lish; *buck*et, *car*pet, for example. When learning a word that starts with an unstressed syllable like tomato, children will often begin by omitting this syllable altogether: 'mato' for tomato, 'tato' for potato, 'bwella' for umbrella and so on. If the word has three syllables, the unstressed syllable is again likely to be omitted, especially when it appears in the middle of the word: 'efant' for elephant, 'pifore' for pinafore, etc.

Constraints on production rather than comprehension

When the child can only say 'bwella' or 'soo' for shoe, etc., he is struggling to approximate to a word that he is well aware of in its adult form. This can produce some amusing interchanges between child and adult – and would certainly caution against patronising a young word learner! For example, Berko and Brown (1960) report the following exchange in connection with a child's plastic fish – pronounced 'fis' by the child:

> Adult (imitating the child): "This your fis?"
>
> Child: "No – my fis!"

Child continues to reject adult's pronunciation until

> Adult: "This is your fish?"
>
> Child: "Yes – my fis"

Similarly when children appear to fail to distinguish between two different names in their attempts at pronunciation, such as 'guck' for jug and duck, or 'mouth' for 'mouse', they can clearly differentiate the items when asked to draw or fetch the objects in question (Smith, 1973).

6.8 THE VOCABULARY SPURT

In their second year of life, children will use about as many 'real' words as non-words, but when they have vocabulary size of 50 words or so (very roughly at an average age of 1 year 9 months) real words will dominate non-words in a ratio of 3 to 1. At this stage, most children will show what is known as a **vocabulary spurt** – a sudden and rapid

Panel 6.8 The vocabulary spurt

- There is a very rapid increase in vocabulary size at around the child's second birthday
- However, there is huge individual variation in the actual number of words children will have at this age

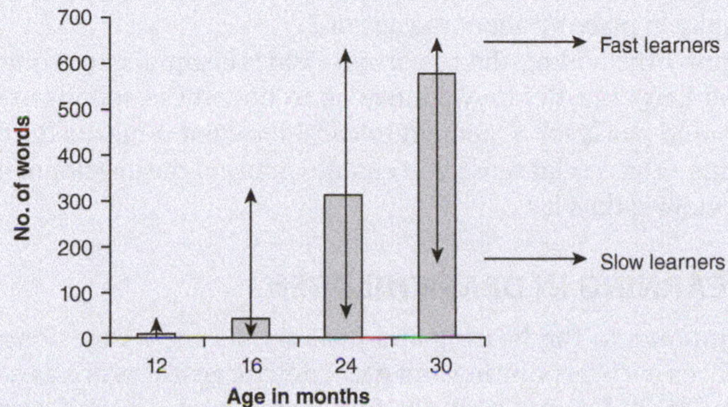

The median number of words in a child's vocabulary between 1 and 2½ years of age – also showing the range of variability across slow and fast learners

(Data from Fenson et al., 1994)

- Some think that the spurt is due to better motor control; others think that children suddenly have an 'insight' into the fact that words have meanings and are eager to acquire them
    - Both of these are likely to be true

expansion of their lexicon. Because of the very large variability in degree and rate of speech development, it is not possible to tie this down to a typical pattern, but some idea can be gained from data collected by Fenson et al. (1994), who distinguished between slow, fast and median learners. The vocabulary spurts for the groups are depicted in the graph in Panel 6.8. Researchers disagree about the cause of this spurt; for some, the acceleration in speech is symptomatic of a general improvement of motor control (Kent, 1993), whilst others argue that children gain an 'insight' into the principles of naming (Dore, 1978; McShane, 1980). It is hard to define what such an insight might be, but it is roughly along the lines that 'things have names'. A third argument is that children learn about words – their stress and intonation patterns – and so become able to categorise words into types, making it easier to add on a new exemplar: 'bucket', 'ticket', 'racket', etc.; whilst others have tied it into the growing ability to classify objects themselves (Gopnik & Meltzoff, 1987). It is possible that all these are factors that contribute in some way to the rapid expansion of vocabulary in the second year of life, which could explain why it is so difficult to identify a clear age at which this 'spurt' appears (Ganger & Brent, 2004).

Vocabulary size apart, children will continue to struggle with the pronunciation of some words until they are about 3 years old. By this age, a typically developing child will have mastered all the vowel and consonant sounds in her native language. Difficult sounds, however, can continue to give trouble up to around the age of 5; in particular, the liquid consonants 'r' and 'l' producing confusions such as 'lip' for 'rip', and fricatives such as 'th' producing confusions such as 'fin' for thin. Correct pronunciation of all common sounds, including the difficult consonant clusters at the start of words (like 'snip' and 'scrape'), is usually in place by about the age of 7.

Difficulties notwithstanding, the 1-year-old child is beginning to acquire the elements of an articulated language. Before we move on to how these sounds are mapped onto meaning, we should pause for a moment to consider what it means for the young child who lacks hearing – the crucial sense that enables many of the developments of language that we have reviewed thus far.

6.9 WORD LEARNING IN DEAF CHILDREN

The element common to the hearing and deaf child's early experience is the use of non-vocal gestures such as pointing and gaze; deictic gestures are as common in deaf children as they are in hearing children. But, by the onset of such gestures, typically developing children will have moved towards speech-like sounds, whilst deaf children will not. Furthermore, when hearing children start to string two elements together, they will do so with words, not gestures. Nevertheless, deaf children develop gestures spontaneously and when they start to combine them (a point and gesture for 'hat', for example), they will do so at the same age as hearing children start to combine words. To approach a true language, however, there has to be a substitute for those arbitrary re-usable elements that we call words. Substitutes for sounds are signs. Like words, signs are part of a culturally transmitted system for sharing meaning, and like words, signs have to be used in a consistent and intelligible way. Deaf children may be taught a sign language but, in the first two years, they may be unlikely to be exposed to signing unless one or both parents are also deaf. How easy is it for a deaf child to move from gesture to sign and start to use signs in a language-like way?

Much of the research on this topic has been carried out with children taught American Sign Language (ASL). ASL and BSL, the British equivalent, have nouns and verbs, but unlike English, sentences are unlikely to use the subject noun explicitly. In Britain, deaf children may be taught manually coded English instead (MCE), which is somewhat different and with a greater focus on the grammatical structure of English. As the age at which children are introduced to ASL (or MCE) is widely variable – depending on the extent of their hearing loss and age of diagnosis – it is hard to draw firm parallels from such sign languages to speech-based language development. Nevertheless, research on deaf children with both hearing and deaf parents is helping to show how the path to language differs for deaf children.

In dyadic interactions, it seems that hearing mothers of deaf babies latch on to the infant's focus of attention and vocalise about it at the same time. This sometimes results in a failure to catch her child's attention and develop some mutual interaction with regard to the object of interest. Research at Bristol University found that deaf mothers, by contrast, would catch the child's attention first, then sign or say the word for the referent before using a sweeping gesture to direct the child back to the object (Woll & Kyle, 1989). By the age of 2 years, deaf children with deaf mothers were found to be 30% more communicatively interactive than deaf children with hearing mothers (Gregory & Barlow, 1989). And so, although they are deprived of the advantage of hearing speech, deaf infants can still develop effective communication with their parents using signing. For many children, this will soon be supplemented with speech reading (silent lip-reading), so that they too will be able to share to some extent in the phonological words of the hearing community.

Panel 6.9 Word learning in deaf children

- Children who can't hear will develop deictic communicative gestures just like hearing children
    - Deaf mothers of deaf babies are more effective at deictic communications
- They are likely to combine gestures at the same age as hearing children combine words
- Sign-language is a formal language system that can be taught to children from a young age. The commonest in English are
    - *American Sign Language* (ASL)
    - *Manually Coded English* (MCE)

CHAPTER SUMMARY

Children learn to speak through visual and auditory imitation. The process of learning how to articulate vowel and consonant sounds leads to babbling, which is coupled with a clear intention to communicate with others. Imitation and feedback from mothers and carers is important, but the process is also highly self-motivated and self-regulated. Mutual interest in objects shared between child and adult gives rise to naming rituals that will eventually lead to the child understanding and producing its first words.

LOOKING AHEAD TO CHAPTER 7

We have seen how interactions with adults enable babbling to turn into recognisable speech. But there is much more going on in these interactions than the learning of articulation. At all times, the adult is using the shared articulatory code to inculcate the infant into a world of shared meaning. There is every sign that children want to convey this meaning themselves. This requires a very special dynamic to operate between child and adult, as we see in the next chapter.

CHAPTER 7

THE ACQUISITION OF WORD MEANINGS AND THE DAWN OF PHRASE SPEECH

Language is the ultimate means of interacting meaningfully with others. The reason we can do this is because we have words. Obviously. Well, not quite. In fact when you think about it, spoken words are meaningless sounds and their meanings have to be learned in two senses if they are to become part of a true language. First, in terms of what they refer to in the world, but also in terms of the type of thing they refer to, such as objects (nouns) and actions (verbs). Words have to be learned, in short, as parts of speech. These achievements will be covered in this chapter.

ACQUIRING A LEXICON

Now able to speak in words, what sorts of things do toddlers want to say? As we have already seen, many first words that the child is encouraged to repeat are names for objects in the visual field that the child is interested in – 'bow-wow', 'teddy', etc. Names for things do indeed account for a large proportion of the child's lexicon around the vocabulary spurt, across a large variety of languages – though exactly what proportion has been a matter of some dispute (Bloom et al., 1993). But acquiring object names is not simply a matter of having things labelled during naming rituals as we see next.

LEARNING LANDMARKS

7.1 Names for objects. You should know what sorts of words children learn first and how we know this.

7.2 Overextensions. You should know what these are and be able to cite some examples. You should be familiar with hypotheses that try to account for how children learn to add new words to their lexicon.

7.1 NAMES FOR OBJECTS

Names for objects – or nouns – are certainly likely to feature in early word learning because of the social context of sharing an event with an adult in which different objects feature – like having breakfast, or a being read a story in a picture book. Objects in the world and depicted in storybooks, e.g. milk, bunny, train, can be pointed out easily – and more easily than, say, an action like running or eating. This suggests that the speech stream heard by children will tend to isolate naming words first. Early research by Eve Clark from Stanford University used diary records from mothers regarding the first 50 words uttered by children in a variety of different languages (Clark, 1973). Out of 10 categories of word type recorded by at least 50% of the sample, 8 were nouns. These categories were: people (e.g. 'daddy'); food/drink (e.g. 'milk'); body parts (e.g. 'nose'); clothing (e.g. 'shoe'); animals (e.g. 'kitty'); vehicles (e.g. 'car'); toys (e.g. 'ball'); household objects (e.g. 'keys'). These basic data were confirmed subsequently, following the development of an important standardised test for language acquisition: the **MacArthur Infant and Toddler Communicative Development Inventories** (Fenson et al., 1993). Used in clinical practice and research this is a checklist filled out by a parent or caretaker as well as (sometimes) by an examiner.

However, the very explicitness of the act of object naming can bias our perception of its relative frequency as compared with naming an action. Gelman and Tardif (1998) established that children learning either Mandarin Chinese or English as their first language would use more object words when reading a book, but more action words when playing with mechanical toys. As the latter situation may make verbs less conspicuous within the overall interaction, it could explain why their data was somewhat discrepant with the estimate of noun production (as a proportion of total vocabulary) recorded with the MacArthur inventory checklists. It was indeed later established that mothers were actually under-reporting the use of action as opposed to object words when completing the questionnaire. This makes it hard to give a precise estimate of early noun use relative to that of other words. Finally, as with all syntactic categories at the one-word stage, it is not always clear whether a child is using a noun such as 'door' to mean the object or the event

Panel 7.1 Names for objects

- Learning what words mean is a very significant achievement – the child has to pick out the relationship between a particular part of a speech stream and its *referent*

- It seems that children pick out *nouns* (words for things) first, as these form 80% of their early lexicon (as measured by some inventories)
    - This may be because the interactive context of language acquisition tends to focus on shared objects of interest
- Inventories are often filled out by parents or caretakers
    - So it may also be partly because it is easier to be aware of nouns in the child's own speech
- The noun categories are fairly universal:
    - people
    - animals
    - food
    - body parts, etc.
- Nouns are more likely to be elicited by picture books, but *verbs* (words for actions) by playing with mechanical toys

of opening. Nevertheless, it is universal to all languages that what appear to be nouns are in evidence early on during vocabulary development, and that these nouns seem refer to the kinds of things that are probably universal in all child-rearing environments.

Now think a bit about the cognitive challenge in discovering exactly what the noun means. When, for example, the mother points out a dog in a storybook picture, and says 'doggie', this could be one of a thousand different sorts of dog, and depicted in any form, from a cartoon to a photograph. You learned in Chapter 2 that the infant's perceptual system is designed to establish invariances within classes, so that with sufficient exposure, many variations of e.g. dog will eventually be distinguished by their invariant properties – and this will even apply across pictures. But the child still has to connect the arbitrary *sound* 'doggie' with the relevant class. When a toddler hears the word 'doggie', how does she know that it refers to one of many, and not just that particular spotty dog in her picture book (which is also quite possibly depicted wearing clothes, standing on its hind legs and talking!)? And when is she able to use the word 'doggie' appropriately herself?

7.2 OVEREXTENSIONS

In fact children do make mistakes in word use at the early stages and are quite likely to use a noun inappropriately. The over-generalisations that children make when learning to name have long been noted by adults – a favourite anecdotal example being the use of the word 'daddy' not only for daddy but also for the milkman, the man next door, etc. These generalisations are called **overextensions** and have been well documented in early research by Eve Clark. Occurring most often between the ages of 1 year 6 months and 2 years 6 months, they can account for up to 40% of the early vocabulary (when its size is less than 100 words). They may last for anything from a day or two to several months. The common feature of overextensions across all languages is that they tend to be based on a generalisation from the *shape* of the originally named object – exactly what would be expected if the child were trying to classify it. Some examples from English reported by Clark (1973) are given in the table in Panel 7.2. However, the child may also latch on to some particularly salient aspect of the thing named such as texture, sound, smell or movement. For example, Clark found that a word used first of all to denote 'train' ('sch') was then applied to any machine that a made a noise, whilst a word for 'dog' ('wau-wau') was subsequently applied to a range of soft and furry objects.

It is widely accepted that overextensions are *not* because of a failure to classify and differentiate these objects at a perceptual level. Thomson and Chapman (1977), for example, showed that children who might apply the word 'ball' to various other round objects could nevertheless pick out the ball versus an apple or orange, etc. in a comprehension test with pictures, where they would be asked to e.g. 'show me the ball'. Overextensions, in other words, are children's responses to their own gap between production and comprehension. They use a handy word, when no other one is available to them. As a consequence of this, when the appropriate new word is added to the lexicon, then that particular overextension no longer occurs.

Panel 7.2 Overextensions

- When children acquire new nouns there is an initial tendency to overextend them to similar objects
  - This is not a failure to classify –
  - just a restriction on vocabulary

Word	Domains to which word is applied				
Bow-wow	Dog(s)				
Bow-wow		Dogs, Cows, Horses, Sheep			
Bow-wow			Dogs, Horses, Sheep		
Moo-moo			Cows		
Bow-wow				Dogs, Sheep	
Moo-moo				Cows	
Gee-Gee				Horses	
Bow-wow					Dogs
Moo-moo					Cows
Gee-Gee					Horses
Baa-lamb					Sheep

As new words are acquired the over-extended domain of the first word is reduced. (Adpated from Clark, 1973)

- Children seem to infer that new words must refer to new objects and, in that way, their lexicon becomes expanded and more focussed
  - This is called the *Principle of Contrast*

Overextensions represent a transient phase in word learning. The more significant fact about learning first words is the rate at which they are acquired. Whilst vocabulary spurts are highly variable in character across children (and not exclusively to nouns), the generally accelerated rate of noun acquisition in the second half of the second year has led to the argument that there is a general principle at work which goes beyond the idea that children simply learn that things have names. It suggests that children at this stage are aware that a *new* name is likely to refer to a new object. This has been called the **Principle of Contrast** (Barrett, 1978; Clark, 1987) or **Mutual Exclusivity** – a similar idea put forward by Markman and Wachtel (1988). For example, if a child can already understand the word 'ball' (as evidenced by a correct choice of object when asked to 'hand me the ball'), they are likely to map a new word, such as 'ladle' onto an object for which they do not already have a name, i.e. an object other than the ball. There is considerable debate as to whether (a) children are involved in a *lexical* exercise by simply mapping novel names to novel objects (rejecting the known object as the referent, as it already has a name), or (b) they are involved in more of a *social pragmatic* exercise, i.e. assuming that the speaker would have used the familiar name if they meant the familiar object. Although Markman et al. (2003) acknowledge the second of these possibilities, they also argue the case for the simple lexical exclusivity principle, and indeed by the age of 2 or so, children may have been doing both of these things. That is, they use the lexical rule of new names for new objects *and* social pragmatic rules fairly rapidly (i.e. people don't use a new word without a reason) to infer how a new word maps to a referent. What is ultimately of importance is that children will come to use the name appropriately in their own speech. As for storybooks, it does seem that reading them with an adult does indeed promote word learning, provided it occurs prior to sleeping (Williams & Horst, 2014).

UNDERSTANDING WORD TYPES

Children are not just interested in things – they are also interested in people and actions for which special word types beyond nouns are needed, such as proper nouns and verbs (e.g. 'Jenny', 'sit'). The meanings of words are tied to their type – or grammatical status – from the very start; that is, the particular role they will come to play in a full phrase or sentence. The grammatical status of words in a sentence helps to determine their meaning. Take, for example, the sentence 'Chomper rolled on the grass and wagged his tail'. You can tell that Chomper refers to a particular individual because of the use of the proper noun or name. It is signalled by the fact that it the word isn't preceded by another part of speech – the definite or indefinite article indicating that it is one of a class as in 'the dog rolled on the grass' or 'a dog rolled on the grass'. Followed by the pronoun 'his', we even know that Chomper is a male. But when children have yet to acquire sentence structure, how are these different parts of speech learned?

LEARNING LANDMARKS

7.3 Proper nouns. You should know what these are and be able to cite a study showing when their function appears to be understood.

7.4 Function words and action words. You should know what these are and the rough age at which they appear in children's language

7.3 PROPER NOUNS

Names for individuals or **proper nouns** satisfy the principle that children seem to apply from early on: a unique thing has a unique name. The person (or animal) can be pointed to and it will have distinctive features that specify it uniquely rather than as one of a class. The unique names for family members ('Mummy,' 'Jamie', 'Grandy', etc.) will of course appear early in speech, but is their function as proper nouns really understood? The main challenge is to differentiate the use of the proper noun from the use of the common noun that might also be used in those circumstances – e.g. 'Rags' versus 'the dog', for the family pet. To comprehend this, the child has a clue from the context in which the word is heard – the use by the adult of the article 'the' or 'a' – that allows children to make this distinction. One of the first studies that demonstrated that young children could understand the significance of an adult's omission of the article was carried out

Panel 7.3 Proper nouns

- Names or *proper nouns* are important to children and are identified by the lack of the definite or indefinite article, e.g.
  - 'Chomper' versus
  - 'the dog'
- Although children are likely to omit the article themselves, studies with nonsense words show that they can understand when a proper name is being used

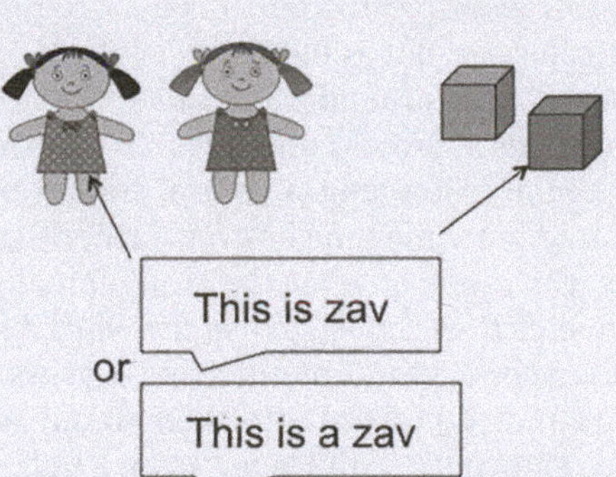

When the article (the/a) is omitted as in the top case, 2-year-old girls will assume the nonsense word refers to the particular doll (dark hair) indicated by the adult. No effect is found for simple objects

(After Katz et al., 1974)

in a now classic article by Nancy Katz and colleagues at McGill University, Montreal (Katz et al., 1974). Fifty-five children of around 2 years of age were given either a pair of dolls with different hair colours or a pair of differently coloured blocks as illustrated in Panel 7.3. The experimenter initially described one of the two blocks or dolls using a nonsense **trigram** (a three letter word usually made of a pronounceable consonant–vowel–consonant string) such as 'zav'. In the common noun condition, the experimenter said 'this is a zav'; whilst in a proper noun condition, the target doll or block was referred to without the article: 'this is Zav'. When asked to put 'the' zav on the table, the children in the common noun condition picked either of the two blocks or dolls, but when asked to 'put Zav' on the table, only the named doll was selected. In this study, the only significant findings were obtained for girls – possibly because of their greater experience with dolls, but interestingly nevertheless, girls showed a significant bias towards selecting the right doll when it was named without the definite article. No effect was found for blocks. Apart from showing an early appreciation of the way a proper noun is used in conversation, this study also shows that the girls were learning the appropriate context of use in that dolls are more likely to have proper names than objects.

7.4 FUNCTION WORDS AND ACTION WORDS

Names are not the only type of first word to appear. A loose category of other words, sometimes known as **function words**, contains an assortment of expressions that are associated with a salient action or event, e.g. 'bye-bye', 'uh-oh', 'up', 'down', 'more' or 'all-gone'. A little later than nouns and function words, words that refer more specifically to actions, such as 'drink', 'fly', 'open', etc., appear in the vocabulary of English-speaking children. We would call these action words verbs, but researchers are cautious about applying such a strict definition before there is a clear use of grammatical parts of speech. (Note that some verbs such as 'drink', 'fly' and 'open' also refer to nouns or adjectives.) Given the variability in early word production, it is hard to pin down the appearance of action words to any particular age, but as Behrend (1995: 254) has put it, whereas noun acquisition seems to prevail from around 13 months, the acquisition of action words seems to be the 'the thing to do' at around the age of 20 months. Interestingly, this is not the case in all languages. Children learning Japanese, Korean and Mandarin Chinese produce action words at around the same time or even earlier than object words.

As with object words, the range of what the child actually means has to be determined by the context in which they choose to use the word. Clark (2009: 82) refers to a case in which children between 1 year 7 months and 2 years 5 months were observed to use the word 'door' as an action word – to refer to any action involved in gaining access to something, like removing a jar lid, a nut from a bolt, or even the clothing from a doll! An idea of verb comprehension and production at 20 months is provided by data collected Goldin-Meadow from 12 children as summarised in the graph in Panel 7.4 (Goldin-Meadow et al., 1976).

The precise meaning intended by young children when an action word is produced in isolation is even harder to determine. First, it is not clear whether the word refers to the whole event – does 'jump' refer to the act of jumping (like a verb would) or does it include the person doing the jumping – the **agent**? Second, the transient nature of actions themselves gives a complex temporal aspect to action words. A verb can describe

Panel 7.4 Function words and action words

- Some of the child's vocabulary consists of *function words* that refer to certain activities or events. e.g.
    - 'allgone'
    - 'more'
    - 'bye-bye
- They will also use words that seem to be verbs but are often conservatively called *'action words'*, e.g.
    - 'drink'
    - 'fly'
    - 'going'
- These start to appear in abundance about seven months later than nouns, i.e. at about 20 months
- As with nouns, comprehension of verbs precedes production

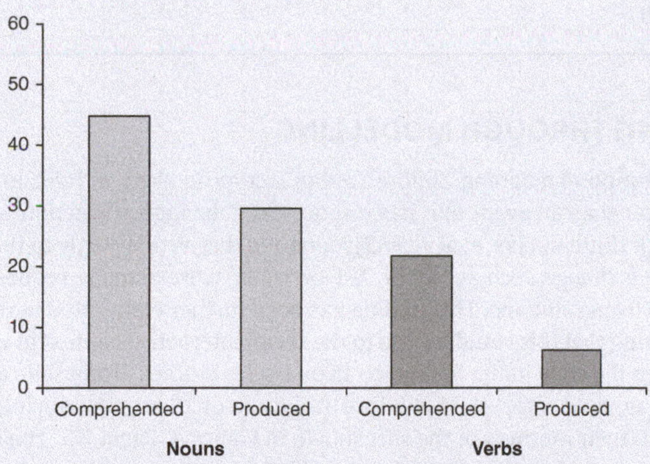

The mean number of nouns and verbs understood and produced by 12 children around the age of 2
(Data from Goldin-Meadow et al., 1976)

- Because they are first produced without tense endings, it can be hard to determine from early verb use whether they refer to future, current or past events an intention to act ('I am going to push it over'; 'are you going to pick it up?'), an event as it is actually occurring ('see him dance'; 'look I'm flying') or an event that has occurred ('the car was hit by a truck'). Now bear in mind that children will not themselves be using the sentence frames and word endings like -ed and -ing that help to disambiguate these different uses. So our 2 year olds may repeat words such as 'push', 'fall down' or 'catch' in a play situation where it is unclear whether they are talking about a current or recent event. Just as noun use reflects the context in which the child learned the noun, the temporal meaning of an action word – past, ongoing or future – is also learned from the context. This is explored in the next section.

LEARNING MECHANISMS

LEARNING LANDMARKS

7.5 Learning through modelling. This section introduces you to Tomasello's social pragmatic approach to language learning. You should be able to illustrate this with study of the child's acquisition of action words.

7.6 The child → mother → child dynamic. You should understand how the study of noun acquisition demonstrates a complex dynamic of interaction between mother and child.

7.5 LEARNING THROUGH MODELLING

In terms of its temporal meaning, children are in fact more likely to refer to future and current events rather than an event that has just occurred during early action word acquisition (Behrend, 1995). Huttenlocher et al. (1983) identified this as due partly to the fact that many verbs signifying a change such as 'sit' or 'fall' or 'open' were actually requests for future or ongoing actions from someone. This finding has been further elaborated in research by Mike Tomasello showing that this could be due to the social interactive context in which the words are introduced to the child in the first place. In one of his studies (Tomasello & Kruger, 1992), he and his colleague videotaped 24 children at the age of 15 months during two 15-minute interactions with their mothers of the sort shown in Figure A, Panel 7.5. The researchers distinguished three separate types of occasion on which a mother would use a verb. For example:

Impending: 'Are you going to spin the top?'

Ongoing: 'Look the top is spinning'

Completed: 'You spun it'

Panel 7.5 Learning through modelling

- Tomasello's social pragmatic theory of language acquisition can be illustrated by experiments on the acquisition of action words
- These can be used to refer to an impending, ongoing or past event
- When the child stars to use these words himself, it reflects the context in which the mother was most likely to have introduced that word a few months earlier
  - This is most likely to be the *impending* context

A A verb introduced by a mother in an impending situation is more likely to be used by the child in a similar situation six months later (After Tomasello & Kruger, 1992)

- The context of use can also direct the child to use a word as either a noun or an action word
  - This can be demonstrated using new nonsense (*nonce*) words

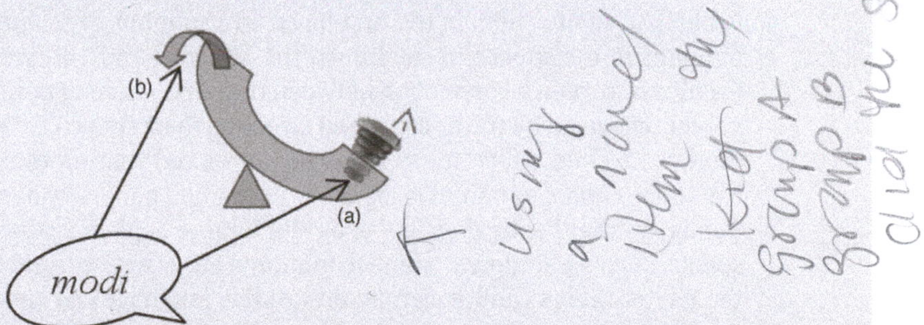

B A novel catapulting action is shown with various objects. In condition (a) the word 'modi' is mentioned only in connection with the object and in condition (b), the word 'modi' is only mentioned in relation to the catapulting. When asked to 'show modi' 88% of children in condition (a) showed the novel object whereas 75% showed the novel action in condition (b) (After Tomasello & Akhtar, 1995, with permission)

The greatest proportion of action utterances by the mother were in the impending mode – either to direct the child to carry out the action, or in anticipation of an action the child was about to carry out. When the children's own productions were measured at 21 months, they too were most likely to use action words in the impending situation – the situation in which verbs were most commonly heard. Tomasello uses results such as these to remind us that word learning is not just about a mapping from word to world, it is also about the **social pragmatic** uses of language. That is, the practical context in which a user conveys meaning.

But what about learning that the word is a verb or action word in the first place – rather than, say, a noun referring to an event (the way we may say 'we are going to dance' versus 'we are going to a dance')? How, in short, does the child learn not just the meanings of words but also the meanings of word types – the 'nouniness' of nouns and the 'verbiness' of verbs? The answer to this is really only clear when children are capable of multi-word strings, as we shall see from more of Tomasello's research in Chapter 8. But in a study with Nameera Akhtar (Tomasello & Akhtar, 1995), he showed that social context helps to differentiate the different functions of nouns and verbs. They exposed children aged around 27 months to a nonsense word, such as 'modi', where an adult used the word either in the context of introducing a new object or a new action as illustrated in Figure B, Panel 7.5. The child's own use of the word subsequently the context of use – it was used like a noun when learned in a new-object situation but as a verb when used in a new-action situation. In a second study, the authors then showed that the use of the new word as a verb could also be induced if the adult engaged in preparatory behaviours that encouraged the child to perform the action before the new word was produced. When no such preparation was given, the child learned the word as a noun.

7.6 THE CHILD → MOTHER → CHILD DYNAMIC

Tomasello's approach is sometimes called **usage theory**. We might think of this as a focus on the mother → child interaction. However, careful pioneering work by Julian Pine and colleagues at the University of Nottingham has pointed to an important qualification. Children don't just absorb what they hear – they also directly influence what the mother is likely to say to them in the first place. In a number of studies focussing on the number of nouns in the speech of children at the 50-word and 100-word stages, Pine and his colleagues observed a correlation between the percentage of nouns used by the child and the percentage used by the adults when directing their speech to the child (e.g. Pine, 1994) – a mother → child effect. It has long been observed that mothers will tailor their language use to the child's apparent level. Using nouns and generally descriptive language – 'see the bunny' or 'that's a big doggie' – to a child is more explicitly *educational* than using *directive* speech such as 'sit down', 'come to mummy', etc. Hampson and Nelson (1993) showed that the use of nouns (and generally descriptive language) by the mother around the child's first birthday predicts the child's fluency at 20 months, but only for children who were already early talkers at the time of their first birthday. This suggests that the more educational style was being used with children who were further along the path to phrase speech. Once again, this reminds us of the subtle dynamic between mother and child – yes the child starts to reflect the mother's speech, but the mother is also taking a lead from the child. In other words, the dynamic is more like child → mother → child.

It also follows from this that if you are interested in measuring how the mother's input affects the child's language acquisition (along the lines of Tomasello's approach), then it is important to try to first partial out the initial effect of the child's language on the mother. When this was controlled for in the data collected by Pine and his group (Pine et al., 1997), they, in fact, found no remaining correlation between the degree of usage of nouns and descriptive speech by the mother and the child's subsequent use of nouns and descriptive speech in their first phrases. So whilst the child will acquire the *meanings* of nouns and descriptive terms from interactions with adults, the *extent* to which they use them in their own early speech does not seem to be a simple function of exposure. Rather, that would seem to come from the quality of interaction that the child has with the adult as we see next.

The complex interplay between child and adult, and how it impacts on language acquisition, has now been subject to careful quantification using **longitudinal** studies that observe the changing dynamic of child/adult/child interaction across that crucial second year of life. One such study was carried out by Elise Masur and Janet Olson from Northern Illinois University where 20 mother–toddler pairs were videotaped at 10, 13, 17 and 21 months (Masur & Olson, 2008). They examined interactions (in both verbal and non-verbal domains) *following* an act of imitation by the mother or infant. For example (in the vocal domain), if the mother said 'duck' and the infant imitated by saying 'duck', it was the next act by the mother that was of interest. Were they 'return imitations' (a part or whole imitation of a verbalisation or action) or were they more likely to simply take the form of a social reinforcement of the action? An example of a return imitation by the mother in the vocal domain would be 'yes the duck'; whilst a socially reinforcing vocalisation (without return imitation) might be laughter or 'is he swimming?' Similar analyses were made in terms of the infant → mother → infant exchanges. The graph in Panel 7.6 gives a sample of their findings, from the vocal/verbal domain, in which the changing role played by the mother in scaffolding speech through return imitation is clear in the way she shifts towards a relatively high level of 'return' imitations at 21 months. The child, by contrast, moves towards more social responses to the mother's act of imitation. In other words, these behaviours have a reciprocal relationship. The mother tends to reserve her direct verbal return imitations until the child is actually attempting to imitate words, which was at about 13 months in this study, showing her focus on encouraging the child to speak intelligibly. The child, however, is not trying to teach the mother to speak and therefore imitates in order to learn – not to teach. It is not so surprising therefore that in the case of the child, the drift in the verbal/vocal domain is away from simple imitation to social responding – often including into those responses additional words that weren't just direct word repetitions. The authors noted that 'those children whose language would accelerate most during the second year were already behaving differently at the end of the first year of life, long before they were truly verbal.' In other words, they were the ones already starting to acknowledge a verbal imitation from Mum with a social response, showing again the complex social dynamic operating from child to mother.

It is still impossible to tell from this what actually causes the more advanced children to be more socially responsive to language in the first place, and there will certainly be large genetic variability and environmental factors at work as well, affecting both child and parent. If there is a universal aspect to all of this it is surely that the adult's intuition is to be sensitive to developmental progress of the child, and, in that sense, to follow it like a guiding hand rather than a relentless teacher. And if there has to be an egg before the chicken here, it is, as ever, the child's own efforts to gain mastery over a new skill.

Panel 7.6 The child → mother → child dynamic

- Mothers adjust the style and content of their speech to the child's language level
  - They are less likely to use nouns and descriptive speech to children under 1 year old who seem to be slow talkers
  - When this is factored out, degree of usage by the mother does not predict degree of usage by the child
- Children's language is not a simple reflection of the language of the mother but rather of how she adjusts her language as the child develops
- *Longitudinal studies* show that mothers move from general social reinforcement of the child's attempts at imitating words towards direct 'return' imitation of these words during the second year of the child's life
  - In the meantime children become more socially responsive to their mother's vocalisations during imitative exchanges

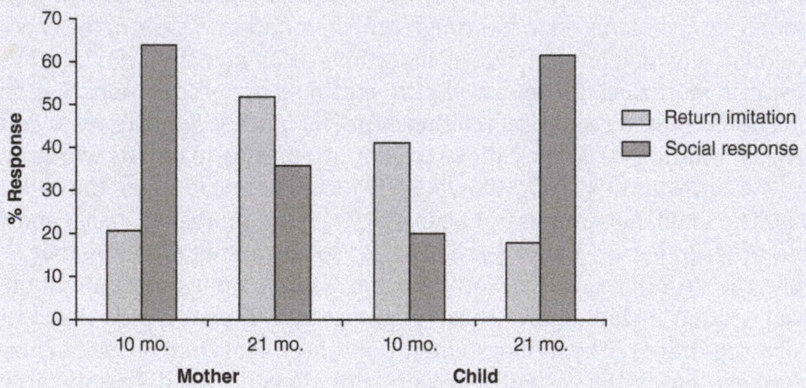

Between the ages of 10 and 21 months, toddlers start to respond to their mother's vocal imitations with a 'social' response that will also include some non-imitated words of their own, whilst their mother will start to show more direct ('return') imitation of their toddler's increasing attempts to imitate words

(Adapted from Masur & Olson, 2008, with permission)

THE DAWN OF PHRASE SPEECH

LEARNING LANDMARKS

7.7 Holophrases and frozen phrases. You should know what these terms refer to and why it is important to distinguish them from true phrases.

7.8 Interactive learning at the frozen phrase stage. You should know how segmentation in the mother's speech can help the transition from frozen phrases to true phrase speech. You should be able to cite evidence from the Trackton children showing cultural differences in how this is enabled. You should have considered to what extent children can learn from older siblings.

7.7 HOLOPHRASES AND FROZEN PHRASES

It is not just words but words within a grammatical structure – a phrase or a sentence – that give it its real power. Even if children can distinguish object words from action words, each on their own are deeply inadequate by themselves to convey to others the precise focus of the intended meaning – 'doggie' may actually refer to the fact that 'the dog *is barking*'; 'daddy' might mean 'Daddy *is sleeping*'. Multi-word combinations make these precise meanings explicit. So do multi-word strings arise by simply combining elements from a core vocabulary of nouns and verbs (or nouns and prepositions, or nouns and adjectives)? It seems that it is not quite as simple as that and the paradox is that learning whole phrases *first* helps them discover how to separate the phrase into parts of speech that can be re-combined in new and untrained ways.

First of all, it has already been pointed out that a single word – apparently a noun or verb – can already appear (from the context) to convey whole meaning – 'kitty' (is sleeping), 'drink' (milk). The impression is so strong that these are intended to convey a greater meaning than the single word alone has led to the expression **holophrases** to describe such utterances. Although they may contain what might appear to us to be two parts of speech, such as a noun and a verb, the way they are enunciated and the way they are used to convey single whole meanings suggests that they have not been put together from those parts but learned as a totality. So, at around the 50-word stage, children are likely to produce some actual multi-word phrases that sound like single utterances that always seem to come in that particular combination, such 'siddown' ('sit-down'), 'anawone' ('another-one'). As far back as the 1970s, John Dore argued that

Panel 7.7 Holophrases and frozen phrases

- Sometimes a single word appears to refer to a whole situation; these are known as *holophrases*
  - For example, 'drink' may refer to both the verb (the act of drinking) and the noun (the drink)
- Single words don't necessarily give way to multi-word phrases in the strictest sense
  - A toddler's first multi-word utterances are sometimes called *frozen or unanalysed phrases*, e.g.
    - 'allgone'
    - 'siddown'
  - They appear from the context to have been learned as if they are single words

holophrases seem to conform to one of three types of expression: referring ('see-doggie'), communicative (e.g. a request such as 'want-juice') or predicating (e.g. where an object and action are combined, such as 'kitty-sleeping') (Dore, 1975).

And so, even when uttered as if composed of separate parts of speech, they are sometimes described as **frozen** or **unanalysed phrases** if their use seems to be restricted to specific requests and descriptions, such as 'here-you-are', 'what's-that?', 'I-get-it'. From the child's point of view, a frozen or unanalysed phrase is simply a more complex 'word', but from an objective point of view, the use by the child of such phrases is hugely important. Why? Because it means that they are already producing appropriate word combinations in their speech. So the child's own production of the word combination as a totality could be one important first step in learning how to compose the combination in word by word fashion – and there is strong evidence that this is indeed the case.

7.8 INTERACTIVE LEARNING AT THE FROZEN PHRASE STAGE

In the complex interplay between child and mother, we need to be clear as to what each contributes to the learning process. In the context of frozen phrases, what the mother can bring when she hears the child use these phrases is not just about meaning, it is also about word separation and word order. Information about the word boundaries can come from the way the mother repeats the phrase back to the child, i.e. how it is acoustically segmented – 'sit down' rather than 'siddown', 'all gone' rather than 'allgone', etc. And the input from the mother could offer other useful feedback to the child, not just by carefully enunciating word boundaries but also by isolating the words within the phrase before re-using them within a different phrase – 'see the dog', 'that's a doggie', or substituting a similar type of word in the same place in the phrase – 'see the doggie – see the bunny'. So, to take an example, the child may learn to say 'kitty-sleeping' as an unanalysed phrase for the family cat in its basket; but when she hears the mother utter a similar phrase such as 'Connie sleeping' to describe her baby sister, she has the basis for picking out the invariant action word (sleeping) and separating it from the word describing the agent – the noun or proper noun (kitty, Connie). The value of frozen phrases was confirmed by Pine and Lieven (1993) in a longitudinal study of 7 children from 11 months to 1 year 8 months old. The percentage of frozen phrases within the first 100 words of each child varied from 4% to 23%, but there was an extremely strong positive correlation between the prevalence of these phrases and the emergence of genuinely productive word combinations later on by the child.

We have concentrated so far on the dyadic relationship between child and mother, where the latter is likely to explicitly scaffold, expand or re-segment the speech back to the child. But it is important to note that the child can also learn from the **polyadic** environment, where it hears the speech of many others, including siblings. Is this useful to the child and, indeed, how far can such an information-rich environment foster early language development *without* explicit scaffolding and one-to-one interaction with an adult?

Cross-cultural variations in the child-mother-child dynamic at the frozen phrase stage

A unusual opportunity to compare and contrast the kind of child-centred language learning that is typical of most first world countries with an alternative approach was provided by an ethnographic study of two communities in the Piedmont Carolinas area of the United States (Heath, 1983). One community (predominantly white) responded to their children's language learning in the ways you have just been reading about. A neighbouring community living at a place called Trackton brought a different social history and cultural attitude to bear on their children. In particular, the child's mother did not give any special attention to the sounds their baby made even when these could be regarded as meaningful. As Heath observes:

> Trackton adults believe a baby 'comes up' as a talker, adults cannot make babies talk: 'when a baby have sump'n to say, he'll say it'. (1983: 75)

Young toddlers raised in this environment are therefore going to have to rely considerably on what they can make of what they hear going on around them rather than benefiting from child-centred speech. Accordingly, there are a lot of instances of directly echoed frozen phrase speech in the texts quoted by Heath. Here, Lem (19 months) is picking up frozen phrases in a conversation going on between the author (Heath) and Lem's older 4-year-old sibling (Benjy):

Heath: "I can't go dere, no road dere"

Benjy: "You can turn right dere"

(Then) Lem: "Can-turn-right-dere"

The boy, Lem, was also observed to spontaneously use overheard frozen phrases such as 'give-it-to-me', 'I-dunno' as stock expressions for a variety of meanings at first, and learning – not from speech uttered back, but rather from reactions by older children and adults – 'the variety of meanings a single utterance can have' (p. 81).

These findings are important because they show that there is a certain robustness to the process of acquiring the basics of language that doesn't exclusively depend on the style and quality of mothering. It also illustrates again that, provided the child is ready to imitate whole phrases, then a certain amount may be learned from simply listening to others.

Learning from siblings

Whatever the culture, all young children may have older siblings from whom they can learn phrase speech. In cultures that actively foster early speech, older siblings have been found to use CDS when talking to an infant brother or sister, making vocal adjustments similar to those made by adults (see Chapter 4, page). Sachs and Devin (1976) found that 4 year olds would spontaneously use a higher pitch, shortened utterances and repetitions when talking to a younger child or a doll that was supposedly 'learning to talk'. However, Tomasello and Mannle (1985) found that children aged 3–5 years are less likely to expand on a toddler's utterance to keep the attentional focus on a particular thing or topic in the way that the mother would. In fact these investigators found that siblings would actually ignore around 83% of their younger sibling's utterances as compared with 21% by the mother. Nevertheless, the fact that older siblings will select a level of speech that is closer to that of a toddler's could perhaps be an intuition to create a linguistic environment that is easier to learn from (just like choosing the right level of French class or guitar lessons at night school). But so far, there is very little evidence that children will benefit from exposure to the direct or overheard speech of an older sibling (as compared with the mother), at least in terms of vocabulary size. In fact, if anything, being a first-born or only child is somewhat more likely to promote vocabulary development than having older siblings to learn from (Fenson et al., 1994; Lee, 2011). This could be because of the greater need to be active in learning to speak when there is no older brother or sister around to do it for you! Insofar as there is any effect of observational learning, it does, once again, seem to relate to the pickup of those important frozen phrases. Pine (1995) found that second-born children were found to have a significantly higher percentage of frozen phrases in their speech than first-borns at the 100-word stage.

Panel 7.8 Interactive learning at the frozen phrase stage

- Not all early multi-word speech is in the form of frozen phrases but, where the child does make these utterances, it can prompt the mother into making the word boundaries clearer
  - Through enunciation, e.g. 'all ... gone'
  - Or re-using one of the words in another context

- In some societies mothers do not offer much linguistic feedback to children; an example comes from an American community at a place called *Trackton*
  - These children used more frozen phases in their early speech but they soon picked up word segmentation from listening to others speaking around them
- Children learn from feedback from siblings as well as from their mother; having an older or brother or sister is likely to increase the likelihood of frozen phrases in the second-born child
- But brothers and sisters are less likely to 'correct' their younger sibling's language than the mother and so this effect is probably due to observational learning

CHAPTER SUMMARY

Children acquire a lexicon of meaningful words first in terms of object names (nouns), function words such as 'bye-bye', and action words (verbs). Learning the meanings of words is highly influenced by the social context in which the word is introduced by the adult, and this predicts how the word will be used by the child. Mothers tend to adjust their vocal input to children in terms of the child's current levels of ability. The use of frozen phrases such as 'allgone' is a common precursor to multi-word speech, and is sometimes used by the mother to draw attention to how a phrase can be segmented into separate words.

LOOKING AHEAD TO CHAPTER 8

In the last two chapters, we have seen how the child progresses from non-speech-like sounds right up to the building blocks of sentences – meaningful words – and this has led to thinking about types of word, such as nouns and verbs. So now we are beginning to brush up against one of the most debated areas in psychology. It is what children do next that causes all the argument – they put separate parts of speech in the correct order. We shall review the development of sentence production in the next chapter.

CHAPTER 8

THE EMERGENCE OF SENTENCE STRUCTURE

Whether it is for a practical purpose such as making an arrangement for a meeting, or for more descriptive acts such as recounting past experiences, what we really have is not just words but language. Words within a grammatical structure provide one of the most powerful cognitive instruments imaginable. How can mere sounds capture so much of human experience, imagination and intent? This question lies at the heart of one of psychology's greatest debates (see e.g. Hauser et al., 2002; Jackendoff & Pinker, 2005). Quite what gave the impetus for the evolution of this amazing skill is probably one of the most hotly debated issues in all psychology. At the core of this debate is the fact of children's rapid progression from speech-like sounds to real language in the second year of life. This led many to believe that there is something specifically about language that sets humans apart from all other species. This may be wrong, and we will not delve into this particular evolutionary issue here, but you may wish to follow the various lines of argument in, for example, Christiansen and Kirby (2003). As mentioned in Chapter 1, it also gave support to the idea that the human capacity for language is innate. As you will see from this and subsequent chapters, the innateness arguement has been countered somewhat by research demonstrating the role of direct exposure to the grammar in the heard speech of adults. The viability of this 'learning' approach has even been formulated in formal mathematical terms (Hsu et al., 2013). Either way, there is an undeniable and remarkable flowering of language in the human child from the age of about 18 months, and we take a look at this now.

As you have seen, this is the point where children are really only just beginning their journey into phrase-based language. Now think about the separate words in a phrase – even just two syntactic units – noun and verb – and you can see that when combined, they can extend expressible meaning exponentially. For example, if a child has six separate nouns and six separate verbs, he can say 12 things in total. But if he can put them together in agent–action relationships, he can say 6 × 6 things (36) and if he can put every noun in the position of recipient as well as agent ('daddy push'/'push daddy'), he can say 12 × 6 (72) – six times as many as he could with his single words. Of course, this is only an illustrative example – children do not learn word combinations in such tightly structured ways. But they do, nevertheless, show a dramatic rise in the amount that they can communicate once they start combining words by themselves.

So how does this come about? To understand one side of the argument, we need to go back to the rumblings of a scientific earthquake that took place in the middle of last century: the publication of Chomsky's *Syntactic Structures* (Chomsky, 1957). Following the excitement caused by his concept of a **Universal Grammar**, the implications were obvious to many. Children do not appear to repeat, for example, the first (or last) two words in a heard sentence (e.g. 'The man ...', 'Should we ...', 'A large ...', '... with me', '... the street'). They construct instead mini-sentences composed of the very core (noun and verb) parts that constitute Universal Grammar: 'drink milk'; 'doggie bark', etc. The recent evidence on holophrases reviewed in the last chapter has modified this popular claim somewhat, as these can quite often derive from 'echoing' the first or last part of a heard sentence. But in the main, children's first sentence-like utterances are novel and self-produced. For many distinguished writers, this was (and still is) clear evidence of the innateness of human language based on a kind of intuition about parts of speech and how they should be ordered within sentences (Pinker, 1994, 2011).

More recently, the other side of the argument has gained impetus from looking a bit more closely at how grammar emerges, giving way to 'usage'-based accounts of how children learn directly from adults – and we shall be returning to this approach throughout the chapter. In fact, neither approach on its own offers a comprehensive explanation of how and why children learn to use appropriate word orders, and why some grammatical forms are easier/harder than others. But in the light of evidence generated by this debate, we certainly have a fairly detailed *picture* of the stages in the acquisition of grammar, the contexts that promote learning, and some of the cognitive challenges that language learning presents to the young child.

THE EMERGENCE OF MULTI-WORD SPEECH

LEARNING LANDMARKS

8.1 Conveying meaning from word combinations. You should know at what age this starts to emerge and the types of utterances commonly made. You should know whether bilingualism affects this.

8.2 Understanding actor versus patient. You should know what is meant by the linguistic roles of actor and patient and you should be able to cite evidence that children understand this difference by the middle of their second year.

8.1 CONVEYING MEANING FROM WORD COMBINATIONS

So when do true word combinations start to appear? The stages of language acquisition are not so much related to age, but rather to particular universal landmarks. Children generally start to use words in combinations when they have a vocabulary of around 50 words, which, on a very rough average, will occur at about 18 months. Progress can be slow at first, but speeds up at around the second birthday. We know from the MacArthur-Bates Inventory that, on average, children will have over 20 phrases in their repertoire by the age of 28 months. Whilst males lag slightly behind females in this regard, the greatest variation is due to individual differences. At 28 months, the fastest 25% of language learners will be using around 32 phrases in their speech, whilst the slowest 25% will be using only five or so.

So what things do children actually say with their phrase speech? Important pioneering work on the acquisition of early language was carried out by the psycholinguist, Dan Slobin at the University of California, Berkeley in the 1970s (Slobin, 1971). He collected data from children learning languages as diverse as English, Finnish and Luo (a Kenyan language) and found that in all of these, early two word utterances were most likely to fall into the categories of:

Request: such as 'more', 'want' or 'give' (e.g. 'milk')

Location: such as 'there' (e.g. 'book')

Negation: such as 'no', 'not' (e.g. 'wet')

Description: using action words such as before a noun (e.g. 'hit ball') or after (e.g. 'cot away')

Possession: using a possessor such as 'daddy' in conjunction with the object possessed (e.g. 'chair')

Modification: using an adjective such as 'hot' in conjunction with a noun (e.g. 'pepper')

Others at around this time such as Lois Bloom at Columbia University and Roger Brown at Harvard, made similar observations (Bloom, 1970; Brown, 1973), leading Brown to conclude that children's early word combinations conformed to a small set of meanings or **semantic relations**. Brown's list of these was based on observations of children learning Finnish, Swedish, Samoan, Spanish, French, Russian, Korean, Japanese and Hebrew. Some, as you can see, are very much like the categories of location, possession and modification as identified by Slobin:

Object and location: 'cup table'

Possessor and possession: 'mommy dress'

Entity and attribute: 'box shiny'

Demonstrative and entity: 'dat money'

The remaining ones contain more explicit use of action words but they still overlap with Slobin's categories:

Action and location: such as 'go park', 'sit there' (included in Slobin's 'location')

Agent/action or action/agent: such as 'mommy come' or 'eat grape' (Slobin's 'request' would be included in this)

Agent and object: such as 'mommy sock' where the context implies an action with the object (included in Slobin's 'description' category).

There isn't a perfect overlap between the categories of every investigator. But, the precise division by category is not important – the main thing is the content of these word combinations – conveying relations between people, objects, actions, place and possession. In other words, what children say is fairly universally predictable by what they want to comment on.

Learning two languages

But what is not universal of course is the language being learned. So we can ask if difficulties are caused by having to acquire two languages – usually the consequence of having parents with two different native tongues, and who use both to each other and their child. Does this make it doubly hard for the child to acquire meaning and syntax? It would seem not. Case studies on bilingual children suggest that they start to differentiate the languages they hear from an early age, and that this differentiation allows them to learn the meanings and grammar that are specific to that language. For example, a detailed case study of a girl learning both English and Spanish from the age of 6 months by Deuchar and Quay (2000) found two distinct phonological systems by the age of 2 years 3 months. By the age of 1 year 10 months, she had acquired a lexicon of 330 words, 146 of which had an equivalent meaning in both languages. As the authors point out, this shows that the Principle of Contrast (see Chapter 7, Section 7.2) applies within a language rather than across languages – otherwise children would reject what were apparently synonyms for words that were already in their lexicon. Although young bilingual children often mix words from both languages in their early utterances, such as (in this case study) 'zapato (shoe) gone' or 'cuchara (spoon) floor', Deuchar and Quay argue that these are simply the result of a restriction on the available vocabulary in the other language. By the time the child is making two-word utterances, aspects of grammar such as word endings, start to appear in ways that are specific to each language, and in this, and other case studies (e.g. Lanza (1997), who studied two children learning Norwegian and English), it has been found that, by the age of 2, children seem able to use the context supplied by the adult speaker to use either or both of their acquired languages – or only one if the person they were talking to happened to be monolingual. But whilst it could not be said to be twice as difficult, learning more than one language *can* have some detrimental effects depending on a variety of factors relating to the rearing environment of the child (Hoff, 2014).

Panel 8.1 Conveying meaning from word combinations

- Word combinations start to appear as a function of vocabulary size rather than age
- A rough average would be two-word combinations when there are about 50 words in the child's repertoire (on average about 18 months)
- These convey core meaning in various ways, e.g.
  - a noun followed by a verb
    - 'doggie bark'
  - a verb followed by a noun
    - 'drink juice'
  - a verb followed by a preposition
    - 'lift up'
  - a noun and a function word
    - 'Mummy bye-bye'

- Children's earliest phrases reveal an interest in the 'here and now'
- Across cultures, the commonest types of meaning contained in early utterances are:
  - requests
    - 'want milk'
  - location
    - 'there book'
  - description
    - 'doggie bark' (event)
    - 'hot pepper' (object)
  - possession
    - 'Daddy chair'
- Being raised in a bilingual environment has no major adverse effect on this process
  - Children seem to be able to keep two languages separate from one another

Drawing by Miller

8.2 UNDERSTANDING ACTOR VERSUS PATIENT

In the last chapter, you saw that children acquire nouns quite early, but there has to be some caution about assuming that the child uses these words as nouns in the grammatical sense. What actually is the grammatical sense? Well when a noun is used in combination with a verb within a sentence, its role is also to convey *either* a thing doing/

Panel 8.2 Understanding actor versus patient

- Nouns can describe inanimate things such as 'ball' or an animate things such as 'monkey'.
- If the noun is the person, animal or thing that is being described ('the ball is red') or that is doing something ('the *monkey* ate the banana'), then it is known as the *subject* or *actor*
- If the noun is the person, animal or thing that is at the receiving end of an action ('the monkey ate the *banana*'), then its is known as the *object*, *recipient* or *patient*
- A famous study by Hirsh-Pasek and Golinkoff found that children understand this difference in heard sentences by 16 months
  - Toddlers would look appropriately at the video corresponding to different actor/patient roles:

Look! Big Bird is tickling Cookie Monster
Look! Cookie Monster is tickling Big Bird

being something ('the *ball* rolled down the hill'; '*greed* is the root of all evil'; 'the *fish* are hungry') *or* the recipient of being something or having something done to it ('he kicked the *ball*'; 'she despised his *greed*'; 'let's feed the *fish*'). So a noun as a grammatical unit is something that can be placed before or after a verb. When it is placed before the verb, it is often described as the **subject**, **actor** or **agent**, and as the **object** or **patient** when placed afterwards in a simple sentence. (Strictly speaking it should be called the direct object in these cases; these are more complex cases but they don't apply to early speech.) We know that children understand this difference within a heard sentence even if they do not yet have spoken language. In a famous study by Hirsh-Pasek and Golinkoff (1996), it was found that children as young as 16 months would look selectively at one of two video displays as a function of a verbal description conveying the actor/patient roles ('Big Bird is tickling Cookie Monster' or vice versa). These preverbal children preferred to look at the video as described in the sentence, showing an apparent comprehension of the different meanings as conveyed by word order. We turn our attention now to when they can begin to use the tools of grammar themselves within their own sentence production.

USING GRAMMAR PRODUCTIVELY: NOUNS AND VERBS

When children can use nouns and verbs appropriately and in novel combinations of their own construction, we say they can use them **productively** as parts of speech.

LEARNING LANDMARKS

8.3 Productive use of nouns. You should be able to describe how investigators have concluded that children can use nouns productively at around 2 years.

8.4 Productive use of verbs. You should be able to describe similar experiments investigating verb use and know when and why this develops somewhat later than the productive use of nouns.

8.5 Morphology. You should know what morphological aspects of verbs need to be learned by the child and be aware of which ones seem to be learned first.

8.3 PRODUCTIVE USE OF NOUNS

You may say if a child can actually say things like 'cat jump' and 'drink milk', then surely this all the evidence you need that they can use the nouns 'cat' and 'milk' in a syntactically appropriate way. But as always, we have to be clear as to whether the word order

Panel 8.3 Productive use of nouns

- The ability to use a noun in the role of actor or patient can be studied using nonce (proper) nouns in sentence frames in which the nonce word is exclusively the actor or patient
- If the child can subsequently place the noun in a different role, then it shows a *productive* use of the new word

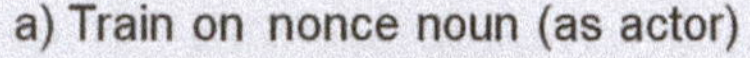

Look! Gazzer is tickling Big Bird!
b) Test for use of nonce noun (as recipient)
Oh! What is happening?
Big Bird is tickling Gazzer

Two-year-old children could re-use a nonce noun in the role of recipient showing that they could use it productively before or after the verb

(After Tomasello & Olguin, 1993)

has simply been echoed from what they have heard, or whether they have constructed the sentences because they know how nouns should be used. How do you test this? Tomasello and Olguin (1993) devised a clever technique in which they did two important things. First, they gave children nonsense proper nouns (called **nonce** nouns) such as Peri, Toma, Gazzer, etc. that were paired in actions with familiar characters such as Micky Mouse or Big Bird (from Sesame street) and the experimenter described an event in a similar manner to the Hirsh-Pasek study (see Panel 8.3). However, the experiment was designed such that the nonce nouns were exclusively heard in a particular position in the sentence – either the agent or patient of an action. After the modelling, the children then witnessed events in which the roles of the characters were reversed. So if there was a description, e.g. '(new word) Gazzer is pushing Big Bird', then Big Bird was now pushing Gazzer. The experimenter elicited a free description of the event by saying excitedly, 'Look – did you see that? What happened?' The investigators found that seven out of eight children aged around 2 years used the proper nouns productively – that is, they were able to use a nonce noun after a verb ('Big Bird is pushing Gazzer'), even though it had only been heard before the verb. Equally they could use it before the verb, even if had only been used after the verb in the modelling condition.

8.4 PRODUCTIVE USE OF VERBS

A very similar methodology was used by Tomasello and colleagues to test for the child's concept of a verb – the type of word that denotes an action (Akhtar & Tomasello, 1997). Once again, the investigators used novel nonsense (nonce) words during modelling sessions to see how productive children would be with these words in their spontaneous speech later. Words such as 'cham' and 'keef' were modelled in play situations where the meaning (such as hair-brushing) was clear from the context. What the investigators wanted to know was whether the child would pair these words with nouns in a novel way that they hadn't actually heard from the experimenter. So, for example if the experimenter had merely said 'look – that's dacking', and the child said, 'Cookie Monster is dacking him' or 'he is dacking Cookie Monster', this would suggest the child understood how verbs work in relation to nouns in sentences.

Tomasello and his team found that children are at least a year older before they show the same productive use of verbs as they do with nouns. Children around 2 years 9 months were very unlikely to extend their use of verbs beyond the precise context in which they heard them. And when introduced to the nonce verb *without* an actor or patient as in 'this is dacking' (whilst being shown the action with two characters), they were very unlikely to give patient and agent information during when asked, 'What is happening now?' They would even repeat an incorrect word order if it was used by the adult, such as 'Ernie the cow tamming', when asked, 'What is happening?' Children around 3 years 9 months, by contrast, were highly likely to 'correct' the word order ('Ernie is tamming the cow') and were also highly likely to extend the use of the nonce verbs beyond the precise examples that had been given and insert them correctly between an actor and patient in their sentences.

On one reading of this, it could be said that children's concept of a verb is simply acquired later than that of a noun, but perhaps a better way of looking at it is to think of a verb as having rather more possible types of uses within a sentence than a noun. For example, some verbs can be used to denote something happening by something on something else such as 'Marty drinks the milk'; 'Mummy washes the baby'. These are called **transitive** verbs, taking both a subject (the actor/agent) and an object (the recipient/patient). Nouns can be slotted into either subject or object roles even if the meaning is highly bizarre ('the baby washes Mummy'; 'the milk drinks Marty'). However, there are many verbs that do not take an object in this way, such as 'sleeps', 'falls', 'trembles', and adding a noun after them renders the sentence ungrammatical ('he sleeps milk'; 'Marty falls baby'). These are called **intransitive** verbs. When a child hears a new or nonce verb without an object being stated – 'he is dacking' (as in one of Akhtar and Tomasello's conditions), for example – it is not immediately clear whether this is transitive or intransitive and it may seem safer to just use the verb in the same context within which it was heard. As Akhtar and Tomasello point out, furthermore, it is also somewhat formal for children to use the transitive forms that would be required either for elaborating on – or for 'correcting' – the sentence given by the adult (producing, e.g. 'the cow is tamming Ernie' as a correct description of what is going on). As the authors point out, children of around 3 years are less likely to make these sorts of third-party descriptions in the first place, and if anything, are more likely to comment on what they are doing themselves, e.g. 'I'm dacking it'. In other words, the experimental procedure of using characters' names in transitive sentences was not likely to be copied by the younger children – let alone used in novel productions of their own construction.

Finally, as we can see from the bizarre examples of 'reversed' sentences given above, there is arguably a greater dependency between the verb and the noun in terms of plausible meaning, than the other way round, e.g. 'drinks' already presumes an animate noun, whereas an animate noun does not presume any specific action. For this reason the

Panel 8.4 Productive use of verbs

- The productive use of verbs can be tested by using nonce words, placed in the position of a verb in a sentence, to see when children will re-use it as a verb in a new context
- One example is to say 'look this is dacking' then play at 'dacking' (a nonce word for an action like hair-brushing) with two characters
- The child is then asked 'what is going on' to see if they can put the new verb appropriately into a sentence
- Children are around 3 years 9 months before they do this
- This could be because verbs have more complicated roles than nouns such as *transitive* (taking an object) or *intransitive* (no object)
- It seems as if children need to learn new verbs in conjunction with a noun (transitively), in order to use it productively later on
    - This is probably due to the fact that verb meaning is often tied to a specific set of nouns, e.g.
        - 'drink', 'hammer', 'kiss', 'fly', 'shine', etc.

The nonce word 'dacking' could refer either to the intransitive action or the transitive action ('dacking the ball')

learning of verb meanings will be linked to particular nouns. For example, the meaning of 'dog' can be extracted in terms of its appearance without reference to its behaviour, whereas the verb 'bark' is hard to decouple from the concept of 'dog'; likewise with 'flies' or 'swims', etc. This even more true of verbs that are used in conjunction with particular inanimate objects such as 'hammers', 'saws', 'cuts' and so on.

The possibility that verbs are understood in a sort of compact with the noun doing the action or being acted upon is supported by a curious finding by Akhtar and Tomasello (1997). This was the study mentioned earlier in which nonce verbs were trained using a description without any nouns at all, such as 'this is dacking'. They found that children under the age of 3 could not subsequently comprehend the meaning of a short sentence in which the trained nonce verb was placed between actor and patient, as in 'make Cookie Monster dack Big Bird', and were as likely to reverse the actor roles as to act them out in the correct order. This suggests that the meaning of a verb needs to be learned in specific relation to the objects carrying out the action.

8.5 MORPHOLOGY

Grammar is not just about word order; it is also about the internal structure of the word. This is made up from **morphemes**, i.e. the smallest unit in a word that can convey meaning. Most words have a **stem morpheme** such as 'dog' or 'drink' that can stand on its own, but they may also appear in conjunction with **inflectional morphemes** that have no meaning in their own right, but which **mark** the particular meaning being given to that word. For English nouns, the only markers are for **case** (singular versus plural) by adding (usually) to the end of the word (something children learn very early), but they can also come in the form of a new word ('mice') or no inflection at all ('sheep'). For verbs, the story is even more complicated. Verbs denote things happening in time: then, now and later. So they have to be **tense** marked. But even the present tense is not straightforward. In English, we can say either 'he dances' or 'he is dancing'. The inflectional morpheme is 'es' in one case, but in the other it is 'ing', *and* it has to take what is known as an auxiliary verb ('is'). The inflection for the past tense is usually 'ed' but there are very many irregular past tense forms as well such as 'bought', 'came' etc.

Some idea of how these and other grammatical forms enter children's language comes from the early work of Roger Brown from Harvard University with colleagues such as Edward S. Klima, Ursula Bellugi and Jean Berko Gleason (see Brown, 1973). The group collected two hours of speech during normal interactions in a home setting from three unrelated toddlers, Eve, Adam and Sarah, every two weeks from the ages of 18 to 26 months (Eve) and from around 26 months to 48 months (Adam and Sarah). During this time all three children moved from one-word utterances to strings of at least four words. Since this pioneering study, a data bank called the Child Language Exchange System (CHILDES) has been set up at Carnegie-Mellon University, Pittsburgh by MacWhinney and Snow to make available large **corpora** of children's language in English and many other languages, so that researchers can be sure which patterns of emergence seem to be generally true of a given language (MacWhinney & Snow, 1985). From the CHILDES data, we know that plural case marking seems to cause as many difficulties for children as tense marking, and they both show the same pattern of difficulties.

For both sorts of inflectional marking, children seem to move from correct use of irregular forms to generalising the regular to the irregular form. In the case of nouns, this would be e.g. 'mice' then 'mouses' before reverting back to the correct irregular. Curiously for verbs, children appear to learn the irregular verb forms earlier than the regular ones that end with -ed. This was noted by Brown (1973) and by Kuczaj (1977) and has been found in many subsequent studies. Also curious is the fact that they seem more likely (at around 21 months) to use the -ing ending than regular -ed endings. One telling ingredient in this pattern, as you may have guessed, is the *frequency* of these endings in the words that children are likely to hear around them. Bybee and Slobin (1982) note that 22 of the first 30 verbs a child will hear are in fact irregular ('came', 'brought', etc.). Akhtar and Tomasello (1997) speculate that the 'ing' endings also may be more frequent in speech to young children – and may be picked up more rapidly for that reason. This is sometimes known as the **critical mass** theory, which is basically the idea that once children have heard a certain ending in a certain number of words, they will start to generalise its use to other words.

Another interpretation of the acquisition of inflectional marking, favoured by those who believe there are some innate intuitions about grammar, is that the irregular forms are first learned by rote or direct imitation, whilst the regular forms are learned because of an innate ability to seek a syntactic rule from an emerging pattern. Once equipped with the rule, it is then mis-applied to the irregular plurals, e.g. 'tooths' and 'mouses'; 'goed' and 'bringed'. Other **over-regularisation** errors occur by attaching the regular ending to the (correct) irregular form such as 'feets', 'geeses', 'wented' and 'camed'. Another argument used by those bent on a nativist interpretation is that the child's over-generalisation errors are self-produced and will not (or should not!) have been heard from adults, and can even be resistant to correction. Here is an often cited example from McNeill (1966: 69), illustrating how the child might over-generalise a regular ending to an irregular case – despite hearing the correct version from the parent:

Child: "My teacher holded the baby rabbits and we patted them"

Adult: "Did you say your teacher held the baby rabbits?"

Child: "Yes"

Adult: "What did you say she did?"

Child: "She holded the baby rabbits and we patted them"

Adult: "Did you say she held them tightly?"

Child: "No, she holded them loosely"

There is still considerable debate about syntactic learning, and how the correct usage eventually emerges for all nouns and verbs (Marcus, 1995; Maratsos, 2000). Maratsos points to the fact that correct and incorrect usage of a verb ending can in fact co-exist for a while in the same child, and argues that the 'competition' between rote and rule-based will ultimately be settled by frequency. In other words, whilst the child cited by McNeill seems impervious to the corrected form used by the adult in that particular exchange, sooner or later the repetition of 'held' – not 'holded' – in heard language will win against the child's incorrect version (whatever the explanation for how that incorrect version came about). So what we can be sure of, despite all the argument, is that children seem to learn that there *should* be morphological rules for denoting number and tense, before their exposure to language finally teaches them what those rules are.

Panel 8.5 Morphology

- *Morphology* is about the internal structure of a word such as a *stem* and a *suffix* (ending)
  - 'dance'/'dancing'
- *Inflectional marking* is the addition of endings to nouns and verbs to denote
  - Plural case
    - 'dog'/'dogs'
  - Tense
    - 'kiss'/'kissed'
- Inflectional marking can appear from about 21 months
  - But children also have to learn many irregular forms as well
    - 'goose'/'geese'
    - 'go'/'went'
- It is quite common for children to produce the irregular form correctly at first (e.g. 'men', 'went'), then overgeneralise the regular ending to the to the irregular forms
  - 'mans', 'goed', 'feets', 'wented'
- There is an ongoing debate as to whether this is caused by an innate tendency to start search for a syntactic 'rule' or simply a question of confusing frequently heard word forms
- Either way, it is thought that frequency of the correct form will eventually cause the child to self-correct

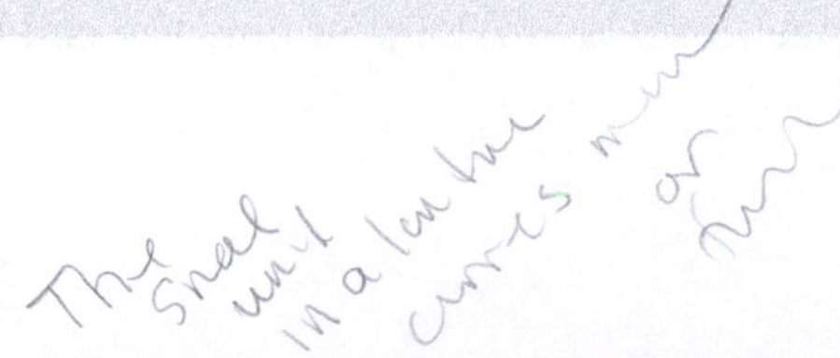

USING GRAMMAR PRODUCTIVELY: PRONOUNS, PREPOSITIONS AND ADJECTIVES

So children can learn how to alter words internally as a function of number or tense by using inflection or even changing them completely (sometimes known as **derivational morphology**). But word forms are often affected not just by what they mean in and of themselves, but how they relate to *other* words in the phrase or sentence. Pronouns are affected by whether they stand in the role of object or subject with regard to the verb, prepositions are affected by the type of action conveyed by the verb, and also whether or not they are learned as an integral part of a well-known idiom ('it's *up* to you'; '*on* the phone'). Adjectives, likewise, are bound to being placed before the noun within a sentence. Learning to use these word forms appropriately and thus productively in their own speech can be expected to pose some new challenges for the child.

LEARNING LANDMARKS

8.6 Productive use of pronouns. You should know the kinds of errors young children are likely to make with pronoun use and cite some possible reasons for them.

8.7 Productive use of prepositions. You should know what a preposition is and when simple spatial prepositions, as well as some common idiomatic prepositions, are acquired.

8.8 Productive use of adjectives. You should know what an adjective is and a suggested reason why they are relatively rare in early productive speech.

8.6 PRODUCTIVE USE OF PRONOUNS

One of the most important set of meaning words for a young child are pronouns such as 'you', me', 'he', 'she'. Unlike nouns, however, pronouns in most European languages may change depending on whether they are in the subject or object position: 'I', 'he', 'she', 'they' change in English to 'me', 'him', 'her', 'them', and in French for example, the familiar word for 'you' would change (from 'tu' to 'toi'). So now the child has to learn not just

Panel 8.6 Productive use of pronouns

- *Pronouns* are the little words that refer to self and other such as 'I', 'you' and 'they'
- They are common in child speech at the time multi-word combinations start to appear (around 2 years of age)
- *Pronominal case marking* refers to whether the pronoun is the subject ('I'/'he') or the object ('me'/'him') of the sentence
- Pronouns referring to self ('I'/'me') are the most commonly used by children in their second year
- But some children make a lot of errors
    - e.g. 'me do it!"

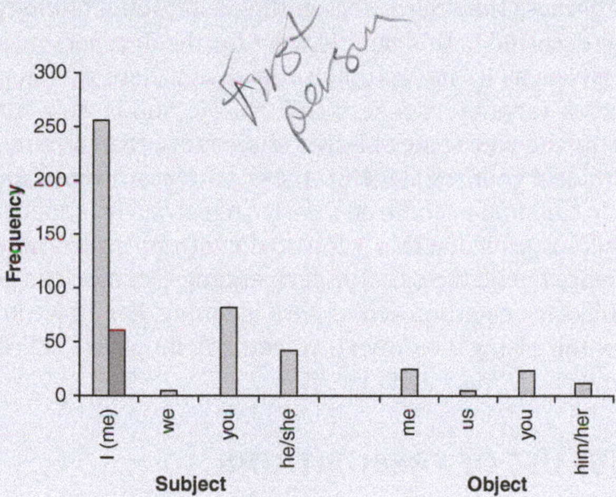

Frequency of pronoun usage by 1 to 3 year olds (n = 11) showing a heavy bias towards first person, both correct and incorrect (dark grey)

(Adapted from Lieven et al., 1997, with permission)

- This implies that getting across important meaning comes before a clear understanding of case marking

what person – or persons – the pronouns refer to but also which pronoun goes in which position, depending on whether it is the subject or object of an action. As with denoting plurality of a noun, this feature is called case marking. Strictly speaking, this means that we are still talking here about learning morphological rules. But let us consider it from the point of view of what the child wants to convey. What do you think she will pick up first? First you know that meaning is paramount, so separating the meaning of 'I'/'me' from 'you' or from 'he'/'him' or 'she'/'her', is actually going to be more important than case marking, i.e. *who* is involved in the action is more crucial than using the right case. You also know that by the time genuine multi-word combinations appear, the child is deploying the words in ways that get that meaning across even if they have never heard an adult use them in that way. So you could predict that constructions like 'me do it' or 'him go' may well crop up in early speech. And they do.

Lieven et al. (1997) analysed pronoun use in 11 children at around 2 years of age, and when each had shown at least 400 multi-word utterances. The results of this study seemed to be fairly typical and they show several things. First, children seem to want to talk about themselves; they were twice as likely to use 'I'/'me' as 'you' or 'it' and not likely at all to use the third person, 'you'/'she'/'they', etc. as illustrated by the graph in Panel 8.6. Perhaps because they were more enthusiastic about talking about themselves, the only errors that occurred in this sample were for the first person, sometimes getting the case marking wrong as in 'me go down'. However, there was huge individual variability in these errors, ranging from zero to 70%. No one is very sure why these case marking errors occur and why some children show more than others, but several investigators think that some children develop these patterns around those specific verbs that are particularly common in children's early speech such as such as 'do', 'want', 'see', 'get' and 'make'. This suggests that this is less to do with trying to apply an incorrect syntactic 'rule', as appeared to be the case for verb endings, so much as a by-product of the child focussing primarily on getting across core meaning. For all we know, it may just be a way of the child emphasising their own involvement, much as the French do when they say 'moi, je ne l'aime pas' – 'me, I don't like it'!

8.7 PRODUCTIVE USE OF PREPOSITIONS

Prepositions are little words that introduce the meaning of a phrase. If you say 'I am going to pass the ball to him', the second use of the word 'to' introduces the idea of someone being a recipient; if you said, 'I am going to get the train to Paris', the second mention of 'to' introduces a spatial concept – a change of location. Note that both those sentences use 'to' twice – its first use is tied to the verb 'going'. In this instance, the usage reflects the fact that 'going' is already being used metaphorically within our language to convey intention. In its primary form – 'I am going to the library' – 'to' simply conveys a change of location. These examples remind us that a huge amount of our language is not always literal in that way, and is often based on the cultural evolution of the language of speech **idioms**. At least some of these idioms seem to come from metaphors. Space is particularly predominant as a meaning metaphor where uses of prepositions such as 'in' and 'into' and prepositional phrases such 'on top of' get across the idea of being in a certain state, but in ways that most of us would never take literally, e.g. 'he is in a pickle'; 'she is really into Facebook'; 'I am on top of things now'. Many, if not most, idiomatic uses are less obvious in terms of their metaphorical meaning (if any), and are no longer traceable to their cultural origins. This applies particularly to prepositions such as 'of' and 'on' as in e.g. 'the election of the President'; 'we made it out of wood'; 'the train arrived on time'; 'let's get on with it'. We rarely stop to think about these words, but when it comes to little children, are some prepositional uses easier to acquire than others, perhaps because their concrete meaning is clearer?

You know from Chapters 2 and 3 that children will understand a good deal about space, occlusion, containment, movement behind other objects, and so on, by their second year. They also seem to *understand* prepositions conveying some of these spatial relations from a very early age. Fisher (1996) used the nonce word paradigm to show that children at 26 months could pick up the meaning of a preposition as cued by its use in a sentence. The children watched as a hand pointed to a duck being placed on a box and heard the scene referred to using a nonce noun (indicating a word for the duck) or a nonce preposition. So in the first case children would hear 'this is a corp'; in the second, another group of children would hear 'this is acorp my box'. These sentences were repeated several times using different ducks. In the test phase of the experiment, all children were shown two scenes side by side. In one there were two ducks, one on the box the other beside the box; in the other, there was a duck and a different object both sitting on the box. They were then asked, 'What else is a corp?' or 'What else is acorp my box?' If children in the first group had by now understood 'a corp' to refer to a noun, they would be expected to look at the first scene. For the second group, on the other hand, if they had successfully learned 'acorp my box' to mean 'on my box', then they would be expected to look at the second. This prediction was confirmed for children with vocabularies of a median size of 75 words.

Another study using looking time measures (Meints et al., 2002) found that children as young as 15 months would look longer at a display representing the spatial relations 'on' and 'under' (a table) following a description of the scene using spatial prepositions, provided they were fairly typical of such a scene (i.e. right under the table, not at the edge). Older children (from 18 months) looked longer at the atypical scene, which the authors interpret as a new understanding of less prototypical situations. But looking time studies do not fully identify children's ability to understand the grammatical status of a preposition. This, as you know, has to be measured using their own productive language. Nevertheless, the comprehension studies do suggest that simple relations like 'on' and 'under' may appear early on in this development.

Panel 8.7 Productive use of prepositions

- *Prepositions* are small words within a sentence that introduce the meaning of the next word, phrase or clause
- The most common concrete prepositions refer to spatial location:
  - 'to', e.g. 'going to the seaside'
  - 'on', e.g. 'on the table'
- Some spatial prepositions appear earlier than others

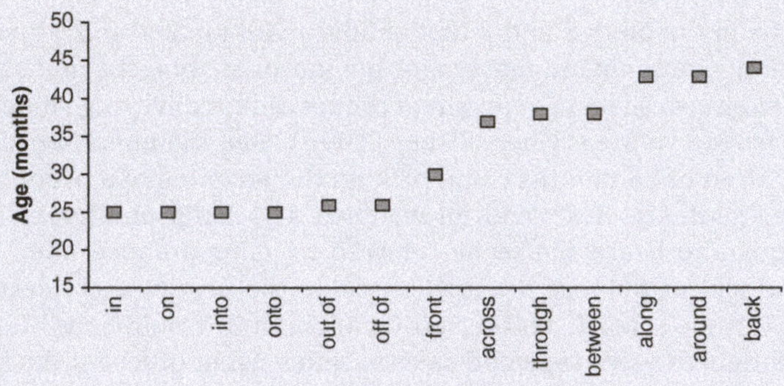

Mean age in months (n = 6) at which different spatial prepositions appear spontaneously in speech. (Data from Internicola & Weist, 2003)

- This is thought to be due to the fact that the later-appearing ones require more than one object to be referenced
  - e.g. 'the cup is *on* the table' versus 'the cup is *between* the jug and the bowl'
- Many prepositions are not concrete but are *idiomatic* – meaning they are part of our cultural usage but with a metaphorical connotation
  - e.g. 'let's go *along* with that'; 'she is really *into* facebook' ...
- ... or no traceable semantic connotation at all
  - e.g. 'the Adoration *of* the Magi'; 'the sentence has been written *down*'
- Idiomatic uses appear with children's first prepositional use, provided they are in common use in the speech used by adults to their children

The use of prepositions in children's early expressive language starts from around the second birthday. It is almost certainly a 'productive' use, insofar as the examples seem to come from spontaneous exchanges that are far in advance of frozen phrase echoing. It also consists mainly of spatial prepositions. Reviewing both comprehension and production in a diversity of languages, including English, Hebrew, Italian, Portuguese, Serbo-Croatian and Turkish, Johnston (1988) found that 'in', 'on' and 'under' could be produced by children aged from roughly 2 to 2½ years, 'next-to' from 2½ to 3½ years, and 'between' from 3½ to 4 years. Internicola and Weist (2003) examined longitudinal data from six children traced from 1 year 10 months to 4 years 2 months, in which they found that 'in', 'on', 'into', 'onto', 'out of', 'off of' appeared at least a year earlier than 'across', 'along', 'around', 'through', 'front', 'back' and 'between', as depicted in the graph in Panel 8.7. As you may be thinking, this is partly due to the complexity of the spatial relations. 'Between' and 'in front of' often require two objects to be referenced in order to understand them in discourse – 'the cow is in front of the tree'. Words like 'through' require an unseen location to be referenced as well as an entrance and exit to be considered ('push the stick through the hole'). Remember that this is also the age at which verbs are used productively.

Does this mean that it is only the simple, concrete spatial prepositions that appear early? You know by now that the appropriate use of early words is learned from the context of utterance by the mother, and certainly the later appearing spatial prepositions like 'through' and 'between' are used significantly less often by the mother in CDS. But when it comes to more metaphorical – but very common – non-concrete prepositions like 'of' ('scared of monsters'; 'tired of playing'), they can be amongst the first to appear (Tomasello, 1987). So the fact that many prepositions are idiomatic does not prevent children from acquiring them. In short, children learn to use prepositions reflecting both the frequency and the context in which they have heard them, and this applies as much to metaphorical/idiomatic as well as concrete uses. Prepositions do not have to be concrete or visual in any way to be amongst the first to appear in the child's own language.

8.8 PRODUCTIVE USE OF ADJECTIVES

Adjectives are descriptive terms for animate or inanimate objects ('*big* dog', '*blue* ball'), concepts ('*nice* day') or events ('*loud* singing'). If we put together the things you have learned about verbs and prepositions, you can probably guess at the fact that adjectives are learned later than nouns, and do not appear in children's speech until the third year. Even at around 2½ years, children, on average, will use around five times as many nouns as adjectives. Like all words, children understand many adjectives before they use them, but studies on their comprehension of nonsense adjectives (e.g. 'this is a daxy one' referring to a colour or shape) show that children are conservative in their generalisations of the nonsense adjectives. That is, they tend not to abstract the property from the thing being described to a range of other things. This close dependency on a particular noun for understanding adjective meaning (similar to what was found for verbs) – makes sense when considered carefully. Properties such as size or texture will mean different things for different objects, such as 'big elephant' versus 'big garden' or 'smooth skin' versus 'smooth music', and something different again when applied to an event, e.g. 'a bumpy parcel' versus 'a bumpy ride'. On the other hand, children can pick up the many and varied idiomatic uses of simple prepositions at an early age, so why should adjectives not be learned from adult speech in the same way? According to research by Sandhofer and Smith (2007) the clue seems to be that, in this case, adults' usage actually impedes the awareness of adjective meaning, because adult's normal usage often fails to explicitly provide the relevant noun that helps to provide the meaning. Almost 50% of object/person referral in adult speech to children will involve the pronoun rather than the noun, e.g. 'this is a red one', 'he is small'. Sandhofer and Smith note that when these sorts of sentences were used (by Mintz and Gleitman, 2002) in nonsense adjective learning tasks – for example 'this is a spoof one' (meaning made of felt) – children need to see more instances of the object being specified before applying it to other things with that property. In their investigation, Sandhofer and Smith found that 2-year-old children with a vocabulary level of at least 300 words were better able to perform comprehension tests when a strong noun was provided, as in 'this the red cup – find the red dinosaur', rather than in the less well-specified context, 'this the red one; find another red one – find the red'. On reading this, you might sympathise with children in the second condition, owing to its vagueness – and it is precisely this sort of ambiguity that is argued to possibly impede the learning of adjective meanings. As Sandhofer and Smith argue, furthermore, the lack of a strong noun in a sentence also makes the syntactic relationship of adjective-before-noun less available in the adult speech and therefore does not provide a good model for the productive use by children of adjectives as noun modifiers. So for both semantic and syntactic reasons, adjectives are a relatively late emerging property of elementary grammar.

CHAPTER SUMMARY

Phrase speech generally starts around 18 months. Using words in their correct position within a phrase shows the productive use of parts of speech and the beginnings of elementary grammar. Nouns, verbs, pronouns and prepositions are all used productively by the age of 3 but the development of case and tense marking endures for some time

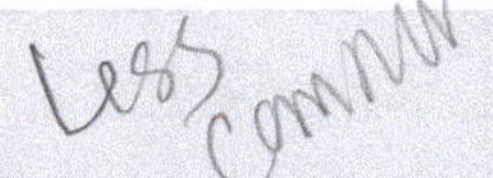

Panel 8.8 Productive use of adjectives

- *Adjectives* are descriptive words that modify a noun referring to an object or event
  - e.g. '*big* dog', '*noisy* party'
- Although children will use adjectives in their own speech at around the age of two to three years, they are much less common in their speech than nouns, verbs, pronouns and (some) prepositions
- Comprehension studies with nonsense adjectives (e.g. 'this is a *dacky* one') show that children learn adjective meanings more readily when a noun rather than a pronoun is used, e.g.
  - 'this is a *red car*, find me a *red dinosaur*' is easier than
  - 'this is a *red one*, find me another *red*'
- As adults tend to use pronouns rather than nouns with adjectives when talking to children, it is thought that this may inhibit their acquisition of precise adjective meanings
- This can prevent giving children a strong syntactic model for using adjectives as noun modifiers in a phrase or sentence

afterwards. Adjectives are less common in spontaneous speech and this seems related to the fact the adults often introduce them in the absence of the noun to which the adjective refers, as in 'the red one'.

LOOKING AHEAD TO CHAPTER 9

Sharing understanding about the world has been one of the major forces for language learning that we have encountered thus far. But we have also come across rules

(Continued)

(Continued)

regarding pronunciation, morphology and syntax that come from the linguistic culture that the child is raised in. Unfortunately for the child, these rules are about to become a lot more complex. And, once again, the way in which these rules are acquired tells us so much more than simply the stages through which language is learned; it tells us how children think.

CHAPTER 9

LEARNING GRAMMAR

With increasing productivity comes increasing emancipation from overheard or imitated speech. The first simple sentences of a young child are therefore not only a testament to the amazing human capacity for language but they also give us a new insight into the child's own mental state. Take questions, for example – it is one thing for a child to repeat back 'bunny' when his mother points to one in a storybook, but when the child singles out something to share with his mother and says 'what bunny doing?' or 'where he going?', there is far greater clarity as to the child's own state of mind and what he wants to know about. So in looking at simple sentences, we are gaining an insight into some of the child's ways of thinking about the world.

Like all cognitive achievements though, there is a price to be paid – and in this case the price is having to learn ever more complex rules – but, as you will see, the pattern of this development makes considerable sense from a psychological point of view.

SIMPLE SENTENCE CONSTRUCTION

LEARNING LANDMARKS

9.1 Appearance of 'wh' questions. You should know the meaning of MLU and the rough order of appearance of question forms.

9.2 Problems with the grammar of questions. You should know what an auxiliary verb is and the kinds of problems that children have with auxiliaries in 'wh'

(Continued)

(Continued)

questions. You should know how question use by parents can help in this learning.

9.3 Problems with the grammar of negation. You should know why negation can produce similar problems of auxiliary use and be able to cite some examples of typical errors at the three main stages of negation use.

9.1 APPEARANCE OF 'WH' QUESTIONS

Some of the earliest important observations about elementary sentence production came from the previously mentioned longitudinal project with Eve, Adam and Sarah carried out by Brown, and his colleagues (see Brown 1973). As the patterns of grammar acquisition show very considerable individual variation, rather than measure specific advances in relation to age, it was measured in terms of the average length of word sequence the child was producing around that time. This measure is called the **Mean Length of Utterance** (MLU).

Where, what and who?

Brown and his group identified three distinct stages in question formation. When they were at an MLU of 2–3 words, the children moved first of all into Stage 1 at which they initially asked a question simply by using a rising intonation at the end of a statement, such as 'sit chair?', 'Mommy eggnog?', 'I ride train?' The main identifiable question words in use at this stage for all three children were 'what' and 'where', e.g. 'what cowboy doing?', 'what's that?', 'where Ann pencil?', 'where milk go?' (Klima & Bellugi, 1966: 200), though as they and others noted, 'what?' questions were not so likely to be understood by the children as 'where?' questions:

Mother: "What did you do?"

Child: "Head"

Mother: "What are you doing?"

Child: "No"

(Klima & Bellugi, 1966: 202)

This is possibly because of the very wide range of meanings that can be associated with 'what' questions (relating both to actions and objects) as compared to the more specific spatial locative 'where?' But it could also be due to the fact that 'where?' questions asked by adults made up 80% of the questions actually put to Adam, Eve and Sarah (Brown et al.,

Panel 9.1 Appearance of 'wh' questions

- When children start to make genuine multi-word phrases, their language level is often measured in terms of *Mean Length of Utterance* (MLU)
- Children start to ask questions at an MLU of only 2/3 words
    - The pattern of emergence has been established by a body of data called *CHILDES*
- Initially these tend to be:
    - 'what', 'where' or 'who' questions, followed by
    - 'why', 'what', 'can'/'can't', and then 'when'
- Question forms become more complex as they incorporate other new word forms such as the pronoun, or the *present participle* of a verb

Drawings by Miller

1969). Using CHILDES data (that we also encountered in Chapter 8), as well as especially targeted studies, others have confirmed that 'where?' and 'what?' questions tend to come first along with 'who?' (e.g. 'who put it in?', 'who's watching?') (Gleason, 2005: 174)

Why, how and what questions and increasing complexity

At the second stage, the questions become more specific in that they become increasingly combined with the new types of words that the child is acquiring such as pronouns ('where my mitten?, 'where me sleep?') and more complex verb forms such as those using the **present participle – or 'ing' ending** ('what soldier marching?', 'why you waking me up?'). There is increasing use of 'why?' questions at this stage, although (and again probably because of its more complex set of meanings), when asked 'why?' questions at this stage, the child may respond inappropriately, as illustrated by these examples from children aged 2 years 10 months studied by Ervin-Tripp:

Mother: "Why don't we bring out the swing?"

Child: "Yes I do"

Mother: "Why don't we sit up-here ...?"

Child: "Me too"

(Ervin-Tripp, 1970: 82)

At the third stage identified by Klima and Bellugi, the questions are now likely to include 'how?', 'what?', and 'can?' or 'can't?' ('how that open?', 'what did you doed?', 'can't you get it?'). 'When' questions appear later than most of these forms and we shall return to this when we consider the child's understanding of time (Chapter 10).

9.2 PROBLEMS WITH THE GRAMMAR OF QUESTIONS

Apart from the complexity of meaning in the 'wh' questions themselves, forming a question requires learning certain grammatical rules and you can already see from the above examples that grammatical errors occur at all stages. Why is this?

Let us look first at what questions require of a child language learner. In questions, the grammatical markers are the 'wh' words, turning statements into queries. The marker is placed at the beginning and then the sentence can be turned round or inverted in various ways, e.g.

'That is a doggie'/'What is that?'

'The man is running'/'Why is the man running?'

'I am making a cake'/'What am I making?'

But the problem for children is that when they are ready to use their language to ask about the world, they are still learning some of the key parts of speech involved in these inversions. Notice that two of above examples use two words taking the role of verb. Here, the verb 'to be', as in 'is' or 'am' is called an **auxiliary verb**. In a statement, it can help express timing as in 'is running'/'was running', though it may not always be necessary, as in 'the man runs'/'the man ran'. However, it does become necessary when a question is asked: 'is the man running?', 'why is the man running?', 'where is the man running to?', etc. Notice that case marking (for number and tense) occurs on the auxiliary rather than the main verb: 'he is running'/'he was running'; 'she does like'/'she did like' – another rule that the child will have to master. At the 3–4.5 MLU stage, children are beginning to quite reliably use the auxiliary especially when asking 'yes/no' questions such as 'are we going?', 'can I eat it?', 'is he coming?' But at this stage they also show some characteristics problems with using the auxiliary in 'wh' questions.

Stage 1 grammatical errors

One of the main errors a child will make when forming his first 'wh' questions is to miss out the auxiliary ('what cowboy doing?'/'where horse go?') – or when an auxiliary is called for, to simply to miss the verb out altogether ('who that?'/'where Ann pencil?'). And because the verb should be case marked on the auxiliary (see above), when there is no auxiliary produced by the child, the case may remain marked on the main verb, as in 'what he likes?'

Stage 2 grammatical errors

At Stage 2, auxiliaries are still unlikely to appear in questions (unless they contain negation, as you will find out later) and as the sentences are a bit longer, more varied in their use of 'wh' words, and more likely to contain a main verb, the missing auxiliary is even clearer: 'where my mitten?', 'why you smiling?', 'what the dollie have?'

These sorts of grammatical errors were captured in an early analysis of children's language by the pioneering psycholinguist, Dan Slobin at Berkeley University. Slobin (1973) introduced the concept of **operating principles**, which are not just linguistic rules but practical solutions to conveying meaning whilst avoiding some of the seemingly arbitrary complexities of grammar. One of these states:

> Look for grammatical markers that indicate underlying semantic distinctions clearly and make semantic sense.

The 'wh' marker at the start of a sentence would be one such example as it clearly flags up a question.

Another operating principle that Slobin detected was:

> Avoid interruption or rearrangement of linguistic units.

This explains why 'wh' sentences are nevertheless difficult. The placing of the auxiliary *before* the noun in a question is an example of rearrangement – 'the man is running'/'is the man running?' The problem with rearrangement is clear both from failures of omission ('why he go?') and then later (when the auxiliary is starting to be used) failures of commission (e.g. 'why he can go?'). Similarly, even when the auxiliary is put in the right place, it is sometimes in addition to putting it in the wrong place as in 'what can he can do?' This is known as a double auxiliary error.

Stage 3 grammatical errors

By this stage, a child may place the auxiliary in the correct position, but fail to have case agreement between the auxiliary and the noun. For example, a failure of number agreement would be as in 'where does the boys go?', and an example of tense agreement failure would be 'did I missed it?' The pressure on children to keep all the parts of speech in agreement may also result in classic verb ending errors such as 'what did you doed?' or 'where my spoon goed?' – forms of verb that wouldn't be correct in any sentence!

Nowadays, psychologist are still arguing over whether the child's difficulties with the placement of the auxiliary is an example of an innate rule system at work or simply a reflection of the gradual process of learning, during which the specific relationships between 'wh' words and their auxiliaries have to be learned bit by bit (Rowland et al., 2005). You will recognise that the second of these possibilities is consistent with Tomasello's usage account. Indeed, he and his colleagues have suggested that children build on **entrenched frames** or frequent combinations that children learn as a unit and then use as a frame for generating the rest of their question. A common unit would be 'do you …', but less common would be 'do turkeys', predicting that errors are going to be more likely with the infrequent form. So for example, it would be less likely for a child to say 'does you drink milk?' than 'does turkeys drink milk?' Careful research using CHILDES data by Caroline Rowland at Liverpool University has given cautious support to the idea that children do indeed build on commonly heard frames for forming sentences. For example, an entrenched frame learned for one child, Becky, was 'do you?' but there was no such learned frame for 'do lambs' leading to the error 'does lambs like apples?' There were significantly fewer errors overall for cases in which an entrenched frame had been learned (Rowland, 2007).

The copula

Auxiliaries may be hard to place in a question but they can also be difficult in their own right, because they tend to be supportive verbs like 'is' rather than vivid action verbs like 'hits' or 'eats'. These verbs can also be used in a form called the **copula**. It is most often based on the verb 'to be' but could also be based on other verbs such as 'to become' or 'to seem'. These are especially non-vivid words semantically because their main role is just to link the meaning between the first and last part of a sentence, perhaps linking a noun or pronoun to an adjective such as 'the dog is happy' or another noun: 'he is a pet'. The copula doesn't interrupt the flow of meaning as in the case of a question auxiliary, as it is placed in the middle (or medial position) within the sentence, but that may not always be obvious to the child because they can usually take a contracted form. For example, the English verb 'to be' may be contracted so that it doesn't stand out from other words, e.g. 'the dog's happy', 'he's a pet'.

So what might make the copula more vivid to the child? On the theory that input from adults can specifically shape the acquisition of grammar, Richards and Robinson (1993) hypothesised that there would be a correlation between 'yes/no' questions put to children using the copula (e.g. 'Is the dog barking?') and their own development of copula use. Why? Because in a yes/no question, auxiliaries go to the start of the sentence, and when they do, they can't be contracted – making them more obvious: 'Is he happy?', 'Are you going?', etc. Richards and Robinson tested data from 33 children aged around 2 years with an initial MLU of just under 2, monitoring their use of the copula (including the contracted form) over the next 9 months and found that there was indeed a correlation between their spontaneous use of the copula and the number of yes/no questions put to them by parents during this period. This correlation was specific to the contracted form only, however, as in, e.g. 'it's a', 'there's a', etc. – so making the full copula more obvious by putting it at the start of a yes/no question can't be the whole story; otherwise you would expect the full copula to emerge first in children's speech. A likely reason for this is that, even if the full form is used for the question, it is not likely to be used for the answer ('is that a doggie? – yes – it's a doggie!'). In other words, the contracted form allows the copula to be learned initially (in non-question sentences) as part of a larger unit before having to work out where it should go as a separate word. This seems to be borne out by the way negative forms are learned as we shall see next.

Panel 9.2 Problems with the grammar of questions

- Questions often require the use of an *auxiliary verb* (based on the verb 'to be') to be inserted before the main verb, e.g.
  - 'why *is* he running?'; 'what *are* you doing?'; 'when *am* I going home?'
- With the first use of wh question forms children will often miss out the auxiliary altogether, e.g.
  - 'where my mitten?'; 'why he sleeping?'
- It has been proposed that this is a way of getting across the core meaning by:
  - starting with the important question word
  - not interrupting the relationship between the main noun and the main verb
- When auxiliaries are used, they are often put where it would go in a non-question sentence, e.g.
  - 'why he can go?'; 'where my mitten is?'
- Even when they are put in the correct place there may be failures of case agreement, e.g.
  - 'where does the boys go?'; 'did I missed it?'
- A *copula* is a form of verb that links a noun/pronoun to an adjective or another noun, e.g.
  - 'he *seems* happy'; 'he'*s* a cocker spaniel'; 'Mary *was* naughty'
    - the emergence of these forms in young children is correlated with the parent's use of direct questioning, e.g. 'does he seem happy?'
- The *contracted form* of the copula appears first: 'he's' rather than 'he is'
  - This suggests that the copula is learned first as part of a larger unit

9.3 PROBLEMS WITH THE GRAMMAR OF NEGATION

'That's not a dog – it's a fox!', 'No – you're not to touch that', 'Don't go in there!', 'I don't want to.' Negatives, or the use of the word 'not', form a very large part of the child's early linguistic environment and you can probably see by now that sentences containing negatives have the lurking pitfalls for children in terms of the use of the auxiliary verb, e.g. 'he is not listening', 'I cannot make it work'. Unlike the 'wh' question marker, which can go handily to the start of the sentence to convey the intention to ask a question, the negative (not) is usually in the medial position, i.e. between the auxiliary and the main verb, unless it is also used as an emphasised imperative, 'No – I told you not to touch that'. And so, even when the auxiliary verb can be used, there remains a problem of 'interrupting' the flow of meaning with the negative. But bearing mind what you learned about the contracted form of the copula in the previous section, you can see that statements with negatives rarely take the full form. In informal speech, an adult is much more likely to use a sentence frame starting 'he isn't (listening)', 'I can't make it work', etc. using a contracted form of the negative, but also sometimes the contracted form of the copula 'that's not a dog', 'you're not'. So having to learn to use negatives can help explain the early appearance of the contracted form of the copula. And just as the contracted form of the copula avoids having to work out where it should go in the sentence, so also could the contracted form of the negative (won't/can't, etc.) help to smooth out difficulties in placing the auxiliary and the negative in the right place as they can be inserted as a single unit.

Despite this, the construction of properly formed negative sentences still takes time and shows a stage-like pattern of errors as found with questions. Consistent with Slobin's idea that children want to place important semantic markers at the start of a sentence, this is indeed what they seem to want to do at the first, 2/3 word stage, using either 'no' or 'not', as in 'no mitten', 'not a teddy bear!' Also as with questions, missing out the auxiliary altogether at first also avoids the interruption of the meaning of the rest of the sentence, producing, for example, 'no the sun shining' rather 'than the sun is – not/'nt – shining' and is consistent with Slobin's operating principle – avoid rearrangement.

By the second stage, children will use the auxiliaries 'can' and 'do' in their contracted form ('can't' and 'don't'), both at the start of a sentence as an imperative ('don't leave me') or in declarative sentences (e.g. ' I can't catch you'). Klima and Bellugi note that this Stage 2 use of the auxiliary in negative statements precedes its use in non-negative sentences, i.e. at this stage, they will not use a phrase such as 'I can catch you'. This is quite consistent with other evidence regarding the later appearance of the non-contracted form, as all non-negative sentences involving auxiliaries 'can' and 'do' have to take the full form: 'you can make it happen', 'I do want to go'.

But by Stage 3, other auxiliaries appear in negative statements in both full and contracted form and the sentences become longer and more complex: 'I am not a doctor', 'you didn't eat supper with us'. But rather like the way the growing use of the auxiliary in questions starts to produce new errors, similar errors appear in negatives also, such as failing to realise that tense is marked on the auxiliary, not the main verb, producing, e.g. 'you didn't caught me', 'I didn't did it'. At this stage, double negatives may also appear as in 'nobody won't recognise us', or even triple negatives, 'I can't do nothing with no string'. The psycholinguist, David McNeill (1966) notes this interesting doggedness with the double negative even when the mother is trying to correct the child (albeit in a rather non-sympathetic way!):

Child: "Nobody don't like me"

Mother: "No, say, 'nobody likes me'"

Child: "Nobody don't like me"

This exchange is repeated eight times

Mother: "No, now listen carefully; say 'nobody likes me'"

Child: "Oh! Nobody don't LIKES me"

Panel 9.3 Problems with the grammar of negation

- *Negation* interrupts the flow of meaning as the negation word is inserted between the auxiliary and the main verb, e.g.
    - 'he does *not* like his dinner'; 'she *cannot* tie her shoelaces'
- Initially they will be put at the start of the sentence with no auxiliary, e.g.
    - '*no* like dinner'; '*no* tie shoe laces'
- Later the contracted verb form is more likely to be used first, e.g.
    - 'he *doesn't*'; 'she *can't*'
- So also is the contracted form of the copula when used with a negative, e.g.
    - '*that's* not a diplodocus'; '*you're* not wearing it'
- These contracted forms help the negation to be used as a whole unit
    - This avoids having to work out where the auxiliary/copula and the negation go in the sentence
- But negations are still hard – when the auxiliary is used in its non-contracted form, it is likely to be incorrectly case marked, e.g.
    - 'I didn't did it'
- or converted to a double negative, e.g.
    - 'Nobody don't like me'
- Questions and negatives combined can cause even more errors, e.g.
    - 'Why he not be a doctor?'

So, to summarise, there are similarities in the development of the use of questions and negatives, both these forms adding the use of the auxiliary to the young child's grammatical repertoire. No surprise then that sentences that are both questions and negatives produce some very strange constructions indeed, such as 'why he can't be a doctor?' (Klima & Bellugi, 1966), or 'why I didn't live in Italy?' (McNeill, 1966). Questions and negatives show similar stage-like advancement with the appearance of some similar errors as attempted sentences get longer and more complex. Contracted auxiliaries and copulas such as 'isn't ('coming here', 'a dog') tend to precede the full form 'it is' both for answers to yes/no questions as well as for the construction of the negative.

Let's now tie the last two bits of this story together. Children seem to produce the copula earlier if they have been asked a lot of yes/no questions. They are also more likely to use the contracted form of the auxiliary/copula with the negative. So what else can questions from adults do? By placing the full form of the auxiliary at the start, the child can see that the contracted form may be an *irregular* version of the full form. For example, 'he can't – he cannot' is a fairly even progression but what about 'he won't' from 'he will not'? This would not be at all obvious without the expanded question form using the regular verb: 'will he do it?' – 'no, he won't'. In other words, questions (and answers) form a complex tapestry of conversational exchange from which all these important parts of speech start to become identified.

COMPLEX SENTENCE CONSTRUCTION

We have traced some of the developments that occur when MLU is increasing from about 2/3 words to about 4/5, but we are getting to the point where MLU ceases to be a benchmark of linguistic development. Once the basic parts of speech are acquired (by about 3 years), sentences can become a lot longer and in a variety of ways. The key to being able to say more is to make sentences out of clauses and there are many ways to make clauses as you will see.

LEARNING LANDMARKS

9.4 Clauses and ways to conjoin them. You should know what a clause is and be able to name three ways in which they can be conjoined.

9.5 Co-ordination. You should know what is meant by an unbound versus a bound connective. You should know what an adverbial clause is and be able to give examples of its use in early speech. You should know what is meant by temporal and causal adverbs.

9.6 Relativisation. You should know the words that introduce relative clauses and why they are very hard for young children. You should know the difference between subject-relative and object-relative clauses and which of these has been found to be harder in general.

9.7 Complementisation. You should know what a complement is in English grammar and be able to explain why some complements are difficult for young children to understand. You should know the meaning of the minimum distance principle.

9.4 CLAUSES AND WAYS TO CONJOIN THEM

One of the simpler ways to extend what you want to say – especially if you are an excited young child – is to combine two short sentences with connectives like 'and', 'so' and 'but' (Harry climbed a tree and/but he fell off', 'he fell off a tree, so he had to go to hospital'. When they are part of a bigger sentence, these little sentences are called **clauses**. A clause, like a sentence, contains a verb. Clauses can be combined – or conjoined – in various ways. The sort of conjunction in the examples just given is called **co-ordination** where words like 'and', 'but' and 'so' connect two meanings to make a deeper point. A second type of conjunction is to use the second clause to actually qualify or **modify** some of the information in the first clause. For example, words like 'who', 'that' or 'which' can modify the noun in the first clause, as in 'Harry, who is in my class, fell off a tree', 'Harry fell off a tree that was not in his garden'. This way of introducing a new clause is called **relativisation**, and the clause it introduces ('who is in my class'/'that was not in his garden') is called the **subordinate** clause because it has a secondary meaning to the main clause. Another use of a subordinate clause is to specify (for example) the time of the event as in 'Harry fell off a tree when he was in the garden'. A third way to conjoin clauses is known as **complementisation**, which combines two meanings but using a short-cut where the words 'that' or 'which' are actually dropped out and replaced by 'to' as in 'I want you to stand on your head' (rather than 'I want that you stand on your head').

This looks like a good deal of new syntax has to be mastered (and you may be having some difficulties following this yourself by now!) but we shall see that, once again, some bits come to the child more readily than others and for good reasons. However, by the time children are at the complex sentence stage, their struggles with language are not marked so much by errors (as in the case of verb endings – though those may still be in evidence at this stage), but rather by order of appearance in their own language. Research using the CHILDES resource conducted by Lois Bloom and her colleagues at Columbia University (Bloom, 1991) and Holger Diessel from the Max-Planck Institute at Leipzig (Diessel, 2004), has revealed some interesting patterns in terms of order of appearance of different complex sentence type. Although only a total of eight different children featured in these projects, the analyses were based on thousands of utterances per child from the age of roughly 2 to about 3½ years. These showed that complex sentences that combine two clauses are a real challenge for children of this age. Why should this be so? By now children have got used to putting extra little words into noun–verb phrases to make them into grammatically correct sentences, like the auxiliary 'is he eating it?' and the negative 'do not eat that'. They can also use the interrogative pronouns such as 'who' and 'which' that are used in relativisation in the context of questions such as 'who ate the honey?' or 'which is it?' So what is so difficult about putting in these little words to link two clauses, such as 'the bear who ate the honey got stuck in the hole' or 'the pizza, which is in the freezer, has cheese on it' (relativisation)? And why are these sorts of conjunction harder than 'the bear got stuck in the hole because he ate the honey' (co-ordination)? As Bloom, Diessel and others have pointed out, there are good psychological reasons why these syntactic forms emerge in a particular order and we shall review this now.

Panel 9.4 Clauses and ways to conjoin them

- A *clause* is a phrase containing a verb
- Two events can be mentioned in a single sentence by conjoining clauses
- The most common way to conjoin clauses in early language is through *co-ordination*
    - This uses 'and'
        - 'He climbed the tree *and* picked the apple'
    - Or 'but'
        - 'He climbed the tree *but* he fell off'
- A second – or *subordinate* – clause can modify the meaning of the first, e.g.
    - 'He climbed the tree *when he was in the garden*'
        - This is an *adverbial* clause
            - It modifies the verb
    - 'He climbed the tree *which was in the garden'*
        - This is a *relative* clause
            - It modifies the subject or object
- Not all subordinate clause are equally easy to use as indicated by their appearance in spontaneous language

9.5 CO-ORDINATION

Unbound connectives

The first connectives used to co-ordinate two clauses are 'and', 'but', 'because' and 'so'. However, it would be a mistake to conceptualise the acquisition of these words simply as ways of making longer sentences. Whilst all these words can and will perform this function, their first appearance (generally just below 3 years) is to link a clause to a clause or statement said by another speaker or by themselves in a clearly (intonationally) separate statement. These are called **unbound** uses and examples (from Diessel, 2004) are:

Child: "Piggy went to market"

Adult: "Yes"

Child: "*And* piggy had none"

Adult: "Flipper's on TV yeah"

Child: "*And* Shaggy's not on TV

Adult: "No, it's not raining today Pete"

Child: "*But* it's raining here"

Adult: "It is called the skin of the peanut"

Child: "*But* this isn't the skin"

Adult: "Hey, what happened?"

Child: "It opened"

Child: "*So* the horsie could get out"

Adult: "How many blankets are you putting on Snoopy?"

Child: "Two"

Child: "*So* he could sleep"

Child: "No, don't touch this camera"

Adult: "Why?

Child: "*Because* it's broke"

Adult: "Is that one better?"

Child: "Yeah"

Child: "*Cause* other one is too small"

Diessel calculated that around 85% of occurrences of these words in children's speech at 3 years old were unbound, reducing slowly but still at around 65% by the age of 5 (Diessel, 2004). When children do start to use bound co-ordination across two clauses, they are most likely to do so with the link word 'and'. The word 'and' was the first to appear in the data base of complex sentences studied by Bloom and her colleagues and also by Diessel, and it remained the most frequent conjunctive used by the children during the two years or so during which the data were collected. One reason for its predominance could be that it can convey a wide variety of meanings. Bloom distinguishes between its additive use – a simple chaining of meaning, as in the child Kathryn's 'maybe you can carry this and I can carry that'. But the same little girl used 'and' at around the same age to specify the order of events in time. 'Jocelyn's going home and take her sweater off', and as a general rule across children, this temporal use of 'and' was a bit later than the additive one. A bit later again (the timing and the precise order varied somewhat from child to child), the word 'and' was used to convey cause and effect as in 'she put a bandaid on her shoe and it maked it feel better' (Peter at 38 months) and 'you push it and it goes up' (Adam at 42 months).

Adverbial clauses

However, some conjunction words tend to be used in a bound way from the start, and these are 'when', 'if', 'while', 'until', 'after' and 'before'. These words appear usually after the age of 3. As well as being connected with the production of bound – and thus longer – constructions, these forms convey some very specific meanings to do with temporal order and conditionality (and we shall consider these in turn below). Because they modify the verb in the sentence – that is, they add in information about the action or event described by the verb – these words are called adverbs, and clauses that are introduced using these words are called adverbial clauses. The adverbial clause that is introduced by these connectives is called the **conjoined clause**.

Temporal adverbs

From this group of connecting words, 'when' is the most likely to be used by preschoolers. 'When' can be used make a point about the past as in 'when we were young we swam in the sea'; the present, e.g. 'when we go to the supermarket, we use a large trolley'; or the future, e.g. 'Daddy will fix it when he gets home'.

The placement of the 'when' clause can be flexible without altering the meaning: 'When he gets home, daddy will fix it.' However, research by Eve Clark and later work by Diessel (Diessel, 2008), found that the vast majority of children's first 'when' conjoined clauses follow the main clause (as in: 'I was crying when my mummy goed away' emerging at around 2 years 9 months, whilst it was five months later before they appeared in the first position (as in 'When it's got a flat tire, it needs to go to the station'). One reason for this could be that children may be unlikely to make a general conversational sort of observation that starts by setting the scene in the distant past ('When they were in Britain, the Romans built a defensive wall'). So one reason for the selective uptake of adverbial sentences may simply be that children use the sentence form that gets their meaning across in the most immediate way, without any scene-setting preamble.

Another consideration, however, comes from the way children of this age understand two other temporal conjunctions, 'before' and 'after'. In a seminal paper on understanding these terms, Eve Clark reports a study in which she asked children aged between 3 and 5 years to act out events described in sentences such as 'He jumped the gate before he patted the dog' using dolls and props (Clark, 1971). As you can see from the graph in Panel 9.5, the children were far more accurate on some sentences than on others. One of the reasons given by Clark is that the easier sentences maintain the order of mention of events in the sentence. In fact this became another of Slobin's operating principles:

> Mention two events in the order in which they occurred.

(In fact, the children in Clark's study were unlikely to use 'before or 'after' at all in their own speech when asked about what happened in the story, and this reminds us that complex sentences using any connective other than 'and' are relatively rare in the spontaneous speech of preschool children.) Clark also points out that 'before' and 'after' are terms that require a more specific mapping to the world of real time than the more global concept 'when' – which can simply denote 'at a time'. 'Daddy will fix it when he gets home' conveys a less precise meaning (Daddy will fix it at a time when he is home) than 'Daddy will fix it after he has had his dinner' (Daddy will do A followed by B), and when you think about it, 'before' and 'after' are usually reserved for these more precise descriptions of order of events. So Clark's analysis offers a cogent reason for why it is that the 'when' connective is more likely to be used earlier than the more precise connectives 'before' and 'after' providing the events are linked in their real-time order. This order of mention principle has also been identified by Diessel (2008), who termed it **iconicity**.

But how do we now explain why the 'when' connective is more likely to be placed second rather than first in the sentence? That is, why 3 year olds are *not* likely to say 'When he gets home, Daddy will fix it'? The order of mention of the events is congruent with their order in real time so the order of mention principle would predict the opposite finding. The answer seems to lie in the use of those words 'he' and 'Daddy'. 'He' is of course a pronoun and will be very much part of the child's vocabulary by now. In a conjoined sentence like this, the use of the pronoun is known as **anaphoric**. That means it refers backwards to an antecedent as in 'The bear eats too much honey and he gets stuck in a hole'. So if the antecedent actually comes second in the sentence ('When he eats too much honey, the bear gets stuck in a hole'), then the speaker has to wait for the main noun and then go back to the pronoun to decode the meaning. The sentence construction goes in a backwards direction.

This is consistent with early findings that children under the age of 5 will use the order of mention of pronouns rather than the meaning of two connected sentences to 'act out' their meaning, thus failing to distinguish, e.g. 'Jane found Susan's pencil. She gave it to her' from 'Jane needed Susan's pencil. She gave it to her' (Wykes, 1983). Later studies of anaphoric understanding in preschool children have established that pronoun to noun reference is less likely to be used in spontaneous speech (e.g. Eisele and Lust, 1996) and this is often called the **directional effect**. For example, in matching a sentence to a picture, children would favour the match, 'When Big Bird held the apple, he touched the pillow' over the backward anaphoric, 'When he held the pillow, Big Bird touched the apple'.

Causal adverbs

Apart from the direction in which words are mapped onto the meaning there is, as always, the issue of the meaning itself. Connectives can convey real-world events which themselves are not necessarily well understood by children at around the age of 3. Examples of such connectives are the causal ones ('It broke because it fell off the table', 'It fell off the table so it broke') and the conditional ones ('If you push it off the table, it will break'). So clues as to their understanding of causality and conditionality come from the ways in which they first start to mention such connections spontaneously.

From the work of Bloom and Diessel, we know that children will express some notions of causality from about the age of 2, using the words 'because' and 'so', but these words will be used first in an unbound manner, i.e. used to connect meaning across two sentences rather than within a single utterance. In fact 'because' and 'so' are likely to be the first words in answer to a question from a parent, as in:

> Adult: "Why do the scissors have to be clean?"
>
> Child: "So I can cut better"

Bearing this in mind, we can think about how they might be incorporated into bound clauses. The clause starting with 'because' is an explanation of something – it adds information. Thinking of it that way, we might predict that the transition to bound uses of 'because' will not be too difficult as the child supplies the event that needs explanation followed by the new information that makes sense of it. However, instead of seeing causal connectives as a way of introducing an explanation, they can also be seen as a formal statement of the explanation itself. Think about this yourself for a moment.

> 'The window broke because Malcolm threw a cricket ball at it'
>
> 'The water spilled because she knocked the tumbler over'
>
> 'I am using these so I can cut better'

Notice that the offering of an explanation following 'because' and 'so' in these examples is not the same as *formally* describing the causal relationship between cause and effect as in 'if you hit a window with a ball it will break', 'if you knock over a tumbler of water, the water will spill', 'if you use scissors, you will cut better'. In these cases, there is a sense that a general physical law is being expressed. Supplying an explanation based on an observed chain of events need make no such presumption, other than the fact that it is useful to have an explanation for the event and we might expect that form of binding to emerge first.

The evidence from children's early language does suggest that they are not trying to convey formal cause and effect relationships. First of all, they are also extremely unlikely to use 'if–then' connections at this age – another indication that they do not see these sentences as conveying a physical rule. And supposing that they *were* trying to express a physical cause and effect relationship using 'because', surely they would have difficulty with inserting 'because' between two clauses on Slobin's 'order of mention' principle. That is to say although 'because' is commonly used in adult speech to connect the consequence with the causal explanation, but the consequence (the second event) is often mentioned first, as in e.g.

> 'The man broke his arm because he fell off his bike'

a form you may expect to be difficult for young children to use.

In fact, an early claim by Piaget (1928) suggested that children make errors when having to complete a sentence such as 'The man fell off his bicycle because' (wrongly supplying 'he broke his arm'). However, the more recent research on children's spontaneous language by Bloom and Capatides (1987), Donaldson (1986) and McCabe and Peterson (1985) suggests such inversions rarely occur in the normal conversational speech of 3–4 year olds. 'Because', furthermore, is more common in the preschool child's explanations than 'so'.

Panel 9.5 Co-ordination

- Children first co-ordinate two parts or clauses in a serial order using *unbound connectives* such as 'and', 'but', 'so' and 'because', e.g.
  - Adult: 'How many blankets are you putting on Snoopy?'
  - Child: 'Two'
  - Child: '*So* he could sleep'

- When they are used within a complete sentence they are called *bound connectives*, e.g.
    - 'You push it *and* it goes up'
- Bound connectives that are relatively easy for children are based on adverbial clauses
    - An early use is with respect to timing, e.g.
        - 'I put my coat on when it was raining'
    - or reason for an event, e.g.
        - 'They can't come cos we're sweeping up'
- But adverbial clauses are much better understood by young children if they reflect the real time-order of events

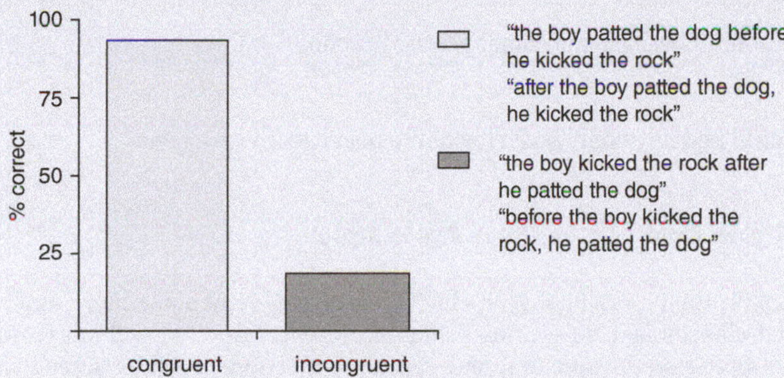

Four year olds could only correctly 'act out' an event with dolls and props when the order of mention was congruent with the order of events. (Adapted from Clark, 1971, with permission)

- *Anaphora* is the binding of a noun and pronoun in an adverbial clause ('the *boy* patted the dog, before *he* kicked ...')
- Regardless of order of mention, young children are very unlikely to use the pronoun first in adverbial anaphoric binding as in:
    - 'When he gets home, Daddy will fix it', preferring to say:
    - 'Daddy will fix it, when he gets home'
- This is called the *directional effect* as it avoids 'backwards' processing of the noun/pronoun relationship

This needs a bit of explaining as 'so' constructions *do* follow the order of mention principle if they are conceived of as expressions of cause and effect, as in:

> 'The ball hit the window so it broke'

The fact that 'so' is rarely used to bind clauses in this way by under-5s, and that causal inversions don't often occur often in their early uses of 'because', suggests that children are not actually trying to connect cause and effect according to physical laws but rather simply trying to provide an *additional piece of information* by way of an explanation. Further evidence for this is that all the researchers in this area note that children in this age range are much less likely to describe physical cause and effect connections anyway – as opposed to socio-cultural causality which obeys no temporal or physical laws, but rather the conventions of a culture, as in:

> Adult (looking a Peter's guinea pig): "Why do you have him? Did you take him home from school?"
>
> Peter: "Yeah because they don't belong in school"

Or

> 'We didn't go anywhere/just stay home because it was all wet'

Or

> 'They can't come here 'cos we're sweeping up'

In summary, in their preschool year, children will gradually make more and more use of adverbial clauses and, as well as using 'and', 'when' and 'if', will start using other connectives that express temporal and causal connections, such as 'after', 'while' and 'since' and 'because'. But at the age of 4 the use of these other words is still rare and they will still be twice as likely to use them in the middle of the sentence rather than at the beginning, for reasons that seem to converge on the need to get the core meaning across in the first clause with additional information in the second.

9.6 RELATIVISATION

Another way of connecting clauses is through relativisation (with 'who', 'which' or 'that'), as in:

> 'The bear *who ate the honey* got stuck in the hole'
>
> 'The pen *you gave me* is broken'

The words in italics mark the relative clause. In these examples, the clause is embedded; it comes between the main noun and the main verb. Like the connectives 'when' and 'because', these clauses modify a piece of information, but in general this embedded relativisation is much less likely to be produced by preschool children than sentences that link clauses adverbially using co-ordinating connectives such as 'when' and 'because', and they are even sometimes difficult *even to repeat back*. Why should this be so?

The first clue is that it is the embedding itself that causes the problem. This was noted in early psycholinguistic research by Slobin and Welsh (1973) when they asked a child (aged about 2½ years) named 'Echo' to repeat back sentences using embedded relative clauses such as:

'Mozart who cried came to my party' (Mozart was a bear)

Echo either omitted the relative clause, as in:

'Mozart cried'

Or replaced it with conjoined connective, as in:

'Mozart cried and he came to my party'

Some clue as to this reasons for this difficulty comes from tracing the earliest uses of clause using 'who', 'which' and 'that'. Diessel and Tomasello studied four children from the CHILDES data base and actually found that between around 2 and 4 years old they would quite often use relative clauses that modify a clause using 'that', but in a non-embedded way that the authors dubbed presentational construction:

'Here's the toy that spins around'

'That's the sugar that goes in there'

In fact 75% of the earliest relative clause were of this form and a further 18% were structurally similar but omitted the word 'that', as in:

'Another picture (that) I made'

'Look at all the chairs (that) Peter's got'

(Diessel, 2004)

Tomasello's research group later conducted a very thorough study with 3–5-year-old English-speaking children in Manchester and German-speaking children in Leipzig to explore this type of relative clause use in greater detail (Kidd et al., 2007). To do this they made three important distinctions.

The first distinction they make is between subject-relative clauses (RCs) where the clause modifies the subject of the sentence, as in:

'Here is the plant *that grew in the garden last summer*'

'Here is the lady *that helped the girl*'

And object-relative RCs where they modify the object, as in:

'Here is the food *that the cat ate*'
'Here is the girl *that the lady helped yesterday*'

They also distinguished, however, between whether or not the subject of the RC is a noun – as in the examples just given – or a pronoun, as in:

'Here is the plant *you grew in the garden'*

'Here is the girl *we helped yesterday'*

Finally they distinguished between the use of an animate subject or object as in girl/lady/cat and an inanimate one as in plant/food.

In one study, children aged between 3 and 5 years were simply asked to repeat back sentences 'like a parrot'. Overall there was a 54% error rate for 3-year-olds and a 38% error rate for 4-year-olds, confirming Slobin's finding that even repeating something back accurately can reveal that they are having difficulties with syntactic construction. Can you predict what they found?

Remember that an over-riding theme in sentence construction is maintaining real time-order of events and this usually means subject acts on object, in which case putting the object first in order to modify it ('Here is the food that the cat licked') is going to be harder than the subject-relative version: 'Here is the cat that licked the food'. As the left-hand graph in Panel 9.6 shows, children were better when they had to repeat a subject relative clause than an object-relative one, tending to convert object-relative clauses into subject-relative ones, as in:

'This the pen *that the boy used* at school, yesterday'

repeated back as:

'This is the boy *that used the pen* at school, yesterday'

As for animate/inanimate, for both English- and German-speaking children this error was greatest when the subject of the RC was animate (as above), suggesting that when two nouns are in competition for being associated with an action, the role will be given to the animate noun. As the authors assert, an animate noun is more 'topicworthy' of an impending action signalled by 'that'. It is more likely to be doing the doing!

What about pronouns? You know that children can learn to use these anaphorically, using them readily when the main noun has already been stated. As the right-hand graph in Panel 9.6 shows, children found it easier to refer to the subject of an object-relative clause using a pronoun ('This the plant she gave to the lady' / 'This the book you read') rather than another noun ('This is the plant the girl gave to the lady' / 'This is the book the lady read').

Panel 9.6 Relativisation

- *Relative clauses* modify one or other of the nouns in a sentence using 'who', 'which' or 'that', e.g.
  - 'The bear *who ate the honey* got stuck in a hole'
- At the age at which children start using adverbial clauses (from about 3 years), they are unlikely to even to be able to *accurately repeat* relative clauses
  - This is thought to be because the clause is embedded between the main noun of the sentence and the main verb
    - interrupting the flow of meaning
- A *subject-relative* clause modifies the main noun (doing the acting)
  - These are easier for young children to produce if the subject is animate than when it is inanimate, e.g.
    - 'The bear *who ate the honey* has run away' would be easier than
    - 'The honey *that was on the table* has disappeared'
- An *object-relative* clause modifies the object of the sentence
  - These are easier if the object is inanimate –than when animate, e.g.
    - 'The bear ate the honey *that was on the table*' would be easier than
    - 'The bear ate the man *that ran away*
- Both reflect a preference for the main subject noun to be 'doing the doing'
  - Object-relative clauses that start with a pronoun, are easier than if they start with a noun, e.g.
    '... the honey *that he put on the table* has disappeared' would be easier than '... the honey *that Chris put on the table* has disappeared'
- This suggests a preference for the simplifying anaphoric device that refers back to a previous part of a conversation (Chris put the honey on the table)

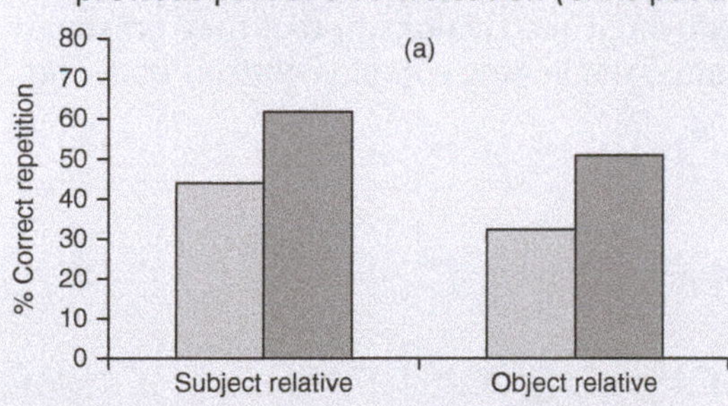

Subject-relative are easier than object-relative clauses for pre-schoolers in general (a), though this is mainly where the subject of the sentence is animate (b), as in 'here is the lady that helped the girl'.

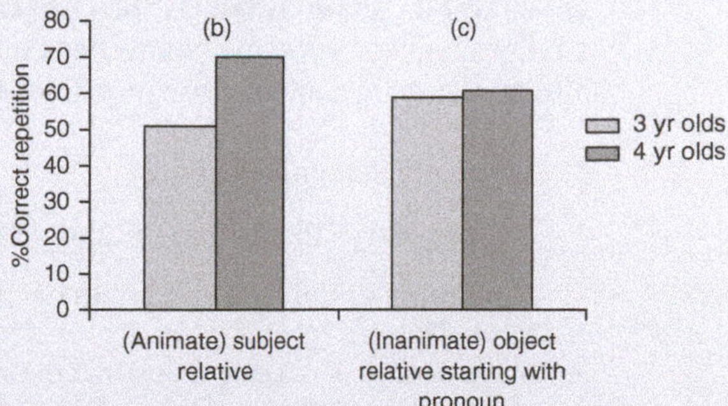

This difference can be reversed for 3 year olds in the cases of (inanimate) object-relative clauses introduced with a pronoun (c) as in 'here is the book that you read)'. (Adapted from Kidd et al., 2007, with permission)

Putting all of this together, preschool children were most comfortable overall with relative clauses that were subject relative and where the subject was animate (e.g. 'This is the lady that helped the girl'). There are various theories regarding all of this and one popular account is based on Tomasello's usage theory, i.e. the forms children are most likely to hear. But this rather evades the issue of why these are more common in the language of adults in the first place. The general principles relating to the expression of meaning – get the key point over first, and how things happen in the real world – people do things to other people or things in real time – go a long way to making sense of this complex story of sentence production.

9.7 COMPLEMENTISATION

If changes of direction in terms of the flow of meaning seem to be a major obstacle to language processing and production in young children, then it would follow that a form that simplifies this flow would be relatively easy. Once such form is the **complement**. A complement clause is another form of subordinate clause to the main one and is usually introduced by a verb. On the face of it, the complement clause is actually quite complex because it doesn't just modify a subject or an object as in the case of the relative clause; it is a sort of mini-sentence in its own right, combining two verbs into a larger meaning. Examples would be:

'I want *to go home*'

'I think *you should put your hat on*'

'He told Mary *not to sing so loud*'

'Mummy asked me *to help*'

'I feel *you are not getting anywhere with this*'

'Are you sure *you're not cold?*'

Complements are many and various and can be introduced by many types of verb in the first clause. Are they easy or hard for young children? Well this time, there really is no answer. In some instances they are simplifying constructions in that they presume a fuller clumsier version – sometimes including the linking complementiser 'that' and often presuming a silent noun or pronoun, e.g.

'I want (that you go home)'

'I told Mary (that Mary/she should not sing so loud)'

'Mummy asked me (that I help her)'

For that reason, it is not surprising that the simpler complement forms appear in the language of children in the CHILDES database by the age of 4 (without the complementiser 'that'). There are two interesting points worth considering. One is that the ease of use – and again the ease with which they can even repeat back some complement forms – depends on familiarity with the verb introducing the complement. So, for example, Kidd et al. (2010) found that repeating the complement clause introduced with the verb 'believe' (e.g. 'Paddington believes he can ski') was harder than with the verb 'knows' ('Ham knows Mickey likes running').

The authors once again point to the fact that children pick up certain syntactic forms as a consequence of lexical frequency in the language around them; 'knows' 'says' and 'thinks' are very commonly used in conjunction with a complement, whereas 'believes', 'bets' and 'imagines' are less frequent verbs. This effect (you could think of it as the linguistic ecology) reminds us of what helps support language learning in general, but, as you have learned in this chapter, some of the difficulties that children have are not just to do with unfamiliarity. It would seem that there is a genuine psychological hurdle involved in acquiring some grammatical forms. Inserting a negative or a relative clause in between the noun and main verb is one of them. And many years ago, Clark and Clark (1977) made a very interesting observation about how this principle can also apply to the complement clause.

Consider:

'She told Robin to play outside'

'He wanted his Mum to come home'

This is straightforward attachment of one clause with another and, as you can see from the expanded (but never articulated) form, it runs smoothly from start to finish with no interruption of meaning:

She told *Robin* (that *Robin* should go and play outside)

He wanted (that his *Mum would come home*)

But what about:

'She promised Robin to make pizza'

'He asked his Mum what to do'

Expand these and you get:

She promised (*Robin* that *she* would make a pizza)

He asked his (*Mum* what *he* should do)

You should be able to guess by now why these particular forms are harder for young children. They interrupt the flow of meaning by covertly referring back to the first noun or pronoun in the sentence. This interrupts the flow of meaning or, as Clark and Clark put it, it disrupts the **minimal distance principle** between the subject of the sentence and the final verb with something coming in between. Very similar, in other words, to relative clauses, as in 'The lady, who was talking to Robin, likes making pizza'.

Panel 9.7 Complementisation

- A *complement* is a subordinate clause that completes the proposition introduced in the main clause – usually by a verb, e.g.
  - 'I believe *you are getting better*'
  - 'He suggested *that we leave early*'
- The clause is introduced by the *complementiser*, which is usually 'that' – and which may be omitted in speech
- Some complement clauses appear as early as 4 years in children's language
  - But they rarely use the complementiser
    - and they are specific to certain forms
- The forms children are most likely to use are the ones introduce with familiar verbs that are often heard in the context of the complement clause, e.g.
  - 'Mummy thinks *I am playing*'
  - 'He knows *it is naughty*'
  - 'Peter told me *to go out*'
- Frequent usage is not the only factor affecting complement acquisition
  - Forms that interrupt the flow of meaning from the subject of the main clause to the verb in the complement clause (such as 'promise') can be very difficult for children right up to the age of 8–10 years.
- These forms are described as violating the *minimum distance principle*

School-age children can find it hard to 'act out' complement sentences that violate the minimum distance principle, such as those starting with 'promise', as in 'Donald promises Bozo to do a somersault'. The child will make Bozo do it instead (After C. Chomsky, 1969)

A very clear example of the difficulty with this sort of complement was provided by a study by Carol Chomsky in which she asked children aged between 5 and 10 years to act out events described linguistically using doll props, Bozo the clown and Donald the Duck (Chomsky, 1969). One task used the complement forms 'tell' and 'promise', e.g.

'Donald tells Bozo to lie down: make him do it'

'Donald promises Bozo to lie down; make him do it'

Out of 40 children, 21 were correct and there was no particular relationship with age; but of the 19 who were wrong (at all ages), 15 were always correct with 'tell' but made errors with 'promise' whether the action was lying down, hopping up or down or doing a somersault. Sorting out the appropriate actor in these complement forms can cause difficulties for some children until well into the school years.

We have reached a point in this chapter where, difficulties notwithstanding, children are in command of many of the tools of grammar and it may be worth reflecting for a moment on how this comes about. Language is a complex blend of our cultural and biological inheritance. Children do seem to have an almost innate understanding of the kinds of words that specify objects and the kinds of words that specify actions. And it is the flexibility and specificity of human speech through articulatory precision (our genetic endowment) that makes it possible to adopt a learned linguistic culture in which meaning can be expressed in many subtly different ways using past tenses, plurals, negations and so on. And although these morphological variations are all learned from others, you can see by now that children don't simply acquire the niceties of language as if they were being taught them in class. When you look closer at what seems to unfold most easily, it becomes apparent that children essentially co-opt those bits of language that seem to get meaning across in the most direct way, modifying and refining their sentence production skills from there on. Whilst children make numerous errors in the course of gradually acquiring adult-like speech, their path to linguistic proficiency makes psychological sense in terms of how we as human primates naturally perceive and understand the world. A final question that may be on your lips in this new era of text-messaging is whether this has any dis-benefits on the hard work children have to do to learn to construct properly spelled and properly constructed sentences. As yet, fortunately, it seems that there are none (Wood et al., 2014).

CHAPTER SUMMARY

Simple sentences are commonly produced first in the form of 'wh' questions. These incur grammatical errors regarding where to place the auxiliary verb. The contracted grammatical form called the copula is thought to make auxiliaries easier to learn. Negation is hard to learn because of similar difficulties with auxiliaries. Complex sentences require two clauses to be conjoined. This is particularly hard for relative clauses, introduced by 'who', 'which' or 'that', as they come in the middle of the main clause and disrupt the flow of meaning. Despite many common grammatical errors, children can usually construct long sentences well before the age of 5.

LOOKING AHEAD TO CHAPTER 10

Language is a tool for expressing meaning. So far, we have seen how ideas, questions and events can be shared through simple phrases and sentences. In this chapter we have concentrated on how the acquisition of this skill maps on to psychological understanding, but it is time to be reminded that language can only express meaning that the child is capable of understanding and that understanding – or cognition – still has to undergo considerable development. Even the way the child perceives the world will develop in important ways during the school years as we see next.

CHAPTER 10

PERCEPTUAL DEVELOPMENT AFTER INFANCY

You may be surprised by the title of this chapter. Can it really be the case that perception develops during the school years? Whilst it is plausible that children take a long time to learn the complexities of sentence construction, surely perception is different? What we perceive is 'out there' and what we perceive with – our senses of vision, hearing touch and smell – are part of our biological endowment. You know now that these senses become more integrated with one another during the first two years of infancy, but what is there to develop after that? In fact, at the age of 2, children are not just struggling to verbally describe what they perceive, how and what they perceive is still in the process of considerable development.

Is this simply a sensory problem? This is harder to answer than you might think. Optometrists have shown changes in visual acuity up to 9 years of age (Semenov et al., 2000) – but what does this actually mean, and how do we distinguish between acuity (sensory sensitivity) and perception? Attempts to answer this question led to the realisation that, psychologically speaking, there really is no such thing as 'pure' vision, or, for that matter, 'pure' hearing or 'pure' touch. These attempts came from an area of research known as **psychophysics**, which finally led to the view that all perception is an active process of comparison and contrast, that is still in the process of developing into the early school years. In today's research we no longer consider perceptual development as a sensory matter but rather in terms of how children become skilled at picking up important information from the world around them.

THE DEVELOPMENT OF CORE PERCEPTUAL SKILLS: PERCEIVING RELATIONS

LEARNING LANDMARKS

10.1 From psychophysics to relational perception. You should know what psychophysics is, the difference between absolute and relational theories, what 'frame of reference' effects are and, specifically, the meaning of the term 'anchoring'.

10.2 The development of relational perception. You should know what the transposition paradigm is and the significance of testing 'far' transposition. You should be able to describe a study that overturned the view that children undergo a shift from absolute to relational responding.

10.1 FROM PSYCHOPHYSICS TO RELATIONAL PERCEPTION

Psychophysics: why that name? When this research area was born (around 100 years ago), some psychologists were suffering from something often called 'Physics Envy'. Their aim was to remove the 'subjective' content of our perceptions on the (mistaken) idea that this would give us a true measure of our sensory skills. The technique was therefore to remove as much surrounding context as possible in order to answer precise questions about how we detect and judge simple stimulus properties such as size, brightness, colour or pitch. For example, at what physical value does one tone sound louder or a light appear brighter than another? This is known as the **discrimination threshold** and the techniques used to measure it go right back to one of the nineteenth century founders of psychology, Gustav Fechner. Of the various techniques he pioneered, one example is to ask participants to compare against a constant standard each of a series of stimuli in terms of e.g. size, loudness, etc. with gradually increasing differences from the standard along that particular dimension. After making many such comparisons, the average value required for perceiving a difference can be calculated.

Psychophysicists were also interested in how participants can actually rank or scale items along a dimension such as size or brightness, and here (and once again deriving from a method devised by Fechner) they would be asked to actually assign a rating on a scale 1–10.

A truly extraordinary amount of argument subsequently raged over an assertion made by most behaviourists in the early part of the twentieth century that such judgments are based on evaluating each stimulus independently and then deciding between them. If you were using a ruler, this would be like measuring something and finding it is 3 cm square and measuring something else and finding it to be 3.2 cm square, so you now know which is the bigger. This is called an **absolute** judgment. The alternative view is that you judge the difference or relationship between the two items directly. This is called a **relational** judgment. The relational theory finally won hands down – basically because it became progressively clearer that the types of comparisons being asked of the participants affected their judgments and this should not happen if every stimulus is evaluated independently. For example, participants were nearly always better at detecting differences during simultaneous rather than successive or serial comparisons, suggesting that having the relation directly visible was helping to support the judgment. This could be put down to the extra memory requirement in a successive judgment, but harder to explain was the finding that, even in a simultaneous task, it is harder to judge that stimuli are identical than that they are different, suggesting that participants are pre-disposed to analyse stimuli in terms of a difference relation.

Frame of reference

Most difficult of all for the absolute theory, however, was the fact that judgments were affected by the other stimuli with which they were being compared. A very convincing case of this is the well-known temperature illusion: dip your hand in a basin of very cold water and the other in a basin of very hot (but not scalding!) water and then plunge both hands simultaneously in a basin of tepid water and judge how it feels to each hand. Another dramatic example is the colour illusion (see http://www.colourtherapyhealing.com/colour/colour_fun/cube_illusion.php). But perhaps the best-known examples of this effect outside of psychophysics are visual illusions. Two of these, the Muller–Lyer and Ebbinghaus illusions, are presented in Panel 10.1. The phenomenon is created by the surrounding context and these illusions show how difficult it is to judge the core stimulus more 'absolutely'. In more everyday sorts of perceiving, we do not even try – relational context is everywhere, and it is the very essence of how we see (and feel) the world.

Panel 10.1 From psychophysics to relational perception

- *Psychophysics* is the study of how we judge the values of physical stimuli along dimensions such as size, brightness, weight and pitch
- *Absolute theories* suggested that we have a sort of sensory scale which allows us to perceive actual values and thus make comparisons between one value and another
- *Relational theories* suggested that all judgments are made with regard to a frame of reference, usually other stimuli of a similar type
- This gives rise to well-known illusions such as the Muller–Lyer (A) and Ebbinghaus (B) illusions in which the perception of identical sizes is affected by the surrounding context

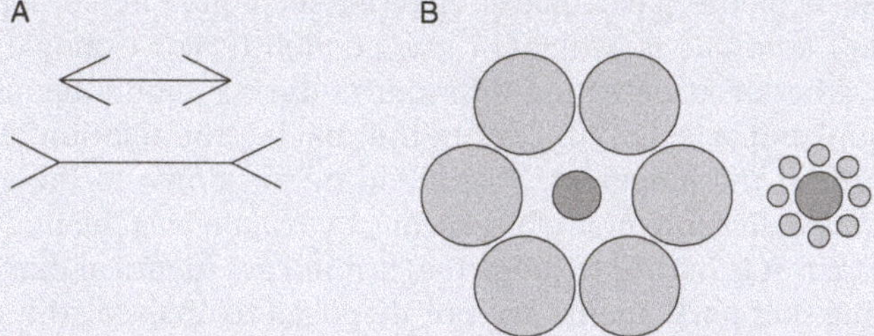

- It is very common to find a value against which we anchor our judgments and this too can distort its accuracy
  - This can happen even when told to ignore the anchor stimulus

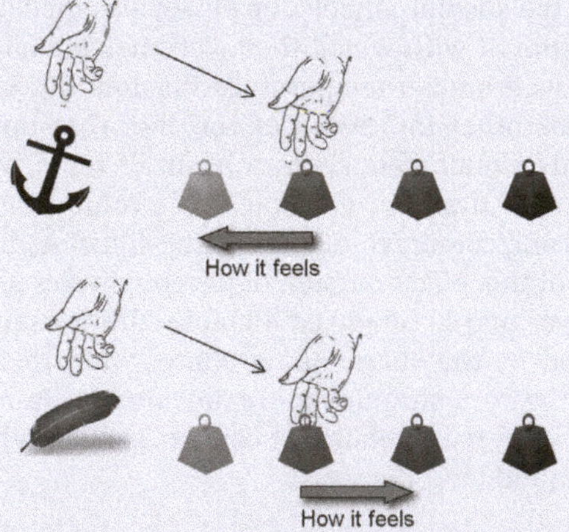

The perception of heaviness will be biased in a 'lighter' than direction if preceded by lifting a heavy object and vice versa. The same is true for other sensory dimensions such as loudness, brightness and so on.

Once it became to be seen as intrinsic to they way we perceive (rather than some sort of experimental artifact), contextual – or **frame of reference** – effects as they were known – became an area of psychophysical study in their own right. In tasks where participants are asked to assign a value along a subjective scale of e.g. size, pitch or loudness, what consistently emerged were **range**, **frequency** and **anchoring** effects. The first of these means that when we assign a particular perceived value on a dimension such as loudness or size from a set of different sounds or sizes, it is always relative to the particular range of stimuli presented. The frequency effect means that we tend to have our values distributed around the middle so that there is the same number below the mid-point as above the mid-point. Anchoring means that we tend to seek a particular stimulus as the end-point or anchor for the range. Usually we will try to find the largest/greatest or smallest/least as the points of reference for our range. But once again, the effect of relational context is almost impossible to overcome and so a stimulus can act as an anchor even if the participant is told to ignore it.

10.2 THE DEVELOPMENT OF RELATIONAL PERCEPTION

So psychophysics tells us that perception lies as much in the relations between things as in the things themselves. Is this something that develops during childhood as a result of knowing about scales and measurement and so on? Or is it a fundamental aspect of human perception at all ages? This question was at the centre of a rather fierce debate in psychology that centred on a paradigm called **transposition**. For many decades, the sticking point in accepting a relational account was a curious finding that suggested that children do in fact judge stimulus variables in absolute terms. We will now review why this appeared to be the case.

In a transposition task, participants would be trained to always choose on the basis of a difference relation. For a young child this simply means training them to select e.g. the larger one of two fixed sizes, following which they would receive a reward, such as a sticker hidden under the correct stimulus. They are then tested on new stimuli that are farther up the size range to see if they transfer this learning (choose larger) to new values. If they do, then this would favour the idea that their original choices were relational and not absolute, because they have to actually ignore the original trained value in order to transpose, as Panel 10.2 illustrates. This is indeed what was found for children as young as 3 years. But there would come a point along the stimulus dimension when young children (and animals) would not continue to choose the larger stimulus (i.e. to **transpose** their choice) and their responding would fall to chance levels. This effect of breakdown at values considerably

Panel 10.2 The development of relational perception

- *Transposition* is the transfer of a trained response to a value along a perceptual dimension such as size
- In young children transposition occurs to stimuli 'near' to the training values but breaks down at 'far' values
- This has been explained in terms of absolute stimulus learning where the *net excitatory response* to a stimulus can be greater than that to the original trained value, at least within a limited distance along the direction of training

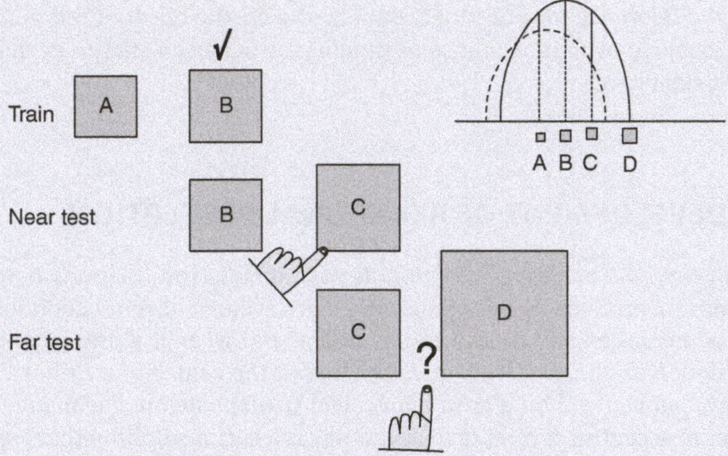

The transposition paradigm and the explanation of transfer of choice based on the net difference between excitation (solid lines) and inhibition (dotted) generalisation curves established during training. Breakdown occurs at values that are outside this range

- But if the children are actually trained on an *absolute* versus a *relational* discrimination, they find the relational one much easier to learn

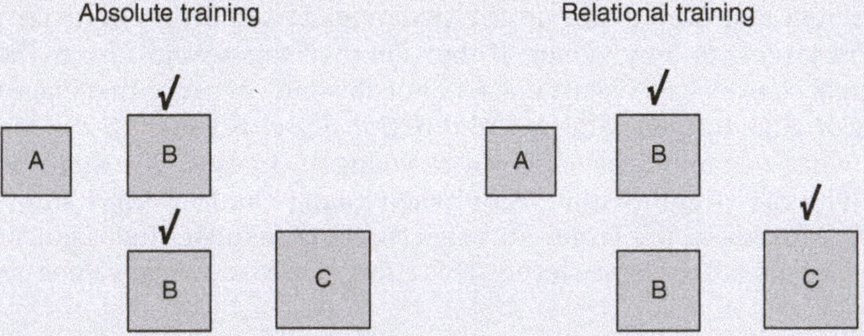

- It seems that younger children are less consistent about the relations they base their judgements on

different from the training ones was known as a failure of '**far transposition**'. As a 'bigger' relation should in theory apply to any set of values, far transposition failure was taken by some as evidence that the children were actually not learning a relation at all, but rather learning to select an 'absolute' size value. This of course raises the question as to why, in that case, they do not continue to select the trained value during 'near' tests also. In support of the 'absolute' theory, a famous learning theorist called Kenneth Spence produced an extremely clever explanation of how near, but not far, transposition might occur, based on classical learning theory concepts (that are very rarely applied nowadays to human learning). Put very simply, Spence argued that when a child learns to attach a response (like choosing) to one of two stimuli, he or she is developing an **excitatory tendency** towards the correct (absolute) value as well as an **inhibitory tendency** to the wrong one (Spence, 1936). If these values are added together, then the overall excitatory curve actually predicts near transposition, but also shows that there will be a point of breakdown further up the range. Panel 10.2 shows how this argument works. Far transposition failure in children was significant, therefore, because it seemed to indicate that young children perceive in a more primitive manner than older children and adults. Whilst we have considered this with respect to size relations, similar far transposition effects were found for other dimensions such as brightness (Reese, 1968).

For quite a while, the belief persisted that children start off perceiving in a qualitatively different way from adults and that they *become* relational perceivers. (For a good example of a developmental theory based on this, see Kendler (1995).) However, in the early 1970s, developmental psychologists at Oxford University had demonstrated that, although young children don't show far transposition, they are nevertheless 'relational' perceivers (Lawrenson & Bryant, 1972). They did this by the simple expedient of giving one group of children (between 4 and 6 years of age) a task in which they were always required to select the same actual size of stimulus, whatever its relation to the comparison stimulus (called the 'absolute' condition). Another group, however, were trained to take the same relative size – under both near and far conditions – called the 'relational' condition (see Panel 10.2). Lawrenson and Bryant found that not only were all the relational tasks much easier for the children, the 'absolute' tasks were extremely difficult to learn. They explained the far transposition breakdown in terms of the fact that as the stimuli become larger, it starts to noticeably affect another perceivable relation, i.e. the difference between the stimuli and the background frame on which they were presented (such as the borders of a stimulus card or the edges of a table). When this difference changes noticeably, Bryant argued, it causes young children to become confused and revert to chance responding.

More recently, Sarris has also shown that children also tend to be more variable or 'unstable' within and across individuals, which fits Bryant's idea that young children are vulnerable to the effects of other, but possibly irrelevant, relations.

We need to ponder this a bit before moving on. Think back to the far transposition effect and why you, an adult, would not find it difficult to solve the task as you could simply tell yourself, 'the sticker is always under the bigger of the two squares'. Is it maybe that children can't *verbalise* the relationship to themselves? Research by Margaret Kuenne in the 1940s showed that although having access to terms like 'bigger' and 'smaller' was not directly correlated with success, children who verbalised the problem in these terms were more likely to show far transposition. This does not indicate a causal connection here as it is possible that a growing perceptual awareness of the common size relationship preceded being able to express it linguistically. Nevertheless transposition is maybe telling us more about how children start to conceptualise the 'right' answer rather than how they actually perceive. Is there any remaining psychophysical evidence that basic perceptual skills change during childhood? And even if there is, does it matter? The answer to both questions is 'yes' as we see next.

THE DEVELOPMENT OF SIZE AND DISTANCE JUDGMENTS

LEARNING LANDMARKS

10.3 Size perception in real-world contexts. You should be reminded of the concept of size constancy and know why size judgments in the real world are also often constancy judgments. You should be able to cite a study showing how judgment of size develops in the early school years.

10.4 Cues for estimating distance. You know the difference between fundamental cues for distance and learned monocular cues, and be able to cite a study showing how the latter develops.

10.5 Velocity estimation in the real world. You should be aware of the problem of safe road crossing in children and be able to cite a study that identifies a change in the way children use velocity information.

Panel 10.3 Size perception in real-world contexts

- Perceiving the sizes of objects depends on making adjustments for distance (size constancy)
- This is measured by asking them to choose one of a range of differently sized stimuli placed at a relatively near distance (the comparison objects) such that is the 'same size' as one placed much farther away (the standard object)
- Size constancy gradually improves over the school years as measured by these techniques

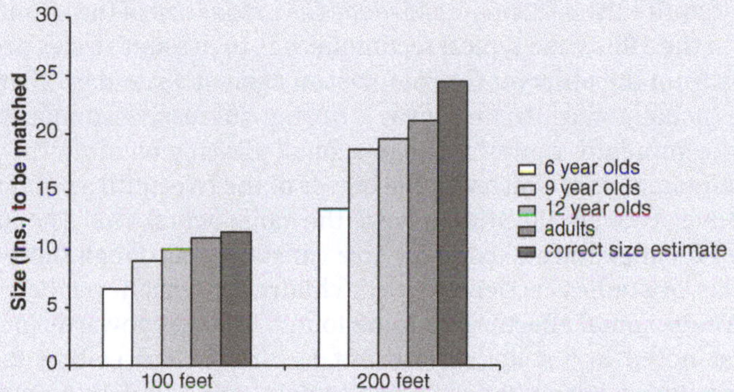

A Age-related changes in assessing the actual size of small objects at two distances. (Adapted from Brislin & Leibowitz, 1970, with permission)

- A common finding is that children will under-estimate the size of the distant stimulus

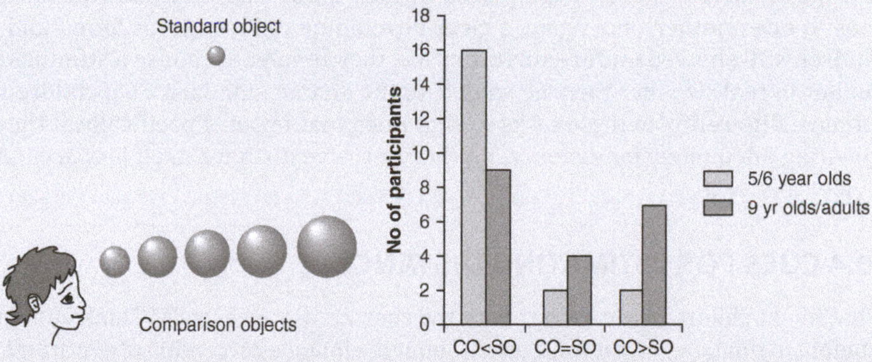

B A schematic representation of a size constancy task and summary results showing a tendency in younger children to underestimate the size of the standard object by selecting a comparison object that was smaller than the standard (CO < SO). (Adapted from Granrud & Schmechel, 2006, with permission)

- They will make this error even if the comparison objects are placed at slightly different distances from the viewer so that they all have the same retinal size

10.3 SIZE PERCEPTION IN REAL-WORLD CONTEXTS

Let us now consider some real-world consequences of the development of size perception. For the most part, objects are arranged at varying distances, and so size judgments are also judgments of distance. Therefore, even more fundamental than judging relative size between objects, is the capacity of the perceptual system to *adjust size estimates in relation to distance.* In Chapter 2 you learned that one of the early stabilising effects of the perceived world is size constancy – the ability to recognise that an object remains the same despite changes in retinal size as it looms or recedes in three-dimensional space. Studies on size constancy with older children and adults typically require the participants to *judge the actual size* of the stimulus. In studies carried out in the 1960s, the typical technique was to present circles presented at varying distances from the observer for comparison against a standard that was at a different distance (usually much farther away). During successive comparisons of each circle against the standard, viewed through a small viewing window, the participant had to make a judgment as to which was the bigger of the two, until a point was reached when the perceiver thought the stimuli were the same actual size. The judgment therefore depended on adjustments made for size constancy. Although there were not many of these sorts of studies carried out with children, it was nevertheless clear that quite large developmental effects were to be found. Changes towards increasing constancy were first noted in a study carried out by Brislin and Leibowitz (1970) and now, over three decades later, the evidence remains the same. In a study by Granrud and Schmechel (2006), children had to make comparisons in much the same way as in the Breslin and Leibowitz study, and as Figure B, Panel 10.3 shows, there was a strong tendency to choose a comparison object that was actually smaller than the more distant standard, thus underestimating its size, or over-estimating its distance. Even when all the comparison stimuli were placed in such a way that they had equivalent retinal sizes to one another, once again, a clear developmental trend was found and younger children still showed **under-constancy**, i.e. they tended to choose a stimulus that was smaller in real size than the true 'match' to the distant standard. So if children actually perceive differently in these tasks – what does that mean? Specifically, if they are not adjusting adequately for distance, do they perceive distance itself less accurately? We review this next.

10.4 CUES FOR ESTIMATING DISTANCE

What might children be learning about the cues for distance itself? Think about this for a moment in relation to what you learned about the infant's perception of depth and distance. Weren't some cues being used from early infancy? Interposition seems to be used from about 2 months as shown by the visual habituation techniques using occluded objects. This cue really only sorts out 'in front of' from 'behind', however. What about relative distance estimations? You may recall that motion parallax – the relative displacement of objects at different distances as you move your head – is an extremely powerful cue that also appears to be utilised almost from birth. But what if there is no opportunity to move your head? A study by Yonas and Hagen (1973) investigated this. Children aged 3 and 7 years and adults had to make size comparisons of items placed at varying distances within real three-dimensional scenes. The participants were either allowed to move their heads to obtain parallax information or were required to keep their heads in a fixed position. As you can see from Figure A, Panel 10.4, when the equally sized comparison object had a retinal size that was 70% of the target (because of increased distance), then 3 year olds succeeded well but only when motion parallax was available.

As you can also see from the figure, however, 7 year olds also performed reasonably well when motion parallax was absent, and adults did well in all conditions. It seems that size constancy improves because children learn to use *additional* cues for distance that can be used when motion parallax is not available. These must have been monocular cues in the Yonas and Hagen study, moreover, as all participants had one eye covered with a patch. In doing this, another normally available cue was eliminated. This is **binocular convergence** (the sensory feedback on how much the eyes have to converge in order to focus) and as it is yet another cue for distance, Yonas and Hagen may have had somewhat improved results under binocular viewing conditions. However, the actual accuracy levels are not what is important here, as these also vary as a function of other things such as the distance between the objects. They key thing is the fact that judgments of relative size in the absence of normal binocular viewing conditions undergo large improvements during development apparently due to increasing use of monocular cues for distance. So what might these be?

Remember the scene from a moving train considered in Chapter 2 in relation to motion parallax. Now think about the train stopping. Your head is still, resting on the window ledge and you are looking out. What gives you a strong impression of distance? It is not just that distant objects (like cows) appear smaller than nearer ones, it is that the more distant scene is somehow compressed, less grainy and features like leaves on trees are harder to detect. This is called **texture gradient**. The texture is also composed of patterns of lines created by things like hedges and roads, which **converge** in relation to distance, producing the effect known as **linear perspective**. In an early study looking at distance judgments in photographic scenes, Wohlwill (1965) found that children from the age of 6 were good at using converging lines to judge distance, though there was a tendency again towards under-constancy. Later, Rosinski (1976) created scenes where they manipulated the nature of these textural cues by projecting stripes over a

Panel 10.4 Cues for estimating distance

- Some cues for distance perception such as interposition are acquired very early (see Chapter 2); others are acquired slowly during childhood
- Size constancy is enabled from early infancy because of one very primitive ability to judge distance
  - This is based on motion parallax created by lateral head movements
- *Texture gradient* is compression of detail with distance
  - It is a *monocular* cue and does not require head movements
    - It takes some time to be used effectively on its own

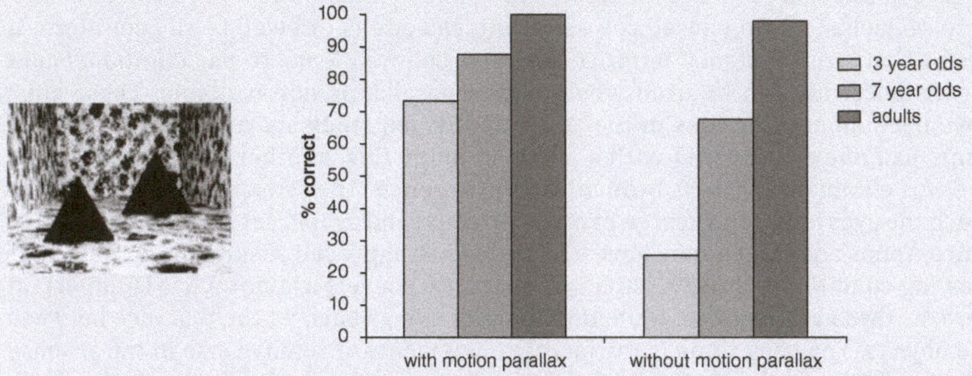

A When head movements are disallowed and only texture gradient is provided, preschool children lose the ability to see that the nearer object is smaller (by 30%) than the more distant object. (Adapted from Yonas & Hagen, 1973, with permission)

- Another textural cue for distance is the *convergence* of parallel horizontal or vertical lines
  - Children seem to be more sensitive to convergence (*linear perspective*) than horizontal compression as measured by a slant judgment task

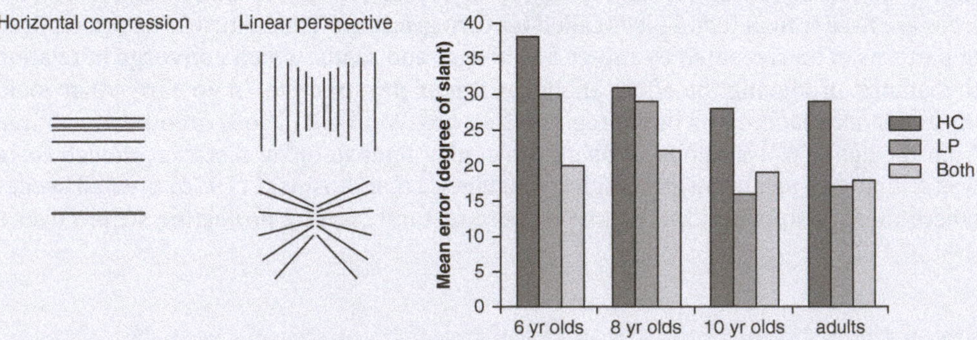

B Children's accuracy in judging degree of slant of a textured surface shows greatest errors when the converging lines are horizontal. (Adapted from Rosinski & Levine, 1976, with permission)

light source. In their simulation, the stripes were presented horizontally with increased compression of the lines (HC). In another, they were presented vertically to create linear perspective (LP), and in another, the lines were horizontal and vertical crossed, thus creating a pattern, which in addition to compression and perspective also altered the density of the squares. These patterns were tilted to create a slanted image and the participant's task was to match the degree of slant as measured by how they manually angled a palm board. This allowed the investigators to see which form of texture provided most information for the children. As Figure B, Panel 10.4 shows, the combined pattern provided most information and was not subject to any developmental change. Vertical slant (depicted using linear perspective) produced almost twice the amount of error in 6 and 8 year olds than in 10 year olds and adults, suggesting that there may be a learning effect for the use of linear perspective in normal everyday scenes. Horizontal slant produced the greatest error for all age groups, although there was some diminution between 6 and 8 years.

Connecting this study with the real world, these findings certainly make sense when you consider the difference between convergence of vertical lines (linear perspective) and the compression of horizontal lines, with increasing distance. The former is readily available in an architectured environment in which the vertical sides of railings and fences offer these cues in abundance and the sides of tops of buildings can be seen even if they are obscured lower down. Horizontal compression is more rare and only likely to be seen in special layouts like railway sleepers. Textured backgrounds with criss-crossing lines are going to be optimal and would also give the most informative background for judging distance. It is almost certainly the relative availability of these cues that explains the timing of their use by children. Overall then, texture through convergence is a monocular cue that takes some time to be acquired.

We have now seen that the use of cues for precise distance estimation, such as texture gradient and linear perspective, is subject to development during the school years, and that this might affect size judgments of remote objects. This raises a question about potentially dangerous real-world situations where both of these have to be calculated fairly precisely in order to judge speed of approach – and, in particular, the speed of an oncoming car. We shall consider this next.

10.5 VELOCITY ESTIMATION IN THE REAL WORLD

There is probably no more important issue in relation to velocity judgments than whether or not they can be made sufficiently accurately to enable safe road crossing by children. British traffic statistics suggest that around 3000 children between the ages of 5 and 12 years are killed each year in road accidents, most of them whilst attempting to cross the road between oncoming cars. The research on this has concentrated in the main on the key behaviours – do children start to cross at the right time when a gap appears in the traffic and do they proceed to cross at the necessary rate? The short answer to this is no, they do not. Younger children start crossing later than adults, though quite why they do so is still not clear (te Velde et al., 2008). Part of the answer may lie in their motion initiation and action self-monitoring, and in that sense may lie with the development of fine-tuned motor skills (applying also to things like ball-catching). However, given that some aspects of depth perception clearly develop, could it be that learning how to judge a 'safe' gap between moving cars is also implicated in learning how to start crossing at the right time?

Panel 10.5 Velocity estimation in the real world

- A disproportionately high number of children are killed every year in road crossing accidents
- There are various reasons for this and one is inaccurate perception of speed between moving vehicles
- Relative distance judgements are not enough in this scenario
    - Estimating time from point A to point B is crucial in estimating speed
- Simulation of relative speed of moving objects shows that children under 10 years do not use time to accurately predict the 'time to arrival'
    - They base their judgments more on distance travelled

Children under 10 years of age predict the arrival time of a slowly moving light more by the distance it has to travel than by calculating how far it has travelled over a certain time. (After Benguini et al., 2008)

To estimate speed of approach, there has to be a calculation of distance travelled relative to time taken, i.e. the decreasing distance of the oncoming car over time. The distance part of this equation should be relatively easy in a real-world situation like road crossing. Although children can utilise monocular cues such as texture gradient for distance, in a road crossing scenario, distance at each point in time would be strongly signalled by the changing retinal size of the vehicle relative to other objects, making other cues less important. And the actual known size of objects like cars and trucks relative to other known objects like houses and lamp-posts makes retinal size easy to interpret. All the more anomalous then that children still make fatal errors in judging when to cross.

A study by Benguigui et al. (2008) has helped identify one reason behind this. In their study, Benguini et al. devised a task in which children had to predict the expected arrival time of a stimulus moving towards a target. The trajectory was simulated by a red LED, which was rapidly switched to give the impression of motion. However, the apparent movement of the stimulus was actually occluded before it reached the target, as illustrated in the diagram in Panel 10.5, and children had to press a button when they thought it would be colliding with the target. They reasoned that the typically slow reaction by younger children to an oncoming stimulus, such as a car, might be due to their making an average judgment of velocity based on distance rather than a precise estimate based on time information. Specifically, it is argued, the younger child uses a fixed distance from the target as a basis for estimating time to arrival. That is, it is based on the distance at which *on average* the car will take a further, say 2 seconds, to be level with the child. The more precise alternative is to calculate the velocity based on time information from sampling visual changes *within* a particular moving trajectory. So, if younger children do not calculate this accurately each time, then they may be (fatally) slow to react when the stimulus is moving faster than average. The test of this is that the child's estimation of time to arrival will be related to the length of the *distance* occluded in the study rather than the length of *time* during which the stimulus was occluded. The investigators found that it was only from 10 years onwards that time information rather than distance became a significant predictor of their children's estimates and that these became accordingly more precise. This goes some way to explaining why the accident statistics continue to show an increase even after 10 years of age. However, the basic visual aspects of road-crossing skills are still relatively under-researched (but see Thomson, 2007 for important new directions).

THE DEVELOPMENT OF FORM PERCEPTION

If changes can occur to the way a child perceives space and distance, then are there any changes in the way they see other aspects the world? This does in fact seem true in regard to what we would call **form perception**, that is the shape or contour of an object. Normally integral with three-dimensional and tactile information, shape and contour are sometimes the only things that signal the identity of an object. This is true of objects at a distance, of two-dimensional depictions of objects, and of objects that are two-dimensional by nature such as handwriting or cartoons. Children need to develop perceptual expertise in all these areas and you may be surprised by some of the things that young children *don't* see. We shall also consider what it means to develop perceptual expertise.

LEARNING LANDMARKS

10.6 Perceptual learning through feature differentiation. You should be able to name a very influential pioneer in the study of perceptual learning and be able to describe her study on letter-like forms.

10.7 Perceptual readiness. You should know who coined this phrase and be able to briefly describe what it means, with at least one example of how 'readiness' based on past experience can enhance encoding of objects in the world.

10.8 Contour integration and brain development. You should know what the Kanizsa illusion is and be able to cite a study showing that even this apparently simple act of perception is subject to development and learning.

10.6 PERCEPTUAL LEARNING THROUGH FEATURE DIFFERENTIATION

A famous pioneer in the area of perceptual learning was Eleanor Gibson from Cornell University. Eleanor Gibson is the 'Gibson' in the famous visual cliff studies with Richard

Walk, but her research also focussed on object perception. She was interested in particular in what develops during childhood in the way children learn important discriminations that are crucial for reading and writing. Her approach to this was based on a concept known as **perceptual differentiation**.

A typical perceptual differentiation study is the one reported first in 1955 (Gibson & Gibson, 1955) – and also Gibson (1991: 300–4). The stimuli were meaningless scribbles. A target stimulus was to be identified from a set of other scribbles, which were constructed according to systematic variations of the target in terms of elongation, orientation, and number of whorls, as depicted in Figure A, Panel 10.6. There were 18 such variations in all. Four targets cards were shown to the participants for five seconds and then mixed with distracter cards in a pack and the participants were simply asked to indicate when they saw the targets. This was repeated until the four correct identifications were made. Older participants made fewer errors on the first trial, as Figure A shows, and they also learned to make the differentiation in the time available, whilst almost none of the youngest group of children did so. This was not a simple failure to comply with the task; the children's data were meaningfully related to the number of differences between the target stimulus and the distracters. The smaller the difference, the harder it was to learn to identify the target.

Another of Gibson's classic studies (Gibson et al., 1962) shows that differentiation is not simply about detection – it is about the relevance of the feature being detected. Once again, the stimuli were rather basic graphic symbols. However, this time they were chosen to be like written letters – an area of perceptual learning that is clearly relevant to the acquisition of reading. Twelve 'letter-like' symbols were used and these were transformed by one of several ways to produce variations. One transformation was to make a break or a close in the symbol; another was to alter the lines to curves; another was to change the orientation by rotation or reversal; and another was to make a perspective transformation – achieved by drawing the symbol as if it was being 'tilted' backwards in space. The participants were children aged between 4 and 8 years and their task was to pick an item from an array (displayed on something like a scrabble board) that was 'exactly the same' as the target displayed above the array. Errors were measured by the number of times a non-identical symbol was picked as the match for a target.

Once again, there were very large age differences as Figure B, Panel 10.6 shows. What was particularly interesting, however, was that there was an enormous effect caused by the *type* of transformation used. If we go through some of these, we can see that this makes sense in view of the fact that these were like letters, and that children were learning to read over the age range studied. Very little learning was required to be sensitive to the line to break change – this is of course a transformation that

Panel 10.6 Perceptual learning through feature differentiation

- Young children can be poor at spontaneous encoding of *feature variation*

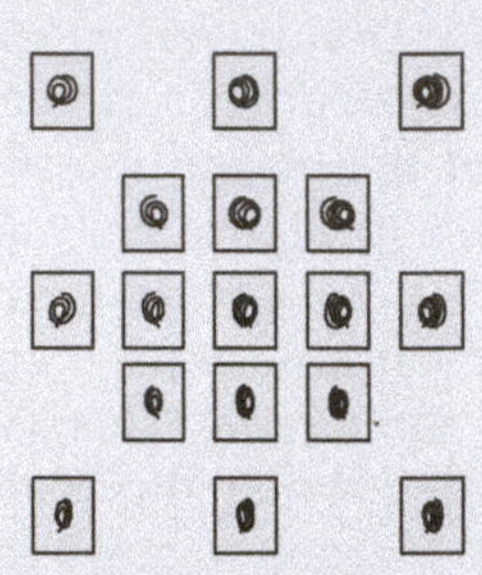

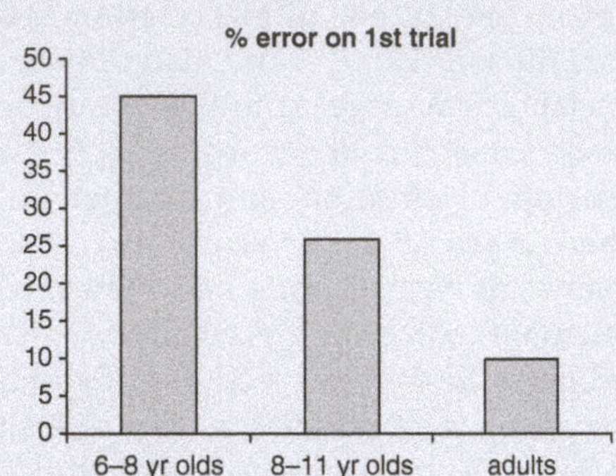

A Errors made when asked to find the exact match to the three targets in the top row (Stimuli and data from Gibson & Gibson, 1955)

- They also have to learn which sorts of featural transformation are important for categorisation
    - And those which simply specify a legitimate change in appearance
- Reading provides a good example as some changes are crucial for letter identification
    - Such as a reversal of *orientation*
        - e.g. b versus d
    - ..or a *break or close*
        - e.g. C versus O
- '*Perspective*' transformations (slant) don't usually matter for these stimuli
    - e.g. letter versus *letter*
- Children show a large reduction in errors if they have to pick out an exact match from different types of transformation of a standard letter-like form

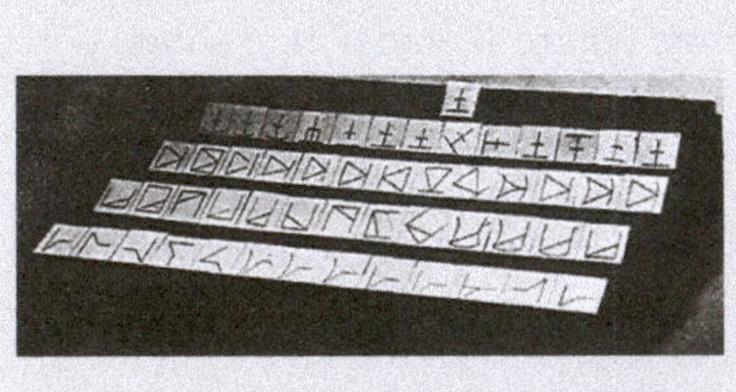

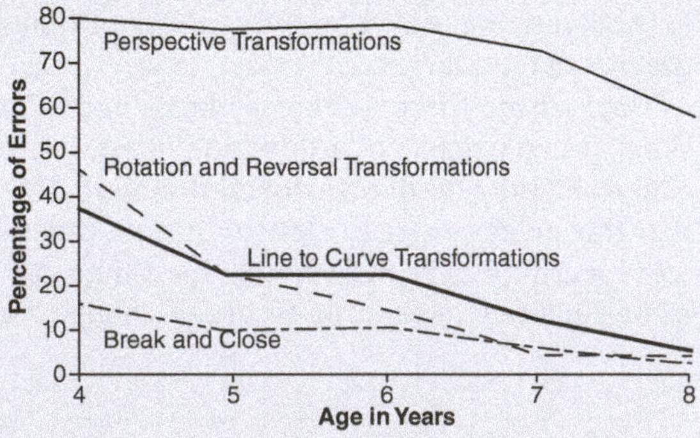

B When children were asked to choose an exact match to a letter-like target, they made fewer errors as a function of age, with greatest learning shown for the types of transformation that are important for letters (Stimuli and graph from Gibson et al., 1962)

- In other circumstances, rotations and reversals don't alter identity

may not alter a rough sketch or drawing, but in the case of written symbols it makes a huge difference to identity. Compare an E with an L, or a V with a W, for example. The lines of a symbol don't just suggest it identity – they *are* its identity. In the case of real-world (non-graphic) stimuli, furthermore, an obvious break or close can also alter shape very dramatically – closed contours are what define the shape of an object. Being sensitive to this transformation both for real-world objects, as well as symbols, could explain its early acquisition. To go to the other extreme, perspective transformations never suggest a change in an object's identity – they simply denote a different viewing angle. It is not surprising therefore that this transformation was not readily used by any age group to determine precise similarity. Somewhere in the middle, and subject to considerable development over the age at which children were learning to read, were the orientational changes. This is an interesting one because, like perspective, orientation does not usually alter an object's identity. An important exception is symbols – compare d with b, for example. It is possible that Gibson's study was picking up the age at which children are learning to attend to this dimension for letters. Line to curve transformations also showed that difficulty decreased considerably between the age of 4 and 8 years. Of Gibson et al's findings, this is a harder one to interpret. On the one hand, variations in curvature are part of the normal variation in handwriting and even a change of case by the same writer will produce such a variation, so we might expect that we learn to ignore it. But such changes can be noted, even if they are discounted as altering the letter's identity – and it may be that 8 year olds get more precise in their definition of what constitutes 'the same' as they become more experienced with handwriting. You may also have noted that there is an ambiguity in any case arising from what is meant by 'the same', which could also explain the poor first trial performance in the Gibson and Gibson (1955) study and the large number of errors for the perspective change. Does this mean the same object or the same depiction of the object? A perspective transformation, for example, could be the same object but a different depiction of it. But although this study leaves some questions unanswered, Gibson's pioneering work on children's encoding of object features has been supported by various avenues of subsequent research, as we review next.

10.7 PERCEPTUAL READINESS

At the time that Gibson was writing, there was a sea change in the way psychologists viewed learning. Around that time, psychology was abandoning classical learning theory as an explanation of children's development, and along with it, the idea that the human perceiver is a passive recipient of information. The new thinking was very elegantly expressed in a seminal article by the famous psychologist, Jerome Bruner (1957). The article was called 'On perceptual readiness' and it essentially suggests that our 'readiness' to see things in the world is because we increasingly supplement sensory information by past knowledge, and in that sense 'enrich' our perceptions. This is interestingly different from Eleanor Gibson's theory, which implies that we become more attuned to the sensory input by simply learning to make appropriate differentiations (rather more in line with a classical learning approach). Nowadays these positions can be reconciled somewhat, as you will see.

So what is 'readiness'? A simple example given by Bruner is the following: adults are presented with **tachistoscopic** (or very short) exposures of nonsense words that vary in terms of their approximation to English. Where the approximation level is zero (e.g. YRULPZOC), participants are only half as good at remembering the letters and the place in the sequence as when the approximation is at level 4 (e.g. VERNALIT). Clearly knowledge of English and how consonants and vowels are distributed allows the reader to be more 'ready' for the more word-like versions and thus they are encoded and remembered better. You may feel that this is not really about the visual world so much as a convention for spelling (in English at least). But a very similar principle of 'readiness' seems to apply to everyday objects. In a classic study by Eugene Gollin of Colorado University, children aged between 2½ and 5½ years – and adults – were shown line drawings of a number of familiar things such as an elephant or an umbrella (Gollin, 1960). However, the line drawings were systematically 'degraded', that is, they varied in terms of the amount of contour and internal detail as shown in Panel 10.7. The least recognisable (most degraded) version of a given object was presented first, followed by the next most degraded and so on. Participants were given a score based on the level required for correct naming of the picture, and so a low score indicated better recognition of an incomplete drawing. Recognition improved with age, and the adults and oldest children were significantly better than the younger ones.

Panel 10.7 Perceptual readiness

- Visual perception is very much to do with 'filling in' from previous experience
- The famous *Gollin test* gives children degraded pictures of well-known objects
    - The picture is completed by degrees to find the cut-off at which children can recognise the object
- There is a huge developmental change in the degree of completion required

 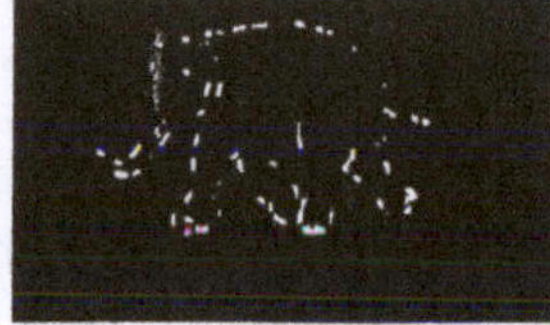 

- Being due to learning and experience in the first place, this effect is subject to practice effects

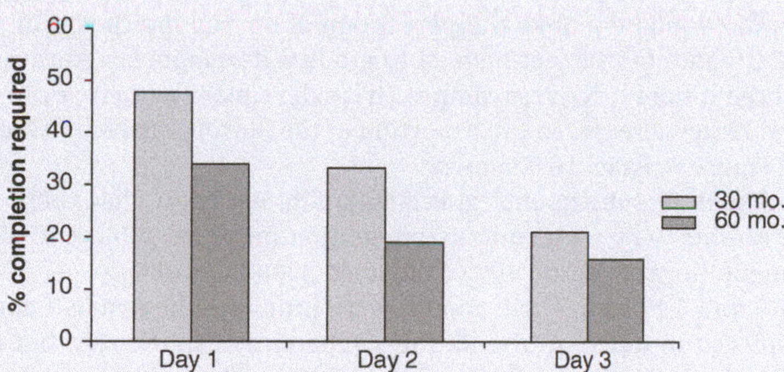

The percentage of completed picture required for 2½ versus 5 year olds to recognise it and the practice effects across three days (Data and images adapted from Foreman & Hemmings, 1987, with permission from Pion, Ltd. London)

The Gollin test has since been computerised by Foreman and Hemmings (1987) and, as the graph in Panel 10.7 shows, still reveals considerable age differences in preschool children. These investigators directly tested the hypothesis that this sort of perception is highly subject to learning and experience and thus re-tested their participants over three days. Comparing the first with the last day, you can see a big reduction in the percentage of completed drawing required for recognition. Most recently, different types of degradation have been compared showing that greatest difficulty occurs when the contour is broken up or cropped, rather than simply blurred (Bernstein et al., 2005), and we shall see shortly why this might be so.

10.8 CONTOUR INTEGRATION AND BRAIN DEVELOPMENT

Let us go back to the simple line drawings used by Gollin. This study demonstrated the dramatic effect of stimulus degradation on children using a few simple lines. Further support for the idea that there is a fundamental sense in which younger children are not 'ready' to see objects from line fragments using **contour integration** is illustrated by the **Kanizsa illusion** depicted in Panel 10.8. You and I 'see' a triangle because we integrate the contours of the broken circles in what the Gestaltists believed to be our innate attempt to simplify the world into complete objects (see Chapter 2, Section 2.8). In this example, the same tendency to 'complete' obscured objects is at work, but this time the geometrical configuration of the incomplete shapes is now creating a powerful impression of a triangle sitting over three 'whole' circles. There are several competing theories about why we integrate the contours of the broken circles as if they form the contour of a larger shape in this illusion. Whatever the reason for it, this tendency does not seem to be innate (unlike the perception of normal interposition – see Chapter 2, Section 2.3), and it is subject instead to gradual development. Abravanel (1982) presented three different Kanizsa shapes (triangle, square and circle) to young children and found large increases in the reporting of the illusory shape between 3 and 5 years of age as Figure A, Panel 10.8 shows.

Now, thanks to subsequent experimentation, we know that there are neurophysiological reasons why such contour integration might be subject to slow growth and development. Kovács et al. (1999) conducted a study involving over 500 children aged between 5 and 14 years. Their stimuli were little lines known as Gabor signals. They were displayed in different orientations, apparently haphazardly, but actually in such a way as to form the broken contour of a shape such as a circle as shown in Figure B, Panel 10.8. These segments were presented against a background of 'noise', i.e. other little lines that did not cohere in this way.

The stimuli were very carefully chosen to correspond to cells in the primary visual cortex that are known to detect orientation. Because of the 'noise', the input has to be received by these local cells, which are themselves indifferent to patterns across the signals. Connecting them together in terms of the overall contour

Panel 10.8 Contour integration and brain development

- The *Kanisza illusion* makes us 'see' an non-existent triangle and three whole circles arranged behind it
- The illusion is much weaker for children

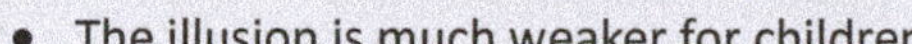

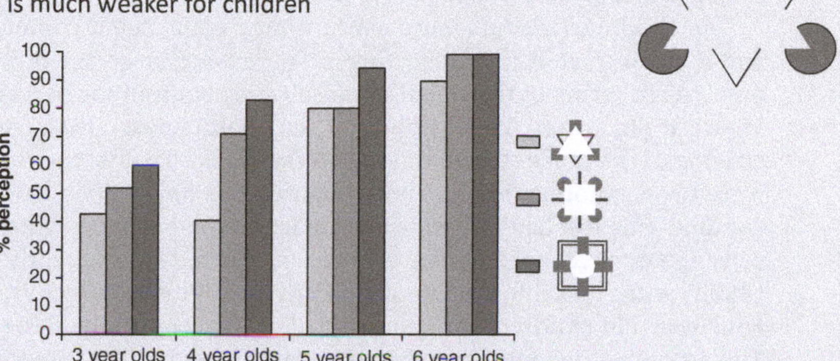

A Changes in the preschooler's ability to perceive the illusory Kanisza figures (Adapted from Abravanel, 1982, with permission)

  - This can be interpreted as showing underdeveloped neural circuitry for integrating across different parts of a figure
- In *contour integration* tests, linear segments are aligned to form a circle within background noise
  - Younger children have a higher threshold for seeing the circle
  - They need reduced noise in order to see the continuity across the segments

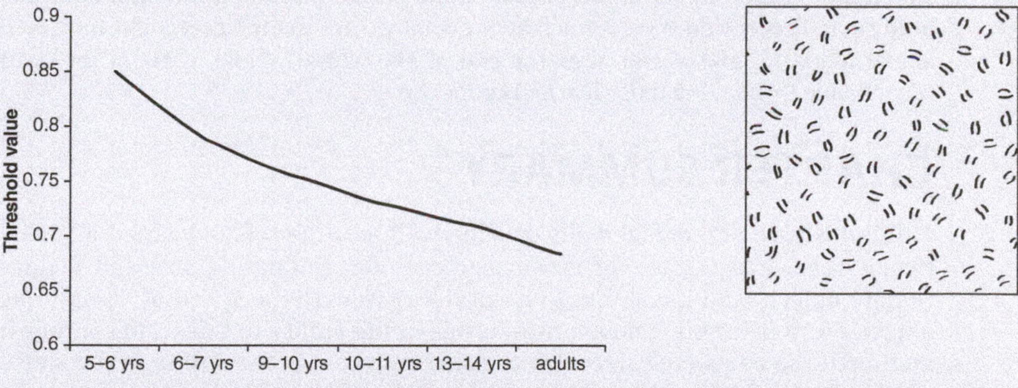

B Reduction in the signal to noise threshold for contour integration as a function of age (Adapted from Kovács et al., 1999)

- Whilst the segments are precisely matched to orientation cells in the visual cortex, it is thought that longer range connections are required to integrate them across the background 'noise'
- Children can learn to see the circles with exposure and practice

suggested by their orientation has to be done in terms of **long-range interactions**; that is, in terms of a more complex mechanism than that supplied by the primary orientation receptor cells themselves. Also occurring as part of ventral stream visual development – specifically the making of new horizontal connections in the visual cortex – it was surmised that these longer-range neural connections were immature at 5 years of age.

The child participants were asked if they could see a contour within the pattern and if so, to trace it with their finger. There were large age differences from 5 years onwards in terms of the signal to noise ratio required for perception of a contour as Figure B illustrates. The visibility of the contour was also varied by increasing the spacing of the noise stimuli relative to the signal. That is, the closer the contour lines were to one another and the more separate the 'noise' lines, the more perceptible the contour. This too had a significant impact on the extent to which children could perceive the circle. A very similar effect was reported subsequently by Káldy and Kovács (2003) with regard to the famous Ebbinghaus illusion, which is shown in Panel 10.1. Four-year-old children were almost half as likely as adults to be subject this illusion. The authors conclude again that the neural circuits that integrate all the contextual information are immature in the younger child, in this particular instance actually producing a more accurate perception.

So what are the reasons for increasing susceptibility to certain illusions and an increasing readiness to 'fill in' incomplete percepts? It might appear from Kovacs' work that the answer is simply to be found in the maturation of the brain. But an equally important finding from the study by Kovács et al (1999) is that the children could *learn* to see the contours. Comparing 5–6 year olds with adults, the authors found that with repeated practice across three days, there was a dramatic lowering of the threshold at which the children (in particular) could detect the contours. So Bruner and Gibson were both right. Perception is very much about what we are ready to see – but this readiness is learned. And now, newer research is now showing us which parts of the brain are responsible for making those learned connections.

CHAPTER SUMMARY

Children's core perceptual skills develop well into the school years. This is in particular regard to the use of monocular cues for estimating size and distance of remote objects and the ability to accurately estimate the speed of an approaching object. Form perception develops in terms of the ability to integrate contour information at the neurological level with consequences for the ability to recognise line drawings and to become subject to certain illusions. All of these are susceptible to learning and experience.

LOOKING AHEAD TO CHAPTER 11

We have seen how perceptual learning can be captured in laboratory situations. But what does it tell us about perceptual learning in general? We do not live in an illusory, degraded or highly fractured world, nor do we normally have to detect contours where none are present, so these may simply be highly unusual cases of perceptual learning. This does not seem to be the case at all, however, as will be elaborated in the next chapter.

CHAPTER 11

PERCEPTUAL DEVELOPMENT AND RECOGNITION MEMORY

In the last chapter, you saw that children learn to make new and more finely tuned discriminations as their perceptions become enriched by past experience. In this chapter, we shall consider how this happens, and its consequences for how important aspects of the world are perceived and remembered.

VISUAL SEARCH AND ACTIVE INTERROGATION

LEARNING LANDMARKS

11.1 Measuring eye movements. You should know how eye movements are measured, and how these change across the school years. You should know which psychologists pioneered the use of eye movements and what they found.

11.2 Visual search and difference detection. You should be able to cite a study showing how poorer difference detection of pictures is related to less efficient scanning.

11.1 MEASURING EYE MOVEMENTS

If perceptual learning is an active process of identifying and processing relevant features of the input, then can we specify exactly what this activity *is*? To answer this, we need a technique that looks at what children look at when they view perceptual stimuli.

Although eye-movement recording with children is rarer than you might think, its use nevertheless extends back to the 1960s. In an early study using photography to record these kinds of normal eye movements, White and Plum (1964) presented children between the ages of 3½ and 5 years with a set of photographic slides of slightly different stick figures, in pairs in a touch-sensitive window. The task was simply to learn the correct stimulus in each pair and to press the corresponding window. A camera recorded eye position three times per second. The children learned to make the discriminations with practice, but this was one of the earliest studies to show that the learning was accompanied by an increase in the number of eye movements on each trial.

Panel 11.1 Measuring eye movements

- Visual scenes are viewed via eye-movements known as *saccades*
  - Pro-saccades are guided externally – such as looking at a fixation point
    - They are useful for looking at oculomotor control
- Saccades can be measured in terms of:
  - latency (time to initiate the saccade)
  - duration (in ms)
  - size or amplitude (degree of visual arc)
  - speed or peak velocity (degrees of arcs per second)
- The most consistent source of oculomotor development persisting into adolescence is a reduction in latency
  - This is usually interpreted as becoming faster at attention switching
- Eye-movement patterns can be plotted through eye-tracking devices
  - Soviet psychologists found that younger children showed *inefficient scanning* of abstract shapes

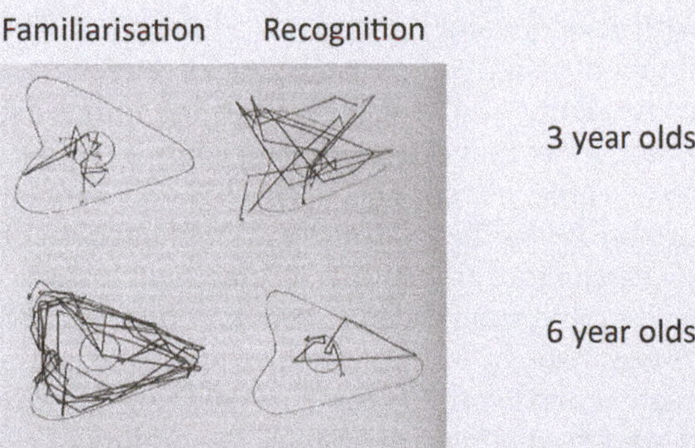

The difference in scanning patterns of 3 versus 6 year olds during study and recognition of shapes. (Adapted from Zinchenko et al, 1962 and reproduced with permission from Vurpillot, 1968)

Is this simply a matter of improved and faster motor control? Since this early study, eye-movement recording has become much more sophisticated and we can be clearer about the answer to this. First of all, let us clarify what is meant by eye movements.

Saccades

These are the muscle-controlled movements of the eye that bring an object into foveal vision. Internally generated (or unguided) saccades are produced when a participant is trying to predict where a target will appear, examine a complex figure or scene, or simply look to a remembered target location. **Prosaccades** occur when the participant has been specifically instructed to look from a central fixation point towards a particular target, such as an object appearing on a computer screen. In normal viewing conditions this means disengaging attention from one part of the visual field to look at another, and is a good measure of voluntary oculomotor control. **Anti-saccades** are another example of guided saccades generated by asking the participant to actually look in the opposite direction from a visible target. All saccades have a measurable **latency** (the time to initiate the saccade); **duration** – normally somewhere between 30 and 120 milliseconds; size or **amplitude** – measured in degrees of visual arc; and speed known as **peak velocity** – normally somewhere between 200 and 400 degrees of arc per second. Saccades are probably best considered for our purposes, however, in terms of the kind of patterns or **trajectories** produced when images are viewed over a period of seconds. In the 1930s and 1940s, corneal reflections were used to record the trajectory of eye movements during picture perception. A more accurate method using a kind of contact lens was pioneered by the Soviet biophysicist Alfred Yarbus in the 1960s, and nowadays such data are based on computerised records of video images using sophisticated eye-tracking devices that can be fixed to the head or even simply positioned in front of the observer.

All these measurements give us some idea of developments in basic oculomotor control. The general finding from studies of saccadic eye movements in children is that the peak velocity and duration of saccades matures relatively early. Whilst this suggests a biological maturing of eye-movement control (and it has been suggested it is related to increased neural myelination), the latency of prosaccades and anti-saccades is often found to decrease with development right up into adolescence. This is accompanied by a reduction in the number of visual comparison errors between the ages of 5–8 and adulthood, showing improvements in disengaging from the initial fixation stimulus. These findings, taken together, show that eye-movement control is subject to developments in voluntary attention switching, not simply improved motor control of the eyes.

This research therefore raises the question of what (if not better eye-movement control *per se*) makes visual search more efficient? Is it something to do with familiarity with the objects being viewed? A rather remarkable attempt to tie together object encoding skills with eye movements was made by a Soviet group of psychologists in the 1960s, in particular Alexander Zaporozhets and Pyotr Zinchenko. What this group discovered first of all was that children would start to voluntarily eye-track the outline of a novel shape at around the age of 5 and that this was associated with better shape discrimination (Zinchenko et al., 1962; Zaporozhets, 2002). An example is given in Panel 11.1. From this you can see that far more systematic tracking was carried out during familiarisation by 6 year olds as compared with 3 year olds. What you can also see is how the older children showed much greater economy in their eye movements giving a clear reason as to why children may become faster at recognition.

So is better tracking causing the better discrimination, or is it that better object knowledge ('readiness') causes better tracking? The Soviet group were also behind a rare attempt to get at this chicken and egg question. One of their team, a lady by the name of Boguslavskaia, tried what was described as a 'forced itinerary' for eye movements – essentially getting children to watch whilst she outlined an object on a blackboard. This passive form of learning did not improve the subsequent recognition of the object, however. The Soviet psychologists concluded that some other form of activity was contributing to the perception of the object, which in turn enabled active tracking and improved recognition of it. This other form of activity was thought to be exploration of the object through touch. This idea became known as the 'touch teaches vision' approach to perceptual development. However, when it comes to things like elephants and human faces, this is perhaps a bit implausible, and returns us to the question of how the developments in visual search (alone) are specifically implicated in perceptual development.

11.2 VISUAL SEARCH AND DIFFERENCE DETECTION

Further development of this important area on this came from French psychologist, Eliane Vurpillot at the University of Rene Descartes in Paris. In a now famous study (Vurpillot, 1968) she asked children to detect differences between pictures of houses with curtained windows, as shown in Panel 11.2. This is very much like the kind of game found on the back of cereal packets today. Vurpillot found age-related improvements in the detection of changes and deletions to pictures of windows. But to this data, she was able to add information on the changes in economy and systematicity of eye tracking across age groups. The ideal way to compare these houses is shown in Panel 11.2, as it systematically compares all windows with their counterparts, but with the least possible total movement of the eyes. Vurpillot showed that there is considerable development up to 8 years of age before this pattern of scanning predominates. Before that, children move from being incomplete and haphazard in checking the windows to more thorough comparisons involving horizontal eye tracking back and forth. The bar graph in Panel 11.2 shows the increase in the number of children at different ages making these sorts of eye movements in relation to their accuracy. If it has occurred to you that these scanning patterns could be induced by the development of reading strategies, then well done. This was a possibility also noted by Vurpillot. However, the fact still remains that more comprehensive and efficient scanning leads to better object differentiation. As Vurpillot (1976) puts it: 'the poverty or extensiveness of this exploration has its effect on cognitive activity since it is by such means that it is provided with the substance of its activity' (p. 276) – where by 'substance' she means the resulting percept.

Panel 11.2 Visual search and difference detection

- Efficiency of visual scanning can be measured in same/difference tasks

Children are asked to look for differences between the houses. The scan path with maximum adequacy and efficiency for difference detection is shown on the right.

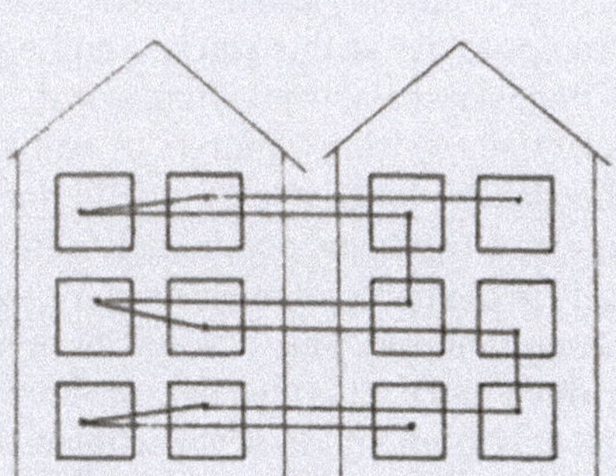

The % of children showing this type of path (bar graph) is related to their ability to detect small differences between the pictures (line graph). (Stimuli, diagram and data from Vurpillot, 1968; 1972, with permission)

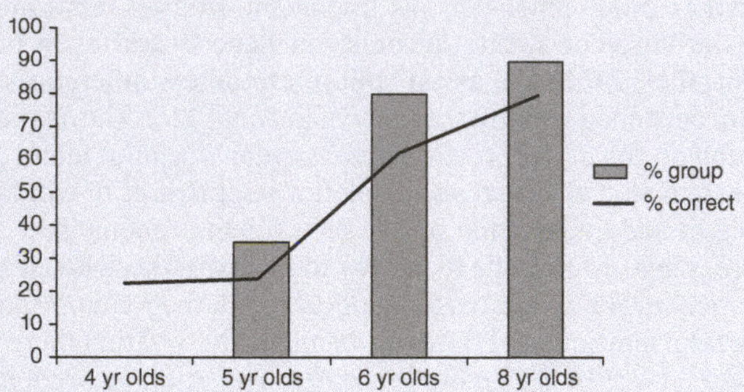

- Younger children show incomplete or haphazard searches
- The most efficient search is one which is systematic but with fewest total fixations

This returns us to the interesting question of what learning confers on perception. That is, whether learning actually enriches our percepts by bringing past experience to bear on what is being currently viewed ('going beyond the information given') - or whether information 'pickup' simply becomes sharper and better tuned (the Bruner/ Gibson debate). Perhaps you can see now that these are different sides of the same coin. As children get better at knowing where to look next on the basis of past experience, they get faster and more efficient at doing so, and their percepts are correspondingly deepened 'in the moment'.

IMPLICIT AND EXPLICIT ENCODING

You are not aware of your eye movements; you may even be surprised by your own saccades if you look into the camera on an iPad or other device. So are there aspects of our perceptual *encoding* of which we are not aware? As this section details, this is indeed the case, with consequences for what we mean by perceptual development.

LEARNING LANDMARKS

11.3 Implicit versus explicit learning. You should understand this distinction and how it can be tested through memory tests.

11.4 Implicit versus explicit face perception in children. You should be able to describe a study that contrasts implicit with explicit face awareness in children.

11.3 IMPLICIT VERSUS EXPLICIT LEARNING

When you recognise your friend's face in a theatre, you have a subjective awareness that you know this person, and others would know that you did because you could point her out and give her name. So when you can point out a particular individual as one you have seen before, then you have two important things. One is that your recognition memory is one you can consciously retrieve. The second is that it is expressible through both verbal and non-verbal behaviours such as naming and pointing. In both those senses, the recognition is **explicit**. So we should consider circumstances in which object perception is *not* explicit and what that means.

Implicit learning. Implicit learning is deemed to have taken place when there is evidence of memory retention but the individual has no conscious awareness of that memory. So, in the absence of naming and pointing, how do we know that such a thing exists? This has been discovered by varying the ways in which **recognition memory** can be elicited. Implicit memory tests with adults characteristically use **priming** techniques. In the case of word memory, a typical task would be to expose participants to

Panel 11.3 Implicit versus explicit learning

- Explicit memories are conscious and can be measured by overt recognition
  - e.g. 'That is an orange'
  - An explicit task might ask a participant to judge whether they had seen a face before
- But many perceptual processes are unconscious and this can be shown by *implicit awareness*
  - This is where there are effects of perceptual learning of which the perceiver is not aware
  - Implicit learning is also often measured using recognition tests
- An implicit task exposes participants to stimuli during a 'distracter' task such as reading a word superimposed on a face or deciding if it is 'famous'
  - This is known as *priming*
- The test of implicit learning would be an effect of learning for the primed stimuli
  - Such as an enhanced Evoked Reaction Potential when looking at the primed face
  - Or a faster RT during the recognition test
    - Even though the participant *does not remember having seen the stimuli*

brief durations of words flashed on a screen. An explicit memory task following this would be to ask the participant to recall the words they thought they had seen, whilst an implicit memory task would perhaps give them something like the 'Hangman' game. This is a game in which only some letters of a word are presented and the participant has to fill in the gaps with any word they please. For example, -a-d-n- could be completed by the words ' (e.g. 'gardens' or 'landing'). Implicit memory is detected when the participants are more likely use a word that they have been briefly exposed to (say, 'gardens'), but have not remembered that fact or been able to recall the word later.

Implicit versus explicit encoding has also been studied in the visual domain, and most often with faces as stimuli. It is much harder to make such a sharp empirical distinction between implicit and explicit memory in a face recognition study, as the participant cannot 'supply' a suggestion for an incomplete face in the way they can with a word. So, one method, using the priming technique, is to expose the participants to a number of briefly presented faces, whilst discouraging any explicit memory. This can be by telling them not to try to remember them – or by having a distracter task which focuses their attention on something else. This could be trying to read a word superimposed on the face

(Yingfang & Chunyan, 2006) or trying to detect 'well-known' faces from the presented set. Following the distracter task, a test set is presented including all the exposed faces together with some novel ones. In Yingfang and Chunyan's study (and others) the measure of implicit recognition memory was an increase in evoked reaction potentials (ERPs) for faces that are classed as 'unfamiliar' by the participant but which were in fact used in the priming phase. The test for implicit memory can also be based on reaction times to the novel versus exposed items. Even skin conductance measures can show unconscious recognition memory (Newcombe & Fox, 1994).

11.4 IMPLICIT VERSUS EXPLICIT FACE PERCEPTION IN CHILDREN

There is not a lot of information on implicit face recognition in children, but what there is suggests that it is explicit - not implicit - face recognition that develops. For example, in a series of studies, Crookes and McKone (2008) used an explicit memory task which was to judge how 'nice' the faces were - and also to remember the faces later. There was a significant effect on recognition for that the test faces were studied in this way beforehand (the primed stimuli) and this effect on explicit recognition memory increased with age. This was contrasted with an implicit condition that measured how accurately participants could identify whether or not a face was 'normal' or 'distorted' (as occurs with a distorting mirror) but there was no instruction to remember the faces. Participants of all ages were better at doing this for the pre-exposed faces but there were no age-related increases in the effect of priming on the accuracy of the judgments of 'normal' as the graph in Panel 11.4 shows. This demonstrates that it is not what children are able to implicitly process that undergoes major change in the school years, but rather how face-related information is stored in the explicit memory system.

The temptation is to conclude that it is this *implicit* recognition that occurs in infancy. You may remember that ERPs showed familiar/stranger discrimination from as young as 6 months - is this implicit memory only? The reason that this is very hard to answer is that conscious aware recognition in a 6 month old (whose cortex is not even fully developed) is unlikely to be similar to that of an older child. So face recognition may well be explicit in young infants but not in the way that it becomes explicit later. Certainly, some have argued that 10-month-old infants have the beginnings of an explicit memory system from the fact that they can remember an action for up to six months as measured by deferred imitation (Carver & Bauer, 2001).

You may also remember from Chapter 1 that it has been argued by Karmiloff-Smith (1995) that cognition can develop through a process of implicit knowledge (stored in the form of 'procedures') becoming explicit. Perhaps this can explain changes occurring after infancy? Much more likely is that two systems are as distinctly different in the infant as they are in the adult. There is no evidence to suggest that the scanning and configurational encoding involved in object and face perception become available to conscious access. And it would be highly inefficient if they did. The information taken in by the visual system during each and every saccade is responsible for resulting percepts but it is not stored consciously as a set of intentional eye-movements. The effects of perceptual learning likewise are not stored consciously as updated procedures for visual scanning.

Panel 11.4 Implicit versus explicit face perception in children

- An implicit face memory test can use pictures of classmates mixed in with pictures of unfamiliar children
  - The *distracter task* could be whether or not the child is smiling

- Children are then asked whether the face is familiar or not
  - They will be faster for primed faces irrespective of whether or not they are already familiar to the child
- Implicit memory does not develop over age during the school years
  - Explicit memory does

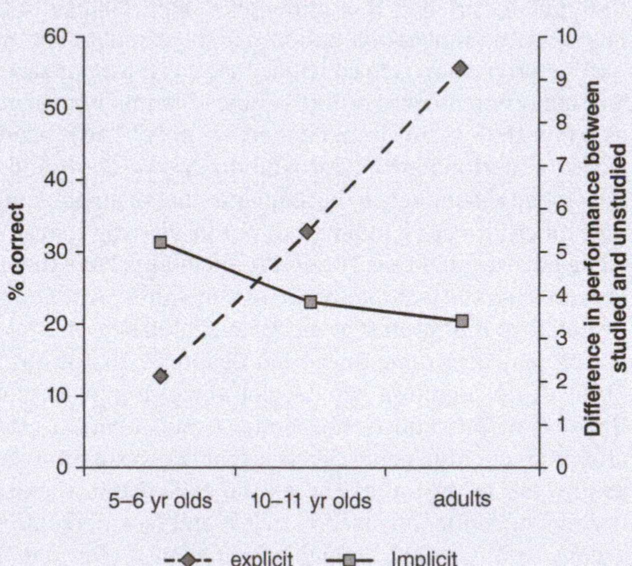

In a study where faces were primed in a 'niceness' rating, recognition memory for the studied items improves with age when participants had been explicitly told to remember the faces later (dotted line).

Priming improved performance on an implicit task with no instruction to remember (judging distortion), but this did not improve with age (solid line). This shows that it is explicit face memory – not face processing – that continues to improve. (Adapted from Crookes & McKone, 2009, with permission)

- Implicit face recognition mechanisms seem to be mature by the age of 5

But the resulting percepts can be stored in an explicit memory system, talked about and recalled in a variety of ways. It is this that we return to now to discover why that develops.

RECOGNITION ACCURACY

The fact that explicit face recognition improves during the school years is an important and significant fact, and perhaps a little over-shadowed in recent decades by the focus on the face perception skills of young infants. But for the explicit enduring memory of faces to become fully mature, there is still a long way for the child to go after infancy, as we see in this section. And, as we shall conclude, the developments in recognition accuracy are not confined to faces.

LEARNING LANDMARKS

11.5 The development of explicit face recognition. You should be familiar with the key findings from a seminal study on face recognition in children.

11.6 From piecemeal to holistic encoding in preschoolers. You should be able to describe at least one study with children that implies that their face perception is piecemeal rather than holistic. You should know why using inverted faces is relevant to this distinction.

11.7 Face recognition in eyewitness situations. You should be able to cite a study using witness identification techniques with young children and describe what was found.

11.8 Recognition accuracy for altered objects. You should be able to cite an example of a study using altered photographs that demonstrates developments in recognition accuracy for pictured objects.

11.5 THE DEVELOPMENT OF EXPLICIT FACE RECOGNITION

So explicit face recognition is about knowing that you have seen a face before and possibly even being able to identify whose face it is. Research on this topic has taken a lead from a seminal study carried out by Susan Carey and Rhea Diamond at MIT and published in *Science* (Carey & Diamond, 1977) (see also Diamond & Carey, 1977). Their participants were 6, 8 and 10 year olds. In one study, their task for participants was to view a photographed face, and to pick out the matching face from a choice of two. Carey and Diamond hypothesised that younger children might make the match on the basis of irrelevant cues such as the clothes being worn by the person in the photograph, or transient aspects such as facial expression. There were four versions of this task. In version 1, the correct match had the same facial expression as in the original but the incorrect match was now wearing the hat and clothes of the original (one type of irrelevant cue); in version 2, this also applied except that the incorrect match now had a different facial expression as well as the clothes and hat of the original. Facial expression is another irrelevant cue but, if used, might have helped to favour the correct match if having a different expression caused the incorrect match to be rejected. So, in the first two versions, the clothing and/or facial expression might be used as a false cue to identity. Although irrelevant to someone's identity, clothing is nevertheless less transient than facial expression, and the authors wondered if same/different expression would be more important than same/different clothing. Therefore, in version 3, the only irrelevant cue (but favouring the incorrect match) was facial expression (clothing did not vary at all), whilst in version 4, the incorrect match again had the same expression as the original but was now wearing different clothes.

The graphs in Panel 11.5 depict the main findings from this study. In the top one, you can see that there is a large improvement with age in being able to overcome the fact that the incorrect match has the same clothing as the person in the original photograph. When this distraction is removed but replaced with an expression distraction, all age groups show a marked improvement (though it was not significant for the higher-scoring group of 10 year olds). In the lower graph, we again see a marked increase in age when there is a clothing distraction with no help coming from the fact that the expression favoured a correct match, and finally, we see all age differences disappear under the easiest of all conditions (version 4) – when the clothing distraction now favoured the correct match even though expression did not. Taken together, this shows that of the two distracters, only clothing was a significant factor, and this resonates with the findings from infants that facial expression seems to be encoded from early on as part of the normal variation within a face. However, it also shows a very strong reliance on the extraneous cue of clothing – sometimes leading to false recognition.

Diamond and Carey (1977) went on to point out that children of this age do not use cues like clothing when it comes to faces that are familiar to them, but it suggested at the time that encoding and remembering new people in terms of the properties of their faces itself may not come readily to school-age children. Specifically, they proposed that children tend to use isolated features for encoding a new face, rather than a holistic or configurational analysis of the face. If you remember, the configurative properties of faces are the geometric relationships amongst the features. Being holistic means taking account of these internal features as well as face contour. Were they right to conclude this?

11.6 FROM PIECEMEAL TO HOLISTIC ENCODING IN PRESCHOOLERS

Possibly because Carey and Diamond used children from the age of 6 in their original study, much of the subsequent research has followed suit and we actually still know surprisingly little about developments in face perception between infancy and 6 years of age. But if they are correct, then we would expect that explicit face recognition by preschool-age children would be even less 'holistic' and more dependent on individual

Panel 11.5 The development of explicit face recognition

- Children's ability to consciously recognise novel photographed faces undergoes considerable development between 6 and 10 years of age
- Their encoding of a photographed person is heavily influenced by extraneous features such as hats and clothing
- They are not influenced by expression, however

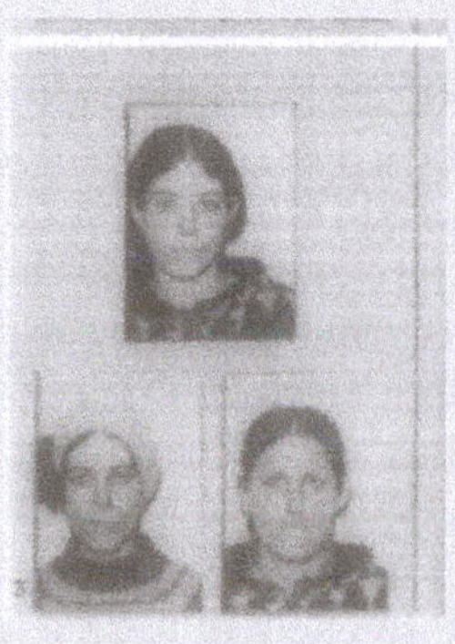

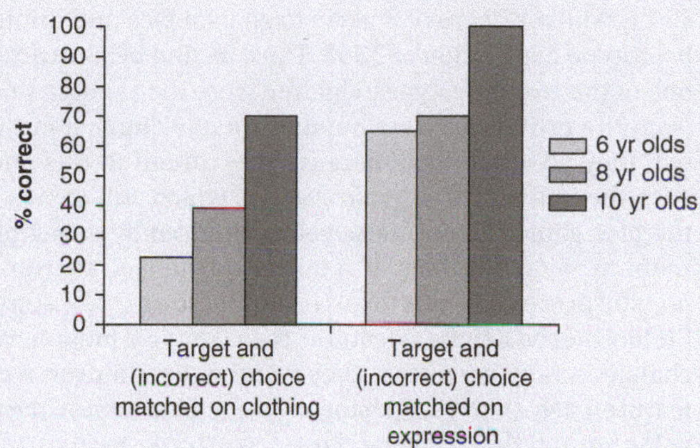

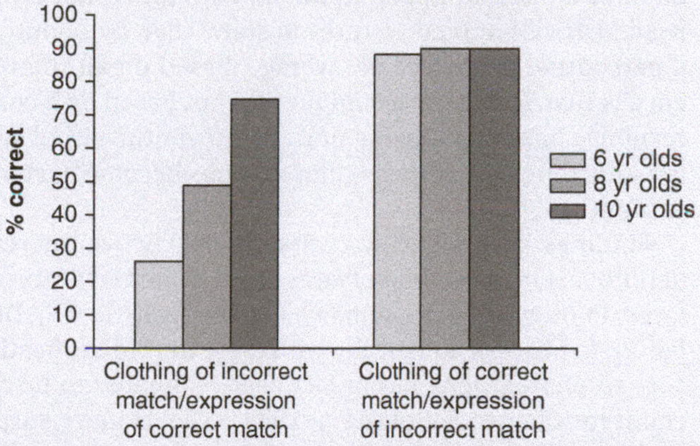

In photo-based tasks, there is a strong developmental trend towards using facial features rather than extraneous features for matching to a target face. (Stimuli and data from Diamond & Carey, 1977, with permission)

features than that of older children. From one of the few studies on this age range (Schwarzer, 2002), it seems that younger children are indeed less holistic and do encode faces on the basis of features, but in a somewhat haphazard way.

Schwarzer studied children between 2 and 5 years of age. Specifically, she wanted to find out if children would recognise a face based on an explicit **prototype**. A prototype, if you remember, means an average representation from a set of exemplars, such as your concept of a typical dog. Schwarzer used four dimensions of face variability in order to suggest the prototypical 'child' or prototypical 'adult' face. These were the contour of the face and the shape of the eyes, nose and mouth respectively. Ascribing a score of 1 to maximum 'roundness' of these features, the child prototype can be expressed as 1111, whilst a score of 3 given to an oval face and minimally rounded features, gives a prototype expression of 3333. Thus, having been exposed to faces that fall readily into one of the two prototypes, children were then shown ones which deviated considerably from the prototype score but only on *one* dimension, such as 3111. The question was will they go with 'adult' because they attend to this one feature alone, or will they go with the holistic/prototypic average, which still comes out as 'child'? Schwarzer made the task game-like for these young children by engaging them in a story that required them to say which 'family' a test face belonged to. Her findings were clear. Almost no holistic processing was found in any of the ages she studied as shown in A in Panel 11.6. Children used separate features to make their judgments. But there was an age-related change in how consistent they were; older children were more likely to use the same feature each time (say, shape of eyes). Schwarzer found a very similar pattern when using stimuli that could be classed as a 'bird' versus a 'plane'. It is worth pausing here to reflect on the fact that these are very different findings from those you learned about in Chapter 2 using animal-like stimuli with preverbal children. If you remember, Younger used artificial animal pictures to show that, by about 1 year old, babies seem to form a perceptual prototype or 'average' based on all the relevant features. The big difference is that Younger's technique was not based on a conscious explicit judgement but a response based on looking time. Whatever the visual system may be able to compute, it is a long time before these computations become part of an explicit conscious judgment of identity.

Findings such as Schwarzer's are instructive, therefore, but they are by no means definitive. Line drawings of faces are in some ways more like patterns than living moving faces. Photographs are somewhat more realistic still. Do young children show a similar failure to process holistically with these too? Identification of faces following prior exposure to photographs has in fact been estimated to be as low as 35–40% for preschool children (Chance & Goldstein, 1984). This is quite surprising is it not? But you should be aware that, since Diamond and Carey's research, there seems to have been a feeling that, in order to really test face encoding (for novel faces), it is necessary to literally use only the face in the photograph, masking other features by the use of a shower cap for example. Using such a method, Mondloch et al. (2003) found poor recognition of the photographed faces between 6 and 10 years of age when viewed in a different orientation. But how often do we have to learn to recognise faces under these circumstances? In using photographs, it would be perhaps be more 'normative' to deliberately use the sort of everyday distracter cues used by Carey and Diamond, so that we can work out why face recognition is so fragile in school-aged children. By keeping them in, but systematically varying them as Carey and Diamond did, we can work out how much reliance young children place on them. This has not in fact been done with very young (preschool) children, but another interesting technique has been used to see to what extent the configurational aspects of the face are processed.

Consider the upside-down faces in Panel 11.6. Now turn the book upside-down. Did you realise that one photograph had been considerably tampered with? The relations we have learned to use to form a prototypical 'face' are subject to frame of reference effects (see Chapter 10). When we encode eye separation, distance between eyes and nose, and shape of mouth (the face 'configuration'), it is relative to the polarity within which we have learned to encode these things, i.e. in an upright position. Switch to the unfamiliar polarity of inverted and we are left with a 'face' impression but accuracy in detecting any geometric distortion of features is hugely impaired. Indeed this illusion was dubbed the 'Thatcher Illusion' at one time when the face of a then current and famous British prime Minister was presented in this way. The effect of inversion was also another of the findings reported by Carey and Diamond in their original article. They found a growing advantage for recognition of photos that were both inspected and tested in an upright position until 10 years of age, but no improvement for photos presented in the inverted position, as you can see from Figure B in Panel 11.6. They interpreted this as due to the increasing use of configurational cues. This developmental trend in the superiority of upright versus inverted faces has been found by others since, such as Itier and Taylor (2004). These investigators also found that ERPs measured during recognition suggested a growing 'tuning' to the encoding of upright faces right up to 16 years of age. The use of inversion thus helps to test for configurational processing without having to remove extraneous features.

Few studies have tried the inverted face condition with little children, but an exception is a study by Brace et al. (2001), which included a 2–4 age range along with older children and adults. As the inverted condition might seem a bit strange, the authors made sense of it by first of all showing them a boy's face in photographic form and naming him as e.g. Jamie. They were then told a story about how he had been kidnapped and taken to a castle by a witch who had turned boys into saucepans (with 'faces'). This allowed the investigators to present a set of nine test faces, which were sometimes all inverted (saucepans hanging upside down). The child was to find the face of Jamie from amongst eight novel distracter faces. Around half to two-thirds of the preschool group were able to identify his face in at least one upright and one inverted condition. Although there were no large differences in the accuracy of identification as a function of orientation, older children, showed the standard superiority of upright over inverted in terms of their reaction times. Notably, the younger age group were actually faster when identifying the target in the upside-down condition, suggesting that the perceptual encoding by the younger children was not yet based on configural properties.

It is important to note that, these findings notwithstanding, not all investigators agree that face perception undergoes real development after the age of 5. For example,

Panel 11.6 From piecemeal to holistic encoding in preschoolers

- Judgments of age of face (adult versus child) by preschoolers seem to be based on individual features rather than a *holistic* average
    - This could be shape of nose or face contour

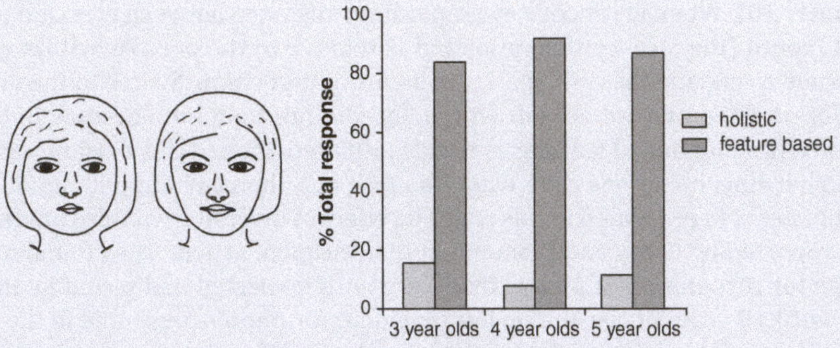

A After being exposed to the set of features that defined an adult's versus a child's face, young children judged test pictures on the basis of single features rather than the average of all the features. (Stimuli and data adapted from Schwarzer, 2002, with permission)

- Older children and adults are more sensitive to the overall geometric *configuration* of a face
    - But this is learned in an upright orientation
- The 'Thatcher Illusion' (based first on a famous British Prime Minister) demonstrates that although we can recognise that the inverted configuration is a face, we may not realise that features have been distorted
- For an unfamiliar face, it can be difficult to pick out the distorted from a normal inversion

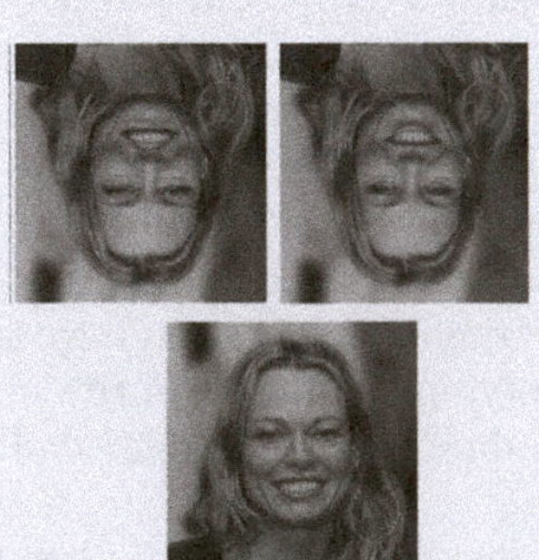

- This is thought to show how we develop orientation-specific configurational face processing
- The advantage for recognising novel faces presented in an upright position develops up to 10 years and beyond

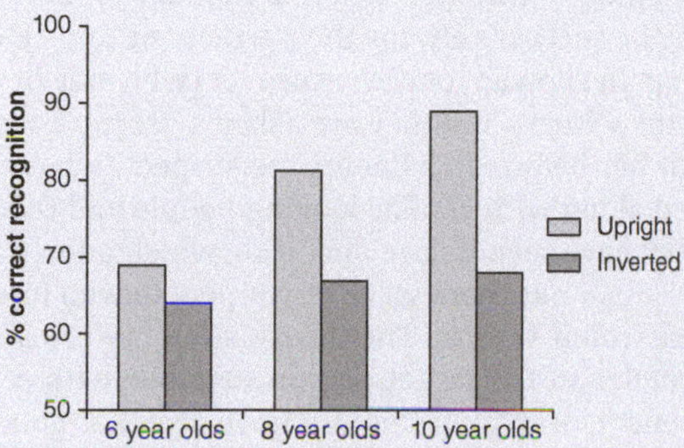

B Development of face recognition is selective to the upright orientation. (Adapted from Carey & Diamond, 1977, with permission)

Crookes and McKone (2009) use their findings from the implicit task (amongst other things) to suggest that what changes is not really about the fundamental mechanisms of face perception. Germine et al. (2011), on the other hand, argue that face learning continues to mature until the age of 30! A resolution of claims of early maturing versus late maturing face perception has been proposed by Weigelt et al. (2014), who suggest that there may be an initial disassociation between the brain mechanisms supporting basic perceptual discrimination and those supporting longer-term memory for faces, and that further neuropsychological research in this area is needed to help clarify the complex relationship between perceiving and remembering. For our purposes, therefore, let us say that there is broad agreement that young primary school-aged children are likely to be less accurate and more piecemeal in their face processing when tested in explicit recognition tests than older children and adults. If this is the case, maybe the more important question is whether that really matters. In fact, there is one real-life situation in which accuracy of perception of a novel face is very important. This is what is known as eyewitness testimony.

11.7 FACE RECOGNITION IN EYEWITNESS SITUATIONS

It is a sad and unfortunate fact that children sometimes have to identify someone who has harmed them. Although the likelihood is that that this is someone they know and can identify easily, what about the occasions when this person is a stranger? Pozzulo and Lindsay (1998) have provided a careful meta-analysis of studies using experimental techniques similar to the identification parade technique used in police investigations (using real people and/or photos). This shows that children in the 3- to 4-year-old age range are often only around 30% accurate in identifications (Chance & Goldstein, 1984) and still only about 50% accurate at ages 4–6 (Marin et al., 1979) – although this estimate is very dependent on the actual technique used. Lindsay et al. (1997) compared and contrasted the method of **lineup** – where a number of individuals are presented, either simultaneously or successively, for the participant to pick out the target – with the method of **showup**. In showup, only the suspect (who may or may not be the criminal) is presented to the witness and they are asked a yes/no question as to whether if they have seen him or her before. In a lineup, the suspect (who may or may not be the criminal) is presented along with similar looking people and the witness is asked if it includes someone they have seen before and, if so, which one. In the study by Lindsay et al. there was no criminal but there were target people who interacted with the participants within a classroom setting. The lineup stimuli were six head and shoulder pictures of people similar to the target person together with a picture of the target person. In one experiment, preschool children were nearly as good as adults (both over 80% accurate) at identifying the female target positively when her photo was presented in a showup. However, in the lineup conditions, the children were also likely to pick out other photos as well; this illustrates a tendency to make **false positive** judgements. So in another experiment with children aged 8 to 15 years, innocent 'suspects' were presented at both the showup and lineup and the rate of false positive responding was calculated for both methods.

Pause before reading on to think about what you would intuitively expect if you wanted to reduce false positives in children's eyewitness testimony. You may think that showup would be the better method as it avoids any distraction from similar looking faces. In fact, it was the other way round as you can see from the graph in Panel 11.7. Being able to compare and contrast across faces seems to help positive identification and is of course consistent with what you learned in Chapter 10 about relational processing.

You have learned that children are less likely to utilise available information even when encoding important stimuli like faces. This is a very significant fact of human cognitive development. The important thing is not so much that children are not so great at encoding faces when young, but rather the question *what makes them better at it*? Is it an automatic process caused by the maturation of the brain, or maybe the enhancement of the ability to remember? In fact, the simplest way to understand perceptual development is to turn these phrases on their heads. The brain matures because we learn to make certain connections – and the connections we make are the ones we need for remembering!

Panel 11.7 Face recognition in eyewitness situations

- The face recognition research indicates that children may be unreliable witnesses when it comes to identifying suspects from their appearance
- Studies with children that simulate identification parades have found that correct identification is highly unreliable in preschoolers and even in school-aged children
  - They are all prone to make *false positive* identifications
- Presenting faces in the standard '*lineup*' mode is less subject to these errors than in '*showup*' mode

Showup: 'Have you seen this man before?'

Lineup: 'Have you seen one of these men before?'
(If yes) 'Which one?'

(Photos courtesy of Dr Kimberley Wade)

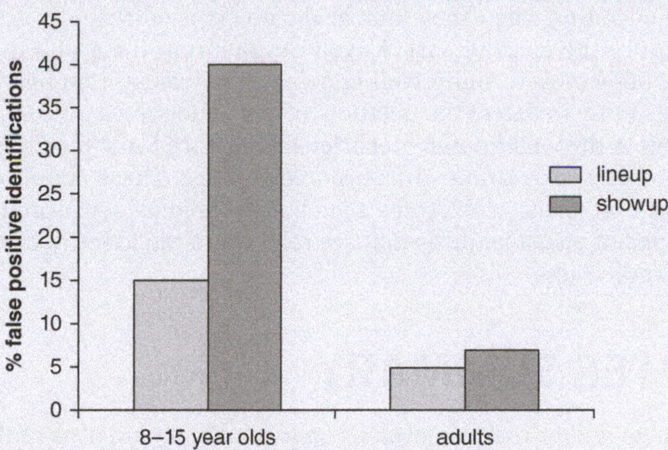

Children are more likely to make false positive identifications in a showup situation rather than a lineup. (Adapted from Lindsay et al., 1997, with permission)

Remembering faces is complex in that it requires many different sorts of connection to be made. On the other hand, children surely have plenty of practice with them – and there is an obvious need attached to this skill. The implication is that in cases without such an obvious demand on the need to be accurate, recognition memory may be especially vulnerable. This is exactly what has been found in studies using photographs of objects or arrangements of objects that have been altered in some way.

11.8 RECOGNITION ACCURACY FOR ALTERED OBJECTS

In a study of explicit object recognition, Shore et al. (2006) presented slides consisting of pairs of pictures and photographs of everyday objects to 6, 8 and 10 year olds (and adults). The photos were alternated with ones in which one object in the pair was now altered by colour, orientation, or by having a part added or deleted, and the participants had to select the side of the slide showing the altered depiction. In this study, orientation changes were the most easily detected, whilst deletions of part of the object were the hardest for all ages. This makes sense. For photographs of e.g. a vacuum cleaner, the visual image is substantially altered by changing its orientation, simply in terms of overall shape of the object against the background. Deletions, on the other hand, have to be searched for. Notice that what is being tested here is not whether children can 'see' that a part of an object is missing, but rather whether their perceptual encoding when they look at the object is sufficiently adequate such that they will notice the missing part. As you can see from the graph in Panel 11.8, even though the objects were quite well known, there was still an age-related improvement in the ability to detect the deletion. In fact, detecting a missing part of an object is a test item in the well-known Wechsler Intelligence Scale for Children (WISC) as it has such a strong correlation with chronological age. These simple change detection tasks tell us that it does take some time before children will spontaneously encode all the important visual features that are relevant to the identity of an object – even a relatively familiar one.

CHAPTER SUMMARY

Children's oculomotor control develops up to adulthood in terms of the efficiency with which stimuli are visually scanned, with correlated improvements on shape perception and recognition. Perceptual development is mainly with regard to explicit encoding; implicit recognition does not develop after preschool age. Explicit face recognition develops up to adulthood and is related to the ability to use configural rather than piecemeal information. Perceptual development also occurs in regard to the explicit awareness of alterations to pictures of objects.

Panel 11.8 Recognition accuracy for altered objects

- Children's spontaneous encoding of relevant object features develops over the primary school years
- Younger children are more likely to fail to notice deletions in photos or pictures of objects

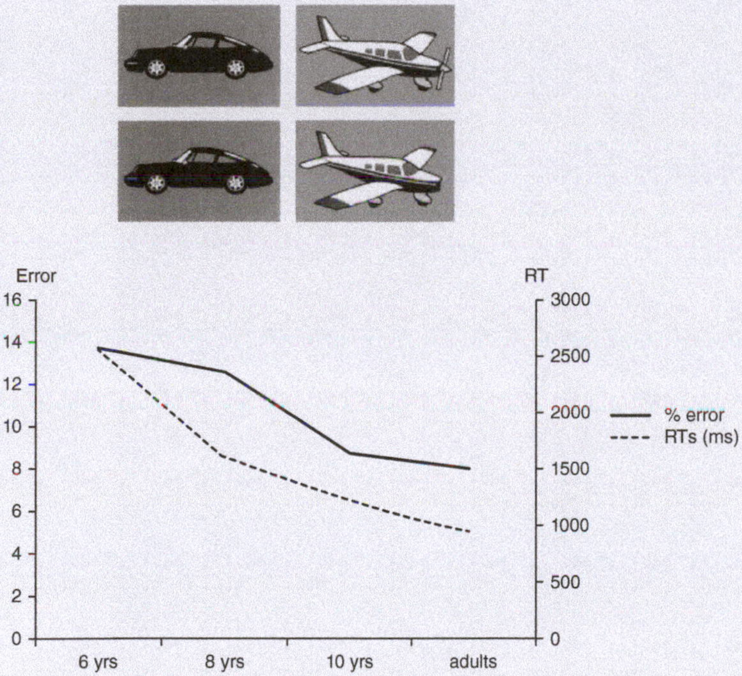

Children are presented with two drawings for 250 ms (top) and after a delay of 250 ms have to indicate which of the two has changed. There are developmental trends in the ability to detect a missing part (as shown) and also in the RTs for correct responses (Stimuli and data from Shore et al, 2006, with permission)

- This suggest that spontaneous encoding of relevant feature information can be sub-optimal in children of primary school age

LOOKING AHEAD TO CHAPTER 12

In this chapter, you have seen how the perceptual and memory systems are inextricably linked with consequences for what children can remember from what they have seen. We have considered this largely from the point of single objects (or faces). But the visual world is a mosaic of many parts. Do these developments also apply to the child's world view of scenes, places and events? The answer is yes, as you will see next.

CHAPTER 12

MEMORY FOR SCENES, ROUTES AND EVENTS

The fact that perceptual learning happens on a significant scale across a wide span of child development has important practical outcomes for what children remember about things they have witnessed. We have already seen that this can have radical consequences for things like identification parades based on face recognition. In this section, we shall return to other important aspects of remembering, such as recognising a scene, remembering a route to and from school or recalling an event.

MEMORY FOR SCENES

LEARNING LANDMARKS

12.1 Memory for depicted scenes. You should know that there are age-related changes in noticing alterations to originally presented scenes and be able to cite at least one study showing this.

12.2 Encoding effects on retention. You should know that retention for scenes decays over time for all ages and understand why memory decay itself does not explain poorer immediate recognition by younger children.

12.1 MEMORY FOR DEPICTED SCENES

A visual scene is rich in detail, contains spatial relationships between and amongst objects, and sometimes has landmarks that may be crucial in remembering the scene in a real-world context. What might we expect regarding children's encoding of scenes? On the one hand, the multiple sources of information in a scene may make it hard to encode. On the other hand, the perceptual 'readiness' hypothesis would predict that

Panel 12.1 Memory for depicted scenes

- Memory for objects depicted within an arrangement shows similar developmental effects to memory for single objects
  - Spatial organisation within the arrangement is often found to improve recognition

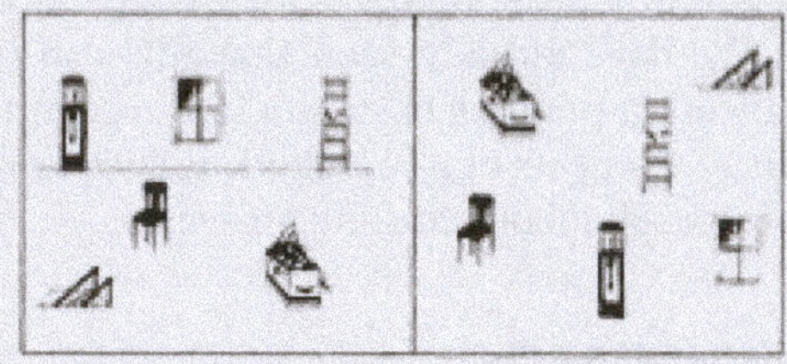

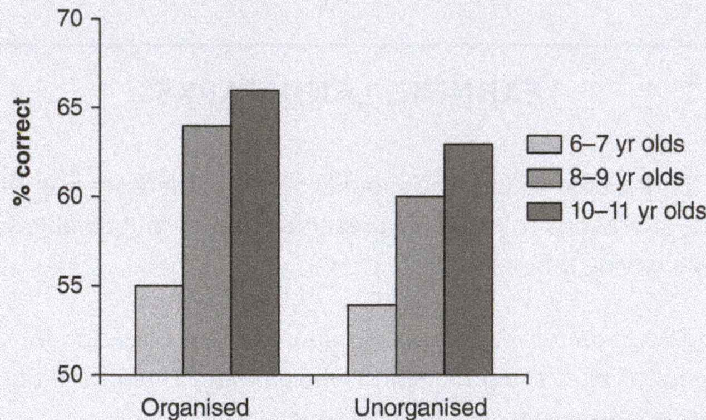

A The effect of spatial organisation on age-related changes in recognising a change to an arrangement of objects (top). Changes include addition, substitution and deletion of one of the objects as well as their re-arrangement. (Adapted from Mandler & Robinson, 1978, with permission)

- Even memory for more conventional 'scenes' can be subject to age-related changes in accuracy and reaction time
  - Though the context provided by a scene can improve memory for landmarks within it

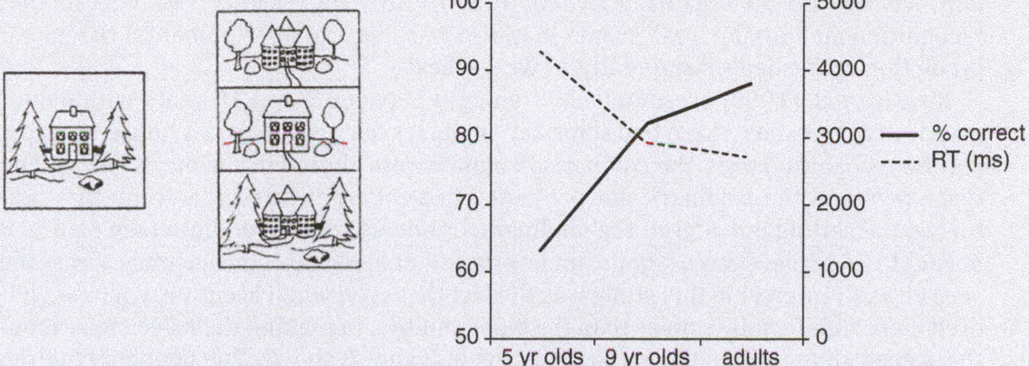

B Age-related changes in recognition accuracy and response time (RT) when an originally viewed scene (above left) is paired during test with a scene that is altered in some way

When the landmark castle or house was presented on its own younger children were worse than when it was presented within a scene. (Stimuli and data adapted from Kirasic et al., 2006, with permission)

the encoding of the important parts of a scene would be enabled by the familiarity of spatial layouts. Certain things are usually 'background', like ground, sky and clouds, whilst key landmarks in a scene are usually buildings. The familiar spatial structure that one would find in a scene is generally thought to enhance encoding. For example, as far back as the late 1960s, it was observed that nursery-aged children were very poor at accurately identifying what was 'missing' from a set of two objects when these were presented as spatially random items (Horowitz et al., 1969). In this study, either real objects or pictures of objects (e.g. cat and box) were presented together and around half a minute later, only one (e.g. the cat) was re-presented and the child had to remember the other item. Three- to five-year-old children (like adults) were considerably better when the objects were presented in a structured scene such as the cat sitting on the box, and in fact they were nearly at ceiling performance. A more elaborate level of spatial organisation involving six items was given to children between 6 and 11 years old by Mandler and Robinson (1978). The child's encoding was tested using a recognition task, where the original scene was presented along with a slightly altered one and the child had to identify the one they had seen earlier. The items were depicted on cards and comprised everyday objects such as items of furniture. These were either presented randomly or within a spatially organised layout, i.e. placed as if they were in an attic (see Figure A in Panel 12.1). There were several sorts of changes in the test cards, including some items being swapped for others, and some being added or taken away. There was a significant overall effect of spatial organisation on recognition accuracy as Figure A depicts, but as it also shows, there was still an age-related improvement for the organised layouts from 6/7 to 10/11 years. This suggests that recognition memory for 'real' scenes may also be subject to developmental change – a prediction confirmed subsequently, as we see next.

Kirasic et al. (1980) presented children aged between 5 and 10 years with photographs of real scenes. These had some key landmark features such as a house or castle. For the recognition tests, the comparison photos were altered in various ways: a scene that preserved the landmark but presented in a different setting, a scene that preserved the setting but altered the landmark, or one which altered both (see Figure B in Panel 12.1). There was a significant improvement in recognition accuracy across the age range. Of interest in this study was the fact that even when accurate, younger children were significantly slower than the older children in making their decisions about the scenes under all conditions as the graph in Figure B shows. The younger children were better nevertheless at encoding the whole scene than at encoding the landmark house or castle, as shown by a poorer performance when these were presented alone with no surrounding context, suggesting that the background enabled the encoding of the objects within the scene.

Some studies have focussed specifically on the degree of structure provided by the scene, and generally, the less familiar structure, the poorer the recognition accuracy, but it is important to note that even when quite familiar items are presented as a scene (such as a watering can and plant), children as old as 8–10 years have been found to make around 35% recognition errors when one of the items was replaced by something else, e.g. a plant instead of flowers (Hock et al., 1978). Scenes can therefore offer more structure to enable encoding but, like objects, they are still prone to recognition accuracy errors in middle childhood.

12.2 ENCODING EFFECTS ON RETENTION

This might prompt us to ask if this is just a question of greater immediate memory decay in younger children, rather than a problem with perceptual encoding. Eye-tracking research might suggest that it is indeed an encoding problem, but then most eye-tracking studies required children to actively discriminate between two objects or pictures. The scene recognition research is usually not based on having participants search for a difference, but simply to decide which of two pictures they had seen earlier. Whatever their encoding, maybe it is also the case that younger children forget more quickly about what they have seen? Certainly children's retention over different time periods seems to be age-related. An example of this is given in Figure A in Panel 12.2, showing data extracted from a study (Fabricius et al., 1993). The stimuli were photos of familiar scenes like a railway or a farmyard, and the graph shows the degree of correct recognition of these

Panel 12.2 Encoding effects on retention

- Scene memory decays in all ages of participant
- But is greater memory decay also responsible for poorer immediate memory of the original material in children?
- When participants are equated for how much they remember during learning, there are no age-related changes in rates of forgetting
- This suggests that what children retain about scenes is a function of what they encode and is not due to faster immediate forgetting of what they have been looking at

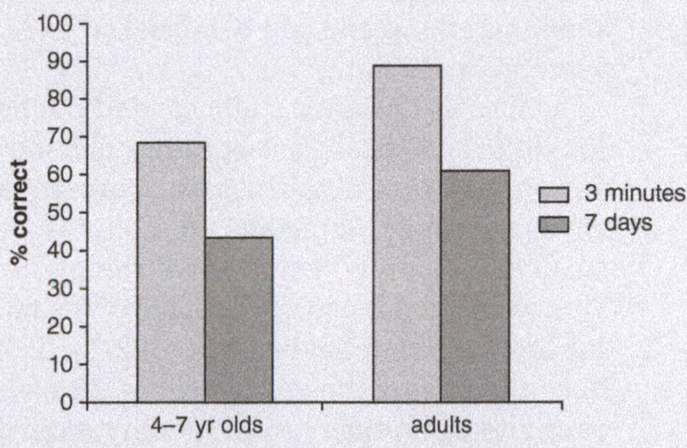

A Children and adults show roughly equivalent levels of memory decay when asked if a scene is one they have seen before. (Data adapted from Fabricius et al., 1993)

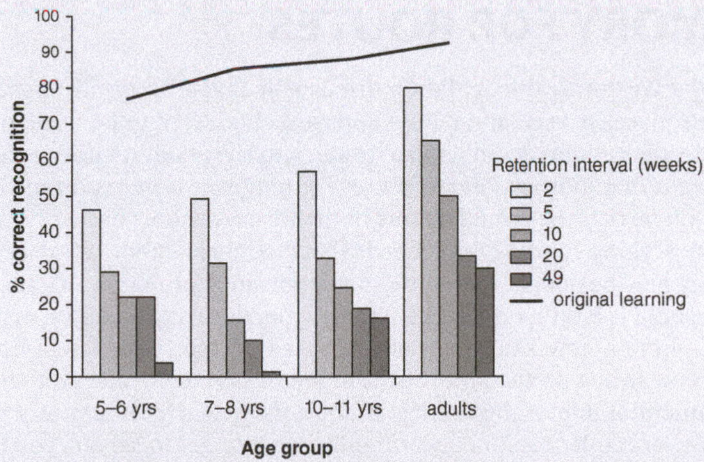

B Children are asked to recognise photos of scenes during a learning phase that are re-presented later amongst new photos. When participants were equated in terms of original learning, there were no significant differences in rate of memory decay. (Data adapted from Fajnsztejn-Pollack, 1973)

scenes as compared with distracters. The distracters altered the scene by substitution of one object. Retention decayed after a short versus a long interval in both ages of participants. But could it that there is *faster* memory decay in younger children between looking at the scene and being asked to recognise it, which makes it *seem* like poorer perceptual encoding?

A cleverly designed study carried out back in the 1970s (Fajnsztejn-Pollack, 1973) sought to specifically answer this question in the following way. A large number of colour photos from magazines were presented to children aged between 5 and 16 years for five seconds. Sometimes the photos were re-presented, up to four times, and the participant simply had to say if the photo they saw was a 'new' one or an 'old' one. This was called the learning stage of the task. Retention was measured (using different subsets each time) at intervals of 2, 5, 10, 20 and 49 weeks after the original learning. Here they were shown subsets of 28 of the original pictures together with 28 new ones and again they had to identify ones they had seen before. The usual age-related differences in performing the original task were found, as well as an apparent faster rate of forgetting in younger children. Both the reduced recognition during learning as well as poorer retention by younger children could be due to more rapid decay of the information in memory. However, the investigators were able to equate their participants for amount of initial learning (their level of recognition accuracy during the original task) and when they did so, there were no age differences in rate of forgetting. This indicates that memory development for scenes, as for objects, is not really about changes in how quickly information is forgotten, but rather how that information is encoded in the first place.

MEMORY FOR ROUTES

In today's Western world, children are usually taken by car or bus to and from school and their places of recreation. But suppose a child were to be taken on foot or by car to a new destination on an unfamiliar route, and they had to either return by themselves or recreate that journey later. Given everything you have read thus far, how confident would you be that they could do this in their early school years?

The first thing you may reflect on is that if scene memory is fragile in young children, then they may be poor at remembering important landmarks on a route. However, travelling a route is a rather different activity from perusing a picture of a scene. Travelling a route offers a new kind of structure based on the sequence in time in which landmarks appear in a particular order. A moment's further reflection, though, will tell you that sequential information alone is not a particularly robust way of remembering a route. For example, a child may remember that to get to school, you drive to the end of the road, turn in front of the shop and then again in front of the garage, and then keep straight until you see a park, and turn into the school gates at the end of the park. Notice that this kind of route memory does not necessarily mean that the child represents the full spatial environment in which shop, garage, park and school are imagined relative to one another – and relative to other landmarks on other routes. Even if they could confidently direct a driver to and from school, would they be able to find their own way to school from a different direction? What would they need to perceive and remember in order to do this?

This is in many ways a psychologically more complex question than many others we have encountered thus far. Why? Well, first of all, spatial navigation is a fundamental and primitive ability that is crucial to survival, and you may remember from Chapter 2 that the ventral stream responsible for 'where' type of information develops in the brain earlier than the dorsal stream responsible for the sort of detailed object perception ('what' information) you have just been learning about. Spatial memory furthermore is thought to be heavily controlled by a very ancient part deep within the mammalian brain called the hippocampus. In other words, it would be not only highly maladaptive but also very strange from an evolutionary point of view if children got very easily lost, when spatial navigation is so highly developed in species like rats. So what we are asking in this section is not so much whether they can learn a spatial route, but how they learn to use 'landmark' information so they can navigate flexibly within it.

Another reason why this is a complex issue is that, at the other extreme, human beings can use maps (unlike rats!). This takes us into the use of a cultural instrument that has to be taught, but it too presumes some concept in the individual of a global spatial layout independently of any route. So our question here is when do children spontaneously construct such a representation for themselves from the space in which they have travelled?

LEARNING LANDMARKS

12.3 Memory for landmarks. You should know the types of landmarks that can be encoded during route learning and be able to describe a study that shows changes in the use of these cues.

12.4 Distal and proximal cues. You should know what these terms mean and know how maze-learning tasks can help determine how they are used by children.

12.3 MEMORY FOR LANDMARKS

In a study of route memory, Hazen et al. (1978) presented children aged between 3 and 6 years with specially constructed environments with landmarks consisting of toy animals.

Panel 12.3 Memory for landmarks

- *Route memory* is based on travelling from A to B
    - o *Landmarks* can help establish this memory
- Travelling a route doesn't guarantee that the landmarks are used to construct an overall spatial representation
    - o This takes longer to develop during childhood than simply remembering the routes and the landmarks

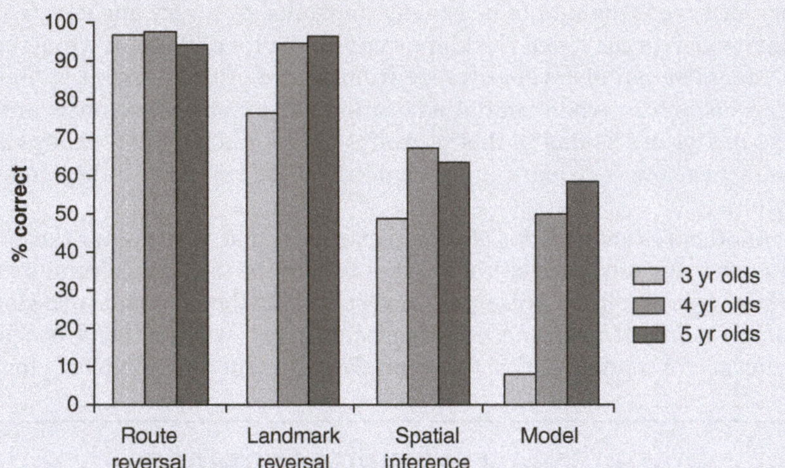

A Children are walked through a 'playhouse' with landmarks in each room. The figure shows the easiest house (four rooms, U-shaped) and the performance across age groups and a set of tests. Memory for landmarks in 3 year olds does not lead to good spatial inferences or model construction. (After Hazen et al., 1978)

- Even preschoolers improve on an easy version of the playhouse task if they are given a simple map first
    - o But map-reading is itself subject to considerable developmental changes during the school years

The environments consisted of 'playhouses' made of collapsible rooms with curtain doors on each wall: one (for 3–5 year olds) was very simple consisting of just four rooms arranged in a square as depicted in Panel 12.3; the other (for 5–6 year olds) was a rectangle made from six rooms. Each room contained a landmark toy.

The study started with a training episode in which children were walked through the rooms in one of two ways: a U-shaped route, or a Z-shaped route. Learning measures were how quickly the child could remember the route, by pointing to which door should be entered next, *and* how well they could remember the sequence of landmark animals when asked which one they would see in the next room. One test measure was whether the child could travel the route backwards, pointing to each correct door on the way and another was whether they could anticipate which landmark animal they would see in the next room. The next test was to work out which animal was on the other side of a dividing wall. Finally, the investigators asked the children to construct a small-scale model of the space they had travelled through using boxes and scaled down versions of the toy animals.

Older children were significantly quicker than the younger ones to learn the routes, but all children learned the routes within a few trials - route-based memory was very good even for the Z-route. Although the children only walked in one direction, reversing the route was the easiest condition, and performed nearly perfectly by all ages under all conditions. Reversing the order of landmarks proved somewhat harder for younger children and was significantly so for the 3 year olds compared with the other two age groups. This suggests that the landmarks were not strongly encoded as part of the route by the youngest children. Nevertheless route memory appears to be much more robust in young children than some of the other aspects of perceptual memory we have been considering.

The tests for the overall spatial representation of the playhouse acquired by travelling the route produced rather different results as the graph in Panel 12.3 shows. Inferring which animal lay on the other side of a dividing wall and reconstructing a model of the house showed very poor performance by the younger children even for the four-room house. This tells us that routes are not easily reconstructed as integrated spaces by children in their preschool/early school years. Further evidence came from various examples of how the younger children could sometimes recreate the right shape of the playhouse but without the correct animal order *or*, in other trials, the right animal order but with no regard to the overall shape.

From all of this we might expect that children cannot use maps until these integrated representations are in place. This is not the case, however. Even preschool children can use simple maps and Uttal and Wellman (1989) found the playhouse task was better performed by children from 4 to 7 years of age when they were given a simple map of the layout before traversing the route. The investigators concluded that the map actually helped to form the integrated representation but they also noted that, even with a map to help them, the younger children were significantly worse than the 6/7 year olds were without a map.

12.4 DISTAL AND PROXIMAL CUES

Does this answer our question as to whether a child could navigate their way to a destination from an unfamiliar origin? Not quite. In Hazen's study, the children knew that they were going back the way they came. Also, the landmarks in the Hazen study were not the sorts of landmarks normally used to navigate. Useful navigational landmarks are things that don't move around – likes trees and buildings – and are usually at some distance from the observer. These are called **distal** cues and, because they are further away, they are also going to be more stable as the observer moves around. A church spire is a better landmark than a front gate. Nearer objects are called **proximal** and some of these may be unreliable if they are moveable and temporary – like parked cars – or the toys in Hazen's study.

Interesting research throwing further light on which cues are encoded during route learning by children has come from techniques developed initially for research on spatial learning in animals. Leplow et al. (2003) used an adaptation of a water maze used with rats, designed to see whether a reward location would be remembered with regard to distal or proximal cues. The apparatus is depicted in Figure A in Panel 12.4. It consisted of a circular wooden floor that was completely curtained all the way round. The floor was sensitive to the child standing on certain key locations that lit up when the child approached. Children aged between 3 and 12 years were told that that some of these locations were places that 'hid nuts' and their task was to remember these so that they could help a squirrel collect the nuts for the winter. The correct locations emitted a tone but only when stepped upon for the first time.

The distal cues were fluorescent paintings of sun, moon, stars and a comet on the curtains. Proximal cues were a mouse and a toy rabbit lying on the floor. After being guided around all the locations and being shown all the cues, the child was required to visit *only* the places hiding the nuts. When they could do this successfully, they were then tested as shown in Figure A in Panel 12.4. Before tests, the child was blindfolded and then taken in a wandering route to the start location. The first test took the child to a location opposite the original. If they simple remembered that a location involved turning right by a certain distance, then they would walk in exactly the opposite direction from the target location. This was a test of whether they were using an egocentric frame of reference. Does this remind you of anything? It should – because it is very like the object permanence test carried out on infants by Bremner and Bryant. If you remember, they showed that infants coded spatial location egocentrically, i.e. with reference to their own body.

However, the use of egocentric cues disappears roughly between 2 and 3 years of age in these types of local search task given to infants (Ribordy et al., 2013). And this fits with what was found for preschool and school-aged children in this larger spatial task. In this first test condition, the children made very few errors, showing that they were not using

Panel 12.4 Distal and proximal cues

- Remote landmarks that are most useful in forming an overall spatial representation are called *distal* and ones that are closer to the observer are called *proximal*
- *Maze learning* apparatus used for research on animal spatial learning can be used to see when children learn to use these cues

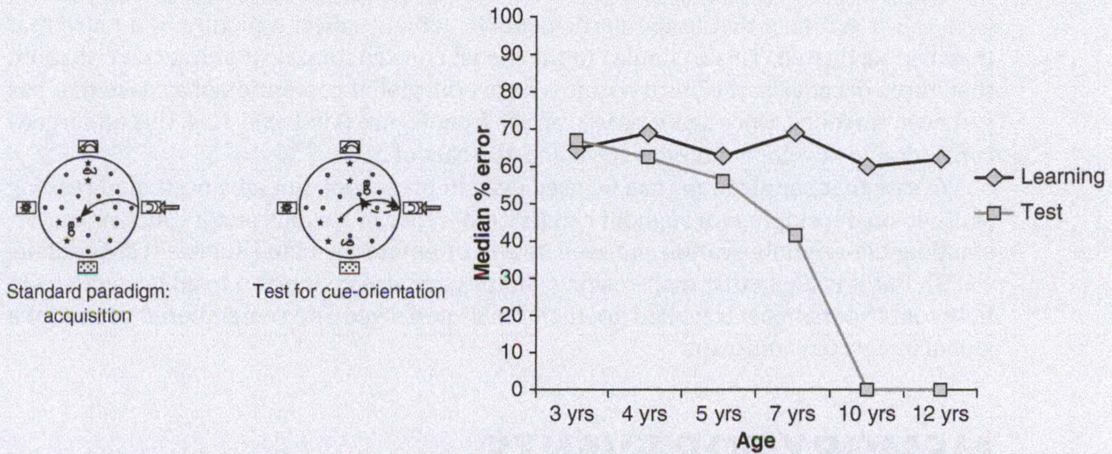

A A maze with target points that light up on approach has two proximal cues on the floor and four distal ones on the surround. Children learn how to find the 'correct' targets (above left). In a test, the distal cues remain in the same place but the proximal ones have been rotated (above right). The large proportion of target finding errors in this condition up to the age of 7 onward shows a lack of reliance on distal cues. (Diagram and data adapted from Leplow et al., 2003, with permission)

- Children's memory of the route as an overall spatial representation can be tested after maze learning using recognition tests

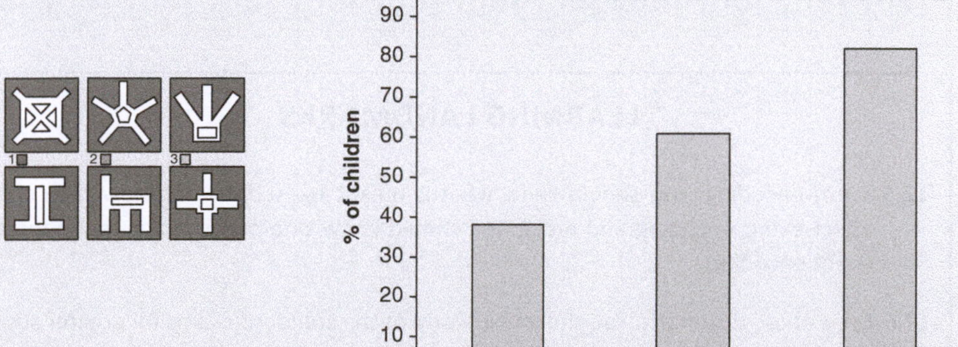

B Percentage of children making recognition errors when given depictions of a variety of mazes and asked to choose the one they travelled. (Adapted from Bullens et al., 2012, with permission)

egocentric cues. This did not by itself determine whether they were using the proximal or the distal cues, so the second (cue-orientation) test used the original start location, but whilst the child was blindfolded, the mouse and rabbit had their positions swapped. Many more errors were recorded in this condition even by children up to the age of 7 as the graph in Figure A shows. This shows that these children had been relying heavily on proximal cues even when distal cues are present to guide them to the correct place.

Similar results have been obtained in a more recent and more complex study by Bullens et al. (2010) using a variety of different mazes, and what is of particular interest here was a sub-task that asked participants to actually select a picture of a maze that they had navigated. This is similar to the model construction task of Hazen et al. more than three decades earlier, as it requires an overall global perception of a space that has just been travelled. Once again, as we can see from Figure B in Panel 12.4, this undergoes considerable development between 5 and 10 years of age.

We saw that simple maps can be used even in preschool, but advanced map reading skills go on developing throughout childhood because of various factors such as understanding the symbols, scaling and even how to orientate the map (Bluestein & Acredolo, 1979). But it is likely that map-reading abilities are also connected to advancements in how routes personally travelled are themselves perceived and remembered as part of a global integrated landscape

MEMORY FOR EVENTS

Another 'real-world' consequence of the development of perceptual encoding is the ability to recall a witnessed or previously experienced scenario or event. Event memory is sometimes known as **episodic memory**. In essence, it means that an event is recalled along with the specific context in which it happened, such as remembering jumping on a bouncy castle at a park at a friend's birthday party. Although it is often part and parcel of memories that are spontaneously recalled, it is easier to measure using specific recognition memory tests.

LEARNING LANDMARKS

12.5 Event encoding. You should know what is meant by 'scripts' and how they can affect event encoding and recall. You should know one other factor that affects event encoding.

12.6 Eyewitness testimony. You should be aware of the standard claims for greater susceptibility to leading questions in young children and know why this is only partly true and how it is related to recall.

12.5 EVENT ENCODING

The ability to encode exactly what happened during an event is thought to be enabled by building a generalised context or **script** for what would normally occur during that sort of episode, so that the important details pertaining to a particular event – sometimes known as a **slot** within the script – stand out against this general experience. These scripts build in the context of time and place that is recalled along with the specific event: 'when we went to the zoo', 'when I was eating breakfast,' etc. But they also help to build a backdrop against which a specific event (or slot) might stand out, such as 'Tom fell into the sandpit', 'Granny had made scones', 'we watched a funny clown'. To try to create event scripts in the laboratory, Farrar and Goodman (1992) set up standard events that children experienced over a number of days. The children were aged between 4 and 7 years and the standard events consisted of dressing up in animal costumes and then going to an 'animal room' where they would engage in a particular activity such as 'being a rabbit jumping over a fence'. 'Deviation' events were meant to represent the sort of thing that would not normally occur in this such as 'being a pig crawling under a bridge'. When they were interviewed a week later, they were asked, 'What did you do when dressed as (e.g.) a rabbit?' (standard event) versus 'What did you do when you were dressed as (e.g.) a pig?' (deviation event). The recall of both the standard and deviation event was at least 30% better for 7 versus 4 year olds. Repetition of the standard event helped older children to remember which activity occurred in the standard event, as opposed to the novel deviation visit. For the younger children, however, repetition actually made them more confused about whether aspects of the event occurred during the standard or deviation visit. These findings are summarised in the graph in Panel 12.5, which shows the number of specific events correctly recalled (as a proportion of the total) by both ages as well as the number of incorrect memories – that is, events that were wrongly attributed to either the standard or deviation condition. You can see that the 7 year olds were still likely to wrongly attribute information to the deviation event, which shows confusion about the episodic information related to the event. Similar findings were obtained in a later study (Farrar & Boyer-Pennington, 1999) in which a standard event (the script) was 'making magic' with an adult dressed as a wizard, and the target episodic events would be some specific change to these activities. This time, however, the episodes (or deviations) were either 'typical' with regard to the script such introducing finger painting, whilst a schema atypical one would be having a snack with the wizard. Once again, 4 year olds showed confusion when trying to remember what occurred during the standard versus the episodic event but this was reduced by repeated experience with the standard event but only for the atypical episodes, whilst it improved recall for both sorts of episode types for 7 year olds. The conclusion is that scripts may help provide a context for encoding an event – especially one that is unusual – but script memory or memory for generalised events is itself subject to development *and* experience.

Obviously then, the more familiar the child is with the usual script, the better their memory for a specific event occurring in that context. Clubb et al. (1993) re-visited memory scores for children's memory of paediatric examinations obtained in an earlier study and found a positive correlation between the aspects of the visit (ear check, blood

Panel 12.5 Event encoding

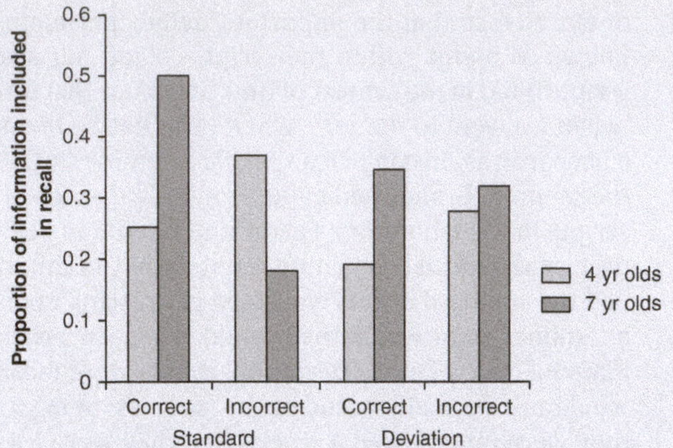

Children are exposed to a standard event such as playing at being a rabbit climbing under a fence as well as deviation events such as being a pig crawling under a bridge. Seven year olds remember more information and are also more accurate overall in ascribing the event to the correct context. (Adapted from Farrar & Goodman, 1992, with permission)

- Sometimes known as *episodic memory*, event memory includes the context of the event
  - Such as time and place
- Familiar contexts can enable event memory
  - These are called *'scripts'*
    - e.g. 'when we go to Granny's'
- Laboratory studies can create scripts using during play
  - Such as pretending to be animals engaged in an activity
- Children would be interviewed later to see how many events are recalled
  - And also if they are attributed to the correct context
- Recall of these events is highly age-related
  - Having control of an event enhances memory of it
- Children's language shows script memory
  - e.g. 'You take your shoes off when you go in'
- as well as episodic memory
  - ' I forgot to take my shoes off at Granny's'
- But both forms of memory develop during the primary school years

pressure, etc.) remembered by 5 year olds and the corresponding event knowledge of what happens on a 'visit to the doctor' which Clubb et al. obtained by interviewing a different set of 5 year olds. (Getting a prize was the best remembered and the most 'known' element of the visit!) Another and related factor that can influence event recall is active involvement in the script and is illustrated in a study by Quon and Atance (2010), which looked at memory for events that happened in the child's recent past. They found that those over which they had more control (e.g. playtime) produced less forgetting for 3 to 5 year olds as compared with ones in which they had less control (e.g. bedtime), which could be due at least in part to greater attention to the details of events that they control themselves. Expressed in terms of standard memory research, this would be known as greater **depth of processing** (Craik & Lockhart, 1972) giving rise to better knowledge and thus better memory.

If event memory is to be tested by interview and contextual prompting, it raises the question of whether children's recall will be influenced by how questions are put to them. You can either ask a child what they usually do when going to Granny's (the script) or what they did yesterday at Granny's (the slot). Brubacher et al. (2011) let 4–8-year-old children engage in a number of activities over several occasions and then either asked general 'breadth' questions' ('tell me what happens') or more specific 'depth' questions ('tell me the time you remember best'). If the breadth prompts preceded the depth prompts, all children remembered more information, but they were nevertheless able to provide specific information about the 'slots' when asked. General questioning and scene setting may enable children's specific event memory, therefore, even if it is really a specific event that the questioner is interested in. However, accuracy and total amount of information recalled does develop with age, which still leaves young children vulnerable to the biasing effect of questioning, as we see next.

12.6 EYEWITNESS TESTIMONY

An important implication of the fragility of event memory in children is that it could be easily disrupted by leading questions that make children think they have seen an event happen. This is particularly important in courtroom or other situations where the child's testimony is used as legal evidence. An investigator famous for her research in this area is Elizabeth Loftus from the University of Seattle. In an interesting review published in 1984 she points out that there was a very long-held belief that children's event memories are faulty because of their suggestibility making them susceptible to 'leading' questions, e.g. 'was she wearing a hat?', as opposed to free recall of what she was wearing. Loftus and Davies point out that the actual evidence for this is mixed. Studies that consider event memory in this sort of context usually involve measures of suggestibility, not just recall. A typical study (Goodman & Reed, 1986) attempted to create a situation in a laboratory setting where children aged 3 and 6 years and adults interacted directly with a confederate during a five-minute game involving arm movements. A few days later, they were asked to identify the confederate from a photo 'lineup' including four distractor males of similar physical appearance, before they were questioned about the event. This took the form of asking objective questions about the room, the man and the game that they played, such as 'Were there any pictures on the wall in the room?' and 'Did the man stand up or sit down when you played the game?' But the children were also asked a set of 'leading' questions such as 'The man's shirt was red, wasn't it?' and 'Didn't the man go like this (experimenter indicates an incorrect gesture)?' Half of these were based on true information; half false. Finally, the children were invited to simply freely recall everything they could remember.

Panel 12.6 Eyewitness testimony

- *Eyewitness testimony* is a practical situation in which event memory is very important
- Increased suggestibility is thought to be an element in poor memory in child witnesses
    - The evidence for this is not as strong as was once thought
    - Young children can resist leading questions about a highly central event
- But they can be susceptible to more general leading questions
    - This is seems to be a direct function of poorer recall

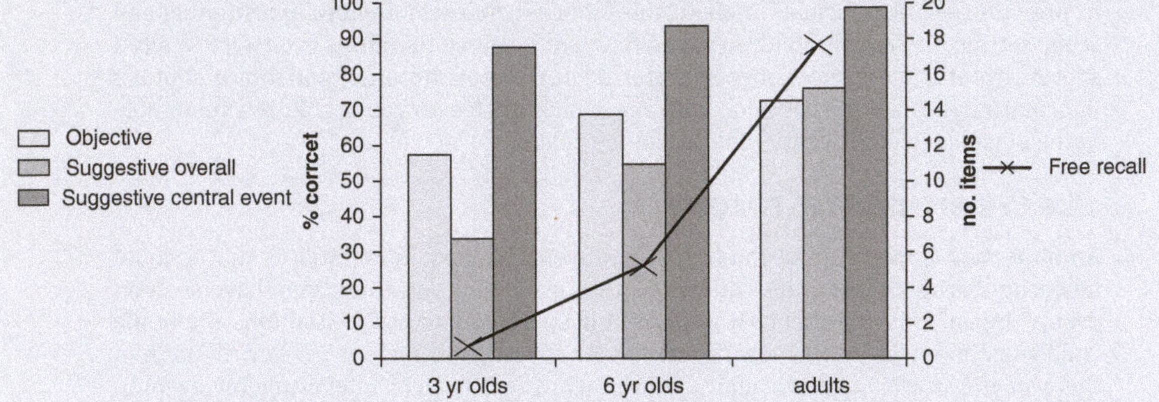

Children played a hand movement game with a stranger and were tested a few days later on free recall; objective questions (e.g. 'what was the man's name?'; incorrectly suggestive questions ('what age did he say he was?'); and incorrectly suggestive about the main event ('didn't he go like this?'). The last did not produce an age effect, unlike the other memory tests. General susceptibility is related to poorer free recall. (Adapted from Goodman & Reed, 1986, with permission)

As you would expect from Chapter 11, the 3 year olds were less accurate than the older children and adults on the photo identification. As for the 'objective' memory for the scene and event, the 3 year olds were significantly worse than the older children and adults – again a finding consistent with what you now know. However, the authors were particularly concerned to see if the younger children would also be more suggestible when it came to resisting the planting of false information. There was indeed a strong age related improvement in the ability to resist suggestive questioning overall as the bar graph in Panel 12.6 shows. This general effect was not found for the arm movements used in the game, however, indicating that where attention was focussed on the most salient part of the event, suggestibility was considerably diminished. Free recall showed a very large age effect as the line graph in Panel 12.6 shows, but importantly, there was very little evidence of incorporating incorrect information from the suggestive questions into the objective narratives of any age group. Weaker encoding of all the information during an event rather than suggestibility *per se* seems to be the main effect from this type of study; if recall is poor, then suggestibility increases when answering questions. Overall, this creates something of a dilemma for those who have to pose questions to children when seeking evidence for a court. Their recall may lack detail, but direct questioning about such detail may lead to false memories under certain circumstances.

VERBAL MEMORY

Events are often simply experienced as heard narratives. From the age at which a child is old enough to sit on someone's lap and be shown a storybook, they will be exposed to events recounted in spoken language. Once we can assume a basic understanding of language, can we also assume that what is understood will be well remembered? Memory for auditorily presented information has, rather disappointingly, been examined most often by psychologists using tasks that do not represent everyday activities like telling a story or giving an oral instruction, such as, 'can you go to the garage and bring back the red watering can and the black bucket please'. Instead, in the tradition of classical memory research, tasks are given where the main point is not to instruct or inform, but simply to remember simple lists of unconnected words or numbers. However, we have learned quite a bit from these tasks about the nature of verbal memory in children as you will see.

LEARNING LANDMARKS

12.7 List recall. You should know what is meant by verbal working memory and which factors affect its development.

12.8 Processing speed and storage capacity. You should know what these terms mean and how they can be measured.

12.9 Recall of narratives. You should know what attentional resource allocation is and why it is important in the recall of heard narratives.

12.7 LIST RECALL

There is ample evidence that the 'capacity' to remember lists increases with age. In fact digit span is used as a part of standardised IQ tests used for children. Using list recall in this way does indeed tell us how one child compares with the 'average' child of that age, but how far can these tests provide an insight into their general abilities to remember heard information?

Initially, the list learning research seemed to support the idea that there is a kind of memory 'module' and that children simply get better at recalling what they have heard in a mechanical sort of way. The sort of short-term storage of this sort of information is described as **working memory** (WM) (and you came across this first in Chapter 4). This captures the idea that there are some active processes required to keep the information fresh until it is needed. In the context of list learning by adults, this was developed within a theory of working memory and is called the **phonological loop** (Baddeley, 1995). For auditorily presented material, it was surmised that the harder to rehearse the words phonologically, the poorer the recall, and that is why it was also known as the **articulatory loop**. Evidence in support of this came from things like the word length effect (Hitch et al., 1989), where longer words are harder to recall than shorter ones ('November' versus 'March', 'unhappy' versus 'sad', etc.). It was hypothesised that longer words impede the ability to rehearse, i.e. that the child's speech rate might be the key. Other phonological factors that seemed to affect list recall was the phonological similarity such that acoustically similar words (e.g. 'cat', 'mat', 'hat') are harder to recall than dissimilar ones (e.g. 'clock', 'fish', 'horse') during the school-age years (Hulme & Tordoff, 1989). But subsequent research has established that recall is not just a function of mechanical rehearsal.

It has been known for some time that another factor is the effect of the familiarity with the items to be recalled – e.g. words versus numbers (Chi, 1978). By comparing known words with non-words, Roodenrys et al. (1993) established that familiarity is as important a factor in children's performance as speech rate in these sorts of list learning tests. You may be thinking – 'but aren't more familiar items ones that are more often rehearsed?' Turner et al. (2000) found that this was not the reason for the familiarity effect when comparing word (familiar) and non-word (novel) lists. Words showed an advantage over non-words for children of 7 and older but there was no relationship between familiarity and the child's reported use of rehearsal.

So even in these simplified tasks, background knowledge seems to play a part. We must also ask what is the everyday validity of these sorts of tests. There is, after all, a sense in which participants *have* to rehearse in these list-learning tasks, as there is no meaningful context for the words being spoken. So perhaps the most important aspect of memory research of this sort is just how much children *do* rehearse when given a list to recall irrespective of how familiar the items. Gathercole et al. (1994) found no evidence for spontaneous sub-vocal rehearsal in 4 year olds and the study by Turner et al. (2000) showed that spontaneous rehearsal is not reliably found in list learning until about the age of 9. If rehearsal alone cannot account for developmental changes in memory span tests in middle childhood, what are the remaining possibilities?

Panel 12.7 List recall

- Memory for auditorily presented information has most often been studied using simple *list recall*
  - These tasks present lists of words and numbers and require the child to repeat them back
- There is a regular increase in the number of items recalled between preschool age and adulthood
  - But it is not clear why
- The *articulatory loop* theory of verbal working memory suggest that phonological factors might impede children's ability to rehearse the lists, e.g.
  - Word length
    - 'March' versus 'November'
  - Word similarity
    - 'cat'/'hat' versus 'clock'/'fish'
- But spontaneous rehearsal has not found to be a major factor in recall in children under nine years of age
- Familiarity with the material to be recalled has been found to be more important than either of these factors
  - This is tested by comparing recall for (familiar) words with non-word lists

12.8 PROCESSING SPEED AND STORAGE CAPACITY

Arising from the days in which memory was seen as a rather independent 'faculty', there was a natural inclination to view it as a kind of box with space for storage, and more recently as the memory in a computer (see the section on Information Processing in Chapter 1). A computer's ability to retrieve information is not just about how much storage capacity it has, but also about how quickly it can process information; the faster you can absorb what is being said the more you can take in over a given time span. It is now recognised that both these things account for developments in recall, though how they actually function together is still a complex issue under investigation. Bayliss et al. (2005) investigated the contribution made by general storage capacity storage and general processing speed to performance by 6–10 year olds during memory games. In one of the games, they were given an array of differently coloured squares that had digits printed on them. They were asked to think of an object associated with a particular colour (e.g. tomato) and then to touch the correspondingly coloured square, noting and remembering the digit on the square for later list recall. The number of items was either 3, 6 or 9. The score on this test was then correlated with an independent measure of storage capacity using a standard digit recall task and also with an independent measure of processing speed using a simple two-choice task on a computer (which presented the children with a frog and a bird and they had to touch one or other as quickly as possible on hearing a low or high tone). The investigators found that performance on the memory tasks was related *both* to general storage capacity and to general speed, showing that neither alone is the single factor that explains memory development.

But we know that familiarity with the material affects recall. So could it be that the faster you process, the easier it is to recall (and thus benefit from) previously stored information? There is a sense in which this is true. Ferguson and Bowey (2005) measured global processing speed using tasks such as having to go through a set of geometric shapes and crossing out the ones that matched a standard. This processing speed measure was found to predict the phonological 'availability' of previously stored words from **long-term memory** (LTM) measured using things like accuracy on oddity tests (e.g. 'gun', 'sun', 'doll'). This in turn predicted auditory memory span in children between 5

Panel 12.8 Processing speed and storage capacity

- Other factors in auditory memory are thought to be:
  - how quickly information can be processed
  - storage capacity
- General *processing speed* is measured by simple RT measurements
  - e.g. the speed of touching one of two items as determined by an auditory signal
- General *storage capacity* is measured by span
  - e.g. for verbal storage by the number of words or digits that are recalled from a spoken list
- General processing speed has been found to be related to developments in memory span
- But both of these are related to phonological 'availability'
- This is measured by oddity detection tests
  - e.g. 'gun', 'sun', 'doll'
- This again shows that general familiarity with words is as important as speed and storage in auditory memory development

and 13 years of age using standard list recall. So general speed of processing is related to developmental change in auditory memory – but not because of rate of rehearsal but because of improved accessibility to already stored phonological information of the sort used in list recall tests.

In summary, list recall studies, have shown that it is not just the 'processes' of trying to remember auditory information that develops in childhood, so much as accessibility and familiarity with the material being used in the tests.

12.9 RECALL OF NARRATIVES

The tasks we considered in the last section are tests of a somewhat artificial nature, where different memory 'processes' are tested separately in simple tasks and then cross-correlated within complex statistical models. Yet in the real-world context of auditory memory, such as listening to someone tell a story, you are often having to listen, understand, rehearse and store information all at the same time. This is referred to as **attentional resource allocation** and refers to having the capacity deal with several things at once. Whatever the developmental changes in storage and global processing, this is likely to be a significant factor in how children remember spoken material.

Montgomery et al. (2009) reasoned that with meaningful narratives, resource allocation would be the most important variable affecting comprehension and memory for a story, as it is important to allocate resources both to the immediate processing of the language as well as to the integration of the new information with previous long-term knowledge. As speed of processing affects how much information can be handled per unit of time, it too should affect how much can be remembered from a spoken narrative. Unlike the list recall tasks (which often only captures temporary memory for meaningless material), for material with a meaningful structure to be processed and stored, phonological short-term memory was argued to be a relatively less important factor. And this is what they found.

The core narrative comprehension task was to listen to three stories: a warm-up story followed by a Shipwreck story and a Dragon story. After hearing these, children aged between 6 and 11 years were asked questions that tested both their understanding as well as recall of the stories. As for ancillary measures, as well as using a standard test of phonological short term memory (the digit span task) and a standard test of speed of processing (how quickly they could find a shape from an array corresponding to a spoken colour), the investigators measured resource allocation by asking the children to listen to sentences that ranged in number from 1 to 6. After each sentence set, comprehension of each was tested by asking whether the sentence could happen in real life ('the lady found a puppy that was furry' versus 'most little chickens can eat a house'), which meant that they had to check the meaning against background knowledge *and* recall the final word of each sentence. They called this a **concurrent processing** measure and it captures the multiple ways in which a narration may have to be comprehended and remembered. When testing narrative comprehension, age accounted for half the variance, but after that was partialled out, a significant contribution remained from the resource allocation measure and also (though to a lesser extent) from the speed measure. No contribution was found for the

Panel 12.9 Recall of narratives

- The factor that most strongly predicts children's recall of heard narratives is their ability to attend to more than one thing at once, e.g.
    - The meaning of a sentence (and)
    - The last word in a sentence
- This is called:
    - *Resource allocation* or
    - *Concurrent processing*

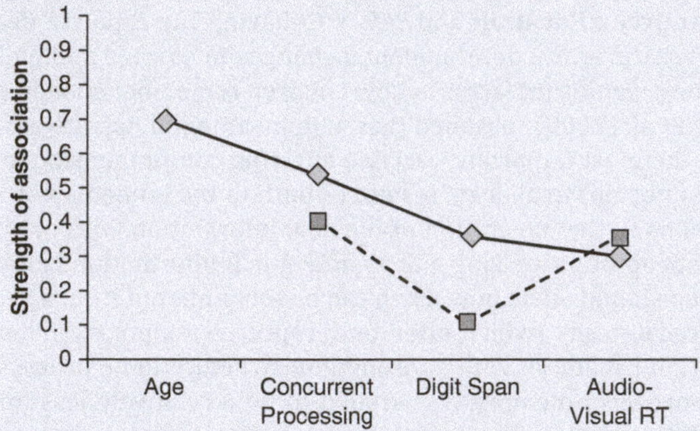

Ability to remember details of narrated stories was correlated with age but also with measures of concurrent processing involving judging the plausibility of a sentence and recalling the last word. Lower correlations were found for the standard short-term memory measure of digit span and lowest of all for speed of processing. The contribution from digit span (phonological short term memory) did not remain when age was partialled out (dotted line) (Data adapted from Montgomery et al., 2009, with permission)

- Memory for narrated events is therefore not a simple function of the 'capacity' to store information
    - Nor the general ability to process information quickly

phonological short-term memory factor after the association with age was partialled out as the graph in Panel 12.9 shows. This identifies resource allocation and speed as age independent influences on narrative memory, and so these seem to help account for the age-related improvements found in story comprehension. The rather stronger effect for speed of processing in other studies we have considered could derive from the artificial nature of some lab tests, such as speeded decision tasks that can impose unusual demands that don't normally apply. Recalling narrated events is not due, therefore, simply to the maturation of storage capacity or processing speed, but also to the complex demands of *attending* to important meaning and relating that meaning to previous knowledge already stored in long-term memory. Clearly it would be circular indeed to then suggest that knowledge is itself acquired by having a better memory! Rather it seems that it is attentional focus and depth of processing at the time of encoding that are the driving forces behind the development of memory. So in this area, as in others, it is children's active engagement with the world 'in the moment' that is the key to their cognitive advance.

In this chapter, we have considered memory for events that are directly perceived as well as described in words. Often both these things are happening at the same time. An obvious question is whether language helps in the encoding of the perceived events by way of adding, enriching or drawing attention to important aspects of the scene or event. Certainly in the study described in Section 12.1 by Horowitz et al., children's memory for objects was improved at all ages if the objects had been named during the exposure period. Similarly, in a study of simple picture recognition, using abstract patterns or real-world objects, Nelson and Kosslyn (1976) found that labelling the pictures at the time of encoding helped all participants to recognise them accurately later. However, it is important to note that naming or verbal labelling does not compensate for the fundamental changes in perception during the school years. In the Nelson and Kosslyn study, even when they had verbally described abstract patterns as e.g. 'brown stripes on a white background', 5 year olds were only 66% correct in recognising these very simple stimuli later, whilst adults were 87% correct. Surprisingly few studies of scene and object recognition subsequently have manipulated verbal labelling, possibly because, even if overt naming is not required, it is very hard to know how much internal or covert language is being used to help remember what is being directly witnessed but this is one area that may become greatly clarified by brain imaging techniques.

CHAPTER SUMMARY

Memory for depicted visual scenes develops through the primary school years, and is generally enabled by structure within the scene. Memory for routes is based initially on the spatio-temporal properties of travelling the route and shows a lack of reliance on distal cues. The ability to form overall spatial representations from routes travelled develops considerably between 5 and 10 years of age. Event – or episodic – memory also develops during that time, and is related to the development of script memory (remembering what normally occurs in that context). Weaker encoding of events can make children vulnerable to suggestibility when being questioned. Memory for verbal information is usually tested through list recall studies that show the effects of speed of processing on information retained. Although this increases up to at least 10 years old, the most predictive elements in what a child will remember from a narrative is their level of attention, depth of encoding, and familiarity with the information to be recalled.

LOOKING AHEAD TO CHAPTER 13

Considering children from the perspective of how they remember what they are told brings us to the point where we really cannot continue without adding in something that has been there all along – the knowledge brought to these things by the ever-present forces of human culture as transmitted through the teaching and language of adults. This does not change the fundamental mechanisms of learning and perception, but it increasingly channels these skills into new ones like learning how to classify things according to convention, how the physical world is measured and how to be more 'objective' when reasoning about the world. As always, difficulties have to be overcome, but – as always – these difficulties make perfect sense in terms of the drive and direction of the child's evolving cognition.

CHAPTER 13

UNDERSTANDING AND REASONING ABOUT CATEGORIES

In this and subsequent chapters we shall review some core elements of world knowledge that are essentially passed down 'by repute'. That is they are explicitly taught to children, if not formally at school then certainly by being raised within an adult culture. This is not just about *content* (Africa is a very large continent composed of many countries; a poodle is a kind of dog; there are 100 pennies in a pound). To be shared with others, many concepts have to conform to certain ways of structuring information. How do you explain what a continent is if a child can't visualise a subdivided space, why all dogs aren't poodles if they can't imagine a subdivided concept, and why 100 pounds is worth very much more than 100 pennies, if they can't grasp the base 10 system? And so, the main focus from now on is on *what it is about children's cognitive development* that can make some shared cultural knowledge hard to assimilate. This chapter focuses on one of the most basic knowledge structuring devices we have: the way we organise the world into classes or categories. Perceptual categorisation has been with us from the start of this book. An infant can perceive a face as a face and 2 year old can perceive something as a bird or a fish. But what level of conceptual understanding does this imply? We are now going to consider how the child learns how classes are constructed, how categories relate to one another (such as poodle and dog) and what can be inferred about an object from its classification.

LANGUAGE AND CATEGORISATION

LEARNING LANDMARKS

13.1 The conceptual challenge of categorisation. You should understand why class concepts can be challenging and how this is related to language.

13.2 Understanding the taxonomic referring function of words. You should understand what is meant by perceptual, thematic and categorical similarity and know which young children find difficult.

13.3 Language and the understanding of conceptual taxonomies. You should be able to cite a study showing how 'naming' nouns support the acquisition of taxonomic classes.

13.1 THE CONCEPTUAL CHALLENGE OF CATEGORISATION

It has been a recurring theme throughout this book that children learn by classifying, so what exactly could be challenging about understanding classes and categories at a conceptual level? Three things make this more than simply learning about the world through direct experience. The first is that, although children classify objects perceptually from infancy onwards, classifying something conceptually may result in a quite different result. Take a quick glance at the photos A and B in Panel 13.1. Which would you group as most similar just on appearance only? Now take a longer look and you will see that two are monkeys, whilst one is an owl. Not just a different zoological species, genus, or family but a different *order*, i.e. avian as opposed to primate. Usually, biological taxa are reasonably correlated with physical similarity amongst members for the very good reason that they share common ancestral lines. But in our world of biological sciences we taxonomise things by many different criteria, not just by external appearance. Some obvious examples are vertebrates, which would include things as diverse as alligators and mice, and insects, which would include head lice but not spiders. So one thing children have to do is understand the difference between what something looks like and what something *is*, according to cultural convention.

The second thing is completely related to the first, and that is to understand that words don't always correspond to something that can be directly seen or pointed at. You cannot *see* vehicleness in the same way that you can see a car, or *see* mammalness in the same way you see a cow. Children who have been exposed since birth to words that refer to things that can be pointed at have to learn that words can describe properties of things that go beyond any visible example, such as 'fruit', or that may not be visible at all, such as the concept of a germ or virus.

The third is related to the first two. Conceptual classification is almost always hierarchical. Eleanor Rosch, a professor of cognitive psychology at Berkeley University, pointed out that all human adults tend to classify things at what became known as **base level** in their everyday encounters with objects (Rosch, 2002). Base level is really the sort of perceptual level at which children learn the names of things such as dog, truck, ball, etc. These have perceivable properties but not at the level of precision that would require a more specific name such as spaniel, dumper truck, cricket ball, and so on. This further refinement is known as a subordinate level. (Don't get too distracted by what constitutes base and subordinate as they are not set in stone, and can depend very much on the context. For example, it might be reasonable to say that a trained show dog judge would consider spaniel as a base level, with Water, Springer, Cocker and King Charles spaniels as the subordinate categories.) The most important point about this is that levels are nested; a 'higher level' subsumes all lower levels. This means that the higher – or, roughly speaking, more conceptual – the level, the less perceivable it is and the more dependent we are on learning from others what constitutes membership of that level.

Finally, learning how to classify from adult guidance can run into confusions arising from questions like 'what is that? – what other things would go with that?' The adult may mean 'spoon' goes with 'fork' whereas for the child it may be that 'spoon' goes with 'coco-pops'. An example is given in photos C in Panel 13.1. The language of questioning children is another challenge as you will see.

13.2 UNDERSTANDING THE TAXONOMIC REFERRING FUNCTION OF WORDS

Taxonomic classification is about knowing to what group something belongs. This is shared knowledge involving facts and usage that have to be learned through language. We are told that a chimpanzee is not a monkey because of various morphological and behavioural characteristics that define it as an ape. A supermarket trolley is not described as a vehicle, though it could be argued to fit the description of a wheeled object designed to transport cargo. The important thing here is not the specific rules of usage themselves, but the fact there is an understanding that words 'monkey', 'ape', 'vehicle' and 'trolley' stand for agreed group membership. It is not up to the individual to decide what 'belongs' in a class or category (for our purposes these two terms may be used interchangeably). In early development, children quickly learn to use nouns to refer to individual objects with perceivable properties, but when do they learn that nouns can also stand for an agreed conceptual class?

One of the things that has made this amenable to investigation is the fact that children are happy to perform natural acts of grouping. In young children these tend to be based on what Markman (1989) has called **thematic belonging**. That is, if you ask

Panel 13.1 The conceptual challenge of categorisation

- Children have to learn that things that are perceptually similar (A) may not be in the same class
  - ... and that things in the same taxonomic class are not always perceptually similar (B)

- Broad classes like 'living thing' or 'vegetable' are rarely defined by shared characteristics that can be directly viewed
  - These depend on language for their definition
- Classes are hierarchically organised
  - This is also has to be explained through language

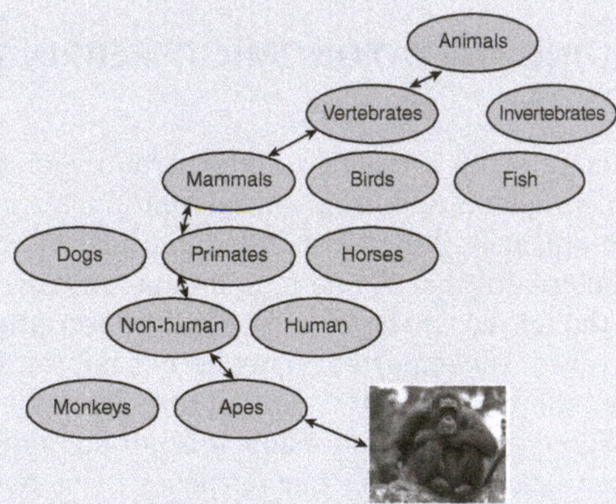

- Children's concepts of similarity are sometimes tested by asking them which pictures 'go together'
  - This often results in a non-taxonomic selection
    - see C above

a child to simply sort objects in terms of what things they think 'go together', they are more likely to link them in terms of a causal or contextual relationship, such as cows/grass, rather than a perceptual or taxonomic one, such as cows/pigs. Both Piaget and Vygotsky had noted that when children were asked to sort coloured shapes into groups, children of nursery age were more likely to make a pattern from the shapes than put them together in terms of colour or shape. In a more recent study, using what is known as a **forced choice technique**, Smiley and Brown (1979) showed children pictures of objects such as a needle or a cow and asked them to choose which of two pictures 'goes best with' (the name of) the picture they had just seen. In each pair there was a choice between a thematically linked picture (such as thread for 'needle', or milk for 'cow') and a **taxonomic** choice (pin for 'needle', pig for 'cow'). The results were quite striking: as Figure A, Panel 13.2 shows, even 6 year olds were more likely to select the thematic choice. Given this tendency, we can now ask at what age children will be sensitive to that special referring function of nouns, which is to identify something not just as an object but as belonging to a class of objects with similar properties.

With her colleague, Jean Hutchinson, Markman explored this with children of 2 and 3 years of age, using a clever technique. For, as Vygotsky also observed, using words that children may have already learned can confuse the issue as to what level of understanding they might have. For example, needle and thread may simply have been heard more frequently together in everyday conversation. Markman and Hutchinson (1984) investigated the effect of using an entirely novel noun in this sort of forced choice situation 'spoken' by a glove puppet. In the control (no word) condition the puppet showed the child a picture of an object, such as a police car or birthday cake, and pointed to the pair of choice pictures, one of which was **categorical** (in this context, this means roughly the same as taxonomic), the other being thematic. So they could choose, for example, between car (categorical) and policeman (thematic) in the case of the police car, or chocolate cake (categorical) and birthday present (thematic) in the case of the birthday cake, when given the instruction, 'find another one that is the same as this'. In the word condition the puppet named the original picture using a nonce word, saying, e.g. 'See this? It is a sud. Find another sud that is the same as this sud'. In the no word condition, there was no significant difference between the categorical and thematic choices, but there was a large and significant difference in favour of the categorical choices in the word condition in which the nonce noun was used. This shows that very young children understand that nouns don't just stand for objects; they can stand for a class of objects based on common properties and going beyond the particular example they are looking at.

Now we come to a problem. If children are building up their repertoire of nouns at this age and language is understood to have this particular function, then why *don't* children use taxonomic grouping in tasks like Smiley and Brown's by the age of 6? More recent research has drawn attention to one very important variable in all of this. Have you figured out what it is? Sometimes the instructions have been in the form of an invitation to find one that 'goes with' another object as in the case of the Smiley and Brown study (and also Piaget's original studies using coloured shapes). Markman and Hutchinson induced taxonomic grouping, by contrast, when children were asked to find one that is 'the same' as the (name of) the original object. If language conveys the meaning of a word, does it not also convey the broader context in which an object should be judged? Of course it does. 'Goes with' can imply grouping based on similarity or almost any other type of connection. 'Same as (name of)' implies something much more conceptual. Several studies since the 1980s have indeed found that children's categorisation does vary according to whether they are asked whether something 'goes with' (usually producing thematic choices) or 'is the same as' (usually producing more taxonomic choices). For example, Waxman and Namy (1997) gave 3 and 4 year olds toy objects and pictures of objects, such as tulip (target), together with daffodil and vase (choices), or carrot (target), together with tomato and rabbit (choices), but varied the instructions across participants. Some were shown the target, whilst it was named, and asked which of the choices 'goes best with this (name)'; others were simply shown the target objects and asked, 'which goes with this?'; and others were shown the object and asked to 'find another one'. In this study, the main finding was that there was often no consistent bias for one type of response over another, but where a bias did occur, the use of 'goes best/goes with' was more likely to provoke a thematic choice, whilst 'find another one' was more likely to produce a taxonomic choice especially in 4 year olds. This not only shows that language can have a subtle effect on children's categorisation; it also shows that they can be quite flexible from an early age as to how to categorise objects.

13.3 LANGUAGE AND THE UNDERSTANDING OF CONCEPTUAL TAXONOMIES

However, it would be wrong to think that this means that taxonomic classification is therefore really quite easy for young children. Taxonomic classification can be difficult for all the reasons listed earlier (learned by repute rather than direct experience, hierarchical, etc.). In the studies we have looked at so far 'taxonomic' has referred to that type of classification that is closest to everyday acts of natural categorisation, because they have been taxonomic classes that also happen to have perceptual similarity (tulip/daffodil) and/or a shared functional context (tomato/carrot); whereas, as mentioned above, one of the things that often makes taxonomising hard is the fact that appearance is not always relevant and the context or function shared by the items is outside the child's direct experience. Think about how many things a child will learn about in their late preschool and early school years that could fall into this category. Here are some: cargo, countries, germs, farm implements, spaceships, planets, soldiers, politicians, symphonies, poisons, predators, cereal crops, explorers and culinary herbs. Think up some more of your own – and then ask yourself, 'how did I ever come to understand *that*?'

This is not an irrelevant question. You may be thinking along the lines of storybooks or exceptionally patient teachers – but is it the words or the context-providing pictures that are most important? So suppose you want to get across the concept of,

Panel 13.2 Understanding the taxonomic referring function of words

- *Taxonomic* classification is based on shared function
  - o Vehicle, money, tools
- Or on biological criteria
  - o Mammal, virus, carnivore
- But when asked which things 'go together', young children tend to choose on shared context
  - o Spoon/bowl rather than spoon/fork
    - This is described as *thematic*

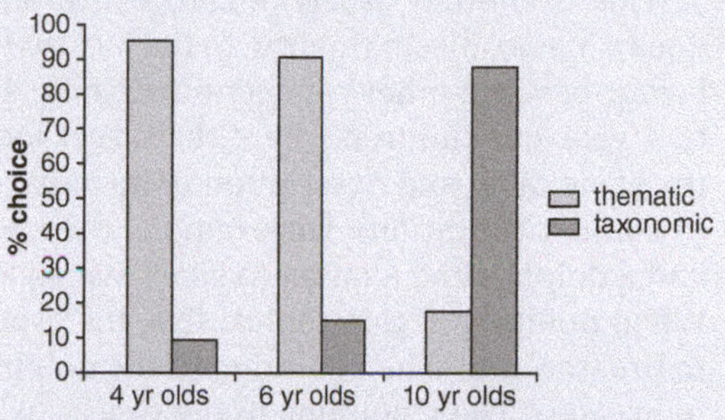

A Children were shown a picture and asked to choose one that 'goes with it'. Younger children made a thematic choice (e.g. milk with cow) rather than a taxonomic one (pig with cow). (Adapted from Smiley & Brown, 1979, with permission)

- But language can direct children towards the taxonomic choice through the use of a name word
- It can also direct via the question itself
  - o e.g. 'find another one' is more likely to elicit a choice based on category in preschoolers than 'find one that goes with'

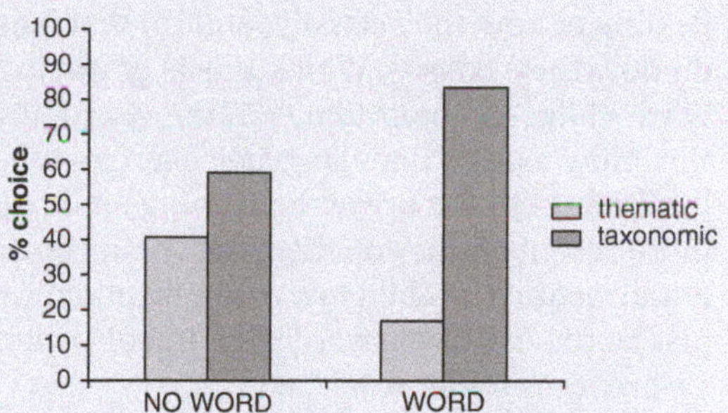

B Children were asked by a puppet to choose another picture 'the same as' e.g. a police car. Only when the puppet used 'puppet language' to refer to the car as a 'sud' and asked the child to 'show me another 'sud' (the WORD condition), did they choose another car (taxonomic) over a picture of a policeman (thematic). (Adapted from Markman & Hutchinson, 1984, with permission)

let's say, a 'missile', to a young child, what is the best way to go about it? How important is it to stress the word 'missile' when you are trying to explain the concept?

Would this new word help to direct the child's attention from the shape (which could otherwise cause e.g. a space rocket or the Gherkin Building to be mis-classified as a missile) and make them consider some other properties that cause things to be given this name?

This is another aspect of categorisation studied by Ellen Markman. That is when does a 'name' direct children to the fact that appearance might have to be over-ruled in favour of some other connection. Gelman and Markman (1986) gave trios of pictures to 4-year-old children where the target looked like one of the choices but was given the same label and description of its behaviour as the other (dissimilar looking) item (a conflict condition). For example, they would be shown a picture of a tropical fish and a dolphin and a target (a shark which looked more like the dolphin than the fish). When pointing to the tropical fish, the experimenter said, 'this fish stays underwater to breathe' and when pointing to the dolphin said, 'this dolphin pops above the water to breathe'. Then, pointing to the shark – which *looked* most like a dolphin, asked, 'see this *fish*; does it breathe underwater like this *fish*, or does it pop above the water to breathe?' In this ambiguous situation, children were significantly influenced by the name ('fish') in their choices and, in their answers, by the verbal description of fish as breathing underwater, when asked the question 'does it breathe underwater?', etc.

So we now know that (a) children as young as 4 years old can understand that invisible, i.e. conceptual, attributes can constitute a basis for classification; (b) that they are flexible in how they classify; and (c) that language has an important directing influence on how they classify. Whilst this is gratifying to know, is it enough? If we are hoping to teach children about things in the world, it is important to be a bit more explicit than this. How exactly does language exert an influence? Although Markman emphasised the importance of the use of the naming noun, e.g. 'fish', in her study, we now know from the more recent studies on thematic versus taxonomic classification that the magic ingredient directing the child towards a taxonomic definition of the ambiguous target may not just be the use of the word 'fish', but also all the other things conveyed in language, such as 'breathes under water', etc.

So, given that naming words themselves cannot always arbitrate between an appearance based similarity and a taxonomic similarity (after all, fish can also look alike in having fins, etc.), how else might language be used to draw attention to the fact some things are alike in ways that are not determined simply by appearance? A probing study into these issues was carried out by Gedeon Deak and Patricia Bauer from the University of Minnesota (Deak & Bauer, 1995). In one of their experiments, one group of pre-school children was given taxonomic pre-training such that with two taxonomically similar toy objects (e.g. large white chair and small red rocking chair) they would be asked 'are these the same kind of thing or different kinds?', and this was followed through with an explanation that tied the name and the idea of 'type of thing' together, e.g. 'That's right, they're both the same because they are both chairs'. Here it was emphasised that things can be called the same thing even though they look dissimilar. For taxonomically dissimilar (but perceptually similar) objects (e.g. shark and dolphin), they would get the feedback, 'they are different kinds of things because one is a shark and one is a dolphin'. A different group of children, by contrast, was given training that emphasised appearance only, so that when asked, 'are these two alike or different?' the follow-through explanations would be, e.g., 'yes these are alike because they both have fins', or (for the chairs), 'yes these are different because one rocks and is red and the other is large and white'. In subsequent tests with new unlabelled objects, this selective training increased the degree to which the taxonomically related item was chosen as the match, when asked 'which is the same kind of thing?', and conversely, the perceptually related one when asked the 'most like' question. This confirms the usefulness of naming when introducing conceptual (as opposed to perceptual) categories but it also shows how children can be directed either towards taxonomic or to appearance based classification on the basis of a more general linguistic instruction. Children's own spontaneous labelling in this study coincided with the type of match they had made, whether taxonomic or appearance-based, showing,

Panel 13.3 Language and the understanding of conceptual taxonomies

- Names have to be used flexibly with regard both to appearance and categorical criteria
- How and when can we influence children to take the taxonomic meaning from a word?
- If the name is stressed in conjunction with a taxonomic explanation, pre-school children can over-ride perceptual similarity

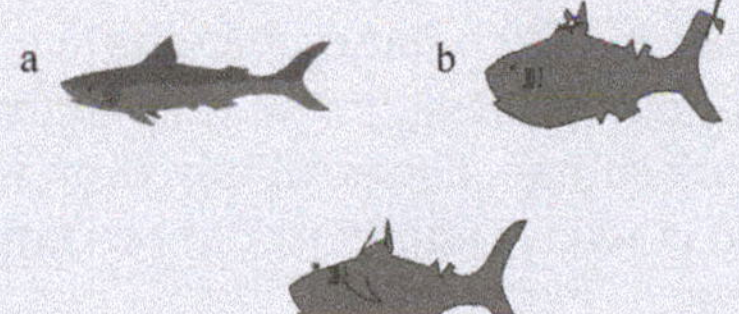

'See this *"fish"* – does it swim under water like a fish (a) or come up for air like a dolphin (b)?'

In the above situation, 4 year olds will generally go for 'swim under water'
(After Gelman & Markman, 1986)

- Linguistic training and instruction can help to direct children of this age to taxonomic *or* appearance based criteria when labelling, such as:
  - 'These are *both the same kind of thing* so they are both fish' or
  - 'These *both have fins*, so they are both fish'

like Gelman and Markman's study, that by 4 years of age, children are able use naming words in ways that can reflect cultural as well as appearance-based criteria for categorising.

CONCEPTUAL HIERARCHIES

LEARNING LANDMARKS

13.4 Understanding the hierarchical structure of classes. You should know that, naming apart, there are cognitive constraints on children's grasp of the hierarchical structure of categories. You should be able to cite evidence for this.

13.5 Collections versus hierarchies. You should know the difference between count nouns and mass nouns and know why children find the latter easier to understand. You should be able to cite a study illustrating this.

13.4 UNDERSTANDING THE HIERARCHICAL STRUCTURE OF CLASSES

It might appear from the above that all you have to do is stress that a shared name implies some shared properties that can sometimes go beyond the directly perceivable. But there is a remaining issue with classification. The words still have to be slotted into a nested structure in which some concepts are more inclusive than others (such as 'flower' versus 'daffodil'). Piaget made this famous in a class-inclusion test that we shall consider in due course. For now, however, let us think of the problem in more concrete terms and consider another of his examples. The situation (Piaget, 1964) was as described next.

The child is presented with eight or more counters in a row, consisting of a random layout of red squares, blue squares and blue circles. In the course of getting him or her to reproduce the row from remaining counters, the experimenter asks a variety of questions using the terms 'all' and 'some'. An example is given in Panel 13.4 (where light grey stands for red and dark grey for blue). Notice that colour and shape terms are not necessarily assigned to a superordinate and base level status (just like flower), but either shape words like 'square' *or* colour words like 'blue' can be used to subsume other subsets within a hierarchical nesting. In the real world, shape is more likely than colour to identify a class or category, with colour as a subset (red and blue hats, etc.).

The question itself suggests this nesting of colour under shape, as it refers to the shape and then asks about possible subsets, and the participant Pierre appears to be thinking of shape as the superordinate when he says 'no there are only two', meaning not all the shapes are circles. Nevertheless, when he is asked about the colour of the circles, he is not thinking of the circles as having one subset (blue) but answers on the basis of both the circles and the squares. Whichever way you look at it, Pierre does not have a clear organisation of the whole set as either colour by shape or shape by colour, as shown in Panel 13.4.

Panel 13.4 Understanding the hierarchical structure of classes

- Piaget discovered that children under the age of 7 can be unclear about nested classes
- In this example, a 5-year-old boy is not using a confident nesting of shape (2) by colour (2) to answer the series of questions

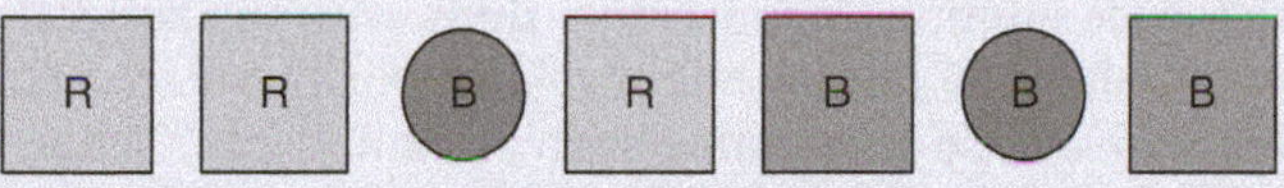

'Are all the circles blue?' Pierre: 'No, there are only two'
'Are all the squares blue?' Pierre: 'No'
'And all the circles are blue?' Pierre: 'No there are blue ones and red ones'
'What are the red ones like?' Pierre: 'Square'

- Neither of the two possible hierarchies (A and B) are being used by Pierre to conceptualise the whole set

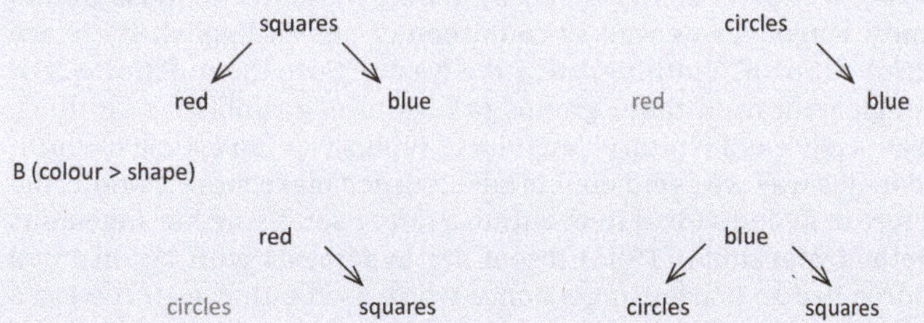

This might seem a bit unfair to the child as there is no obvious reason why shape should be nested under colour or colour nested by shape in this task, and it may be this ambiguity that causes the difficulty here – especially as one subset (red circles) is missing. However, subsequent work by Markman has shown that hierarchical nesting is indeed challenging for children under 6 years of age. Markman showed this through the way that children come to understand different sorts of superordinate nouns, as we see next.

13.5 COLLECTIONS VERSUS HIERARCHIES

Let us go back to what is meant by superordinate nouns. These, by definition, include more things than any of the base level subsets. 'Animals' includes more items than cows, and 'toys' more items than dolls, for example. Yet words like 'animals' and 'toys' are surely prevalent in children's early language and so are they not also capable of understanding these simple **inclusive** relationships? And here is the very important point noted by Markman. Children learn such words initially without necessarily understanding the inclusive principle. For example, Callanan and Markman (1982) observed that children in the preschool age range were happy to use 'toys', 'drinks', 'animals', etc. to refer to collections of things, but were sometimes resistant to naming an individual thing with the collective noun. So, for example, they would happily put 'all the toys' in a box but were resistant to calling an individual toy with a base level name such as 'ball', a 'toy'. When this was examined in greater detail by Blewitt (1994) it was found that children as young as 2 and 3 could in fact apply multiple levels of category name when specifically tested, and that it was more a question of preference of one over the other. They cite an example where the base level name 'hammer' would be preferred over the superordinate name 'tool', and quote a child making this sort of choice, saying it was the 'realest' name for the object!

However, another factor was identified by Markman that could also contribute to discomfort with double labelling. The names we have been talking about are **count nouns**. That is, the superordinate term such as toy, drink or animal is applied to a single item *and* to a collection of similar items by adding the suffix 's'. **Mass nouns** have evolved in most languages as well as count nouns, and in English these are terms like 'furniture', 'rubbish', 'clothing', etc. Here we don't use the indefinite article to refer to a single item from these groups (a furniture, a rubbish, a clothing, etc.). Instead we say 'a piece of furniture', 'an item of rubbish' or 'an article of clothing' and so on, and in this way we avoid double labelling *and* make more obvious the hierarchical structure of an individual item within a larger set. Using her ingenious 'puppet speak' method, Markman (1985) tested her hypothesis with an invented category that children had to learn using a nonce word, used either as if it were a

Panel 13.5 Collections versus hierarchies

- Young children often use a term such as 'toys' as if it refers to a collection rather than a superordinate term that subsumes, e.g. 'ball', 'doll', etc.
- A term such as 'toys' is a *count noun* – an object can be a toy (superordinate) *and* a doll (base-level)
    - Reluctance to call something both 'a toy' and 'a doll' suggests a difficulty in thinking hierarchically
- They have less difficulty with *mass nouns* such as 'furniture' or 'clothing'
    - The term 'piece of' seems to make the structure clearer
        - For example, a chair is a 'piece' of furniture
        - A hat is an 'article' of clothing
- The mass noun involves a specific term to sub-divide the set
    - e.g. 'piece of'
- This is thought to help the child grasp the hierarchical nature of the class

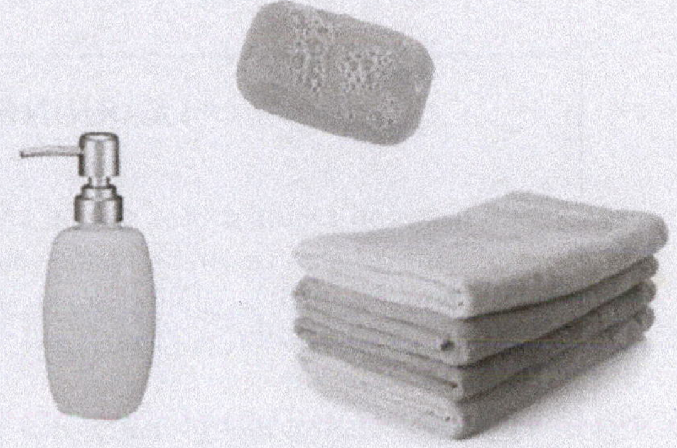

(a) 'Here are some pieces of veb'

(b) 'Here are some vebs'

Preschool children are introduced to items that belong to a new category (bathroom accessory) by a puppet using the nonce word 'veb'. They were better at correctly classifying new items when they had been trained with word as a mass noun (a) than as a count noun (b). (After Markman, 1985)

count noun or a mass noun. One such category included items of bathroom accessory such as sponge, soap, towel, shampoo and so on. The puppet showed pictures of these items to preschool-aged children and said either 'here are some vebs' *or* 'here are some pieces of veb'. When tested with new items and distracters, children who had learned the count noun showed great confusion when asked the question 'is this a veb?', answering either yes or no to everything they were asked, whilst they were more successful in dealing with the question when posed with the mass noun as noun: 'is this a piece of veb?'

REASONING ABOUT CLASSES

As you learned from Chapter 1, Piaget's fascination with the grasp of logic resulted in developmental psychology in the first half of the twentieth century being centred heavily around reasoning abilities. Reasoning by children is a natural extension of how they think, and as we have seen they do not necessarily think of classes as hierarchically structured. We shall now consider how this impacts on how they reason about classes.

LEARNING LANDMARKS

13.6 Inclusion relations. You should know that the logic of class inclusion involves transitivity and asymmetry and you should be able to define these concepts. You should be able to cite a study showing which is harder for children to grasp and what is meant by empirical reasoning.

13.7 Classification and executive skills. You should understand why the development of classification is also about the development of executive control: specifically conceptual flexibility. You should be able to describe how this can be tested.

13.6 INCLUSION RELATIONS

Piaget's most famous test of reasoning about classes (Piaget, 1964) is called the **class inclusion** task, in which he deliberately used the language of taxonomies. He showed children a set of flowers, composed of two subsets (tulips and roses), where there were more tulips than roses, and asked the key question, 'Are there more tulips or are there more flowers?' His finding was that children below the age of 6 or 7 would answer 'tulips', basing their answer on the relative sizes of the two subsets of flowers. This claim has been modified by subsequent research that suggests that children are more likely to get the right answer if the wording of the task is altered to make the set/subset distinction clearer (as in 'are there more cows or more lying down cows') (McGarrigle et al., 1978), but the general difficulties with inclusion relations have been replicated in many studies.

It is important at this stage that we distinguish between the grasp of a logical rule pertaining to amount, and the understanding of what might constitute the larger of two classes, based purely on particular knowledge about the items in them. Piaget argued that, at around the age of 7, children have a concrete understanding of the elementary logic of inclusion. This means that they understand that class A (flowers) is composed of sub-classes B and C (tulips and daffodils) such that they simultaneously grasp that A = B + C and that A – B = C, and so on. This is called an operational structure (see Chapter 1) and a key aspect is that it represents the use of a universal principle that will apply to other things in the real world such as animals and so on. It is not yet truly abstract in the sense that it is tied to these particular instantiations. So we are talking here about what Piaget would call 'concrete operations'. But just how 'logical' is the understanding of class inclusion at this age? We now know from other research that superordinate category words may be used and understood as base level (like 'flower'). And we also know that if children know a lot about base level terms they may be unwilling to re-name a single item with its superordinate ('doll' and 'toy'). It has therefore been surmised (Deneault & Ricard, 2005) that children understand the 'logic' of class inclusion by a sort of default. If a word like 'fish' is relatively poorly known in terms of different types of fish, it is more likely to be given the superordinate role (implying a larger set) in a reasoning task such as 'Are there more fish or more sardines?'

Does this mean that reasoning about real-world categories isn't really based on logic at all? Is the child's reasoning simply an elusive aspect of their individual understanding of different things in the world? Or can we consider the child's grasp of categories as having at least some inherent grasp of the logic of nested hierarchies, albeit in a partial way? There are two logical properties that are entailed by hierarchical classifications. One is known as **transitivity**:

> All Xs are A
>
> This is an X
>
> Therefore this *must be* an A

The other property is **asymmetry**, which means that the above conclusion can only be reached in one direction. Substitute 'Dog' for X and 'Animal' for A and you can say:

> 'All dogs are animals
>
> Bengo is a dog
>
> Therefore Bengo is an animal'

So you can reason upwards from X to A, but you can't reason downwards from A to X; i.e. you *can't* say 'Bengo is an animal; therefore Bengo is a dog'.

The grasp of real-world categorical understanding in terms of these logical properties was measured in a study by Deneault and Ricard (2005). The study was conducted with 5-, 7- and 9-year-old children. Transitivity was assessed at superordinate/basic, basic/subordinate and superordinate/subordinate levels, using nonsense words. For example, basic to superordinate would take the form:

'Do you know what a DAX is?'

'A DAX is a dog'

'If a DAX is a dog, is a DAX an animal?'

Subordinate to basic would be:

'Do you know what a DAX is?'

'A DAX is a collie'

'If a DAX is a collie, is a DAX a dog?'

And subordinate to superordinate would be:

'Do you know what a DAX is?'

'A DAX is a collie'

'If a DAX is a collie, is a DAX an animal?'

Asymmetry was assessed by comparing these forms to the reversed version:

'Do you know what a DAX is?'

'A DAX is a dog'

'If a DAX is a dog, is a DAX a collie?'

As a DAX *might be* a collie, children's justifications of either a 'yes' answer ('well it could be') were carefully noted, and it was followed up with supplementary questions such as 'can it be something else?'

Panel 13.6 Inclusion relations

- A well-known example of reasoning about classes (*class inclusion*) is Piaget's flowers task (below): 'are there more flowers or more daffodils?'
    - Young children will answer 'daffodils' if they outnumber another subset of flowers
- To be able to reason with a classification hierarchy, two properties of inclusion must be understood
- One is called *transitivity* (see I)

I. a transitive inference:
All dogs are animals
Bengo is a dog
Therefore Bengo is an animal

- Inclusion relations require subsuming a smaller part within a larger one
    - So whilst the conclusion in (I) is necessarily true, it is not a necessarily true conclusion in (II)
- This property is called *asymmetry* (see I versus II)
- Children show an earlier grasp of transitivity than asymmetry

II. an incorrect deduction:
Bengo is an animal
All dogs are animals
Therefore Bengo is a dog

Children were given information about a Nonce animal and then asked different questions, e.g.

- A DAX is a collie
    - is a DAX a dog?
    - is a DAX an animal?

(transitivity at two levels)

- A DAX is a dog
    - is a DAX an animal?
    - is a DAX a collie?

(asymmetry; only the upward direction is correct)

(Adapted from Denauld & Ricard, 2005, with permission)

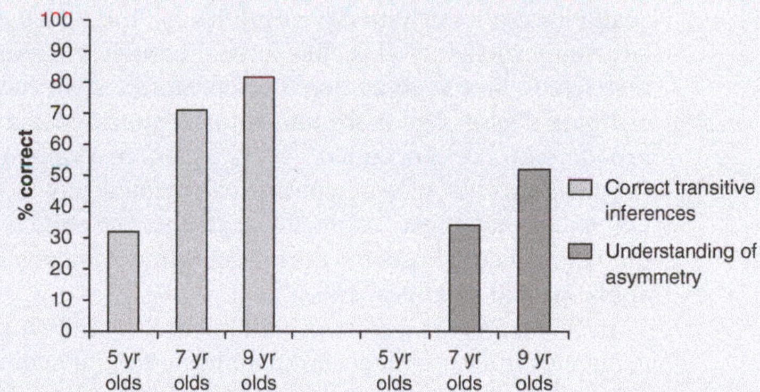

- Children's world knowledge both helps them to reason (they know about animals and dogs) but can also hinder it (it can be hard to generate hypothetical alternatives to the one offered)
    - Their understanding of inclusion relations could be said to be *concrete* but not truly logical

As the graph in Panel 13.6 shows, children improve between 5 and 9 years on transitivity questions (across all levels), and the level at which the categories were introduced made no difference. This cannot be taken to imply that they understand the logic of inclusion relations at all hierarchical levels though, because there was a large amount of faulty 'downwards' inferences committed on the asymmetry questions overall, with 5 year olds failing altogether. Correct answers certainly reflected their understanding of the **indeterminacy** of the relations in their justifications. For example:

> 'A DAX is an animal'
>
> 'Is a DAX a dog?'
>
> 'It could be because you didn't say what kind of animal it is'

This ability to justify their reasoning logically was much better (for 7 and 9 year olds) when they were considering superordinate/basic relations – as above – than in cases where they were asked about the subordinate level, as in:

> 'A DAX is a dog'
>
> 'Is a DAX a Dalmatian?'

... arguing that this could not be the case as Dalmatians already had a name! As the authors point out, the pattern of both success and errors could be explained on the availability of alternative possibilities for the nonce word. A novel term assigned to a large superordinate class like animal implies a larger set of possibilities than a more restricted class such as dog. Furthermore, as we have already noted, basic and subordinate classes are more perceptually specified than the more linguistically defined broader classes like animal. The vividness of a category such as 'Dalmatian' may block the formation of other hypothetical possibilities in the mind of the child. Certainly, taken together, these results illustrate that the child is using acquired knowledge about the world as the basis for reasoning rather than any abstract logical rules that should apply in each and every case.

In short, there is a growing understanding of the logic of nested relationships implied in our cultural use of superordinate, basic and subordinate terms, but even at the age of 9, this is still at an empirical level of understanding. That is to say, children are beginning to acquire the hierarchical structure of specific category names along with those names (Dalmatian, dog, animal) and make some valid deductions from them, without as yet having a clear insight into the general logical structure of categories. This is also sometimes referred to as **empirical reasoning**, and it is important to note that this is not quite the same as Piaget's concept of concrete operations. The difference is that the newer research shows that 'becoming logical' at a concrete level is not quite the all-or-none sort of transition to a new truly logical way of thinking that Piaget claimed to appear at around the age of 7. Even at the level of 'concrete' real-world knowledge, progress is gradual, piecemeal and (still) heavily influenced by the child's perceptions of the world and what they believe names to refer to. This can both help and hinder the process of reasoning logically.

13.7 CLASSIFICATION AND EXECUTIVE SKILLS

Resistance to renaming is one good reason why all the terms acquired at base level in early language acquisition are hard to incorporate into a hierarchical structure where the base level (e.g. car) gets subsumed by something more general (vehicle). On the other hand, you might reasonably ask (and well done if you already have), why is grasping the hierarchical structure so hard in the first place?

What is the difficulty here? It may not be immediately obvious but there is a connection between this difficulty and the struggle that young children have in learning how to plan complex motor actions such as reaching past an obstacle for an object. You may remember from Chapter 4 that the key to this development was in a part of the brain called the pre-frontal cortex. Patients with damage to this area have difficulties inhibiting some actions (motor inhibition) but they also have difficulties in terms of cognitive tasks that require flexibly shifting from one goal-directed response to another. A famous test of this is the Wisconsin Card Sort task, which requires a sorting rule such as 'put all the red-coloured pictures in one pile and the green ones in another' to be switched to a sorting rule based on another dimension of difference such as shape (e.g. 'the round ones in one pile and the square ones in another, whatever their colour'). Once the first rule is established, frontal patients cannot give it up in favour of the new one. This is called **perseveration**.

Being flexible with the way an object might be classified as, say, an apple, a fruit, lunch or a round bio-degradable object makes demands therefore not just on having these different types of concepts available. It also implies the ability to select the appropriate conceptual scheme from a set of possible alternatives. There is an important and subtle point lurking in here in relation to how children become more

Panel 13.7 Classification and executive skills

- Classifying hierarchically requires cognitive flexibility and being able to access different classification levels
  - This is an aspect of executive control
- Flexibility also means being able to use different grouping criteria and to switch amongst them
  - For example to sort things by theme (e.g. picnic, breakfast) and then re-sort by type (cutlery, food, etc.)
- This can be tested by asking children to sort pictures into groups and then asking them to sort the same pictures in a different way
- Children are only able to make two distinct sorts by the age of 6, but three by the age of 9

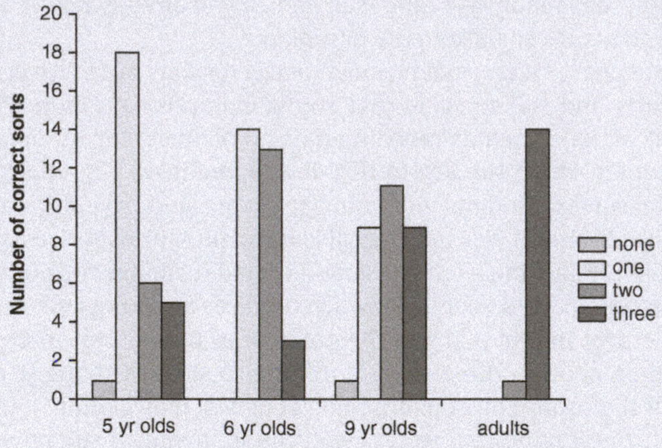

Developmental increase in the number of different possible 'sorts' of the same pictures. (Adapted from Blaye et al., 2006, with permission)

- Preschool-aged children seem unable to classify flexibly within the same trial
  - Though they may do so across trials

logical. To be truly flexible you should not only be able to access the appropriate category levels (superordinate, base level, etc.), you should also be able to switch to a different basis for categorising depending on the context. When a mother says to her daughter, 'see the pretty flower', she is drawing attention to its perceptual properties. When she says (of a raspberry bush), 'the flower will grow into fruit', she is drawing attention to the taxonomic properties of the flowering part of a fruit bush. We know that preschool children can use names in ways that flexibly reflect different criteria for sorting, but just how conceptually flexible can they be and how would you measure it? A solution has been offered by Agnes Blaye of the Aix-Marseille Université. She has argued that what is needed is to look at how many types of classification can be carried out by the same child in relation to the same object. In one study (Blaye et al., 2006) she asked children to sort pictures into different groupings and to name the groupings, but then to try sorting the pictures in a 'new way' (up to three different sorts). The ability to produce multiple sorts increased dramatically with age as the graph in Panel 13.7 illustrates. A further indication that this is indeed to do with executive control and flexible switching came from another study by (Blaye & Jacques, 2009) in which they compared the performance of 3- to 5-year-old children on a match-to-sample task, in which one of three pictures could be matched to a sample on the basis of a taxonomic classification (dog and snail) or a thematic basis (dog and kennel). However, the different sorts of matching could take place across different trials or *within the same* trial. Only 5 year olds were as good at classifying flexibly under both conditions; around half of the younger children were not significantly above chance when they had to 'double classify' within the same trial.

CHAPTER SUMMARY

Categorisation according to conventional criteria can be challenging for young children, owing to the fact that it may involve overcoming perceptual appearance and having to use more than one (level) of naming for the same object. The use of language is important in directing children to how an object is categorised, especially when it involves directing them to taxonomic (rather than perceptual) criteria. The hierarchical nesting of categories is a key cognitive challenge for children as shown by inconsistencies and inflexibility in their reasoning about classes. Classification occurs in tandem with real-world knowledge and familiarity with class names, and this in itself gradually helps to build conceptual hierarchies.

LOOKING AHEAD TO CHAPTER 14

In this chapter, we have seen how the development of categorical understanding depends not just on learning facts, but on the child acquiring the cognitive skills that are involved in moving around in a hierarchically organised conceptual 'space'. In the next chapter, we shall be focussing on the sorts of conceptual structures that are required for an adult-like representation of aspects of the world such as time and space. And again, we shall view the impact of these developments on the child's growing ability to reason.

CHAPTER 14

UNDERSTANDING AND REASONING ABOUT TIME AND SPACE

A child will eventually have to stretch his or her imagination to encompass new ideas about big things in space and time, like the world, the universe, eternity and the future. Small things can be equally challenging – a microbe, a nanosecond, etc. But stretching the imagination depends on having a scale in which to locate concepts such as an inch, foot or mile; a minute, hour, or week, etc. These provide the structures for acquiring knowledge about things we can never experience directly. What would be the point of asking a child to imagine some very, very large space or some very long time if some of these basic concepts are not in place? You would not only get a different answer from every child as to how big the universe is, or how small a 'flu virus, they are likely to be inaccurate on a truly cosmic scale. Indeed our own understanding as adults defeats our imagination when it comes to Planck lengths and billions of light years. And so, rather like the way in which concepts of classes have to be established by cultural consensus, we come to understand and represent space and time in our human experience through our shared cultural use of spatial and also time-related or **temporal** words. For space, these words refer to the three dimensions of up and down, back and front and to the side of. For time: past, present and future.

When it comes to thinking and reasoning with these concepts, however, space and time pose a challenge both to the child and also the investigator. For it is quite legitimate to think of space and time relative to one's own perspective, and indeed there is no other way in which to acquire spatial and temporal understanding in the first place. On the other hand, to be able to share these concepts with others, it is important to take a more objective viewpoint – either in terms of a fixed point in time (yesterday it looked as if it were going to rain) – or in space (a Volvo has just parked behind our car). Being able to do both is a challenge for the child and also to the imagination of the researcher in trying to test this.

As you may already be thinking, space and time are not of course completely independent in our normal experience; if an item moves from place A to place B, then it happens in time as well. Nevertheless, we are quite used to thinking about them as distinct concepts – indeed even today, many people find the Einsteinian concept of space-time very hard to grasp. Psychologically, temporal and spatial concepts pose subtly different sorts of challenges for the developing child and we shall deal with them in turn.

THINKING AND REASONING ABOUT TIME

Our imagination is sometimes defeated by what we are told about the immensity of cosmic time and the seemingly endless duration of prehistoric epochs. Astrophysicist and palaeontologists often use what are called 'geologic analogies' to scale them down to something we have actually experienced, such as the progression of a single day or year. But these analogies help only because we have such culturally shared concepts of time. How well developed are these fundamental concepts in the young child?

LEARNING LANDMARKS

14.1 Understanding temporal referring expressions. You should be able to cite a pioneering study on the acquisition of words and expressions referring to time and have an idea about how this ability develops.

14.2 Understanding past and future. You should know the age at which children can answer questions accurately about future events, and be able to describe how this is tested. You should understand why this ability is limited by constraints on executive functioning.

14.3 Temporal concepts and episodic memory. You should know the difference between episodic and semantic memory and know which is harder for young children and what factors can affect it.

14.4 Temporal decentring. You should know what this means and be able to cite a study testing this ability in young children.

14.5 Temporal reasoning. You should know what is meant by inductive and deductive inference and be able to show how the latter can be tested using a concrete task.

14.1 UNDERSTANDING TEMPORAL REFERRING EXPRESSIONS

Not a great deal is known about the child's understanding of words like day, week, etc. This is probably because it is quite hard to think of a way of determining this without involving other time words, e.g. 'how long is a week?' Also the answer may simply produce a rote answer without understanding: there are seven days in a week, etc. What we do know comes largely from the child's own spontaneous use of temporal terms.

The first study of this was carried out a long time ago by a famous psychologist called Louise Bates Ames at Yale University (Ames, 1946), and it is worth looking at what she found. About 50 preschool children aged between 2 and 8 years were observed over the course of nearly a year and their spontaneous conversation analysed. Specific questions relating to time were also asked of these children and also of older children – up to 8 years old. Ames asked a good many questions – ranging from questions about actual times and dates such as 'when do you take your nap?' and 'when is your next birthday?' to questions about days of the week such as 'what comes after Sunday?' and 'how many minutes are in an hour?' From a wealth of observations and answers, she drew some succinct conclusions, which are summarised here:

- **18 months**. Has little if any sense of the past and future. No time words are used.
- **21 months**. His chief time word is 'now'; he will wait in response to 'in a minute'.
- **24 months**. Has several words which denote future (especially 'gonna') and several words to denote the present ('now', 'today', 'dis day').
- **30 months**. Numerous word for past, present and future time, fewer for past than future; 'tomorrow' is used but not 'yesterday'.
- **36 months**. Expressions of duration such as 'all the time/all day'; can tell how old he is and when he goes to bed; uses a lot of 'when' questions.
- **42 months**. Refinements in use of time phrases such as 'it's almost time', 'a nice long time', 'on Fridays'.
- **48 months**. New words such as 'month', 'next summer'; and according to Ames 'a reasonably clear understanding of when events of the day take place in relation to each other'.
- **5 years**. Can tell what time it is; can name days of week and what day follows Sunday.
- **6 years**. Has knowledge of seasons and an increased knowledge of duration.
- **7 years**. Can tell season, month and time but 'the larger concept of what year it is still beyond him'.
- **8 years**. Cannot only tell the time but 'indicates an understanding of the more generalised concept in his ability to answer the question what does time mean?'

Ames's account gives us a picture of a child whose concept of time is expanding to cover past and future and events of differing durations.

Research since then has been somewhat patchy, but in response to this, Janie Busby Grant from the University of Canberra attempted to gain a more comprehensive and

Panel 14.1 Understanding temporal referring expressions

- Words referring to time (temporal expressions) occur in increasing variety and specificity in children's spontaneous speech from the age of about 2
- We know this from records of spontaneous use as well as experiments that ask children specific questions such as 'how long is a week?'
- Studies suggest that children start by referring to the present, and then to the future more than the past
- Their use of temporal terms becomes more specific
- These data, however, only tell us about usage – they do not probe the child's underlying concepts of time

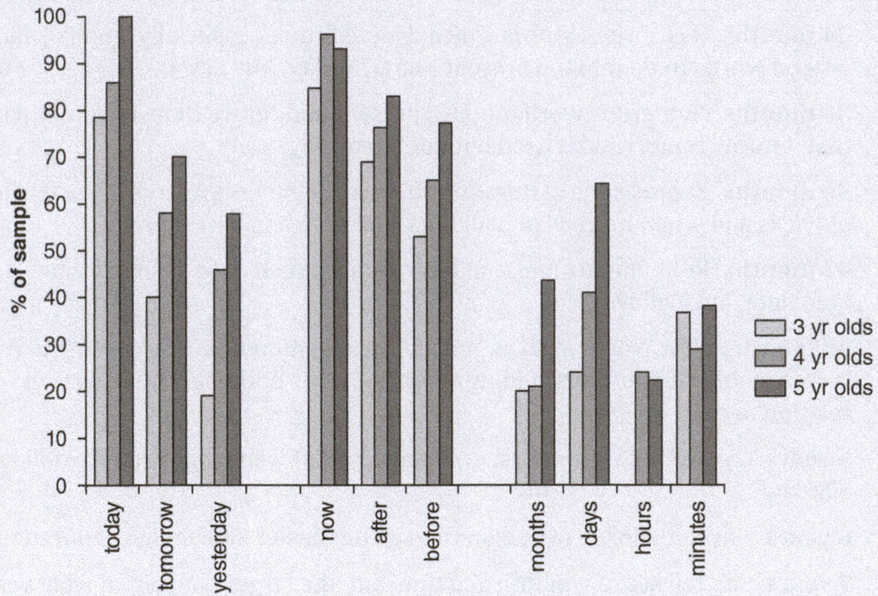

Percentage of a sample of children judged by parents to correctly produce certain temporal terms. (Adapted from Busby Grant & Suddendorf, 2011, with permission)

updated view of children's use of temporal terms (Busby Grant & Suddendorf, 2011). She focussed on 18 of these such as 'today', 'tomorrow', 'yesterday', 'next week', 'last week', etc. and concentrated on children between the ages of 3 and 5 years. Her method was parental interview using a customised questionnaire called 'children's talk about time', where the parents had to report accurate use of these terms. These results are very consistent with Ames' findings from over half a century earlier. Children show a steady increase in the use of these terms but also show a strong bias towards the present, a greater use of terms referring to the future than the past and a much higher use of words represent general order in time (before, after) rather than terms denoting particular temporal units. Some of the data from this study are shown in Panel 14.1.

14.2 UNDERSTANDING PAST AND FUTURE

This helps to flesh out the picture somewhat, but word use alone clearly leaves a lot of questions unanswered. Many of these terms are colloquial – 'let's leave it for now', 'in a minute' (often meaning more than one!), 'yesterday's children' (meaning an other era). The words we use to describe things happening in our own lives may not necessarily reflect a more objective state of affairs. But when it does, it is crucial to understand that only things in the past – and not things in the future – can have resulted in a present state. Other research by Busby Grant (Busby Grant & Suddendorf, 2010) suggests that this emerges roughly around the age of 4 or 5, but varies somewhat depending on the task. It was only by the age of 5 that children were able to answer at above chance levels in regard to story scripts about tomorrow and yesterday. Here the experimenter sets up scripted scenarios such as 'Mindy bought a new toothbrush yesterday/Emma is going to buy a new toothbrush tomorrow' then asks 'Who should I ask if I want to see a new toothbrush now?' However, there were certain memory demands in these scenarios and when better performance by 4 year olds was obtained when the words 'did' and 'will' were used, it raised the question about whether some linguistic terms make more vivid the causal implications of what happens in the past versus what happens in the future.

To avoid such a heavy reliance on the child's understanding of language, Povinelli et al. (1999) looked at how children understood the temporal events in a videotape. Children aged between 3 and 5 years looked at videos depicting events in their own recent past. These were created by filming the child engaged in a game with interesting props, whilst an unobserved adult hid a puppet in one of two boxes behind the child's back. A new game, with different props was started, and this time the puppet was hidden in the other box. After playing the games, the child was invited to watch the videotapes to work out where the puppet 'is now'. Children of 3 years old were not above chance on this game, whilst 5 year olds could work out from the props which of the two films correctly clued the location of the object. From this study, we know that the 5-year-old child can distinguish recent (and relevant) past from more distant past, using visual cues. So what about past versus future?

An answer to this question comes from a study reported by McColgan and McCormack (2008). The scenario presented to the child involved a zoo with five cages and a kangaroo in the middle cage (see Panel 14.2). A doll (Emily) visited cages 1 and 2, placing her rucksack containing a Polaroid camera in the lockers at each cage and then retrieving it before moving on. There was no locker at the kangaroo's cage; she takes out the Polaroid and takes a photo of the kangaroo, puts her camera back in the rucksack and continues

Panel 14.2 Understanding past and future

- A key element in this understanding is the realisation that only the past can affect the ways things are now
- This can be tested using scenarios such as telling the child:
  - 'Mindy bought a hairbrush yesterday; Mandy is buying a new one tomorrow; Who should I visit to borrow one today?'
    - But the child has to remember the information correctly
- Another technique is to ask a child to reconstruct an event in terms of past and future
  - Or plan an event in these terms

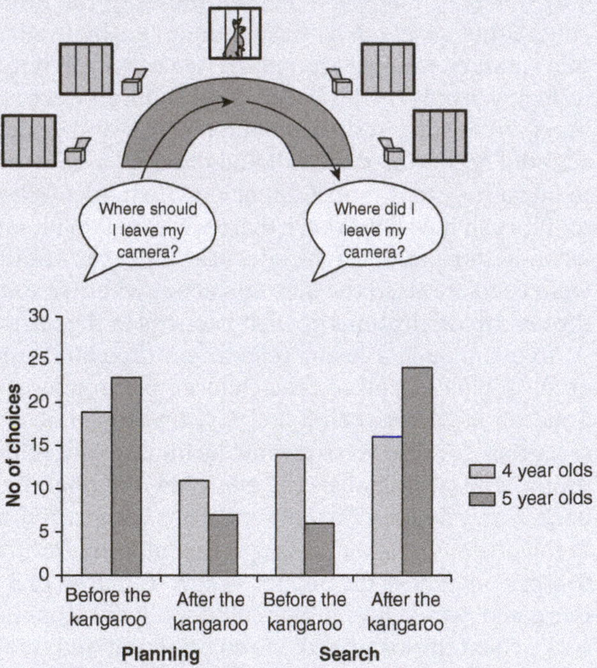

Children are told about a doll's visit to the zoo. She takes a picture of the kangaroo, but loses her camera and the child is asked to work out where she may have left it. In another task, a doll is planning to take a photo but must leave her camera where she can pick it up on her way round. The child is asked to help her decide where to leave it. Only 5 year olds were significantly above chance on both tasks. (Adapted from McColgan & McCormack, 2008, with permission)

- Sorting out past and future *in* the past is easier for 4 year olds if memory demands are reduced
  - In the zoo (search) task, this was done by reducing the locations to only one before and after

to visit the cages. At the end of this, the child is told that the camera is not in the bag and it must have fallen out in one of the lockers (a search task). The child is invited to help Emily find the camera. Clearly it had to be lockers 4 or 5. This tests the distinction between past and future with regard to an event that is already in the past. In a second (planning) task, the child was told that a doll (Molly) wanted to take a photo of the kangaroo when she got to its cage but needs to leave her camera in one of the lockers so that she could pick it up on the way to the kangaroo. Which locker should she leave it in?

As you can see from the graph in Panel 14.2, there was a rise in correct performance with age, and only the 5 year olds were significantly above chance. Being able to plan the future event, however, seemed to develop earlier than the ability to search the past, as 4 year olds were significantly better on the planning task. At first sight, this would seem to suggest that thinking about the relationship between past and future *in* the future is easier than sorting out what *was* 'future' from what was 'past' in the past. Through various manipulations of their procedure, the authors went on to show, however, that 4 year olds passed and were *better* on the memory task when there was only one cage before and after the kangaroo. This suggested that they found it hard to decide amongst two past locations – only one of which was the correct location of the lost camera.

Taken together, all the results from this set of experiments make sense from the point of view of executive control. Reconstructing a past with two possible outcomes makes demands on cognitive flexibility but being able to plan an action (rather than simply remembering one) is also considered a very important element in executive functioning, as you may remember from Chapter 3. So when the memory element was simplified, planning with regard to when the future *becomes* the past appeared more difficult. So is future or past easier for children? The answer is: it depends on how complicated the series of past or future events is to construct or reconstruct.

14.3 TEMPORAL CONCEPTS AND EPISODIC MEMORY

Our own autobiographical memories are not just based on a sense of how distant or long ago something is; we will try to fix it accurately with respect to something else. This is a device that is often exaggerated in crime fiction (e.g. 'I remember the time I went out, because I heard the clock in the hall strike 7', etc.). We may not chronicle events quite so assiduously, but we do all use these types of things to help provide as accurate a memory as we can. Being able to recall the time or place of encoded information is an aspect of episodic memory (after Tulving, 1972), which we came across in Chapter 12. Equally, we will use devices like this to think about the future – e.g. 'if I am going to the wedding the week after next, I will have to go to the hairdresser on my next day off', etc.

How accurate are children in terms of placing events in the past and future? We have encountered this already in terms of connecting the content of an event with the correct time and place (episodic memory). The study by Quon and Atance (2010) mentioned in Chapter 12 addressed this by going on to distinguish between episodic memory, episodic future anticipation and **semantic memory** in young children. The first two involve remembering the temporal context as just noted. Semantic memory, however,

Panel 14.3 Temporal concepts and episodic memory

- Remembering when an event happened (*temporal memory*) is an aspect of episodic memory, as in:
    - I had a banana at breakfast yesterday
- *Semantic memory* is knowledge that is free of a temporal context, as in:
    - We have bananas at breakfast
- Semantic memory for an event seems to be easier to recall than temporal memory for the same event
- Like memory for content, temporal information in episodic memory is affected by the degree of control a child has over the event

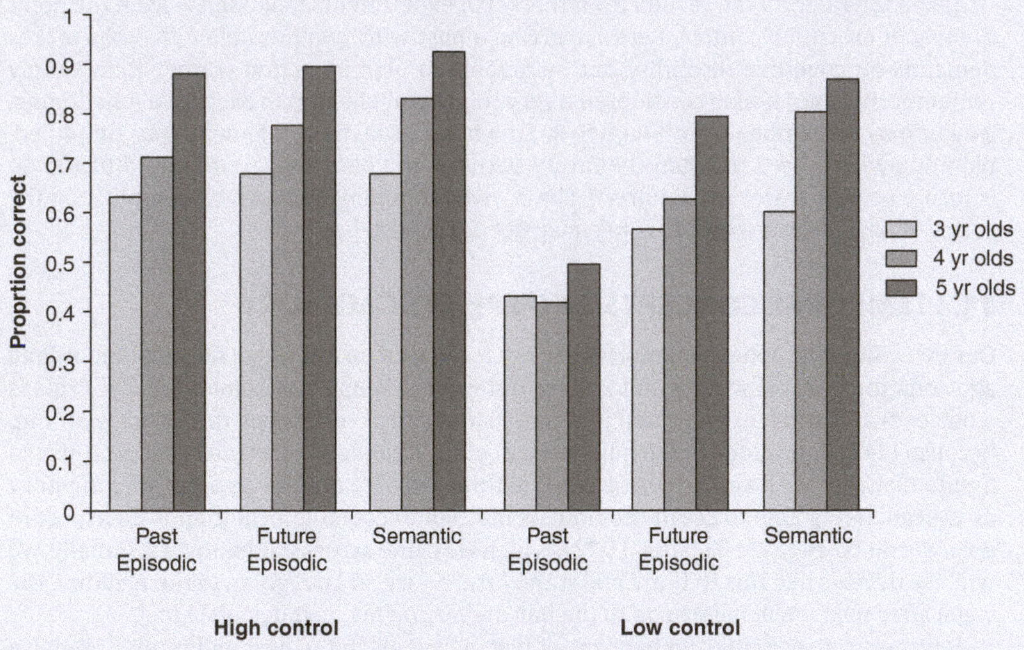

Children were asked questions about e.g. what they ate (*past episodic*) or what they were going to eat (*future episodic*) as well as semantic memory questions. Semantic memory questions were answered more accurately than the temporal questions, but the biggest factor was how much control the child had over the event in question. (Adapted from Quon & Atance, 2010, with permission)

is time-independent knowledge such as 'The moon controls the ocean's waves', 'Asia is the world's largest continent'. Children were asked, for example, the episodic memory question 'what did you have for breakfast yesterday'; the future episodic question 'what do you think you will have for breakfast tomorrow?'; and the semantic memory question 'what do you have for breakfast'. You may remember from Chapter 12 that an interesting manipulation in this study was to consider events over which children have 'high' control (like playtime and going to the park) versus 'low' control (like bedtime and shopping for food). High control events therefore may be more vivid when thinking about their timing, whilst for low control events, they would have a weaker sense of what did – or was about to – happen, and they would be less accurate in placing these events in time. Semantic memory, which doesn't require such knowledge of timing, would be less influenced by control. As the graph in Panel 14.3 illustrates, this is what the investigators found. Age was a significant effect, as was type of question, with semantic memory showing higher scores than the other types. The biggest effect on episodic memory was in terms of the control factor. This is precisely what was found for the *content* of the event as described in Chapter 12. Episodic memory for both content *and* timing of the event therefore develops in children in direct relation to their control and involvement in the event in question.

14.4 TEMPORAL DECENTRING

The studies we have considered thus far put the child at the origin of the event that has to be considered. This means that thinking about past and future may indeed centrally reflect both memory and control over the event. Is there some way we can study the child's understanding of time without this element of self-involvement? This issue introduces a concept referred to as **temporal decentring**. This is not the same as simply remembering the past or planning the immediate future; it is about having a way of thinking about time independently from one's current perspective – where a point in time can be thought of as a point in time when something else happened. In the zoo task, the photograph fixes a point in time when Emily was at cage 3 and a photo was taken, but the difficulty that young children have with this task suggest that they have difficulty accessing this decentred frame of reference.

From various studies, the investigators Teresa McCormack and Christopher Hoerl have concluded that the basic logic of temporal actions is not grasped until at least the age of 5 (McCormack & Hoerl, 2008). In a typical study, McCormack and Hoerl (2005) used an apparatus consisting of a box with a transparent window and two dolls (Sally and Katy) standing either side of the box beside a button. It was demonstrated to the child that if Sally pressed her button, a particular toy would appear, but that a different toy appeared if Katy pressed her button. It was impressed on the child that 'Sally always goes first'. The apparatus was covered with a screen and the child heard both buttons being pressed by the experimenter. When the screen was removed, the dolls were visible but the toy was concealed with a card, and the child was asked what toy would be in the window when the card was removed. Neither 4 nor 5 year olds were above chance on this test, as the graph in Panel 14.4 shows. However, McCormack and Hoerl found

Panel 14.4 Temporal decentring

- To understand the effect of past events on a future or current state of affairs, it is necessary to reconstruct these from a different perspective
  - This is called *decentring*
- Children seem unable to do this before at least the age of 5

Children are shown that two buttons produce different toys in a window in a box; two dolls are allocated one of buttons and the child is told that one doll 'always goes first' or 'always goes last'.

The box is covered; the sound of two button presses are heard and the child has to infer which toy will be in the concealed window.

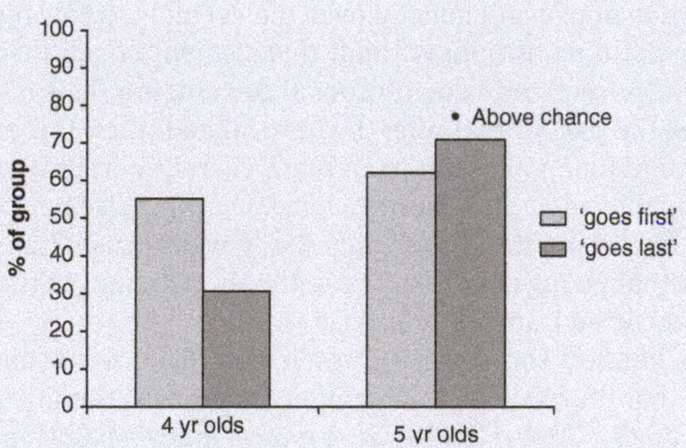

Only 5 year olds are above chance and only in the 'goes last' condition. (Percentage of group passing. Adapted from McCormack & Hoerl, 2005, with permission)

- It seems that young children use immediate memory rather than decentering when working out the order of past events

successful performance by 5 year olds in the windows task when they mentioned which doll 'always goes last' rather than 'first'. The memory demand on recalling the second event is clearly less than that for remembering the first – all of which suggests that they are using a kind of immediate memory rather than a fixed frame of reference for encoding the task that places toy 1 at time 1 and toy 2 at time 2.

14.5 TEMPORAL REASONING

It is in the very nature of time that we habitually make 'inferences' about it: the shadows are getting longer, therefore we are moving towards evening; the post hasn't been delivered, so it can't be 10 a.m. yet. For something as ephemeral and transient as the passage of time, it is reasonable to pin it down as much as possible – it is helpful to have a decentred frame of reference within which to operate to let us infer the timing of other events. But is this true temporal reasoning? Let us think a bit more about what is meant by reasoning. A classic distinction is often made between **inductive** reasoning – based on past experience and **deductive** reasoning, based purely on the logical connections across statements. Inductive reasoning might indeed be: the post hasn't arrived so it can't be 10 o'clock yet (because the post usually arrives at 10). Whilst this is rational, it isn't logical in the deductive sense, because there is no necessary connection between the post arriving and the time – it is a rational generalisation based on what usually happens. But it could be turned into a deductive inference by saying: 'the post always arrives at 10 a.m'.; 'it is 9.30, therefore the post hasn't arrived yet'. The difference is that, in the second case, the statement is called a premise; the term 'always' has to be taken on trust whether or not it is actually true, and so the conclusion necessary follows from that premise. Deductive reasoning is usually based on statements that can sometimes make advanced demands on the understanding of language. We will be considering this form of reasoning in Chapter 16.

In a sense, neither term is useful in telling us how children *start* to reason logically about time. Inductive generalisations are not necessarily logical and formal deductive inferences are still too advanced. What we have considered thus far, such as the Katy/Sally task, would not quite qualify either, because once the events have happened (Sally went first; then Katy; 'what is in the window?'), the answer follows because of inevitable temporal laws. That is why this is sometimes called **event-based thinking** rather than reasoning. So we have an issue that is similar to the one we encountered in relation to class inclusion when we wanted to find out how much children understand *in principle* about the logic of classes, but at a concrete or empirical level. The solution in that case was to insert a hypothetical entity into the reasoning task (e.g. if a DAX is a dog, etc.) and from this we learned about the partial but growing grasp of the logic of classes. Is there some way of looking at reasoning about time but at a concrete (or empirical) level in a similar manner? Inserting a hypothetical entity into a scenario about time would be to ask children about logically *possible* events.

In one recent example doing precisely that, Beck et al. (2006) constructed an apparatus which offered two chutes down which a little mouse could slide as depicted in Panel 14.6. The chute was selected by a child having to turn over either a red or blue card. They also

Panel 14.5 Temporal reasoning

- Thinking about time often involves making general inferences based on past experience
  - o The post has arrived – it must be after 10 a.m.
- This is a type of *inductive inference*
  - o The conclusion does not always follow logically
    - (The postman might have been early)
- A *deductive inference* is where the conclusion is necessarily true based on information presented in the form of premises, e.g.
  - o The post always arrives at 10 a.m.
  - o It is after 10 a.m.
  - o Therefore the post must have arrived
- The premises do not have to be true or based on past experience
- The differences between inductive and deductive inferences are:
  - o the necessity of the conclusion
  - o the ability to consider a hypothetical state of affairs
- Deductive reasoning is most easily tested using language-based tests that present premises (statements) and ask the child to draw a conclusion
- If we want to know how logical young children can be about time, we need a concrete task that doesn't rely on language
- One way to do this is to ask them to consider the logical possibilities that could hypothetically occur during a temporal event they have witnessed

Four- to 6-year-old children made a blind selection of cards that determined which arm of a chute a toy mouse would slide down and 'prepared' a soft landing for it. The red chute had two possible exits that were also selected by a card. When the landing had to be prepared before the card was selected (1.) only 5/6 year olds prepared for the hypothetical possibilities of both exits. (Adapted from Beck et al., 2006, with permission)

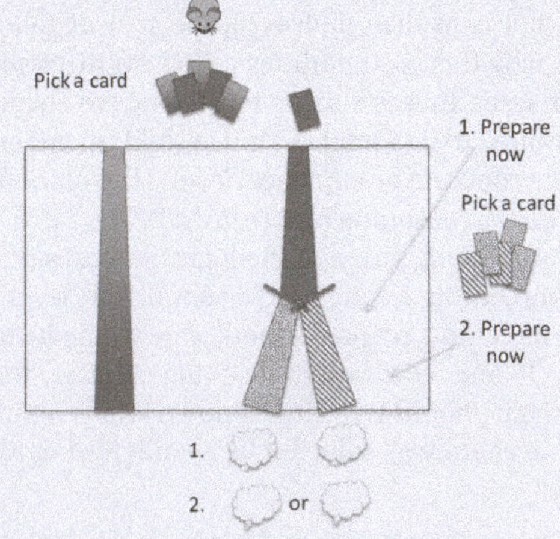

had to prepare for the mouse's exit at the appropriate aperture with a soft landing (cotton wool). If a red card was selected, the mouse would reach a fork in the chute (the key experimental situation). At this point, a further blind selection of cards at the barrier of the fork would determine which arm of the fork it went down next. In one condition, however, the child had to prepare for the mouse's exit *before* it was selected by the second card. This was called the undetermined '**hypothetical future**' condition. Ideally, the child should place two bits of cotton wool as the landing was undetermined at that point: it could *hypothetically* go down either arm. Three and four year olds did not prepare for these alternative possibilities beyond chance levels. A second study suggested that this ability was in place by the age of 5 or 6 and it was only at this age that the children could answer the question, i.e. 'Could he have gone anywhere else?' It is often argued that this requires a kind of 'mental time travel'.

You may wonder why this develops earlier than thinking about hypothetical alternatives in the class inclusion test: if DAX is a dog, is DAX a Collie? (where even 9 year olds might wrongly assert that he is). The probable answer comes back to the fact that temporal events are much less labile than categories. Timing of an event is a fixed property of our world that we have not arrived at by any kind of linguistic or cultural consensus, and so hypothesising about possible alternative events in time will come more easily to children than thinking about possible types of things we call 'dog'.

THINKING AND REASONING ABOUT SPACE

As with temporal concepts, we have to start with a slightly artificial distinction between space and time in order to focus on what is specific to how the child starts to understand the three dimensions of space which they and other objects occupy. We have, of course, been thinking about this since Chapter 2 in terms of children's reaching and finding things in space, since Chapter 3 in terms of moving through space, and again in Chapter 12 in terms of navigating space and using landmarks. So what are we thinking about now that is different from these aspects of spatial cognition? Well, just as with time, spatial experiences are shared and, as well as moving and finding things in space, children need to adopt the cultural practices of referring to space in a certain way and also to view space objectively from a perspective that is not necessarily the one they occupy in the here and now. Just as with time, this requires the ability to 'decentre', and just as with time, decentring is a necessary ingredient for reasoning about space.

LEARNING LANDMARKS

14.6 Understanding spatial referring expressions. You should have an idea of the spatial words that enter a child's vocabulary by the age of 4 and how this relates to their later spatial abilities.

(Continued)

(Continued)

14.7 Spatial decentring. You should know what is meant by 'intrinsic reference' and the relationship between deixis and spatial decentring. You should be able to cite a study illustrating the child's non-deictic interpretation of 'in front of' and 'behind'.

14.8 Adopting another's perspective. You should be able to describe Piaget's Three Mountains task and his findings. You should know why it is important to distinguish taking a decentred perspective from working out what the perspective would look like.

14.6 UNDERSTANDING SPATIAL REFERRING EXPRESSIONS

We know surprisingly little about children's basic spatial concepts like inches and metres. Rather more is known about the words that refer to spatial relations, like 'on', 'up' and 'under'. Once again, we have Louise Ames to thank for an early study of these linguistic terms in young children. If you remember, children ask 'where' questions from an early age and so Ames and Learned (1948) asked children aged between 2 and 4 years a variety of questions such as 'Where is Daddy?', 'Where is the roof?', 'Where do birds live?'. They also just simply recorded their spontaneous speech from behind a screen over an entire nursery school term. Replies to questions showed very similar patterns to spontaneous speech and showed fairly universal patterns across ages. This much you would expect from Chapter 8, where we considered children's use of prepositions (as parts of speech), many of which are spatial in nature ('down', 'to', 'from', etc.), and it was noted that they start to appear around the second birthday. This is consistent with Ames' finding that they did not really appear in answers until around 24 months, though she did find some use of 'up', 'down', 'on' and 'off' from 18 months onwards in spontaneous speech. Given that Ames and Learned carried out their study some 50 years prior to some of the studies reviewed in Chapter 8, it is worth noting that the consistency across this time period, even down to the finding that 'between' appears around 42 months (compare with Internicola and Weist, 2003).

More importantly for the purposes of this chapter, Ames' study throws some light on how their use of spatial prepositions reflects children's growing conscious access to spatial concepts. Ames and Learned interpreted their data in terms of some interesting landmarks in the development of spatial awareness:

- **24 months**. A focus on the 'here and now' in the use of e.g. 'there', 'other side', 'up stairs', 'in' and 'out'.
- **30 months**. A focus on being very precise and exact, e.g. 'right here', 'right up there', 'way up', 'in there'; and the start of references to more distant places, e.g. 'far away'.

- **36 months**. Both 'an increased refinement in space perception' and 'a new and marked interest in space detail' as indexed by words, e.g. 'back', 'over', 'corner', 'up on top'. Ames and Learned observed that children at this age will be able to give directions by saying 'turn left and then turn right' (which reflects the findings reviewed in Chapter 12 that children develop an elementary memory for routes from around 3 years old).
- **42 months**. New spatial relations appear such as 'next to', 'under' and 'between', as well as a combination of both precision and expansion to farther locations as in 'way down' and 'far off'.
- **48 months**. Even more expansive use of spatial terms such as 'far away', 'way up there'. By this age the words in most frequent use are 'in', 'on', 'up in', 'at' and 'down'.

In short, by their fourth birthday, children show a precise and quite wide-ranging knowledge of spatial concepts at least as evinced by their use of these words.

However, does that really bear on their understanding of spatial concepts, or are they simply acquiring a richer and more descriptive vocabulary? As we learned in the chapters on language acquisition, words are acquired to express important meaning, and investigators have noted that spatial meaning first becomes important in the preverbal stages. You know already that this consists of finding objects in space, learning to move through space, and how to interpret the visual cues associated with moving objects. In short, it is the dynamics of the spatial world that are important to the child rather than its static properties. In the Ames and Learned study, the (static) terms 'next to', 'under' and 'behind' were amongst the last to appear in answers to questions and did not appear at all in the records of spontaneous speech. This reminds us that what seems like an obvious description to us (it's 'behind' the occluder) may be represented more dynamically by the children at first in terms of their own behaviour (I have to reach 'over there').

This is of course hard to prove, but it is fully consistent with the findings of the CHILDES analysis of the linguistic corpus, by Eva-Maria Graf from Alpen-Adria University in Austria, which you learned about in Chapter 8 (Graf, 2010). She found that the spatial language of children in the 6- to 10-years-old age range did in fact favour dynamic expressions such as (ride) 'around' or (ran) 'down', over static ones that represented fixed locations, such as (keys) 'on' (the table) or 'in' (this room). Graf also made the important observation that spatial words are very often used metaphorically. She entitles one of her papers accordingly: 'I'm fed up with marmite – I'm moving on to Vegemite'! These colloquial uses gradually increase from the age of 6 until the age of 10 but literal uses of spatial terms prevail at all age groups.

So if spatial language reflects what is cognitively important to children, does spatial language actually predict other spatial skills? It would seem that it does. Pruden et al. (2011) monitored the spatial language of 52 children and their parents over a three-year period, from when the children were just over a year old to when they were aged 3 years 10 months. When the children were 4½ years old, they were than presented with three

Panel 14.6 Understanding spatial referring expressions

- Children start to use spatial referring terms from their second birthday and have a wide vocabulary of spatial terms by the age of 4
- They start with words such as 'here' and 'there' and 'in' and 'out'
- A year later, they will be more exact in their usage, e.g.
  - 'right here'; 'over there'
- And will have more precise spatial terms, such as:
  - 'corner'
  - 'over'
  - 'on top'
- By 4 years they will be able to refer to more distant places:
  - 'far away'
  - 'way up there'
- From 6 to 10 years children increase their metaphorical use of spatial terms as used in colloquial language, e.g.
  - 'she's on Facebook'
  - 'it's in a muddle'
- The degree of spatial language in 3 year olds can predict how well they solve spatial puzzles a year later

well-known tests of non-verbal spatial intelligence. One was to work out which of a set of whole shapes would result from a rearrangement of two separate pieces; another was the Block Design Test in which four or six blocks with red and white surfaces have to be assembled to recreate a larger red and white geometric shape. The third test required the child to make a spatial analogy between a picture, such as bird above a tree, and one of a set of diagrams depicting relations such as a dot above, in or beside a circle. In a clever set of correlational analyses, the authors discovered a significant relationship between the parent's use of spatial terms and the child's ability on the spatial tasks. Of course it is hard to work out the precise cause and effect relationships here. Maybe children already interested in spatial puzzles talk about them in spatial language and/or encourage the parent to do so. Whatever the set of causal connections, however, this shows that spatial language reflects spatial understanding and awareness in non-verbal domains. Just how advanced that awareness is we shall see next.

14.7 SPATIAL DECENTRING

Spatial language nearly always implies a reference point that exists in the here and now, such as 'in front of the *bookcase*', 'behind the *clock*'. That language can be quite ambiguous in several ways. First, polarised objects such as bookcases and clocks have 'fronts' and 'backs', whilst trees don't, so spatial terms can be relative to the object's own front, back and sides under some circumstances. Second, there is also a spatial relationship between the viewer and the object, whatever its polarity. Suppose a clock is facing the wall, whilst being wound up, and someone says 'the key is behind the clock' – this would mean at the clock's 'front'. To be able to use and understand spatial terms accurately, a child must be capable of thinking in terms of different perspectives on the same scene.

Deixis and spatial language

Taking account of the viewpoint of another person is known as **deictic**. Do you remember this expression from Chapter 4? Deictic pointing means taking the mother's viewpoint into account – sharing the object of interest with her as signalled by looking back and forth from Mum to object. So, when it comes to using language to explicitly indicate where something is, deictic means taking into account the viewpoint of a speaker/observer. For example, 'The headlights are at the front of the car' should be interpreted in relation the car itself and its polarity, regardless of its orientation relative to the viewpoint of an observer. This is known as **intrinsic** reference. By contrast, 'Stand in front of the car' could invite someone to stand to the side of the car if their photo was being taken and the photographer was facing the car side on. This would be a deictic interpretation. (Note that we would not call this **extrinsic**, as this term specifically refers to an objective frame of reference like the points of a compass, i.e. fixed and independent of either the object's polarity or any observer's viewpoint. This is a more advanced concept.) Simply understanding how and when spatial terms should be used deictically (relative to the another observer) would be the first indication of decentring in terms of a child's representation of space.

Given what you learned about temporal decentring in Section 14.4, you may not expect children to interpret spatial language in a decentred way until after the age of 5. This is indeed largely what has been found by Christine Tanz at the University of Chicago and also by Maureen Cox at York University from the early 1980s. For example, Tanz (1980) asked children aged between 3 and 5 years to place an object (e.g. a ring) to the 'front', 'side' or 'back of' two types of toy object whilst seated beside the child and facing in the same way towards the objects. These were either polarised with an intrinsic front and back, like a toy car or a pig – or not fronted like a bar of soap. Tanz argued that the more sophisticated response would be to place the objects relative to self *and* speaker, e.g. place the ring between the pig and themselves for 'in front of the pig' even if it was facing away from them. Whilst this might appear 'egocentric' in this context, it would in fact suggest a deictic interpretation of the request, as it would reflect the shared viewpoint of the child and the adult. There was strong developmental change in responding in line with the prediction that an intrinsic interpretation would prevail. All children placed the item relative to the object (e.g. ring in front of pig's face), whatever its orientation and became even more consistent in doing so as they got older. They were particularly consistent in doing this for the polarised objects, which have clear intrinsic spatial properties.

Tanz's situation was deliberately ambiguous in order to find out the child's natural preference for interpreting the spatial terms. This raises the question as to when children can identify the situations when they *should* use an observer or speaker's viewpoint and those when they should use the non-deictic interpretation. A neat method of testing this was used by Cox and Isard (1990) with children aged 5 to 6 years and 9 to 10 years. One of their conditions strongly solicited the deictic interpretation of the expressions 'in front of' and 'behind', saying to the child e.g., 'You're going to take a photo of the (toy) man *in front* of the car. Where should he go?', where the car was sometimes facing away from the child. For 'behind', they were asked 'The man is going to hide (from you) *behind* the car; where should he go?' Again the car was sometimes facing away from the child. In the first case ('in front'), the man should be placed at the side of the car nearest to the child whatever the car's orientation; in the second ('behind') at the far side. In another condition, the child was simply asked to place the man behind or in front of the car, in which case an intrinsic interpretation (relative to the car), would be acceptable. A baseline condition was used for comparison which did not employ the words 'in front of' and 'behind' but simply asked the child where the man should go for a photo of him with the car (implying deictic 'in front'), or where he should stand if he was to hide from the child (implying deictic 'behind').

Children of all ages had little difficulty knowing where to place the man in the baseline conditions. Once again, however, when the spatial terms were used, children of both age groups were strongly inclined towards the intrinsic (car relative) interpretation even when the deictic interpretation was being solicited, as the graph in Panel 14.7 shows. In addition, whilst the intrinsic interpretation appears to be the objective one and, in that sense, 'decentred', Tanz considers that this tendency actually reflects a bias towards being egocentric in children of this age. She argues that the object-centred response is egocentric, as it suggests that the child fails to understand that she shares a viewpoint with the speaker and should comply with the request from that perspective, whatever the polarity of the object.

Does this indicate an *inability* to decentre? Whatever the tendency towards an egocentric interpretation of spatial *language* under these somewhat ambiguous situations, the key question for many investigators has been whether young children are cognitively able to 'decentre' from their own perspective especially when the task explicitly demands this. Cox and Isard's baseline results (without the spatial terms) suggest that they can (at least by the age of 5). But the definitive way to test this is to see if they can *adopt the perspective of another observer at a different position*. As you will see, using intrinsic features can actually enable this ability.

Panel 14.7 Spatial decentring

- Defining spatial position relative to an object is known as *intrinsic reference*
- A spatially decentred viewpoint means taking account of the viewpoint of a third party
  - This is called *deixis*
- This might conflict with the intrinsic reference
- The terms 'in front' and 'behind' seem to elicit an intrinsic interpretation rather than a deictic one in primary school children

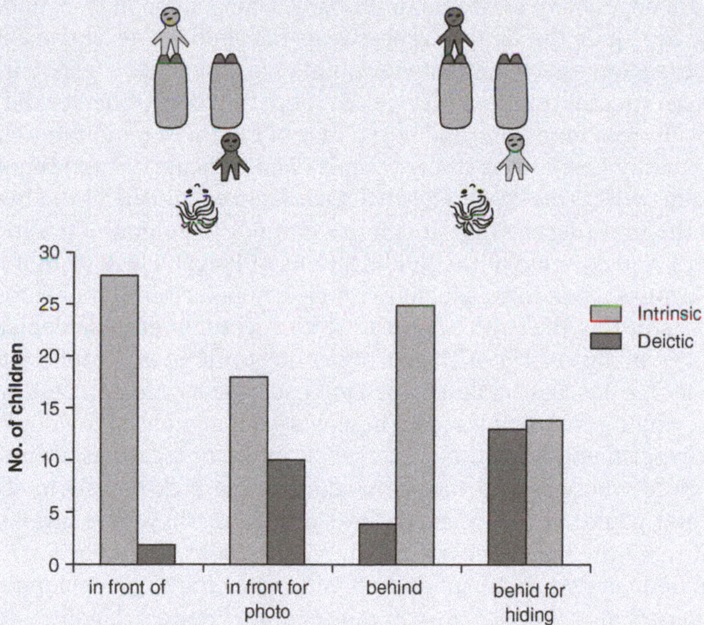

Children aged between 5 and 10 years were asked to put a toy man 'in front of' or 'behind' a car, which elicited a high level of intrinsic interpretations; the man was placed relative to the car's orientation. This bias was still found when the instruction explicitly implied a deictic interpretation (taking a photo of the man 'in front of' or 'behind' the car). (Data adapted from Cox & Isard, 1990)

- It has been argued that this bias is actually a sign of egocentricity in children's understanding of some spatial words

14.8 ADOPTING ANOTHER'S PERSPECTIVE

The concept of egocentrism in development was made famous by Piaget, who regarded it as one of the hallmarks of pre-logical thought. He famously devised a measure of egocentricism using a spatial task called the **Three Mountains Task** (Piaget & Inhelder, 1967). This task presented the child with a model of three differently shaped Swiss mountains of different heights and with features marking each summit (cross, snow cap and house). Children were asked to identify the scene from the viewpoint of a doll placed at different locations around the model either by picking a photo from a set that depicted the scene from the doll's perspective, or by placing the doll in the position that would correspond to the position of someone taking the photo. They were also given an opportunity to reconstruct the doll's view using their own model mountains. Piaget found that children generally failed this task until around the age of 7, and that the predominant error was in selecting or reconstructing a view that corresponded to their own.

There are clearly two elements to this task. One is the ability to understand that the doll would not share the same perspective as the child – a decentring skill. The other is to be able to reconstruct what that viewpoint would look like – a spatial skill, sometimes described as 'mental rotation' (Cooper & Shepard, 1973). The second of these can be quite difficult even for adults, and in the case of the three mountains could be expected to be affected by just how spatially complex and difficult it is to remember this sort of layout to start with. This is precisely what has been established by subsequent research. To assess the first (decentring), it is important not to confound it with second (spatial complexity), and so some of the modifications of Piaget's task simplified the mountain scene to layouts using toys, usually with clearly polarised dimensions. Using Piaget's method of requiring the child to select the correct photographic depiction of another's viewpoint, Fishbein et al. (1972) used either one or three of the following toys: a mouse, a doll, a Santa, a bus and a soldier. Each toy had a clearly demarcated right and left side (e.g. Santa waving with one hand). These were depicted as shown in Figure A in Panel 14.8. The experimenter positioned herself at different locations around the table away from the child who was told that he would have to pick the photo showing what the experimenter could see from each of these positions. They were given the prompt 'I am looking at (e.g.) the mouse now – which picture looks like what I can see?' Even with this simplified version, Fishbein and his colleagues found a developmental increase in accuracy across his age range. As you can see from Figure A, having three as opposed to just one object was also a major factor and children were around 8 years old before they were 80% accurate with three easy-to-remember objects.

This was also found by Borke (1975), but he also used a second method in addition to the pointing method employed by Fishbein's group. This was to turn a turntable so that the model corresponded to the view of a Sesame street character (Grover), who drove in his car around a scene. This method elicited much higher levels of correct responding even in scenes with as many as eight different items, which indicates that the method of selecting a correct picture is part of the difficulty. But there was still no such improvement using the turntable with Piaget's mountains. So, here it seems that it is the *lack* of intrinsic spatial features and discriminability in the mountains task that makes it especially difficult.

The ability to realise that the doll would have a different perspective can therefore be acquired quite early if the scene itself is relatively easy to discriminate and thus remember. But as you may have been thinking, some spatial vectors are surely easier to discriminate than others. 'In front of' and 'behind' are very different in terms of the intrinsic properties of polarised objects (face/ponytail; bonnet/boot, etc.) as well as in terms of how they would occlude another object from an observer's point of view. However, this is much less true of right and left; indeed many adults find these body-relative terms quite confusable. This was one of things explored in a recent study by Ziegler and Acquah (2013) which updates the research on this topic in several ways (see Figure B in Panel 14.8). First of all, it confirmed that children *can* adopt the perspective of another from at least 6 years of age with regard to the main front/back and left/right dimensions of 3D space. This was established by showing them the locations of four model objects in a geometric layout until they could remember all four locations. They then covered each object with a box and placed a doll into the centre of the layout. The doll was rotated so that it faced all four positions in turn. The point of the task was to see if the child could point to the object at the front/back/left or right of the doll, which meant the child had to separate his own left/right from that of the doll. (Left and right were aided by giving the doll a blue sticker on one hand corresponding to one on the child's hand and using this as a prompt in the instructions.) Although accuracy was high overall, it was indeed lower for left/right than for front/back locations. Of further interest in this study is the fact that a similar task was presented on a touch screen, but without the layout. Here children as young as 5 were shown images of the four objects and the characters but they had to learn the layout in relation to the character through a verbal description alone. They were then tested on the locations of the objects from the original position of the character as well after being told that the character had turned to his left or right. Accuracy was lower than in the actual objects condition but showed the same pattern of errors, with most occurring in the left/right orientation.

We have seen that children can adopt another's perspective from quite early on after all, by effectively placing themselves in the position of the observer in the mind's eye, provided that the spatial scene is itself relatively easy to mentally rotate and transform. This ability to be objective about space is a qualifying condition to be able to 'reason' about it. But sometimes the term spatial 'reasoning' or 'inference' is loosely used to refer to situations that involve working out where a hidden object may be at a given point in time by remembering a sequence of hiding locations – tasks that are sometimes given to toddlers. This is not quite the same as hypothetical reasoning, however. Why? Let us think back to the mouse study by Beck et al., described in Section 14.5 above. After the mouse had safely landed from one arm of the chute, another question the child was asked was, 'What if he had gone the other way, where might he have landed?' In their apparatus there were three choices: the other exit from the branched chute; the exit of an unbranched chute; and the place where he landed. This is a hypothetical question as the child had not actually witnessed the alternatives. Despite this, 3 year olds were nearly perfectly correct in choosing one of the 'other' exits of the chute. However, remember that they were poor at preparing *in advance* for a possibility that he might land at either of two exits and also (at this age) poor

Panel 14.8 Adopting another's perspective

- Piaget used the term *egocentricism* to refer to the child's inability to take another's perspective
- His famous test of this was based on a three-dimensional model of three mountains in which the child had to select the viewpoint as seen from someone else's perspective
- This required decentring and an ability to mentally rotate the spatial layout
- Subsequent research has found that this type of spatial rotation can be hard for children under 7 years

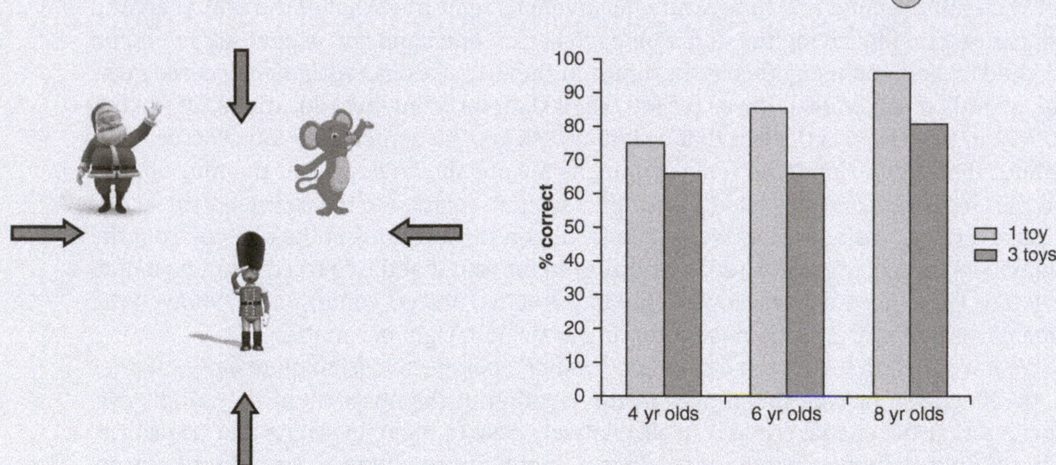

A Even when given objects with distinct left/right sides, children can find it quite hard to predict different visual perspectives on the same layout. (Adapted from Fishbein et al., 1972)

- Recent research shows that if the task is simplified to a 4 × 4 layout, children as young as 5 can work out what would be to the front/back or left/right of a doll when it is rotated inside this layout

B Children learn the location of hidden objects and then have to work out what would be in front/ behind and to the right/left of a doll rotated within the layout. (After Ziegler & Acquah, 2013)

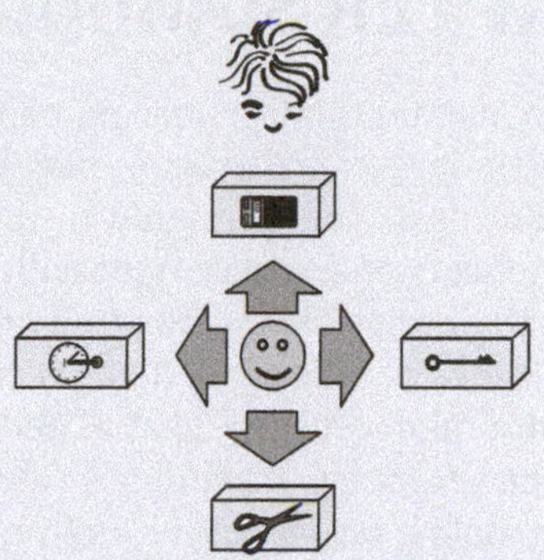

- Children understand from early on that someone else may have a different spatial perspective from their own (decentring)
  - But knowing what that perspective would look like (rotation) depends on the spatial complexity of the scene

at contemplating the 'open' question posed simply as 'could he have gone anywhere else?' So why are these hypothetical questions harder? What is the difference between the task of deciding where *else* the mouse could have landed and where it *might* land?

One answer is that, in the second case, the child has to mentally travel into a future where nothing is determined, whilst in the first they can solve the problem by simply thinking in the present tense. It has landed here (X); that leaves landing locations (Y and Z) empty. It is in the nature of observable space/time that something cannot be in the same place at the same time, and so it is not so hard to reel off the alternative possible locations, when the current location is known. For the future hypothetical case, various possibilities have to be imagined within an undetermined future where nothing is known. It would seem that it is reasoning about hypothetical events in space *and* time that takes far longer to develop. This has very real implications for how well children may be able to deal with future risks such as the possibility of a car appearing from a side-street when they are about to cross the road.

CHAPTER SUMMARY

Children use temporal referring expressions from an early age, but have some difficulty in the preschool years in making simple inferences about what has happened in the recent past. This is related to their episodic memory, which in turn is affected by the complexity and involvement with the event in question. Temporal decentring means placing themselves in the position of another observer and also develops in relation to the complexity of the event being reconstructed. Spatial terms also appear early on, and like temporal decentring, spatial decentring can depend on how difficult it is to reconstruct the geometry of another's viewpoint. Children are likely to use the polarity of an object to define terms such as 'in front of' and 'behind', but object polarity can help them adopt the perspective of another observer. Children can consider hypothetical outcomes in space more readily than possible future outcomes in time because of the determinate nature of space versus the indeterminate nature of future time.

LOOKING AHEAD TO CHAPTER 15

You have learned from this chapter that children are beginning to think and reason about time and space by the school years and in ways that go beyond their own immediate perspective. But an acid test of reasoning 'beyond the self' is to have to work out what inferences might be made by other people. This takes us to the famous Theory of Mind tasks that often use spatio-temporal scenarios as the basis for the studies. In that regard we shall be continuing on from the themes in this chapter. However, it also raises other issues that get to the very heart of what it is to be able to think beyond the self, as we see next.

CHAPTER 15

REPRESENTING OTHER MINDS AND THE DEVELOPMENT OF SYMBOLIC THOUGHT

In the previous chapter, we have seen how children's knowledge can extend beyond their own viewpoint in time and space, even allowing some elementary logical reasoning about hypothetical possibilities. Of considerable recent interest to psychologists, however, is when they are able to make their own inferences about the world as well as *at one and the same time* represent the inferences and thus beliefs held by another. This is hard to test if the child and the other person have the same belief about the world, e.g. they both know that a ball has disappeared from the garden because a dog has just run off with it. Sharing knowledge about the world is in evidence in fact from the earliest deictic behaviours of looking and naming in infancy. Having the ability to hold your own belief about the world whilst also being able to *separately represent* what someone else might know about the world becomes really clear when that other person currently holds a belief that you know to be wrong. Interest in this issue has thus centred on a clever paradigm known as the **False Belief test**. A child witnesses a change in the spatio-temporal location of an object (dog runs off with ball) but knows that a friend who has moved away from the scene does not, and the question is whether the child understands that the friend now holds a false belief about the current location of the object. This paradigm has attracted interest for several reasons. Understanding that others can hold different beliefs from their own is crucial aspect of their social development, but it would also show that they understand the difference between reality and a *mental state*. Finally, in order to hold such a distinction in their own heads, they must have a certain kind of representational flexibility. Although the roots of this flexibility arise very early in the context of play and imagination, language is the ultimate tool for symbolically representing both the real and the imaginary. The mental representation of other minds and symbolic development are thus strongly intertwined as you will see.

FALSE BELIEFS AND THEORY OF MIND

LEARNING LANDMARKS

15.1 The False Belief test of Theory of Mind. You should know the meaning and origin of the expression Theory of Mind and be able to describe the first false belief task given to children.

15.2 The Sally-Anne Test and autism. You should be able to describe the Sally-Anne task, understand its relevance to autism and know what was found.

15.3 Theory of Mind: a meta-analysis. You should know who carried this out, and what was found.

15.1 THE FALSE BELIEF TEST OF THEORY OF MIND

What is now commonly known the **False Belief test of Theory of Mind** originated in research by Heinz Wimmer at Salzburg and Josef Perner at Sussex University using a task based on a toy character called Maxi (Wimmer & Perner, 1983). The expression Theory of Mind (**ToM**) was borrowed from research by Premack and Woodruff (1978), who studied whether chimps could be trained to 'deceive' other chimps about the location of food, which would imply that they recognised others as having different 'minds' from their own. This did not come easily to the chimps and led Wimmer and Perner to ask the very interesting question as to whether children acquired this understanding naturally and if so, at what age. Their research implied that it did, and that it emerged around the age of 4. Partly because of the robust difficulties shown by children younger than this, and partly because it quickly became associated with a 'deficit' in children with autism (which we will come to presently), ToM has often been described as if it is an all-or-none ability that suddenly appears as a fully fledged skill. You probably know by now that nothing in development appears in an all-or-none fashion and this turned out to be the case with ToM.

Let us start with Maxi. In the study by Wimmer and Perner (1983), a story with props created a situation in which Maxi had a mistaken belief about the location of chocolate. The basic scenario is shown in Figure A in Panel 15.1. Maxi puts his chocolate in one cupboard; his mother transfers it to another cupboard in his absence. The key question put to the child is, 'Where will Maxi look for his chocolate?' and the child can answer by pointing; a point to the original location being correct. In this study, 3 year olds failed the false belief question, as shown in the graph in Figure A and this held true even when they were cautioned to 'stop and think' first. As the graph shows, 4 year olds improved in a condition in which the object completely disappeared (was eaten) rather than relocated to another cupboard, as the authors surmised that having two cupboards might have caused some confusion. This study also included an interesting variant of the deceit task, as the child was asked what Maxi would *say* about the chocolate's location to someone he wanted to deceive (his brother). This is particularly difficult because the deception (Maxi says the chocolate is in a new location) has to be based on the child's understanding that Maxi is himself wrong (the chocolate really *is* in the new location)! The authors found a strong relationship between the child's ability to answer the false belief question correctly and the ability to make Maxi state a deceptive utterance to his brother. So across these interesting variations of their task, Wimmer and Perner concluded that ToM emerges after the age of 4.

Perner and his colleagues revisited this research three years later (Perner et al., 1987) and introduced a variation that is now in common use. To ensure that the child really understood that another person could be misled into a false belief, they introduced a false belief in the child's own mind. Here the child was shown a Smarties box, which would normally be expected to hold sweets. However, on opening it in view of the child – but not a friend of the child who was behind the door – it was made clear that the Smarties box actually contained pencils (Figure B, Panel 15.1). So what would the child think the friend would think – now having had his own experience of false belief? Although the majority of 3-year-old children (75%) remembered their own false belief, less than half were correct regarding the 'friend's belief'. However, there was a significant increase in correct responding across the 3-year-old sample, lending support to the view that false belief understanding emerges at around 4 years.

Notice that the children who succeeded on the Smarties task were able to hold two different representations about their *own* beliefs – an ability that is necessary for things like pretend play. Children can pretend a matchbox to be a car, or a banana to be a telephone, precisely because they know the difference between a true state of affairs and an imagined one. Research on pretence (which we shall come to presently) has shown that this ability is in place well before the age of 4. Alan Leslie (then) at Oxford University elaborated a detailed theory about this ability, which he called **metarepresentation** (Leslie, 1987). This is the simultaneous awareness of two primary representations (e.g. banana/telephone) that become specifically linked in a new (meta)representation. The question is what makes the metarepresentation of false belief so hard? For Leslie it is the fact that there is no already existing primary representation – that is precisely what the child has to work out when thinking about someone else's belief. Perner and his colleagues, on the other hand, concluded that what seems to *newly* emerge at the age of 4 is the ability to assign *conflicting* truth-values at one and the same time – a slightly different idea. But all investigators agreed that the ability to hold two representations of an object, as evident in pretend play, would be a necessary precursor to what Perner et al. (1987) describe as 'the conceptual complication' of false belief. An absence of this core ability would certainly be expected to affect ToM abilities and this is one of the things that was tested by using children with autism as we see next.

Panel 15.1 The False Belief test of Theory of Mind

- *Theory of Mind* (ToM) was first used by comparative psychologists studying the ability of apes to intentionally deceive competitors for food
- It has since been used to study when children can make the distinction between their own true belief and the false belief of another
- The original task used characters played by dolls in a narrative
    - o The child is witness to the relocation of an object of which one of the characters is unaware
        - The key question tests the child's ability to understand that the character now holds a false belief about the object's location
- A later version used a false belief about the contexts of a sweets container about which the child was originally deceived
    - o The child was shown the true contents and the key question related to the belief of a friend who had not

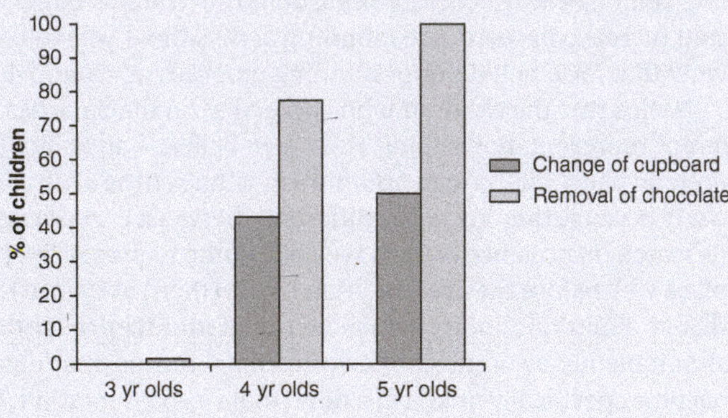

A Children are told a story in which a character called Maxi puts his chocolate in one cupboard and whilst he is gone, his mother moves it to another or removes it altogether. The child is asked 'where will Maxi look for his chocolate?' (Percentage of children passing. Adapted from Wimmer & Perner, 1983, with permission)

- Success on ToM tasks emerges at about 4 years, but can vary with task difficulty

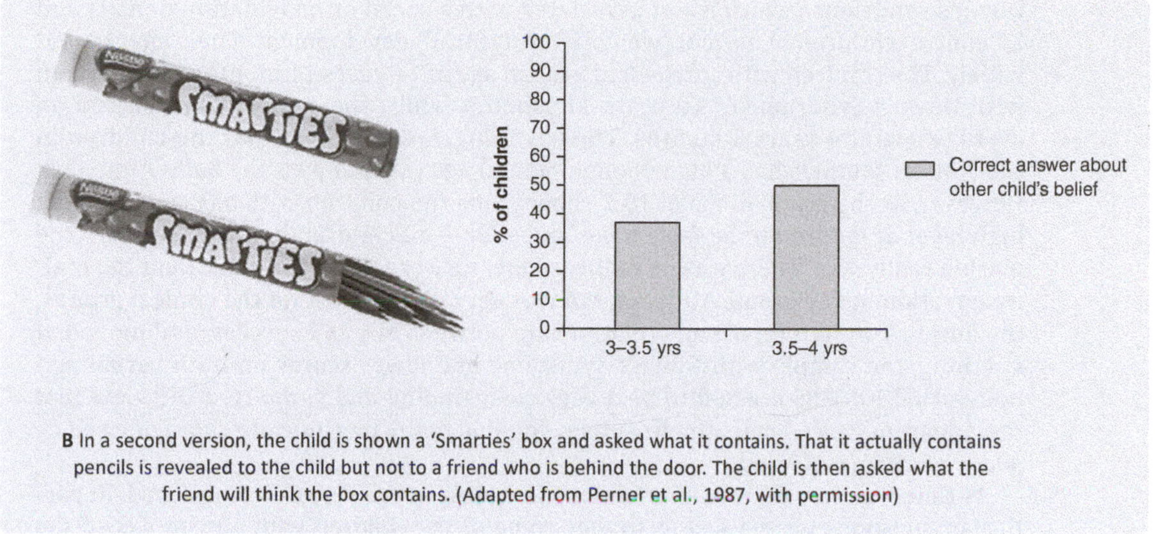

B In a second version, the child is shown a 'Smarties' box and asked what it contains. That it actually contains pencils is revealed to the child but not to a friend who is behind the door. The child is then asked what the friend will think the box contains. (Adapted from Perner et al., 1987, with permission)

15.2 THE SALLY-ANNE TEST AND AUTISM

At around this time, the now well-known Sally-Anne version of the false-belief test was introduced by Baron-Cohen et al. (1985) also using dolls as the key characters The scenario this time is that the Sally doll puts her marble in a basket and then leaves; doll Anne moves the marble to a box and then Sally returns (see Panel 15.2). The task included the key question, 'Where will Sally look for her marble?', and included two important control questions – a memory question: 'Where was the marble in the beginning?', and a reality question: 'Where is the marble really?' This simple version of the task has attracted enormous interest because it was the first time it was given to children with autism. At the time of the study, autism was still a relatively rare condition and relatively unknown to the general population. Clinicians, however, were increasingly aware of some characteristic impairments that are usually manifest by the second birthday and two were particularly relevant to ToM. One is a difficulty in reciprocal social interaction – essentially an apparent indifference to the needs, wants and desires of others. The other is impairment in pretence and imagination such as unwillingness to participate in 'make-believe' games.

Back in the 1980s, the speculation was therefore quite reasonable that autism may turn out to be, in essence, an impairment of Theory of Mind – or as Baron-Cohen et al. (1985) phrased it, a failure 'to employ' a Theory of Mind. To test this, the authors compared the performance of 20 children with autism, 27 children with

Down's syndrome (which is not associated with a social or imagination deficit) and 27 control children of normal (we now say 'typical') development. Their ages varied widely. The children with autism had a mean age of 11 years 11 months, the children with Down's Syndrome of 10 years 11 months, whilst the control children had an average age of 4 years 5 months. The key thing, however, was that the children in the clinical samples had a high enough mental age (MA) to pass the Sally-Anne test. However, as the graph in Panel 15.2 shows, only the children with autism showed a high level of failure on the false belief question – all children pointed to where the marble really was. There was no failure of memory or failure to understand the reality question in any group. Although MA was very variable within the clinical groups, the authors did not report any relationship between MA and success, and indeed, if anything, the sample with Down's syndrome had lower scores on both verbal and non-verbal IQ. This seemed to be a very clear finding and supported the view that the apparent lack of empathy in autism could actually be clinically characterised as a lack of Theory of Mind.

As time went on, the situation became less clear as the research burgeoned. In particular, questions were asked as to why some of the children with autism *passed* the Sally-Anne test if ToM is an all-or-none deficit specifically associated with the disorder. The relationship with language was also revisited, most notably in a longitudinal study by Happe (1995), who *did* find a very marked relationship between success on the task and verbal mental age. Baron-Cohen himself went on to expand the theory into a concept he called 'mindblindness'. What he was proposing was that individuals with Autism Spectrum Disorders (ASD) have a deficit in thinking about any mental states – not just those of others. This focussed the research back on to the representational challenges in thinking about pretence and imaginary states of affairs in general and we shall come to that (and how it might relate to language) in due course.

One cause of failure in ToM does not exclude others. So to what extent is ToM (also) a social phenomenon – requiring at least an *interest* in what others would think? Baron-Cohen's subsequent (and current) research has to some extent pointed back towards the social demands of ToM in a new theory of autism in which he views it as an extreme version of the 'male brain'. His research team at the Autism Research Centre in Cambridge measured levels of prenatal testosterone in mothers who gave birth to babies subsequently diagnosed with ASD. Their findings led them to promote the view that these high levels are responsible for an extreme male personality. This is associated with somewhat anti-social tendencies as identified in a questionnaire known as the Autism Quotient (AQ) (Baron-Cohen et al., 2001), as well as other characteristics associated with ASD such as attention to detail and mild obsessiveness. It was also correlated with subsequent performance on ToM. But as he was considering autism as a *variable* clinical expression along a basic personality continuum, Baron-Cohen could now account for the fact that failure on ToM by individuals with autism was not necessarily inevitable.

Panel 15.2 The Sally-Anne test and autism

- *False Belief tests* depend on an awareness of the minds of others and an ability to represent a 'non-real' state of affairs
- The social and imaginative impairments in children with Autism Spectrum Disorders (ASD) suggested that they might fail ToM tasks even after the age of 4
- The Maxi version of the task was used in a study in which a doll character (Sally) is absent whilst her friend (Anne) relocates her marble

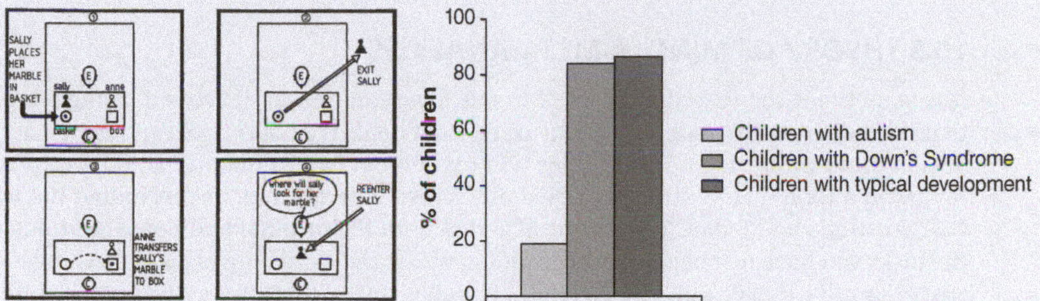

The Sally-Anne task was given to children with autism children with Down's Syndrome (both with a mean age of around 11 years), and children of typical development with a mean age of 4½ years. Only the children with autism failed. (Diagram reproduced with permission and data showing percentage pass rate adapted from Baron-Cohen et al., 1985)

- The difficulty shown by children with autism on ToM tasks is now thought to be a general problem with understanding mental states
- It seems likely to be related to verbal intelligence

It is not clear if the 'mindblindness' identified by Baron-Cohen's research is an additional element in the pathology of autism, or is it itself the consequence of a form of extreme egocentricism due to social indifference. Whilst the explanations still vary as to why children with autism fail on ToM tasks, the relationship with this disorder is sufficiently well established for ToM tasks to be included in the general profiling of individuals with ASD in clinical research (where the four-year cut-off first established by Wimmer and Perner is the expected 'norm'). It is also important to be aware that it is now very clear that autism itself – known as a Complex Neurodevelopmental Disorder – is a highly multi-factorial condition which departs from the trajectory of typical development from a very early age, in many different ways and with cause/effect relationships that are notoriously difficult to disengage. Mentioned in this book primarily because of the deep connection with the development of ToM tests, autism, as well as other neurodevelopmental disorders, is a fascinating area of study in its own right and should you wish to pursue this in greater detail some useful references are Frith (2003), Volkmar and Paul (2005), Howlin and Charman (2011) and Waterhouse (2013).

If ToM is to help inform the understanding of autism *and* typical development, it is important that researchers are confident about what it measures. Issues have already been raised about how language and the conceptual complications of the task may influence results. Let us now look to see what we can assert with confidence about ToM in the light of the substantial follow-up research with typically developing children.

15.3 THEORY OF MIND: A META-ANALYSIS

It is sometimes the case that there is so much varying research around a single topic that it is necessary to pool the results to see what holds true of the research as a whole. Such a **meta-analysis** of ToM studies was carried out by Wellman et al. (2001). They reviewed a total of 178 studies carried out across several countries including the UK, USA, Australia and Japan. These ranged across both the original and new variations of the tasks you have just been reading about in which the child witnesses something that a **protagonist** (Maxi, Sally, the 'friend', etc.) does not. Whilst there were some differences across countries in terms of actual scores at different ages, the developmental patterns were the same for all. So what were those patterns? The authors sought to see if there was a genuine developmental change in ToM. The alternative was that there is a basic ToM competence in all preschool children over the age of 2½, but it is simply obscured by task factors that make it 'too difficult' to demonstrate this competence. If this is true, then those factors should impact selectively on the younger groups. This is not what was found. Wellman et al. found that that there was a genuine change across the preschool years and some factors did indeed make the task harder, but for all children at all ages:

- **Motive**: making the deception meaningful to the child had a significant effect overall. That is, there was more correct responding when it was made clear that the transformation/translocation was actually designed to 'trick' the protagonist.
- **Salience**: a similar finding was found in terms of drawing attention to the mental state of the protagonist, e.g. by explicitly commenting on the fact that the protagonist did not witness the change.
- **Participation**: a similar finding was that the degree of involvement of the child improved their performance (as also found with the basic encoding of a

temporal event mentioned in Chapter 12). Helping to set up the props or make the transformation improved performance.

- **Presence of target object**: just as Wimmer and Perner found that having the object disappear completely (the chocolate was eaten, or the Smarties box was actually empty) made it easier to answer the false belief question, so it was found within the meta-analysis.

Other factors did not seem to be particularly important, and these included:

- **Type of task**: that is, whether the task was of the Sally-Anne (spatio-temporal) or contents (Smarties) variety.
- **Type of question**: there was no real effect of asking where e.g. Maxi would 'look', 'think' or 'believe' where his chocolate was.
- **Depiction of characters and objects**: by now both the protagonist as well as the transformed/translocated object had been an actual doll or prop, a drawing of a story character or object, or a real videotaped person or object. This made no overall difference.

These findings from the meta-analysis show that there is a robustness to the ToM phenomenon that cannot simply be pinned down to some extraneous aspect of the task. By the time it was published, however, there were already diverging opinions as to what Theory of Mind really is. No one was really suggesting that young children employ a 'theory' in the scientific sense involving being able to state it explicitly, as in the case of Copernicus having a theory that the Earth revolves around the Sun. Nevertheless, ToM was seen by some investigators, such as Josef Perner and Henry Wellman himself, as a sort of informal intuitive theory that is specifically about the minds of others – not least that others *have* minds. This view became known as the **Theory Theory** approach. The alternative was to see ToM as just one of many different sorts of reasoning task, and thus subject to the same cognitive constraints as the sorts of reasoning we have come across already and explicable in those terms. One finding from the meta-analysis consistent with this is that children showed the same developmental trend in correctly answering questions about *their own* false belief regarding e.g. the content of the Smarties box when they first saw it, as found when asked about *another's* false belief about its contents – a finding first noted by Gopnik and Astington (1988). Attributing *any false belief* may be the source of the difficulty.

In short, the intuitive theories that children might have about other's minds do not always lead them to make a clear distinction between their own beliefs and the false beliefs of others, nor even, sometimes, between their own current (true) and past (false) beliefs. Why? We shall consider some reasons in the next sections.

Panel 15.3 ToM: a meta-analysis

- ToM has generated an unusually large numbers of research articles
- A powerful means of reviewing the totality of articles is to pool the results across studies
  - This is called a *meta-analysis*
- A meta-analysis of ToM studies of typically developing children confirmed that success generally appears around 4 years of age
  - This is despite variations in versions of task (Maxi, Smarties etc.), props used (drawings, dolls, etc.) and the wording of the question
- It also identified factors that can affect performance (see below)
- There is no evidence that 3 year olds fail simply because of a higher impact of these factors at a younger age
- The idea that ToM success indicates an intuitive 'theory' that other people have minds is called *Theory Theory*
- Others view ToM more in terms of general cognitive mechanisms to do with representing falsehood

Performance on false belief is improved if:

The relocation or change of contents is a deliberate trick (**Motive**)

Sally'/Maxi's/the friend's absence during the switch or change of contents is made obvious (**Salience**)

The child helps to set up the props (**Participation**)

Maxi's chocolate disappears rather then is relocated (**Presence**)

When results of 178 studies across several different countries and different versions of the ToM tasks were compared, findings emerged from the pooled data indicating how the task could be made easier. (Findings summarised from Wellman et al., 2001; Sally-Anne cartoon by A. Scheffler)

THEORY OF MIND AND EXECUTIVE FUNCTIONING

We have now seen that ToM bears on more than one type of cognitive skill. At its broadest, you could say that the ToM task makes demands on the child's representational flexibility. It requires flexibility of symbolic thought to allow metarepresentations, and also the specific representation of falsehood. The concept of flexibility has in fact been raised before within this book. It was discussed at a basic behavioural level in Chapter 4 in connection with how the infant learns to control complex motor sequences – and at a more conceptual level in Chapter 13 in connection with being flexible about how things can be classified. This sort of flexibility is thought to be related to executive functioning. So ToM seems to bear on symbolic abilities but also possibly on executive control. In this section we expand on how executive functioning might bear on ToM performance.

LEARNING LANDMARKS

15.4 Executive functions, response flexibility and attention switching. You should know why attention switching is relevant to the executive demands of ToM tasks. You should be able to describe the Windows Task and know what it revealed about children with autism.

15.5 Executive functions, representational complexity and second-order belief. You should be able to describe a second-order test of ToM and what it has revealed. You should be able to relate this to executive functioning and autism.

15.4 EXECUTIVE FUNCTIONS, RESPONSE FLEXIBILITY AND ATTENTION SWITCHING

If you remember, a key element in executive functioning (EF) is *response inhibition* – and we considered this at the simple level of inhibiting a reflexive movement in young infants and also people with damage to their frontal cortex. But these patients also fail at the more conceptual level of inhibiting a classification strategy as classically tested in the card sorting task known as the WCST (Wisconsin Card Sort Test) in which cards have to be sorted into correct piles based on the types of shapes displayed on the cards, the number of shapes or their colour. If you remember from Chapter 13, a rule such as 'sort by colour' can be learned by patients but when it is suddenly switched to a different one such as 'sort by shape', the first sort rule will persist causing perseverative errors.

It is known that the more **prepotent** (or compelling) the original response, the harder it is to inhibit it. So how does that relate to representational flexibility and ToM?

Think about a 3-year-old girl looking at a green cupboard in which Maxi's Mum has just put the chocolate bar – and the need to answer the question (correctly) by pointing to the other (blue) cupboard, which she knows does not contain the chocolate! Add to this the fact that executive functioning (EF) is known to be generally impaired in children with autism, with specific questions surrounding their inhibitory control (Pennington & Ozonoff, 1996), then small wonder that many people have considered ToM as a test of EF and, in particular, of response inhibition.

One of the first people to advance this idea was James Russell at the University of Cambridge, using a 'windows' task, which required children to engage in a simple act of deception. Russell et al. (1991) used the task with 3 and 4 year olds but also with 7–15-year-old children with autism or with Down's syndrome. The task is depicted in Panel 15.4. First the child learned during a training phase that they could obtain a chocolate reward only by pointing to the empty box rather than the box containing the chocolate, otherwise the chocolate went to the experimenter. The child then viewed the contents of the boxes through windows that could not be seen by the experimenter and they continued to be encouraged to stop the experimenter from winning by pointing to the wrong box. Over the course of 20 trials they found that the majority of 3 year olds could not consistently point to the wrong box, as the graph in Panel 15.4 shows. Of the four exceptions to this, three of them were the only ones in this group who could respond to the false belief question in a version of the Sally-Anne task. For 4 year olds, by contrast, only two were less than 100% correct, and the majority were completely correct. All children in this group passed the false belief test. The children with autism performed like the 3 year olds, however, whilst the children with Down's syndrome performed more like the typically developing 4 year olds. The need to inhibit competing responses to reach a goal state is a classic aspect of EF, so the results from the Windows Task could certainly indicate inhibitory problems in autism, connected with suspected weaker connections between their prefrontal cortex and the motor regions of the brain (O'Hearn et al., 2008). A study with typically developing 3 and 4 year olds, moreover, showed a strong predictive relationship between their inhibitory control on some simple tasks (such as pressing a button to a yellow cue but not a blue one) and success on false belief tasks (Flynn, 2007). However, it is not clear whether the key development in children *without* autism in ToM tasks is due exclusively to a better general control of inhibitory mechanisms. It could also be due to an improved and clearer mental representation of the goal state (get the chocolate) and/or of the belief of the protagonist, because, as Russell et al. (1991) argue, the clearer that representation becomes, the more its salience will outweigh any other.

These latter possibilities are highly elusive as it is only possible to infer the strength and clarity of a mental representation such as 'she thinks her marble is in the basket' from behavioural measures. However, it is possible to see if making that representation more complex affects performance in ToM. It may be a foregone conclusion that it would (of course), but knowing more precisely how it affects performance across a range of ages at least allows us to consider the representational element independently – very much as it was done in the variations of the Three Mountains task. We consider this next.

Panel 15.4 Executive functions, response flexibility and attention switching

- ToM has been thought to make demands on *executive functioning* (EF)
  - Particularly with regard to *response inhibition* and *attention switching*
- The ToM task can invite a particularly compelling response (point to the true location of an object) which the child must inhibit
- If this is a cause of difficulty then it should be shown in independent tests
  - Especially in children with autism who have known EF impairments
  - But not in mentally aged matched children with other (non-EF) sorts of learning difficulty
- This was tested directly by a game known as the *windows task* with children of typical development as well as children with autism or Down's Syndrome (aged from 7 to 18 years)

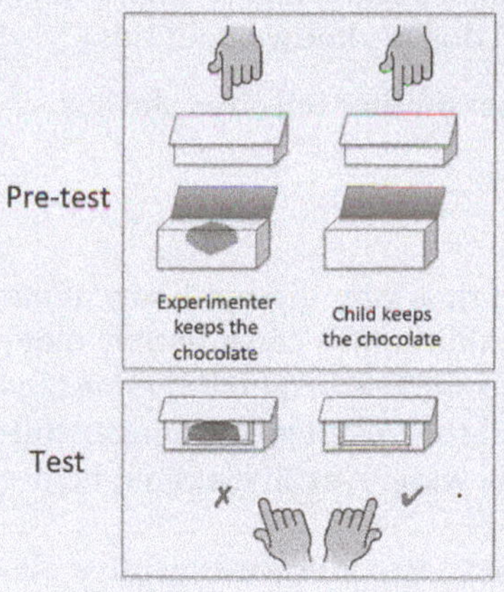

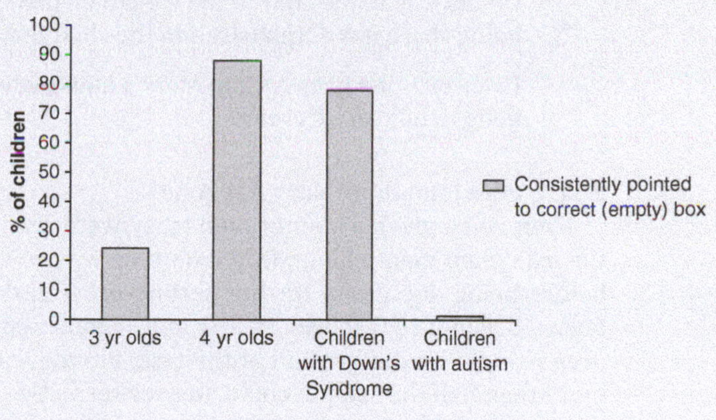

Children are rewarded with chocolate by *not* pointing to a box that they know contains the reward but that experimenter cannot see. Children with autism are unable to inhibit the response to the baited box and the experimenter 'wins'. (Adapted from Russell et al., 1991, with permission)

- This points to the requirement in ToM tests to inhibit a prepotent response and switch to another
- But also that the *salience of the alternative viewpoint* (the experimenter does not know the correct location) needs to be strongly represented if a potent cue is to be ignored
  - Both of these may be deficient in autism

15.5 EXECUTIVE FUNCTIONS, REPRESENTATIONAL COMPLEXITY AND SECOND-ORDER BELIEF

One way to vary the representational complexity of the protagonist's belief in ToM is to make the spatio-temporal relocations of the object harder to keep track of in working memory (WM). This is precisely what was done in a development of their paradigm by Perner and Wimmer (1985). Instead of solving the answer by having to think, 'I think s/he thinks', now the participant has to solve it by thinking 'I think that he thinks that she thinks.' This was called **second-order belief** and is almost impossible to imagine without an example. So here it is.

The central false belief task involved a story created by using three-dimensional layouts with dolls and props (see Figure A in Panel 15.5) . The essence of the story is this:

- Two children, Mary and John, want to buy an ice cream from the man whose ice cream van is in the park. Mary needs money and returns home, whilst the ice-cream man assures her he will still be in the park when she gets back.
- Whilst she is away the man decides to sell his ice cream outside the church instead, and John sees him leave the park for the church.
- On his way to the church the ice-cream man sees Mary and tells her where he is going (here it is emphasised to the child that John doesn't know about this).
- Later on, John goes over to Mary's house where her mother tells him she has gone to buy an ice cream.

Where does John think Mary has gone?

Even when given a memory aid (they were reminded that John did not know about the ice cream man telling Mary where he was going), children are considerably older before being successful on the second-order task than on the original versions, as Figure B, Panel 15.5 shows. Perner and Wimmer checked this result with younger children using a similar version of the task, but the children were over 6 years old before more than half the sample could answer correctly.

The second-order false belief task confirms that ToM tests involve executive elements. There is considerably more information to keep track of in comparison with the standard Sally-Anne task and it was also found within the task itself that giving the memory aid significantly improved performance (by nearly 20%). Working memory is another EF factor implicated as a possible deficit in autism. The second-order task is also arguably more 'mentalistic' because it requires understanding another's belief about a belief rather than an objective fact. On both those counts, the prediction would follow that individuals with autism would find second-order tasks particularly difficult. This is what was found by Baron-Cohen (1989) using 10 children and adolescents with autism aged between 10 and 18 years and a similarly aged group of individuals with Down's syndrome. Both groups performed less well than typically developing 7-year-old children, who were highly successful. (It should

Panel 15.5 Executive functions, representational complexity and second-order belief

- The executive demands of ToM tests could be increased if the contents of the false belief are made more complex
- One way to do this is to use a *second-order* version of the false belief task, e.g.
  - He thinks that she thinks that ...
- This makes it harder to hold all the information in working memory
- And increases the demands on *mentalising*
  - It forces the participant to think about someone's thoughts about thoughts rather than thoughts about the world (first order)

A A story is presented involving two key episodes. In the first, John buys an ice-cream in the park but Mary has to go home for some money. In the second Mary, sees that the ice cream man has left the park and gone to the church but John doesn't know this. The child is asked where John thinks Mary will go for her ice-cream.

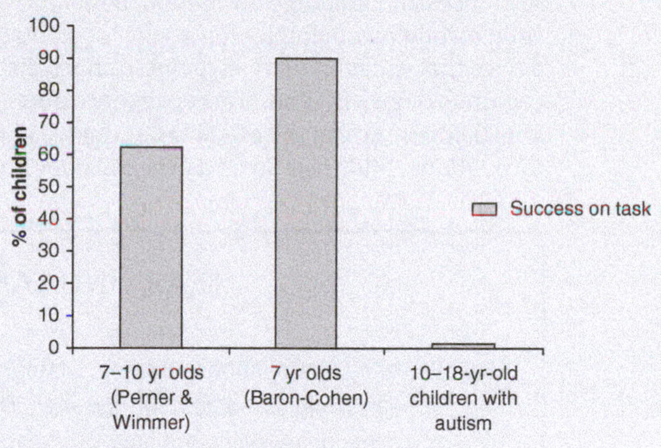

B Typically developing children are about 7 years old before they can reliably answer the second-order ToM question. Children and adolescents with autism failed entirely. (Adapted from Perner & Wimmer, 1985, and Baron-Cohen, 1989, with permission)

be noted that there were more memory prompts in Baron-Cohen's version of the task.) However, of particular interest is the fact that the entire autistic group failed this test as Figure B, in Panel 15.5 shows. Half of those who failed used a first-order false belief justification for the wrong response: 'He knows the van is at the church', but half did not mention belief states at all, saying, e.g., 'It (the van) is at the church'.

The EF analysis of ToM thus confirms that the ability to switch flexibly from one's own knowledge to another's false belief will be affected by the representational complexity of the held beliefs. But it also suggests that this itself may be related at least in part to the ability to hold the narrated information given in the tests in WM. But before concluding that EF factors seem to account for all the findings, there is yet another aspect to this. That is, the child *has to be able to represent a falsehood.* What bearing might this (also) have on performance? We consider this next in connection with the symbolic demands of false belief tests.

SYMBOLISATION, LANGUAGE AND THEORY OF MIND

Executive factors impact on false belief performance in terms of overcoming prepotent responses and holding information in memory. But neither of these is independent of the child's ability to mentally represent the protagonist's view. There has to be a cognitive device that can hold this viewpoint in sharp distinction to the child's own viewpoint. That cognitive device is **symbolic representation** – specifically language. Children can speak long before they can solve ToM tasks, but we know that their language goes on developing throughout childhood. So let's now consider how symbolic abilities might affect ToM.

LEARNING LANDMARKS

15.6 Pretence, imagination and symbolic thinking. You should know when pretence first appears in children's play, the age at which they can still be confused by the 'reality' of an imaginary event and how this relates to the understanding of symbolisation.

15.7 Language and false belief understanding. You should know why it is thought that language ability mediates the relationship between symbolic understanding and false belief. You should be able to say what aspect of language in particular may be responsible for this.

15.8 Understanding falsehood as a speech act. You should know why understanding 'lying' might relate to ToM. You should know what a speech act is and how this concept can explain further advances in understanding the intentions of others through their language.

15.6 PRETENCE, IMAGINATION AND SYMBOLIC THINKING

We have already encountered the idea of 'metarepresentation' and specifically of representing something that is false. This can sound a bit dry and academic, but it is in fact central to the very concept of childhood. Consider everyday acts of 'let's believe', such as pretending a stick is a hairbrush, a matchbox a car, or that a dolly is eating 'ice-cream' made of Play-Doh. Or indeed that the child him- or herself is a 'princess', a 'monster' or a 'pirate'. These play behaviours are in evidence from as young as 18 months (Piaget, 1962; Friedman & Leslie, 2007), and Piaget was one of the first to note the obvious connection with the beginnings of what he called **semiotic functions** – using something to stand for, or symbolise, something else. This could be an imitative gesture – like hand-washing or hair-brushing actions – but it is most likely to be language itself. From almost the moment they can speak, the imaginative routines of children are supplemented with words that help them in their play. There is perhaps no richer account of these behaviours than in Piaget's *Play, Dreams and Imagination in Childhood* (1962). To take just a few of his numerous examples (from Jacqueline, aged around 2 years):

- She took an empty box and moved it to and fro saying 'motycar'.
- She filled her hands with shells and said 'flowers'.
- She moved her finger along the table and said 'finger walking ... horse trotting'.
- She let some gravel trickle through her fingers and said 'it's raining'.

These acts of pretence suggest a facility with using language in a way that can flexibly represent both the real and the imagined. In pretend play, however, the imaginary scenario *is* the reality for the time being. The language maps perfectly onto what the child is thinking. In the case of ToM, Perner and others have argued that the child must be able to be able to separate the language clearly from the thing it is representing (the **referent**). In other words, to explicitly understand that language *is* symbolic. Unless this separation is clear in the child's mind, then it would be difficult to understand that the something might be misrepresented. Notice that this is not a difficulty in representing something that is false (as in pretence) but in representing the fact that the *representation* is false.

Numerous studies on children's engagement with fantasy and pretence in stories have supported the idea that this separation between language and referent is indeed not well established at the ages before ToM success. Whilst children seem to lap up scary stories, they can in fact become a little frightened due to the power of the symbol and their weak grasp of the fact that it is only 'words'. Many parents will have anecdotal evidence of this, but an interesting experimental study was conducted by Harris et al. (1991) in which they asked children to imagine (for example) a monster that wags its tail, and then told, 'now make a picture of that monster as it comes chasing after you'. They were then asked, 'that monster in your head – were you really scared when it came chasing after you or just pretend scared?' Although 4–6 year olds were quite able to distinguish real from 'fantasy' items, at least half of them acknowledged to have felt some fear. On a more objective measure of this finding, the authors then asked 3 to 5 year olds to imagine a box with a scary monster that would bite their finger off if they poked it through an aperture, or a box with a puppy, who would lick their finger instead. Four out of 20 older, and 7 out 20 younger children claimed that there really was a puppy and a monster in the boxes, but even for those who know it was 'just pretend', the vast majority were actually cautious about approaching the monster box and preferred to use a stick to poke into an aperture in the box than their finger! Subsequently, Samuels and Taylor (1994) found that even when the 'scary' factor is taken out of fantasy events as depicted in pictures (e.g. a moose cooking in a kitchen), children around 3 years 10 months did not distinguish these from everyday pictures (such as a girl riding a horse) when asked if they could happen 'in real life'.

To resist believing in a mere representation of an event, it is important that the (purely) symbolic role of the representation is understood. So when do children begin to have this kind of awareness? An answer to this was given by a study by Judy DeLoache that looked at elementary symbolisation without the confounds of using language. In this experiment, a miniature toy was shown being hidden under an item of miniature furniture in a scale model of a real room, and the child then had to retrieve the real one from the corresponding location in the real room. This was a deceptively simple game, used to answer an important question: can children use a symbolic representation of a hidden toy to locate the toy in the real world? The dramatic finding, published in *Science* (DeLoache, 1987), was that children just under 3 years of age generally failed, whereas children just over that age generally succeeded. DeLoache and colleagues argued that the difficulty arose from having to represent the model both as a reality *and* as a symbolic representation. They subsequently performed a very interesting variation to demonstrate this (DeLoache et al., 1997). Here they introduced a condition in which the model was created by 'shrinking' the real room to model size. This was made into a credible event by a magic 'shrinking machine' as shown in Panel 15.6. When the toy and room were 'shrunk', children of 2½ years old now succeeded on the task. The authors argued that this was because there was no longer any demand on the dual representation of referent (room) and a symbol (the model), as the room had now become a smaller version of itself and all the child had to do was remember the location.

The idea that children have to learn the dual role of any symbol as both a symbol, and also as an object in its own right, echoes arguments we encountered in relation to metarepresentation. DeLoache's research shows that this is a general aspect of becoming representationally flexible, and that it does not just apply to false belief. Rather it suggests that false belief understanding is just a special case of something far more general that is happening at that age. As you know, one of the things that happens from the age of 2½ is the explosion of language. However, to elaborate on that idea, we need to be sure both if and how language expertise may be important here.

Panel 15.6 Pretence, imagination and symbolic thinking

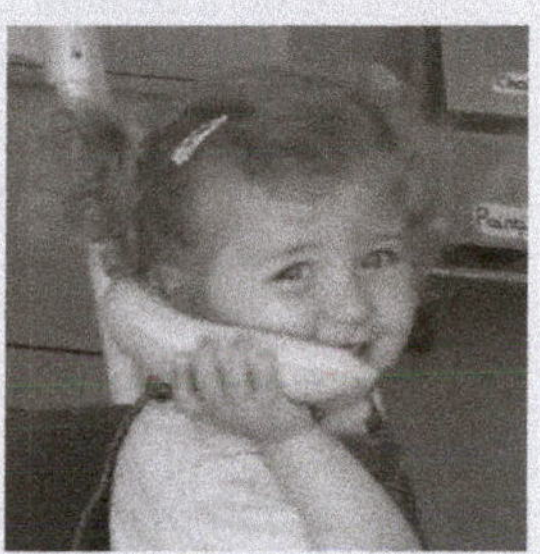

- Toddlers engage in imaginary play behaviour from the second year of life
  - They can use objects as substitutes, e.g.
    - a stick as a hairbrush
    - a banana as a phone
  - And also engage in pretend actions
- These behaviours are often accompanied by language
  - 'It's Mummy ironing'
- But the language of pretence is not always clearly separated from reality in the child's mind
  - Children of up to at least 6 years old can become 'scared' by imaginary creatures during story-telling
- This suggests that they do not clearly separate the symbol (the word) from its referent (the thing it stands for)
  - Thus a 'monster' can become real in the child's mind
- Elementary symbolic awareness has been tested in a task that uses a toy in a model room to represent an object in a real room
- Being able to explicitly understand that a symbol is (only) a representation and that it can be separated from reality is thought to underlie false belief understanding

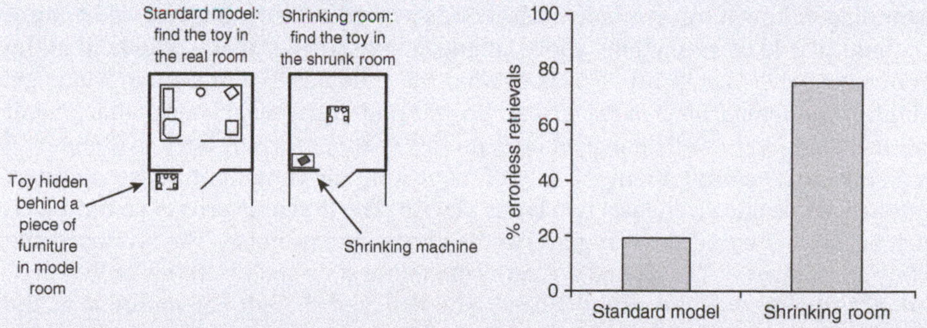

Children aged 2½ years could not locate a hidden object when a model toy in a model room symbolised a real one in a real room, but were able to do so when the toy and model were magically 'shrunk' and the symbolic element was removed. (Task and data depiction extracted from DeLoache et al., 1997, with permission)

15.7 LANGUAGE AND FALSE BELIEF UNDERSTANDING

If language development is strongly related to symbolic awareness as in the Scale Model task, and also to false belief understanding, then these three abilities should be strongly correlated. To test this, Walker and Murachver (2012) gave a set of tasks to 59 children aged between 2½ and 4 years comprising: the standard scale model task of DeLoache (1987); standardised tests of language comprehension and production; and a version of the Sally-Anne (false belief) task. The authors also looked at the other factor implicated in ToM: Executive Functioning (EF). One of the EF tests was an auditory WM task in which the children had to remember the names of pictured objects, another was an inhibition task (in which they had to switch from turning a knob to flicking a switch to obtain a toy) and the last was a version of the card sorting task (WCST).

A small extract of the results of this study are depicted in Figure A, Panel 15.7. Language abilities across the sample predicted performance on the False Belief task and also on the Scale Model, and abilities on these two tasks were themselves related. But that was not all. Using statistics that specifically test whether the predictive effect of Scale Model performance on subsequent false belief performance can be explained via a third variable (language abilities), the authors found that 'around 75% of early scale model performance on later false belief understanding was by way of language'. That is to say language ability is responsible for or **mediates** the relationship between scale model (symbolic) and false belief abilities. EF abilities also showed some correlative relationships with both scale model and false belief scores. For example, EF measures at 30 months predicted scale model performance at 36 and again at 42 months, and inhibition abilities and set-shifting in particular predicted false belief abilities at 48 months. The development of EF is thus confirmed in this study as an important factor in false belief (and, it turns out, also in scale model tests). Unlike language, however, EF did not seem to mediate the relationship between these two abilities (symbolising and false belief). This study then highlights the separate roles of *both* language *and* EF in the development of ToM.

It makes intuitive sense that increasing use of language is likely to lead to a better understanding of how it can symbolise falsehoods as well as truth, but can we be more specific than this? Is there anything about language in particular that would help in the context of false belief? Let is just go back to what the child has to represent in language, 'Sally thinks *that her marble is in the basket*'. Do you remember what we call this type of grammatical form? Very well done if you can do this without turning back to Chapter 9! Yes it's a **sentential complement** – a way of truncating the content of the second part of a sentence. It specifically follows two types of verb. The first are verbs of communication such as 'say': 'she said she was going to the shops', and promise: 'she promised she would buy some sweets'. The second are verbs of mental state such as 'think' or 'believe': 'she thought the bus would come at 3 p.m.'; 'she believed she left her umbrella at the bus stop'. (Remember that in these forms the word 'that' (the complementiser) is rarely included in the speech of children as young as four.) The complement, furthermore, can have a truth value that is separate from the truth of the overall statement. It may be true that she believed she left her umbrella at the bus stop – but her belief might be false. Do you see the relevance to false belief tasks? The sentential complement allows a specific symbolic representation of a false proposition. If this argument is along the right lines, then training or special exposure to these forms should enable children to perform the false belief task.

In a very interesting study, this was precisely what was carried out by Hale and Tager-Flusberg (2003). First of all the authors selected 60 children around the age of 4 who did not as yet use the sentential complement. This was pretested via a story in which a character says she is doing something whilst really doing something else. The child was asked what the character *said* she was doing (e.g. cutting up paper) whilst being shown a picture that depicted her doing something else (cutting her hair). A correct answer to the question 'what did she say she was cutting?' ('some paper') would show they could use the sentential complement. Because they intended to train children on using the complement, the authors used a control condition on another linguistic construction, so that any benefit from training on complements would not be confounded with more general linguistic training. This was a linguistic construction that you also know from Chapter 9 to be hard for children at this age – the relative clause. So once again children were pretested to establish that they were not already likely to use the relative clause at the start of the experiment. Here they had to answer question about a story character introduced with a relative clause (e.g. 'the boy *that had red hair*') to see if they were able to use this clause themselves in their answer. They were also pretested to make sure they could not yet solve false belief tests. Before training, performance was at or below 20% correct on all three pretests.

The children were allocated to one of three training groups. For the false belief group, the task was repeated and children were now given feedback and hints when they failed (e.g. 'but remember Cookie Monster did not *see* Ernie hide the cookies'). For complements training, the feedback following an incorrect response was, for example, 'but remember the boy *said* "I kissed Grover" but he really kissed Big Bird', and for relative clause training (e.g.) 'remember the boy kissed the girl *that* jumped up and down'. Four training trials were then given on all the tests on each of two training sessions. All children were posttested on all three types of task.

Training significantly improved performance on all three abilities, but as Figure B in Panel 15.7 shows, complements training also significantly improved performance on false belief posttests, whilst the reverse was not the case. The effect was not due to general linguistic training, as relative clause training had no effect on false belief performance, as you can also see from the graph. The investigators were careful to emphasise only the syntactic aspects of the training, and specifically avoided mental state verbs such as 'think' or 'believe'. They did not therefore favour the idea that they were enhancing a general insight into the minds of others as the Theory Theory account might suggest. Rather, they interpreted their results to suggest that 'the structural knowledge of specific language constructions actually fosters the ability to explicitly attribute mental states to oneself and others'. This conclusion makes considerable sense of everything that is known about Theory of Mind and its relationship with Verbal IQ in autism.

Panel 15.7 Language and false belief understanding

- Symbolic awareness is related to growing linguistic skills between the ages of 2½ and 4 years
- Significant correlations have been found between symbolic awareness (using the scale model task) and subsequent false belief abilities
  - The factor underlying this relationship seems to be the growth of linguistic abilities

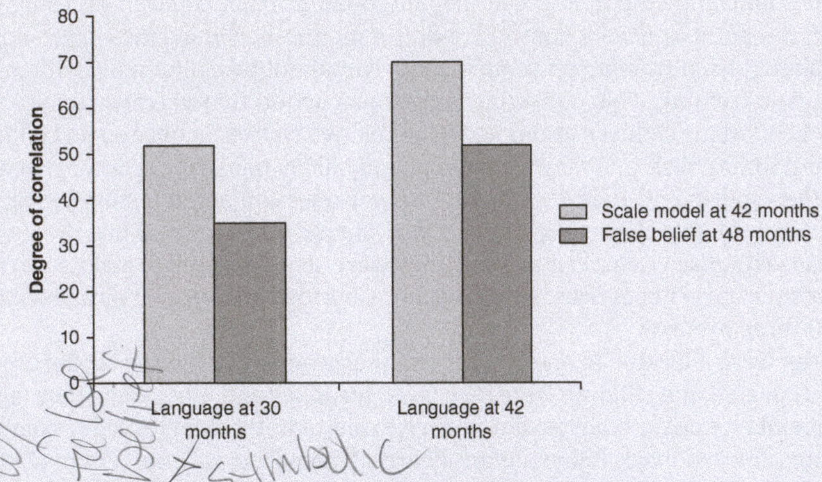

A Standardised tests of language skills show strong correlations with performance on scale model (symbolic understanding) and false belief tests. The correlations increase in significance across time. (Adapted from Walker & Murachaver, 2012, with permission)

- It has been argued that growing language ability *mediates* (is responsible for) the relationship between symbolic understanding at 2½ and later success on false belief tests
- One aspect of language development that occurs from around the age of 4 is the use of the complement
  - This follows verbs of communication and mental state
    - She said *she was going out*
    - He thought *he left his umbrella at the station*

- Because they grammatically separate the content of a thought from the rest of the sentence, the complement can also convey a false belief
    - Sally thought *her marble was in the basket*
- Training 4 year olds specifically on the use of the complement enhances false belief performance

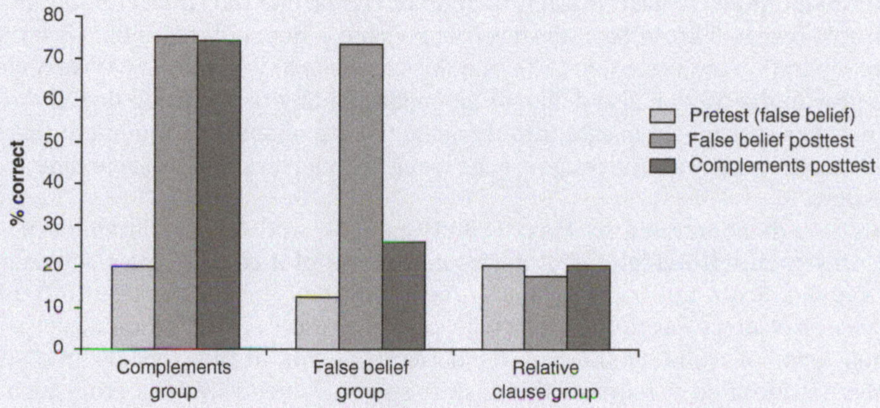

B When children are specifically trained on using the complement to answer a question it enhances performance on complements posttest and also on false belief. False belief training only enhances false belief performance. Control linguistic training (relative clause) has no effect on either. (Adapted from Hale & Tager-Flusberg, 2003, with permission)

15.8 UNDERSTANDING FALSEHOOD AS A SPEECH ACT

One question remains unclear, however. False belief paradigms have used the falseness aspect because if everyone (experimenter/child/story character) held the same (true) view of reality, it would be very hard to tease apart the child's own representation from the representation of another. Falseness in that sense was a kind of experimental device. But several times in this chapter we have raised the question as to whether there is something that is specifically hard about representing a *false* representation. Being able to linguistically state the propositional content of the representation (she thinks *that her marble is in the basket*) may indeed be one reason why this is hard to do, but even this possible link with language is slightly opaque in false belief tests, because no one has actually uttered a false statement. It may have occurred to you by now that there is a more obvious and everyday case of linguistic expressions of falsehoods than laboratory tests of false belief. And that is the concept of lying.

A lie is not just a false statement such as 'the moon is made of blue cheese'. That sort of falsehood is prevalent from the earliest stages of childhood, when absurdities, talking animals and imaginary beings populate the child's whole world of play. A lie is a special kind of **speech act**. A speech act is an utterance that has a very specific type of communicative intent – like 'inviting' or 'congratulating'. In the case of lying, this is the deliberate intention to misrepresent to another rather like the concept of deceit from which ToM research arose. So at the level of language, it demands more than just the linguistic separation of the content ('she said *she was going to wait for me*') as we reviewed in the previous section. It also demands an understanding that a lie is a lie if there is an intention to deceive – an insight into the mental state of another. You might therefore expect that the ability to 'understand' lying would develop around the same time as ToM. And it does.

This was demonstrated by Maas (2008) using 4- and 6-year-old children. They were presented with videotaped stories consisting of a conversation between two children (e.g. Scott and Lori). In one of the conditions (insincere intention), one of the story characters lies to the other with regard to a promise. The insincerity of the promise was conveyed by showing the actual thoughts of this speaker in a speech bubble. A simplified version of this task is shown Panel 15.7. The story also concluded by showing whether or not the intention was sincere in terms of the outcome (e.g. the promise to help is not fulfilled). Maas then asked the children both about the 'promise' made to the listener (e.g. 'Do you think Scott promised to help Lori?'), as well as whether or not it was a lie ('Do you think Scott lied to Lori?'). She also asked them the same questions from the perspective of the listener in the story (e.g. 'Does Lori think Scott promised?'). Understanding the falseness of the lie has to take account of the contrast between the contents of the thought versus the speech bubble as well as the outcome. This did not cause a major problem for any age of child. They all distinguished the insincere condition from a sincere one and degree of success on the lie judgment was correlated with passing first-order ToM questions in 4 year olds, as we might expect.

Maas's study made another interesting point, however, in connection with the understanding of a speech act. This arose because of an age-related effect in the understanding of 'promise'. As a speech act, a promise is subtly different from a lie, and should simply reflect the contents of the utterance at the time – i.e. a pledge to do something. You may promise to take your little brother to the zoo, but if you are prevented from doing it, it does not mean you were lying. And so, even if the story character used the 'promise' to lie, the fact that they promised is in fact true! This, in other words, should be quite independent of the actual outcome. Maas found that 6 year olds seemed to be using this distinction. This was evident in the fact that even in the insincere condition they (mostly) correctly answered 'yes' to 'do you think (Scott) promised?', whilst correctly answering that Scott had in fact lied. The 4 year olds, by contrast, did not view the promise as a promise in the insincere condition, treating

Panel 15.8 Understanding falsehood as a speech act

- Representing falseness through language is implied by ToM tests but it is made quite explicit in the act of lying
  - A *speech act* conveys a particular communicative intent
    - Lying is the intention to deceive
- Four year olds seem to understand that a character has 'lied' in a story setting where the character's thoughts are pitted against what he actually says
  - This understanding is correlated with success on ToM questions

Children were given a story in which a character makes a promise that is a sincere or insincere (pictured) as depicted in the thought bubble and also by the actual outcome of the story. Four year olds were adept at identifying a lie, and their performance was correlated with performance on false belief. Only 6 year olds correctly judged a promise in terms of the content of the utterance rather than the actual outcome. This did not extend to the case of second-order understanding (from the story listener's perspective). (Adapted from Maas, 2008, with permission)

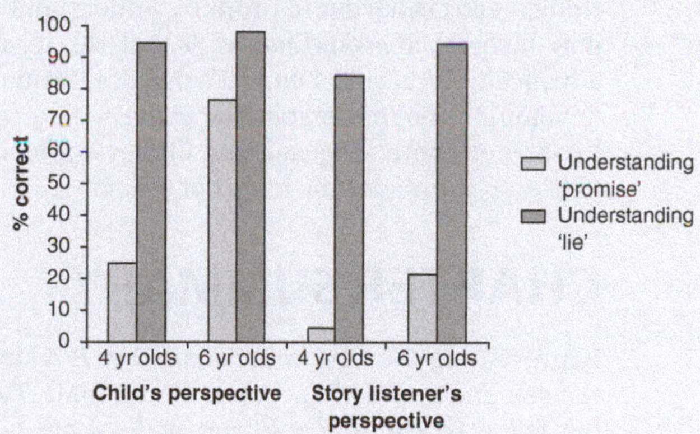

- At this age no distinction is made between a 'lie' and a 'promise'
  - A promise is also a speech act
    - It should reflect the content of the utterance rather than whether or not it was fulfilled
- Being able to represent the mental contents of other people in terms of speech acts that may not reflect reality is an important step in being able to deal with ToM type of tasks

it as if were a lie, because of the outcome of the story (in which the promise was not fulfilled). This development in 6 year olds did not extend to the second case, however. That was where the answer was to be based on what they thought the *listener* (Lori) would think. This of course requires representing another's thoughts (Lori's) about another's thoughts (Scott's), which we know to be a type of second-order belief. And indeed Maas found a significant relationship between the performance of 6 year olds on a second-order false belief and their ability to maintain the promise/lie distinction in the 'other's' perspective condition. Understanding language as a speech act that can be separated from the 'reality' it refers to is thus an important development in children's abilities to represent the minds of others. It is also central to the ability to answer hypothetico-deductive questions, as you will see in the next chapter.

The findings reviewed in these last sections do not imply that language development actually causes such subtle distinctions to be represented in the mind of the child. Rather, language allows these distinctions to become explicit to the child. Whilst language is a fine-tuned tool for making meaning explicit, this does not happen all at once, as we have seen already within this book. As language develops, this tool for representing the world and the intentions of others becomes more and more available. But as we have also seen, advanced language also make demands on executive control. A long embedded sentence ('Mary thinks that John thinks', etc.) is harder to produce, understand and remember than a simpler one. You may also recall from Chapter 9 that the term 'promise' can sometimes require an advanced hierarchical unpackaging of information, which could also explain the later development of understanding promise in terms of a speech act. In short, it isn't hard to see how both language *and* EF development are highly related to the developing ability to represent the minds of others.

CHAPTER SUMMARY

Representing the false belief of another is a strong test of being able to reason beyond the self and is called Theory of Mind (ToM). Typically passed at around 4 years of age but failed by children with autism, ToM has been variously regarded as a measure of representational flexibility and executive functioning (EF). The EF factors particularly implicated in normal (and abnormal) development of ToM are working memory and response inhibition, though others see the failure of ToM in autism as due (also) to a fundamental inability to represent mental states. There is a strong relationship between ToM and linguistic abilities, especially the ability to separate linguistic symbols from their referents. This reflects the importance of the ability to symbolically represent the content of another's belief in ToM, especially in terms of 'speech acts'.

LOOKING AHEAD TO CHAPTER 16

Theory of Mind research has not led us to a single skill or ability that suddenly appears at the age of 4, but to an interplay of different elements of the child's growing cognition – executive functioning, language and symbolic awareness in particular. This leads us to ask if the maturing of all these skills marks a kind of end-point as far as symbolic awareness is concerned. The answer is a definite 'no'. In fact, at the age at which children pass standard ToM tests, they will robustly fail on certain other 'symbolic' tests that might appear on the face of it to be much less demanding than having to represent the minds of others. Indeed, as you will see from Chapter 16, it is eventual mastery of these tests that will denote their own possession of an adult-like intelligence.

CHAPTER 16

SYMBOLIC REASONING AND LOGICOMATHEMATICAL THINKING

In this final chapter, we are going to come full circle and take up the topic that started Piaget on his long journey into the mind of the child in order to reveal the origins and growth of symbolic reasoning and logicomathematical thought. We have already seen the many ways in which children can gradually adhere and adopt some of the logical implications of real-world situations such as the inclusion relations entailed in the hierarchical organisation of class names (Chapter 13), the hypothetical possibilities of what might occur in a given spatio-temporal event (Chapter 14), and what *should* be in the mind of another observer of a particular event (Chapter 15). But we have also seen that children's 'logic' can be partial even at the age of 10, and that their 'symbolic' understanding is not always freed from its moorings in the real world. In this chapter we are going to look more closely at when and how children can apply logical rules at a more abstract level – by seeing commonalities across situations, or understanding logical entailment implied purely by the language of relations. Finally, we shall turn to mathematics itself.

SYLLOGISTIC AND CONDITIONAL REASONING

This belongs to a broad class of inference problems called **propositional logic**, meaning that two statements are logically connected in such a way such that a third proposition can be deduced, i.e. taking account of what follows from a given **antecedent**.

LEARNING LANDMARKS

16.1 Syllogistic reasoning. You should know what a syllogism is, what is meant by incongruent problems and what we have learned from them.

16.2 Deontic reasoning. You should be able to cite a study showing that deontic is an easier type of conditional reasoning than indicative reasoning, and understand why.

16.3 Counterfactual reasoning. You should be able to give examples of this and know what problems it can cause for children.

16.1 SYLLOGISTIC REASONING

A syllogism comprises two statements called **premises** from which a conclusion is deduced. If the conclusion follows logically it is said to be **valid**. It is not a requirement for the premises to be true. A famous example is:

Premise: All men are mortal

Premise: Socrates is a man

Conclusion: Therefore Socrates is mortal

Socrates was course a (male) Greek philosopher, and so philosophers are fond of this next example, to make the point that one or both premises may be false, but the conclusion is still valid:

All women are mortal

Socrates is a woman

Therefore Socrates is mortal

For a child, a good example of valid reasoning from false premises might be:

All cows eat nothing but pizza

Daisy is a cow

Therefore Daisy eats nothing but pizza

These kinds of false premises are sometimes called **incongruent** or **misleading**. That is to say inconsistent with real-world knowledge. (Some researchers use the term 'counterfactual', but we shall reserve this term for a more specific scenario that we come to presently.)

So making inferences from incongruent premises really forces the child to separate the symbol level of meaning from real-world knowledge. The age at which this ability appears depends on several factors. One of these is how well the child can actually imagine the incongruent state of affairs. This was shown in a study by Dias and Harris (1990) with 4- and 5-year-old children using problems such as:

All fishes live in trees

Tot is a fish?

Does Tot live in water?

Children were presented with up to three different cues to help them imagine these false premises, such as trying to imagine that these things occur on 'another planet'. As the graph in Panel 16.1 shows, each of these increased correct responding to significantly above the level found in the 'no cue' condition. The improvement was related to a significantly higher number of **justifications** of their answers referring appropriately to the fact that e.g. 'you told me (or 'we are imagining') that fishes live in trees'.

So when can children spontaneously take the linguistic statements at face value? Moutier et al. (2006) found that by the age of 8 years, children were at levels of over 80% accuracy on judging syllogisms such as:

All elephants are hay eaters

All hay eaters are light

So all elephants are light.

What do children have to do to pass these reliably every time? A suggestion by Moutier et al. was that they would have to learn to inhibit interference from what they know to be true. This should sound familiar to you by now. Difficulties in inhibition are associated with executive functioning and its development, and this was one plausible source of difficulty in Theory of Mind tests. But in the case of incongruent syllogism, there is the additional factor of having to suspend disbelief.

They called this the inhibition of **belief-bias**. Essentially, they have to think in terms of 'pretend' classes where members violate the rules of classes they already know about. This makes sense of an early finding by Hawkins et al. (1984), who found that entirely fantasy-based syllogisms such as:

Every Banga is purple

Purple animals always sneeze at people

Do bangas sneeze at people?

were solved much more easily than incongruent problems that violated world knowledge such as:

Glasses bounce when they fall
Everything that bounces is made of rubber
Are glasses made of rubber?

Panel 16.1 Syllogistic reasoning

- A *syllogism* is a form of inference in which a conclusion is drawn from two connecting statements
  - These are called *premises*:

    All dogs like cheese
    Henry is a dog
    Therefore Henry likes cheese
- Neither premise has to be true for the deduction to be valid
  - False (incongruent) premises can thus isolate the child's ability to reason from their world knowledge:

    All fishes live in trees
    Tot is a fish?
    Does Tot live in water?
- Children seem to be able to do this from about 4 years old if they are enabled to imagine the false premise

Four- and 5-year-old children are better at solving an incongruent syllogism when told to try to imagine the false premise, told to think of it occurring on another planet or given the statement with increased intonation. (Example and data from Dias & Harris, 1990 with permission)

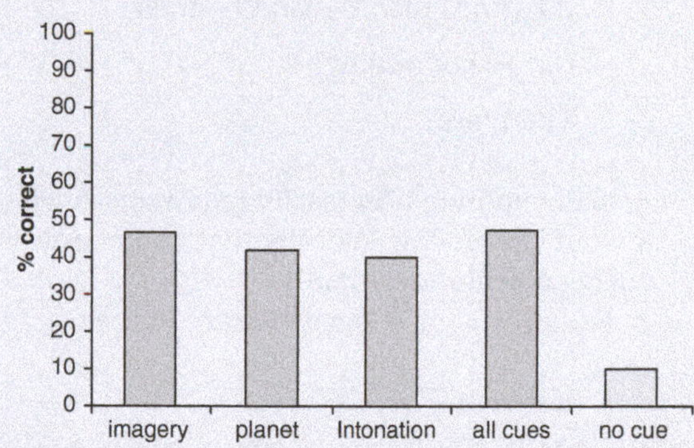

- The difficulty in solving these is thought to be a difficulty in inhibiting their world knowledge
  - This is called *belief bias*
- It is therefore easier for young children to deal with completely imaginary problems such as:

  Merds laugh
  Animals that laugh don't like mushrooms
  Do Merds like mushrooms ?
  (After Hawkins et al., 1984)

In short, children gradually become capable of solving syllogisms, but their ability to apply strictly logical rules to them seems to develop well into the school-age years – at least as measured by reality-violating examples. So is it possible to look at hypothetico-deductive reasoning without having to violate real-world expectations? We consider such a case next.

16.2 DEONTIC REASONING

This is a particular type of **conditional reasoning**, which means that the propositions are connected through 'if/then' logic:

> If P then Q,
>
> P
>
> Therefore Q

e.g.

> If it rains Chomper will get wet
>
> It is raining
>
> Therefore Chomper will get wet

You may know that is called reasoning from **modus ponens**. Now consider this:

> If P (rain) then Q (wet Chomper)
>
> Not P (not raining)
>
> Therefore?

Actually nothing necessarily follows here. The answer 'not Q' (dry Chomper) is wrong; it would not follow logically that Chomper is not wet (e.g. someone may have thrown a bucket of water over him!).

Equally wrong is the backward inference:

> If P then Q
>
> Q (wet Chomper)
>
> Therefore rain

for the same reason that you don't know what else might have happened to Chomper to make him wet.

However, if Chomper is *not* wet, then you *can* argue that, 'Therefore it is not raining'. This is called **modus tollens**:

If P then Q

Not Q (dry Chomper)

Therefore not raining (valid)

It has been shown that adults typically fail to draw the valid conclusion from modus tollens, unless the context is made really meaningful. Here we come to a famous example that you may know. It is called the four-card problem (Wason, 1966). Participants are told that every card has a letter on one side, a number on the other. Two are displayed letter-side uppermost (E and K); the other are number-side uppermost. The participants are given a conditional rule that states:

If there is a vowel on one side, then there is an even number on the other side

(If P then Q)

and asked which cards must they turn over to verify the truth of that rule. Fifty-three percent of adults correctly asserted that the E card should be checked. However, 46% also thought that the 4 card should be turned over to look for a vowel – the *invalid* backward inference of the form:

If P (vowel) then Q (even)

Q (even)

Therefore P (vowel)

In fact the correct second card is of course the 7 card to check (by modus tollens):

If P then Q

Not Q (not even)

Therefore not P (not a vowel)

If there *is* a vowel on the other side, the rule is false.

If you are confused by now, you are not alone! Only 4% of Wason's participants selected this card.

An astonishing increase to over 80% correct was found later in a follow-up by Johnson-Laird et al. (1972) when the rule was posed in terms of something meaningful to British participants familiar with current postal regulations. Here the vowel and consonant were replaced by open and sealed envelopes and odd and even numbers by four- and five-pence stamps. The participants had to verify the rule: if the letter was sealed it had to have a five-pence stamp. It was easy to deduce that the four-pence stamped letter had to be turned over to make sure it was not sealed! The meaning connecting stamps and envelopes helped them draw the inferences correctly.

Panel 16.2 Deontic reasoning

- This is a type of conditional reasoning
  - o It follows an 'if/then' rule
    - If it rains (*antecedent*)
    - My dog will get wet (*consequent*)
- To *verify* the truth of a rule (if X then Y) you have to check that the antecedent always results in the consequent
  - o It's raining – so the dog should be wet
- But also that the absence of the consequent is not preceded by the antecedent
  - o My dog is dry – and it is raining (rule disconfirmed)
- This is called *indicative* or *epistemic* reasoning
  - o Checking the truth of an epistemic rule is known to be difficult for adults
- Unless it is interpreted as a violation of a regulation
- *Deontic* reasoning makes this type of reasoning explicit in the form of *permission rules*
  - o If you put on your coat
  - o Then you can go out to play
- Children are able to reason deontically from the age of 4

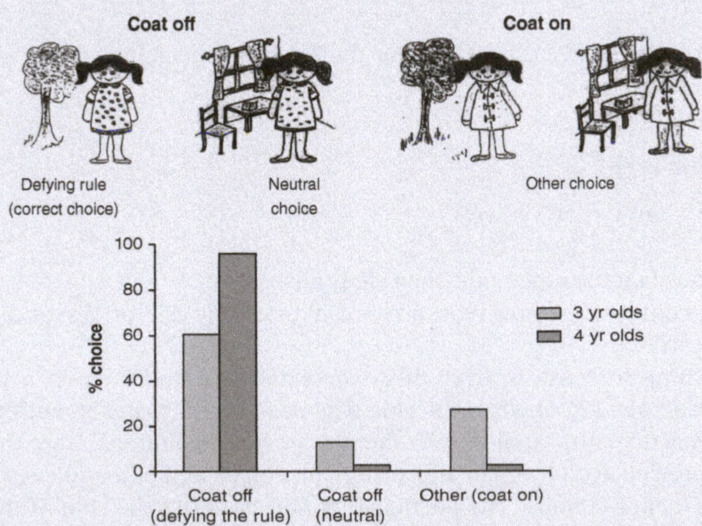

A Preschool children can correctly select the picture of the girl defying a permission to play outside only if wearing a coat. (Stimuli and data from Harris & Nunez, 1996, with permission)

- There is a bias in favour of deontic over indicative reasoning that increases during childhood and persists into adulthood

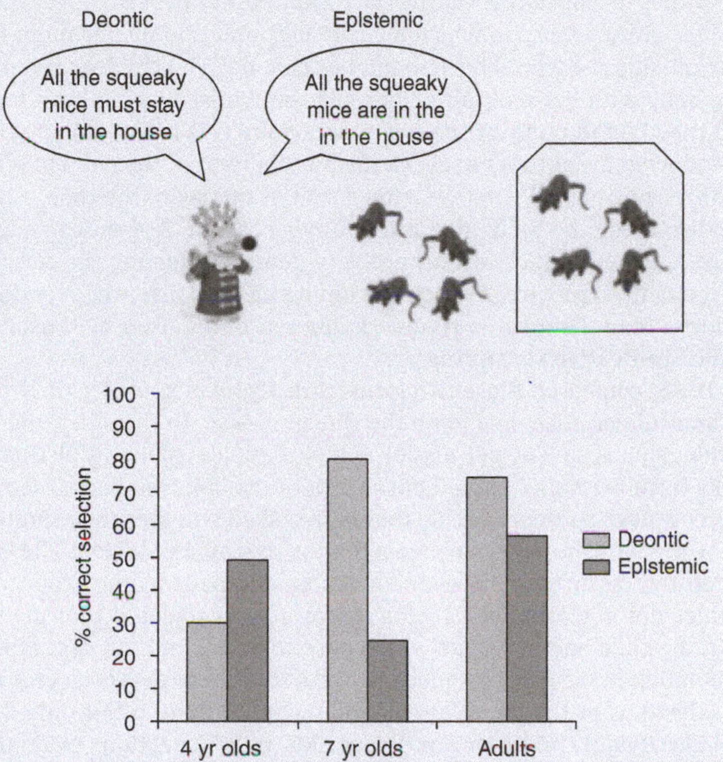

B An authority figure (Queen mouse) states a rule about rubber mice. To check whether the rule has been violated, the rubber mice outside the house have to be squeezed to see if they squeak. This is performed correctly by 7 year olds and adults but only when it is expressed as a permission rule. (Adapted from Dack & Astington, 2011, with permission)

So let's go back to children with our question as to what might be meaningful for them. Children are not accustomed to verifying the truth of a rule (even about stamps), but they are used to obeying them! Examples are:

If you put your coat on

Then you may go out to play

Clearly this requires a kind of understanding about a social contract with an authority figure. A child will be very used to Mum saying, 'Put your coat on before you go out to play'. But when does a child really understand the conditional logic that only *if* those conditions are met, *then* will the consequence follow? These are called **permission rules** and this is what is meant by **deontic reasoning**.

One of the studies to look at this was by Harris and Nunez (1996). Three- and 4-year-old children were given a story in which a girl (Sally) was told by her mum that 'if she wanted to play outside she would have to put her coat on'. The children were given pictures showing Sally with her coat off or her coat on whilst playing both indoors and outdoors, and they had to point to the one where Sally was being naughty (outdoors, coat off). This allowed the authors to check the possibility that the child might as easily go for any picture showing Sally not wearing a coat. If this were the case, a neutral but non-logical choice would be Sally indoors with her coat off. As you can see from the graph in Figure A, Panel 16.2, children were very good at selecting the correct picture only and not the neutral picture. Deontic reasoning has consistently been found to be easier for children than the form of rule-verifying reasoning used by Wason (which is sometimes called **indicative reasoning**).

Cummins (1996) compared these two forms directly by means of a story involving a toy cat and some rubber mice, including the Queen mouse. In the story, the cat would pounce if the mice squeaked. The permission rule was exclaimed loudly by Queen mouse: 'All the squeaky mice *must stay* in the house ...'. Here the children had to see if the rule was violated (by squeezing the mice). So they were asked whether they should squeeze the mice that were in the house or the ones that were playing outside. The contrastive indicative condition was an equally vehement statement made by the experimenter: 'All the squeaky mice *are in* the house ...'. Here the game was to see if the rule was really true, and again the child had to decide which mice to check. In both cases they needed to check the violation of the rule by squeezing the outdoors mice. Three year olds made 60% correct selections in the deontic (rule following) condition but only 37% in the indicative (rule verifying) condition. For 4 year olds, these selections were at 80% and 30% respectively.

It is, of course, important to consider the communicative context of these tasks. In one case, the statement is a command made by the authority figure (a queen mouse), whereas the indicative condition is more neutral. The possible influence of this factor was investigated by Dack and Astington (2011) who, in a replication of Cummins' study, made Queen mouse utter both the indicative statement (which they called the **epistemic** condition) as well as the command, to equate the presence of an authority figure in the two conditions. As the graph B in Panel 16.2 shows, the bias towards the deontic form was actually no longer found for preschool children who were not above chance on either form in this study. But when performance was above chance (for 7 year olds and adults), it was only on the deontic form. The authors surmise that what is developing here is a sensitivity to the different communicative force of a command as opposed to a statement. Deontic reasoning does seem to be easier then than indicative (or epistemic) reasoning but that is a difference that initially grows rather than subsides during development, and is related to understanding the communicative intent of the speaker.

This also helps explain a general feature associated with all reasoning tasks that require the child to engage in certain types of game. This has often been noted with regard to Piaget's conservation tests where the child is repeatedly asked if there is 'more here or more here, or are they both the same?', and it has been mooted that younger children may think the intent of the question is to get them to reconsider their first response ('both the same') leading to the incorrect second response ('more here'). It could also include some of the Theory of Mind tests, such as having to point to a box that does not contain the reward in order to *obtain* the reward, and also to accepting the premises of incongruent reasoning tests, such as, 'all cows eat pizza, Daisy is a cow; what does Daisy eat?', etc. In these situations, the experimenter is also an authority figure and is really asking the child to implicitly 'go along with' what must sometimes seem a rather bizarre exercise. The social context of 'testing' itself is also part of what the child needs to explicitly understand and in a way that is related to understanding language as a speech act (Chapter 15) insofar as they need to be complicit with why the question is being put to them in this way.

16.3 COUNTERFACTUAL REASONING

This is another form of conditional reasoning, taking the form not so much of 'if, then' as 'what if'. **Counterfactual** reasoning is a special case of this. It is about making inferences about what might have happened (but didn't). You may remember that we considered something like this in relation to a 'concrete' scenario (a toy mouse going down one arm of a chute and landing at an exit point) when children were asked, 'could he have gone anywhere else?' This is what is called an 'open' counterfactual question, which means that the child does not have to explicitly generate a different set of antecedent/consequent relations, such as the specific proposition, 'if the green card had been selected instead then the mouse would have gone down that chute'.

Is there any way to test counterfactual reasoning with children but at this more demanding conceptual level? Rafetseder et al. (2013) constructed a story scenario in which a doll's mother puts candy on a high shelf that can be reached by a boy and taken to his room, but not by his little sister. When Mum puts it on a lower shelf, only the sister can take it to her room, as the boy has his leg in plaster and can't bend down. Children aged from 5 to 14 years were able to work out where the sweets would be if they were placed on the lower shelf and the girl came (in her room) or upper shelf and the boy came (his room), and so on. But they were also given counterfactual questions that forced them to reconsider the whole event (e.g. top shelf/boy comes), such as 'where the sweets would be if the girl had come instead'.

Panel 16.3 Counterfactual reasoning

- This is a form of 'what/if' conditional reasoning
  - It involves reconstructing what might have happened under other circumstances
  - Possible circumstances:
    - If the chocolate is up on the shelf then my sister can come for it
    - If I don't put it on the shelf the dog will eat it
  - The actual circumstances:
    - I put the chocolate on the shelf and my sister came
  - The *counterfactual* questions:
    - Where would it be if my sister had not come? (Ans: still on the shelf)
    - Where would it be if I had not put it on the shelf ? (Ans: in the dog)
- During story scenarios, children can show difficulties on counterfactual questions up to at least 10 years of age

If Chocolate on top shelf and boy comes
Then chocolate goes to his room

If Chocolate on bottom shelf and girl comes
Then chocolate goes to her room

The chocolate is on the top shelf
The boy comes – where is the chocolate?

Counterfactual question: where would it be if the girl had come instead?

Can't reach top shelf

Can't reach bottom shelf

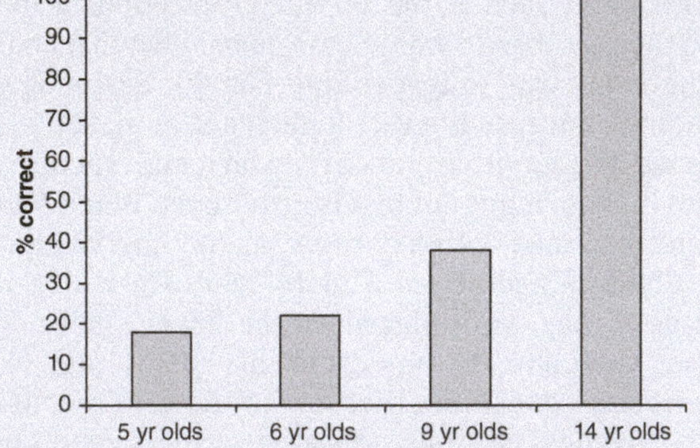

A Children are given conditional stories and have to reconstruct alternative possible outcomes. The graph shows performance for the counterfactual question – in which the relationship between the antecedent (top shelf) – and the event (girl comes instead) has to now be completely reconsidered – as she can't reach the top shelf. (Adapted from Rafetseder et al., 2013, with permission)

- Taking account of a different possible antecedent/consequent relationship can be measured by retrospective pleasure or disappointment, e.g.
  - You have won £100 on a lottery, but with a single change of number, it could have been £1000 or just £10.
- Adults can retrospectively reassess their pleasure in the light of 'what might have been' but children under 5 years do not

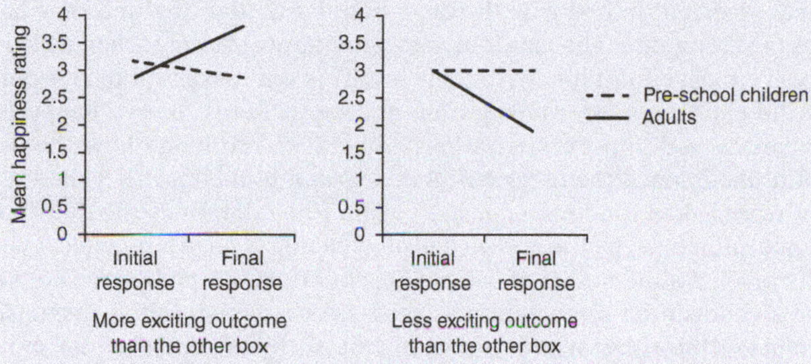

B Participants rated the pleasure that a story character would feel on opening a box to find a gift. Adults, but not children, readjusted this score subsequently in the light of whether opening the other box would have been a better or worse option (Adapted from Amsel et al., 2003, with permission)

The graph in Figure A, Panel 16.3 shows that from two experiments with this sort of structure, it was found that children under the age of 10 found it difficult to answer counterfactual forms of question.

In this study, the same antecedent (sweets on top shelf) had to be reconsidered in relation to a different possible subsequent event (girl comes instead of boy). You could also have asked what would have happened if Mum had not put the sweets on the shelf at all (a different antecedent). This difference is common in everyday use. A person falls off a ladder and breaks their leg. Someone is sure to say to them, 'it could have been so much worse – you could have broken your neck!' But if the injured party says, 'but if you hadn't asked me to climb the ladder in the first place, I wouldn't have broken my leg!', then they are using counterfactual reasoning – coming to a logical conclusion by considering a different possible antecedent.

A common context for this sort of reasoning is often in terms of pleasure or disappointment at the way things turned out in relation to what might have happened, e.g. 'If I had put a zero (different antecedent) instead of a seven, I would have won the lottery'. And suppose you had won £100 and were feeling pretty pleased about it, how would you feel about that win when you learn that if you had put an eight instead of a seven, it might have been a £1000? So when do children become influenced by these sorts counterfactual 'ponderings'? Not until after the age of 5 it would seem. Amsel et al. (2003) gave preschool children a game in which two dolls open one of two boxes, each receiving the same toy inside. The second box was opened to see what the doll 'might have' received. In one case, it was a better toy than the one they had; in the other, a less exciting one. The children answered appropriately when asked whether the dolls were pleased initially with their toy. This was assessed by a 4-point rating scale that the children used, ranging from not happy (sad) to very happy (sad). The children also showed appropriate ratings when asked to judge how the doll would have felt if it had opened the other box. As the graph B in Panel 16.3 shows, however, when they were asked the initial question again ('how happy is the doll?'), their ratings were not influenced by the knowledge of what might have happened, as compared with adults given a similar sort of game. Subsequent research by Weisberg and Beck (2012) gave children an opportunity to reassess their *own* initial response (rather than that of a doll) to either winning or losing tokens by turning over one of two cards. They found that children as young as 4–5 seem to experience regret that they 'could have won more' when the second card was turned over. It was only by the age of 6 to 7, however, that they experienced relief after a loss when discovering that they could have lost more. This places the first emergence of counterfactual abilities at before 5 years old, but it should be noted that the children were encouraged to reconsider their initial responses. We have no way of knowing if this would have occurred to them without prompting. In short, the ability to reconsider responses to outcomes can tell us that counterfactual reasoning can be employed from about 5 years of age, but there is no simple answer to when this will occur spontaneously during development.

Conditional reasoning is an important tool for deriving new knowledge. But, you may remember that Piaget's original interest in logical reasoning was about the child's ability to understand the logic of relations. We look at this next.

RELATIONAL AND QUANTITATIVE REASONING

If conditional reasoning is about abstracting what connects antecedents with consequents, then relational reasoning is about abstracting what connects one relationship with another.

LEARNING LANDMARKS

16.4 Analogical reasoning. You should know what this means and be able to cite two examples of how it has been tested in children and what was found.

16.5 Reasoning with numerical quantifiers. You should know what these are, the kinds of difficulties shown by children and what is meant by Mental Models and figural effects.

16.6 Reasoning with dimensional quantifiers. You should be able to describe figural effects in transitive reasoning, a famous study demonstrating transitive reasoning in preschool children and what was subsequently concluded from this area of research.

16.4 ANALOGICAL REASONING

Analogical reasoning tests the explicit awareness of relational similarity based on a structural property of a scene or event. A common example would be:

Horse is to Foal

As Sheep is to ?

This test is based on a **classical analogy** and the convention for representing this symbolically is:

horse : foal :: sheep : lamb

The ability to understand classical analogies is tested by asking the participant to supply the last item in the sequence (e.g. 'lamb' would have to be selected from a set of non-analogous alternatives such as 'wool' or 'piglet'. This ability is so strongly related to cognitive development that it features as a subtest in some IQ test batteries such as the WISC. Analogies require what is sometimes called **relational mapping** and it gives us some insight into how they can 'abstract' a common relationship across situations. So when can children show this mapping?

An apparently simple case of analogy is shown in Figure A in Panel 16.4. The common relationship is of course 'house of'. Goswami and Brown (1990) used this test with 4-, 5- and 9-year-old children, asking them which picture was need to complete the sequence.

Panel 16.4 Analogical reasoning

- An *analogy* is a structural similarity across two scenarios
    - Horse *is to* Foal as Sheep *is to* Lamb
- A classical analogy test might present this in picture form
- Another test is to see if it can be adopted to solve problems

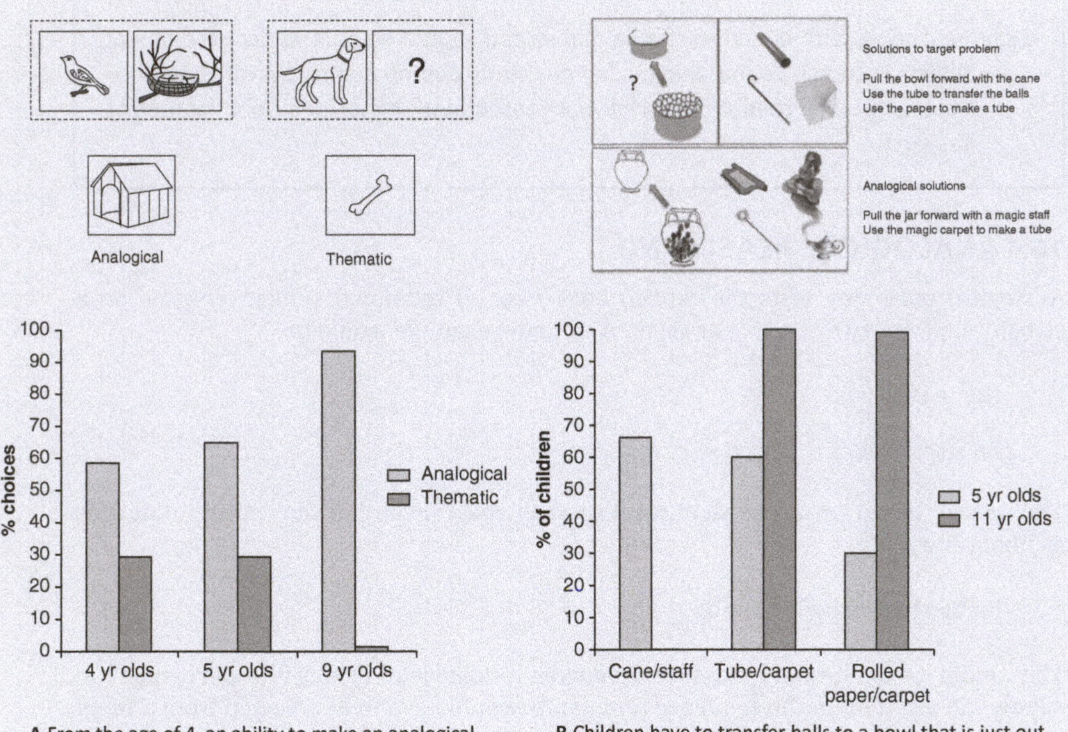

A From the age of 4, an ability to make an analogical choice can overcome the tendency to make a thematic one in a classical test. (Adapted from Goswami & Brown, 1990, with permission)

B Children have to transfer balls to a bowl that is just out of reach, using available tools. The story analogy concerns a genie needing to transfer his jewels. Younger children adopted the analogy but mainly where there was high perceptual similarity. (Adapted from Holyoak et al., 1984, with permission)

- Children of around 6 years old sometimes transfer a story analogy to a solution even when it is not appropriate

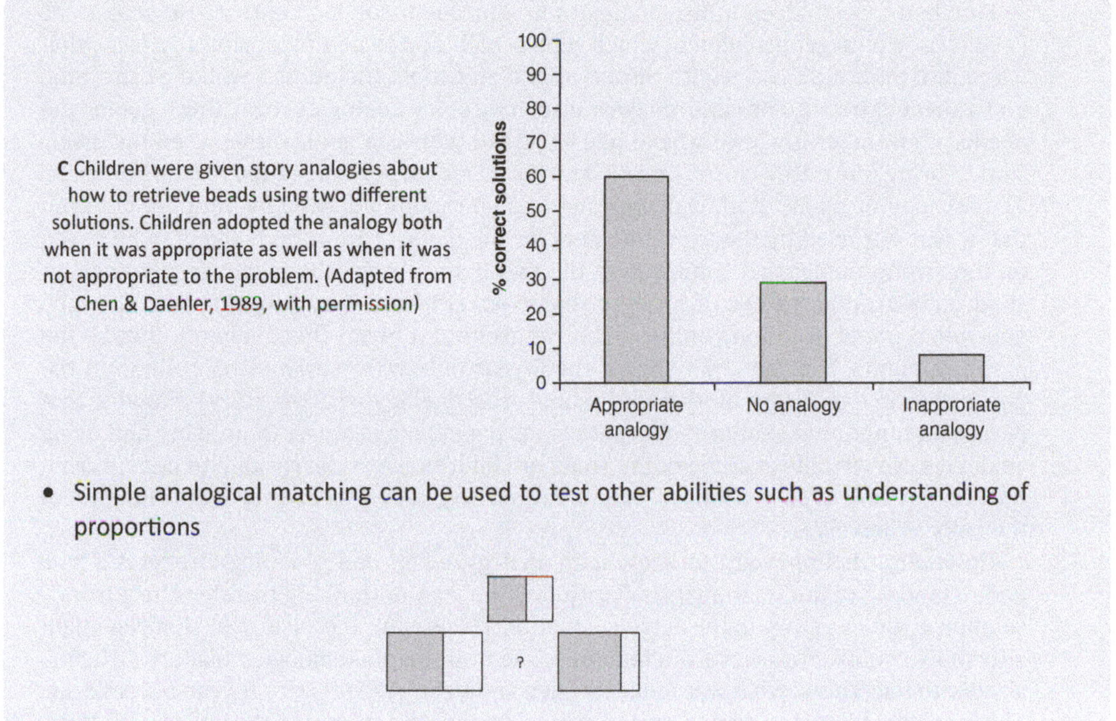

C Children were given story analogies about how to retrieve beads using two different solutions. Children adopted the analogy both when it was appropriate as well as when it was not appropriate to the problem. (Adapted from Chen & Daehler, 1989, with permission)

- Simple analogical matching can be used to test other abilities such as understanding of proportions

They used an important control condition in which only the the single test picture was presented and they had to choose another picture that 'fitted best' with it. As you know from Chapter 13, this could well induce the thematic choice expected at this age (i.e. 'bone' rather than 'kennel'). These choices did occur but they did not outweigh the (correct) analogous choice. As you can see from the graph, the analogous over thematic selections increased with age.

Another line of research is to ask when children are able to utilise analogies in order to solve problems. A well-known example of this with adults is based on a famous study by Duncker (1945). The key task or **target problem** was how to treat a patient's tumour with radiation without destroying surrounding tissue. Only 5% of college students succeeded in finding a solution. Subsequently, however, Gick and Holyoak (1980) presented this problem together with an analogy involving a story about an army general trying to attack a fortress without his troops being destroyed by mines – the solution being to split up the army into small converging units too light to trigger the mines. This increased the chance of a correct solution to the target problem (use weak harmless rays that converge on the tumour) from 10% to 20%, and up to 75% when it was 'hinted' that they may like to think about the story.

So when can children utilise analogies in a problem-solving context? Holyoak et al. (1984) used a target problem in which rubber balls had to be transferred to a bowl that was out of the child's reach with the use of available tools, including a walking cane, tube and a sheet of paper. The children were given two story analogies regarding a genie who needed to transfer his jewels from one jar to another. The genie either used his magic staff to bring one bottle closer, or rolled up his magic carpet into a tube to transfer them. The analogy of magic staff/walking cane was so readily adopted by younger children that it was not used by the experimenters for the older group, and is likely to be based on the strong perceptual similarity of the two items. As for the magic carpet analogy, children of around the age of 11 were able to benefit from it by adopting both the tube and rolled paper solution (unlike a control group not given this analogy). But, as the graph in Figure B, Panel 16.4 shows, the 5-year-olds were resistant to rolling up the paper to form a tube (the more precise conceptual analogy with the story), showing that perceived functional similarity (carpet versus paper) plays a part in noticing and using analogies. Nevertheless, some of the younger children were clearly able to benefit from the analogy and even verbalised their solutions to make it clear they were thinking of the balls as 'jewels'.

However, it is important to know if an analogy, when one *is* adopted, reflects a true understanding of the relational similarity, or simply an unthinking transfer effect from a solution given in a story to the current situation. If this were the case, then children might also show negative transfer from inappropriate or unhelpful analogies that are structurally dissimilar. This is what was found by Chen and Daehler (1989) for 6-year-old children. The target problem was how to retrieve a bead floating in water near the bottom of a glass. In one version, an available solution was to add water to raise the level; in the other to reach the bead by adding a spoon end to a stick. These were not interchangeable; in the first version no spoon was available; in the second the water level could not be raised high enough. A helpful analogy for the first was in the form of a story about a thirsty bird who used pebbles to raise water in a container. For the second it was a story about a monkey combining sticks to reach bananas outside his cage. These stories would clearly not provoke a solution if there was an attempt to use them in the 'other' context. As the graph in Figure C, Panel, 16.4 shows, children were both positively *and* negatively influenced by the stories as compared to a control group. So insofar as recognition of analogy is concerned, this seems to be present from preschool years, but we have to be cautious in ascribing a deep and spontaneous understanding of the nature of the analogy at this age.

If children can use analogies, then we can use this skill to probe their understanding of relationships that can be hard to assess using other methods. Some have used analogical reasoning to test the child's comprehension of 'proportions' using geometric shapes (Spinillo & Bryant, 1991), 'slices of pizza' or numbers of chocolates (Singer-Freeman & Goswami, 2001), where the child has to choose an equivalent 'share' across e.g. differently sized pizzas. Performance is highly variable depending on the relative difficulty of the proportion itself and whether the amounts are continuous (pizzas) or discontinuous (chocolates). This tells us that whatever the capacity to adopt analogies, what crucially develops is the ability to comprehend the relationship in question.

So let us return to what lies at the very heart of relational reasoning: understanding relations and, in particular, how symbolically expressed relations are themselves logically interconnected. This is what Piaget meant by **logicomathematical** structure and we look at its developmental origins next.

16.5 REASONING WITH NUMERICAL QUANTIFIERS

You may remember from Chapter 13 that at around the age of 7 children can answer a problem such as:

> 'All bears are animals
>
> Barney is a bear
>
> Is Barney an animal?'

However, they may have more difficulties at this age if you said:

> 'All bears are animals
>
> Barney is an animal
>
> Is Barney a bear?'

Their difficulty with 'downwards' inferences where the answer is indeterminate (he might be) was related to their knowledge of how names can refer to things at different levels of generality in the real world. The key element in logicomathematical inferences about class inclusion is that they can be drawn purely through the symbols that express the relations themselves and not through any world knowledge about the names or the classes themselves. An example would be:

> 'Some wuggits are figgots
>
> All figgots are wuggits
>
> Are there more wuggits or more figgots?'

The relationship between the **quantifiers** 'all' and 'some' makes it necessarily true that wuggits is the more inclusive class. So what can children infer from relational terms like these? An obvious place to start might seem to be the child's understanding of quantifier language in everyday contexts – and it turns out to be very far from logical! Since a very interesting finding by Donaldson and McGarrigle (1974) it has now been established across several replications that children find difficulty in using the basic quantifiers 'all' and 'more'. Their study included questions about toy cars placed inside garages and arranged on two shelves as shown in Figure A in Panel 16.5. A key finding was that when 4 year olds were asked, 'are all the cars on "this" shelf?', they would (correctly) deny that the top row had 'all the cars', but a significant proportion asserted that 'all the cars' were on the short (garages all full) row. Most of these children referred to the empty space in the top row to justify their answers (e.g. there's 'one missing'). In a replication study by Freeman et al. (1982) it was found that errors also occur to the question, 'are all the cars in *a* garage?' in situations in which there was an empty garage, but it was found the level of error could be significantly reduced if the empty garage was occupied by something else (such as a boat). As Figure B in Panel 16.5 shows, similar difficulties have been found by Brooks and Sekerina (2005) with the words 'every' and 'each' – in children under 9 years of age when they had to choose which of two pictures of alligators in bathtubs fitted statements using 'each', 'every' and 'all'.

These results might suggest that reasoning with quantifiers like 'all' and 'some' may be a late development. On the other hand, depicted situations also have distracters (such empty bathtubs). Supposing you said to them (in the absence of any picture): all the alligators are bathing; some bathers use soap. Are all the alligators using soap? This form of task has been used to see when adults can use the quantifiers alone to form pictures in their mind. You may have done something just like this yourself when thinking about the wuggit example given above. Tasks like these have been extensively studied by Philip Johnson Laird and his colleagues. He did not use bathing alligators but human professions such as Artist, Beekeeper and Chemist, and a standard form of the task would be:

'All the Artists are Beekeepers

All the Beekepeers are Chemists'

And the reasoner has to state what can be inferred from these A–B; B–C relationships. In this case it is that all the As are Cs and that (at least) some of the Cs are As. This is not something that could be deduced (validly!) from world knowledge about artists and chemists and so it relies on how the reasoner constructs some sort of mental depiction. This could be a set of overlapping circles:

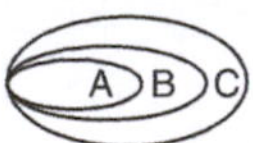

Alternatively, Johnson-Laird (1983) has promoted the idea that adults use placeholders that represent the item relationships in the order in which the information is presented and that the conclusion is reached by following a path through the connections from A to C:

Artist	Artist		
↓	↓		
Beekeeper	Beekeeper	Beekeeper	
↓	↓	↓	
Chemist	Chemist	Chemist	Chemist

Panel 16.5 Reasoning with numerical quantifiers

- The logical relationship between 'all' and 'some' permits deductive inferences that are not based on world knowledge
    - These terms are known as *quantifiers*
- The understanding of quantifiers in natural language shows that young children do not abstract the numerical implications of the terms

A Preschool children were shown a set-up with toy cars in garages on two rows. They correctly denied that all the cars were on the top row but most asserted that 'all the cars' were on the lower row. (After Donaldson and McGarrigle, 1979)

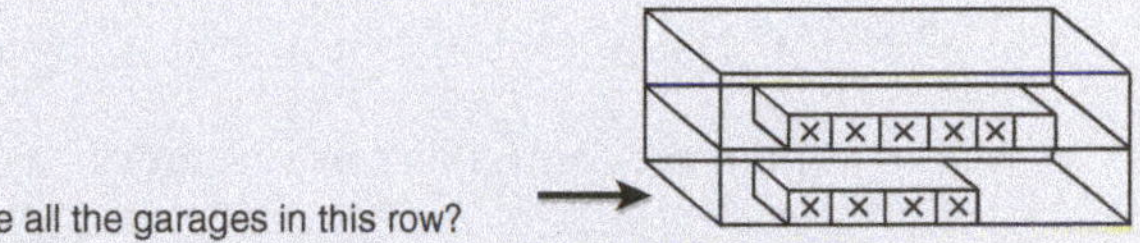

'Yes' answer justified by pointing to empty garage in top row

- Reasoning with quantifiers at the purely symbolic level can be tested by asking what can be deduced from premises stating arbitrary all/some relationships such as:

All of the footballers are runners
Some of the musicians are footballers

- The inference: *therefore some of the musicians are runners* is much easier for adults and children when the syllogism takes the linear form A–B and B–C as in:

Some of the musicians are footballers
All of the footballers are runners

- This is known as the *figural effect*
    - It is thought that this is a reflection of the ease with which a *'Mental Model'* can be created from the order of the statements as they come in (Johnson-Laird, 1983)
- Children of 9 years can solve these problems but only with the easier form of figure

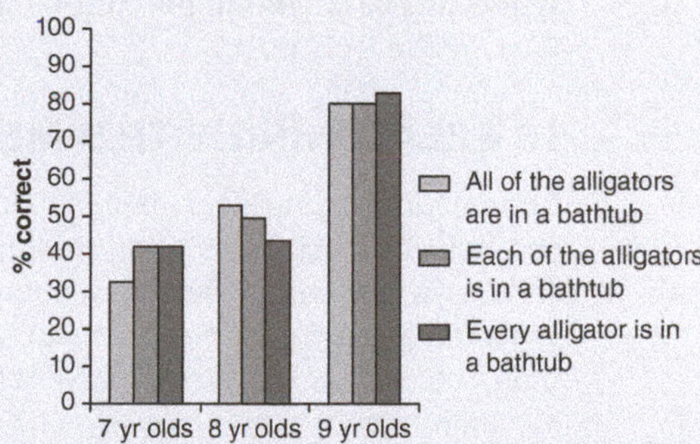

B School-aged children made similar errors when asked to select the picture matching statements with quantifiers, 'all, each' and 'every'. (After Brooks & Sekerina, 2006, with permission)

He called these **mental models**.

Is it possible for children to make deductions from any of these sorts of statements? In studies with children aged between 9 and 12 years, he used premises such as:

> 'Some of the musicians are footballers
>
> All of the footballers are runners'

And the children were asked what other things could be said about these people. In the above example, it is that some of the musicians are runners (and vice versa). However, it also presents the premises in the form A–B; B–C. It could have presented this way:

> 'All of the footballers are runners
>
> Some of the musicians are footballers'

This changes what is known as the **figure** of the syllogism to B–C; A–B. Johnson-Laird found that, as with adults, children's performance varied widely in terms of the figure (Johnson-Laird et al., 1986). Where the terms came in the correct consecutive order (allowing the 'path' to be followed easily), 9 year olds were able to draw a valid conclusion at a level of 60% correct, but less than half that level for the problems where the terms were out of that order.

So the answer to the question regarding when children can reason with quantifiers seems to depend on how the premises are presented. But 'all' and 'some' are also about discrete (discontinuous) quantities and so they require thinking numerically.

It might be expected, therefore, that relational reasoning may be found earlier with syllogisms based on simple continuous quantities, such as bigger than and smaller than. We consider this next.

16.6 REASONING WITH DIMENSIONAL QUANTIFIERS

Dimensional quantifiers express extent along a dimension such as size, brightness or pitch. This brings us to an intelligence test item that started Piaget thinking about children's reasoning when, as a young man, he worked in the laboratory of the famous psychologist, Alfred Binet. It was this: 'If Edith is fairer than Suzanne and Edith is darker than Lilli, who is the fairest/darkest?' This is known as a test of **transitive reasoning** – do you remember this expression from Chapter 13? In that context we were taking about downward and upward inferences from a superordinate to a subordinate class, or vice versa. Here we are talking about a linear inference where e.g. Suzanne, Edith and Lilli have to be ranked in order to find the answer. There has been little challenge to Piaget's finding that children find purely linguistic tests of this sort rather difficult, and are not likely to solve them reliably until around the age of 11 years. However, it has also been known for some time that one of the difficulties arises (as with Johnson-Laird's tests) from the order in which the information is presented (Hunter, 1957; Clark, 1969), and that children can solve these tests much earlier using the form that maintains the same serial direction or 'path' through the premises such as 'Tom is taller than Harry; Harry is taller than Bill, who is the tallest?' This is called **isotropic** (A > B; B > C or A < B; B < C). **Heterotropic** figures are all the others, such as B > A; B > C or A > B; C < B, etc. Even when these can be solved, they take much longer and it is thought that extra time is needed to mentally re-order and convert the premises to make them isotropic. Nowadays we would see the extra processing steps as adding to the working memory (WM) load and thus showing another effect of EF on problem solving. But it also tells us that children seem to make a sort of linear ranked model of 'greater than' and 'less than' statements and this became known as using a **spatial paralogic** (De Soto et al., 1965; Huttenlocher, 1968).

It was also becoming evident from research by Clark (1970), Donaldson and Wales (1970) and others that the relations expressing 'greater than' and 'less than' themselves might add a further WM demand. Relations that we might think of as relating to the negative pole of a dimension, such as 'smaller', 'worse', etc. seem to take more time to process. This is called the **lexical marking** effect. It appears from independent research using simple questions to children such as 'Is a cat smaller than a cow?', that this is because terms like 'smaller than' are actually first processed as 'not bigger' by children of up to 9 years of age (McGonigle and Chalmers, 1984). This produces the striking result that they can be faster to deny that 'a cat is bigger than a cow' than to assert that it is smaller! Can we separate out WM and marking effects then, in order to establish a rough age at which we can say that children can, in principle, make a deductive inference about dimensional relations? A study by Oakhill suggests that children are largely – though not completely – correct at answering the isotropic form at around the age of 8. The problem was given to children in the forms of statements on cards and in one condition, they simply had to answer question such as 'who is best?', following the information printed on cards: Ann is better than Carol; Carol is better than Mary. However, performance dropped to chance levels with heterotropic forms, especially when they were combined with marked terms.

The superiority of the isotropic form introduces another problem, however. For it raises the possibility of a correct answer being arrived at by a kind of 'echoing' of the relation stated in the first premise rather than real deduction. Think about it:

'Tom is taller than Harry; Harry is taller than Bill; who is the tallest?'

If this is mentally converted to Tom = tall; Harry = not tall, etc. then Tom is the only one exclusively described as tall. This is known as **end-point labelling** and the way round it is to use extra relations (A > B); B > C; C > D; (D > E), where the key question is not about the end-points but the internal comparison B v D. Just to make sure, it would also be important to describe the relations in both directions: (B < A); C < B; D < C; (E < D). So B is described as both 'bigger than' and 'smaller than', and likewise D. Now a correct answer to B v D must surely mean that it is through logically combining the relations described in the premises BC and CD, and not through 'echoing'. This is called a five-term (as opposed to a three-term) series problem.

Panel 16.6 Reasoning with dimensional quantifiers

- These tasks convey extent along a continuous dimension such as size, e.g.
    - Tom is *taller than* Sam; Sam is *taller than* Harry; Who is the *tallest*?
- They are subject to figural effects
    - Unidirectional premise presentation is called *isotropic*:

      A > B; B > C and A < B; B < C
    - The others are called *heterotropic*, e.g.

      B > C; B < A into A > B; B > C
- Isotropic but not heterotropic forms can be solved from about 8 years of age
- These verbal tasks were thought to introduce two main problems:
    - Having to remember verbal information
    - A labeling bias such that 'end-points' might suggest the solution
- When these elements were controlled for, children as young as 4 seemed to be able to make a relational deduction

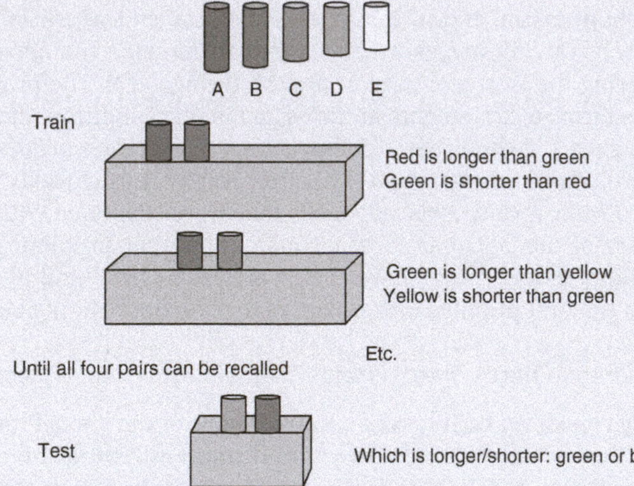
A B C D E
Train
Red is longer than green
Green is shorter than red
Green is longer than yellow
Yellow is shorter than green
Etc.
Until all four pairs can be recalled
Test
Which is longer/shorter: green or blue?

A 'Invisible' size relations were trained in pairs from AB to DE, and then in random order until the child could repeat them. Four year olds were highly successful on tests of all pairwise relations including the crucial pair B versus D which was not subject to labeling bias. (Adapted from Bryant & Trabasso, 1971)

- Subsequent research showed that this result was dependent on the children first learning the pairs in isotropic order
  - Only 7 year olds succeed where the training presentation is in random order (heterotropic) throughout
- Reaction times measured during transitivity tests have since demonstrated that the inferences can be based on a 'read-off' from a mental array
- This is different from making a logical deduction of the form: B > C; C > D therefor B > D, etc.

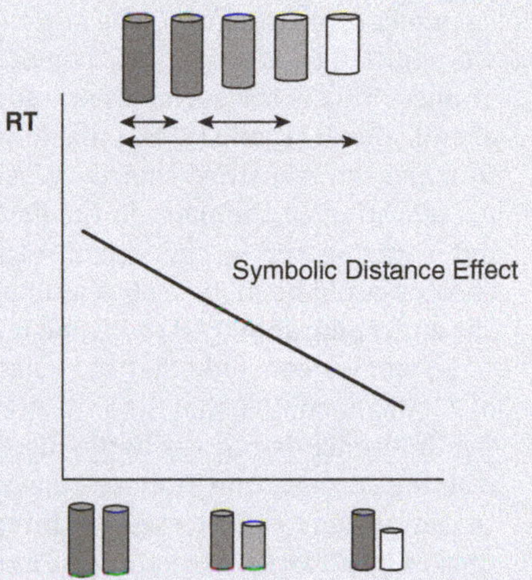

B Reaction time measures (RT) suggest that items are integrated into a mental array during training, such that more distant items are more discriminable, explaining why RTs to training pairs during tests are actually longer than to the test pairs such as BD. (After Trabasso, 1975)

Several decades of research resulted in a famous study that incorporated all these elements, conducted by Peter Bryant and Tom Trabasso at the Department of Experimental Psychology in Oxford and published in *Nature* in 1971. It was even reported in *The Times*, for it claimed that children could make transitive inferences as young as 4 years of age (Bryant & Trabasso, 1971). Their study presented a five-term series in the form of pairs of sticks presented in a training box (see Panel 16.6). The actual sizes were not revealed, but the children were verbally trained on each pair-wise relation until they were at extremely high levels of correct responding for all four pairs. Then they asked about the relationship between all the other items including B and D. This showed very high levels of correct responding by preschool children on this important pairing suggesting they could make a logical deduction at this age.

This was not, however, the last word on the topic. The presentation of each pair within a training box caused some to speculate on whether the children were actually forming a spatial image of the relationships such that the end-point A – and by proximity, B – was associated with the 'longer' end of the box and/or whether the training itself induced a correct representation. The latter of these concerns was due to the fact that children were initially trained on AB, then BC, then CD, then DE, before training on all four pairs at once. This is the serial presentation you now know is called isotropic. It was finally established by Kallio (1982) that it was this factor alone that enabled preschool children to make the transitive choices. When the presentation used the box but with random presentation of the pairs in the first phase of training, 4 year olds failed the BD test, but it was passed by children of 7. Later, Schnall and Gattis (1998) found that transitive choices could be made by 6 year olds if both spatial and temporal information were linear and 'congruent' (AB to DE and left to right).

So can we conclude that size relations are combined deductively from about the age of 7? An alternative that fits with all the evidence from children and adults is that deductive inference is not really the mechanism at work in the first place at least in these training studies. Tom Trabasso, the co-author on the original paper in *Nature* later found that adults and children seem to **integrate** the relational information during the training phases into a larger structure-like a rank order or linear array as suggested by the earlier spatial paralogic accounts. Reaction times measured during the test phase showed this very clearly in the form of what is known as the **Symbolic Distance Effect**, as shown in Figure B, Panel 16.6. Notice that this means that answers to the BD question are actually faster than to the connecting pairs. This is quite different from the predictions arising from a deductive model that would mean that the relations would have to be retrieved from memory and then combined.

What this tells us then (again) is that children, like adults, reason by making mental representations, rather than by applying formal rules of deduction. However, their ability to use logical deduction to solve (untrained) verbal three-term series problems seems to be in place by the age of 11, even though it may still be subject to figural effects. And using logical deduction to sort out more numerous or more complex sets of relations is something some of us never achieve.

THE EMERGENCE OF MATHEMATICAL THOUGHT

The language of mathematics is one of the most powerful tools of the human mind. Unlike almost every other thing you have learned about in this book, however, its acquisition is not a natural or inevitable consequence of growing up. It is our cultural heritage from the very special minds of very special thinkers. We have Euclid to thank for the first coherent ideas about geometry, Newton for inventing calculus so that he could describe planetary motion, and Leonhard Euler for a huge amount of modern mathematical notation . We don't have to discover these things for ourselves. We are taught them. And so we must at least have access to the cognitive tools that make these thoughts possible. Yet what we have just seen is that children converge on ways of reasoning, which although entirely rational from a psychological point of view, don't seem to bring them any closer to the formulaic manipulation of symbols that constitutes a system of formal logic. In that sense, mathematics departs from everyday reasoning - and becomes a system in which we simply have to place our trust. This is why the transition to mathematical thought can be a tricky (some would say painful!) process for school children.

LEARNING LANDMARKS

16.7 Number systems and enumeration. You should understand why having a count alphabet is not the same as being able to enumerate and you should know two principles required if counting is used in order to enumerate.

16.8 Number systems and calculation. You should understand why the formal properties of number creates a new challenge for school-age children when learning elementary addition and subtraction and be able to describe at least two principles they have to learn.

16.7 NUMBER SYSTEMS AND ENUMERATION

In countries with formal schooling, children will have begun elementary maths from around the age of 7 at the latest. In many countries like the UK it is considerably earlier and may even begin in preschool. From this we might predict that there may be a considerable psychological gulf in the first instance between how children like to think about numbers and how they *have* to think about numbers. And there is.

The first element is the count alphabet - the words that represent digits. The invention of simple tallying or count systems goes very far back into our prehistory; the earliest recorded was in the form of notches carved into bone about 35,000 years ago and by 8000 BC, there were many different types of number signs (Bellos, 2010). To tell the story of (most) modern children, we will assume the use of Arabic numerals, which at first children will learn as words rather than as digits (Benoit et al., 2013).

Learning the count alphabet comes very easily to children: 'one', 'two' and 'three' feature amongst the first words acquired - not least because of their use in story books, rhymes and ways of getting children to button up their cardigans. But to use count words for the purpose for which they were invented - that is, to enumerate (count the total) - at least two key principles also have to be understood (Gelman & Gallistel, 1986). One is that the words have to be mapped onto each and every single individual unit in the set to be counted. This is called **one-to-one correspondence**. The second is that the last item in a count sequence also represents the total number of the items counted. This is called the **cardinality principle**. There is ample evidence that both of these take a good bit longer to acquire than the count alphabet itself. Difficulties with one-to-one

Panel 16.7 Number systems and enumeration

- Numbers systems are cultural inventions
  - Their most fundamental use is to count or keep a tally
- Children acquire count words before they understand counting principles:
  - *One to one correspondence*
    - Each word must mapped on to each and every member of a set
  - *Cardinality*
    - The last word counted stands for the total number in the set
- Children show a fragile grasp of both these principles for small numbers by the end of preschool
  - What they still have to learn is that the number system is independent of the procedures of counting

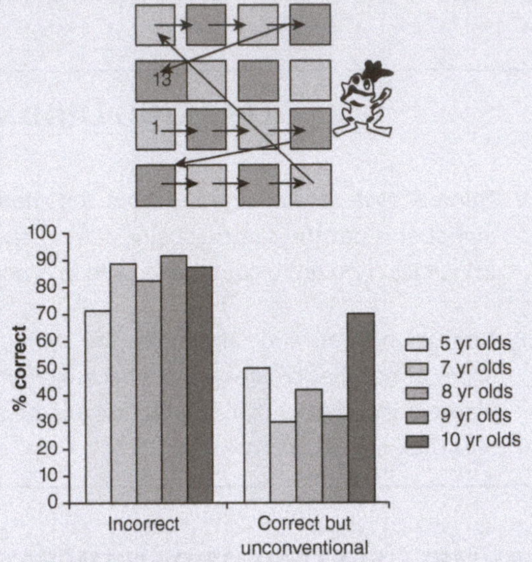

Children watched a toy frog count squares out loud – either in a conventional top to bottom/left to right order or in an unconventional order. They found it much easier at all ages to detect an incorrect count using the conventional method, than to confirm a correct count using the unconventional one. (Adapted from Kamawar et al., 2010, with permission)

correspondence were made famously evident by Piaget's number conservation task, in which children judge one of two rows of counters as 'having more' when they are spread out, creating a longer row (see Panel 1.1). Since then, it has been well established that young children will use things like the density of dots in an array or the length of a line of counters when asked 'more' or 'less' questions. This is a perfectly rational approach to assessing quantities quickly, and is highly developed in some non-human species, especially chimpanzees (Tomonaga & Matsuzawa, 2002). A fragile ability to match arrays on the basis of number alone (one to one correspondence) can be found in preschool children with very small sets of two and three items (Mix, 1999), but the key point is that they often don't spontaneously use their available counting alphabet to enumerate the sets, despite the fact that they are encouraged to count from an early age. As children approach school age, there is greater understanding that larger numbers need to be counted if asked to supply a given amount (Fuson, 1988). This shows the beginnings of an understanding of the cardinality principle. By around 5 years then, children have at least some grasp of one-to-one correspondence and cardinality, but to what extent does this reflect a deeper understanding of the *logic* of number relations?

One logicomathematical implication of the cardinality principle is that the number has a particular place within a linear system. This is called a **rule of succession**, such that that, if X = 4, the word denoting X + 1 (5) must be the next word in the count sequence. This knowledge is hard to separate from the sequential behaviour of counting up. However, it also means that a number denoting number X – 1 (e.g. 3) *precedes* the number denoting X. By giving preschool children a set of tasks, Sarnecka and Carey (2008) were able to establish the level at which their participants were operating in these terms. The first task was a 'give n' test, in which children were simply asked to give (a dinosaur), e.g. one, then two, then three lemons, etc. By a mean age of 3 years 8 months, some children were fairly accurate up to numbers 5 and 6, and were also very much more likely than the other (generally younger) children to count up, especially for the higher numerals. But on another test, two identical amounts were placed on two plates (five bears and five bears) and then the child was shown one being moved over to the other plate. They were not given time to count and were simply asked 'which plate has six?' and also 'which plate has four?' This time only half these children were above chance, suggesting that understanding a change of amount from X to Y occurs in two directions is a further principle yet to be understood.

So counting up and 'knowing' amounts are interlinked in early development. But this is precisely why learning the logic of number is a particular challenge. Children need to be able to count as an activity tied to the real world. How else will they learn what numbers mean? And where can they start their count, if not from 1? To understand the number system, however, they have to eventually divorce the activity of counting from the logicmathematical properties of the numerals themselves. The numbers being counted stand alone and apart from the visuospatial properties of what is being counted. A clever demonstration of this was devised by (LeFevre et al., 2006) and used in a large longitudinal study by Kamawar et al. (2010).

Children aged 5, 7, 8, 9 and 10 years took part in a game in which an animated frog (Hoppy) counted squares arranged in rows on a computer screen. The child had to monitor Hoppy to see if he made a mistake. Using small numbers ranging from 3 to 13, Hoppy was either correct or incorrect, but sometimes he also counted in an unconventional manner as illustrated in Panel 16.7. As the graph shows, children of all ages were adept at detecting a wrong count by Hoppy, but failed to confirm that Hoppy's count was correct when he took an unconventional path through the set. This strong allegiance to a highly linear count procedure has both good – and not so good – implications for how they come to deal with basic calculations as we see next.

16.8 NUMBER SYSTEMS AND CALCULATION

Addition seems to be a natural extension of counting. But before addition is properly understood as a numerical calculation, at least three principles have to be grasped. One is the relationship between the first and second amount (or **addend**). If the cardinality principle is in place, then the cardinal value of the first amount should allow the next amount to be added *on*. If this is understood, then the linear procedure of counting up (from 1) can be waived – adding and counting start to become separated. This understanding was tested in a study by Kornilaki (1994) in which 5- to 6-year-old Greek preschool children were shown a purse and told that it contained 8 drachmas. They were then given 7 more and asked how many now? Without having been taught yet that 8 and 7 'makes' 15, the answer can be arrived at by counting out 7 onto 8. Nevertheless, the children who could answer correctly showed a prevailing tendency to add *up* from zero – even pointing at the purse whilst they counted the 'invisible addend'. A similar effect was found with British preschool children, which seems to disappear by the early school years (see Nunes & Bryant, 1996). This is another indication that the cardinality principle lags behind basic counting.

Second and third principles are **commutativity** and **additive composition**. This first means that adding sets in different orders still results in the same sum; 3 apples added to 4 pears has the name total number as 4 pears added to 3 apples. The second means that a total set is decomposable in different but equivalent ways. For example, 10 = 5 + 5 *and* 10 = 7 + 3 *and* 10 = 2 + 4 + 4, and so on. As Piaget pointed out, this also allows subtraction to be grasped as part of this decomposition of a whole: if 7 + 3 = 10, then 10 – 3 *must* equal 7, etc.

In the context of real objects, additive composition seems to be relatively easy for children by the age of 5 or 6. Canobi et al. (2002) found high levels of performance by 4 to 6 year olds in tasks involving distributing sweets to two bears with statements such as 'Bill gets three blues and then a box of reds' (these were known to contain 16 sweets), 'whilst Kate gets a box of reds and then three blues. Do you think they have the same number of Smarties?' However, problems with additive composition have been found in more abstract verbal arithmetic where children have to really think about the relationship between the parts and the whole. Riley et al. (1983) found that simple verbal addition problems were solved easily by 6-year-old American children when they were of the additive/subtractive form 'Joe has eight marbles and he is given three more/gives three away; how many does he have now?' The same children showed difficulties, however, when the problems were expressed in what is described as a **static distributive** way, such as 'Five of Martin's fish are yellow, and three are blue; how many does he have altogether?' Notice that this does not simulate the sequential action of adding *on* to an amount. Similarly, subtraction is hard when described in this more static way, as in 'Joe has eight marbles and Tom has five; how many more does Joe have than Tom?'

Panel 16.8 Number systems and calculation

- Conformity to a linear procedure – rather than insight into number principles – is evident in early addition
    - When given items to add to an amount they already have (the *addend*) preschool children count the total from 1 rather from the cardinal value of the addend
- Addition depends an understanding that numbers can be combined in different ways, e.g. 7 + 3 = 10 and 4 + 6 = 10 and 10 – 4 = 6, etc.
    - This property of number is called *additive composition*
- Adding using the decimal system, e.g. 10 + 4 = 14, is a more advanced form of additive composition as it involves combining units of different values
- Playing with currency can lead to this understanding of additive composition and more advanced counting (adding on or the use of number rules)

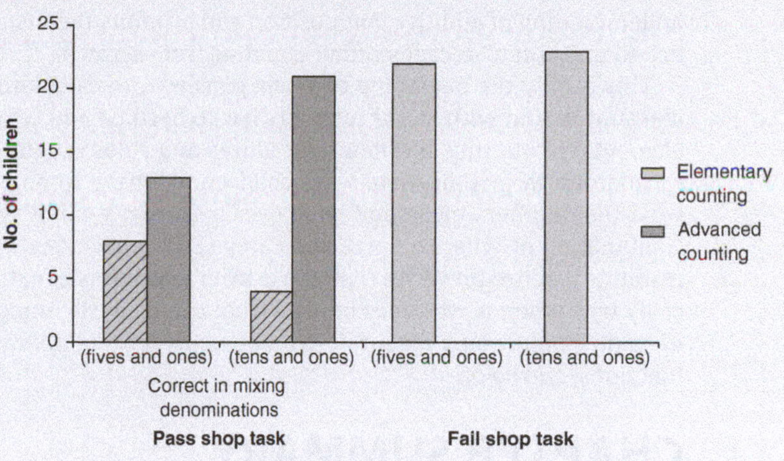

Five- and 6-year-old children had to mix coins of different values in a shop game. Some could succeed on this whilst still at the elementary count-up stage (hatched bars), suggesting that mixing amounts might prompt later insight into true additive composition and advanced counting. (Adapted from Krebs et al., 2003)

Simple addition and subtraction can be performed using learned rules (such as 8 plus 7 equals 15), but larger sums have to be calculated according to cultural devices for making this easy and economic. Within the base ten or **decimal system**, we divide up numbers, into units, tens, hundreds, thousands, etc. The base ten system is thought to be based on a very obvious way of counting using our fingers, and as such it can provide a natural abacus. Indeed Terezinha Nunes has provided a fascinating account of how prevalent finger counting is in 'unschooled' street children, and even in children who are still learning to count at school (Nunes & Bryant, 1996). But this skill is based on learning how a calculation can be read off directly from fingers or beads of an abacus, not through mental calculation.

The crucial insight for additive calculation is that the decimal system allows numbers to be combined not just in different ways but also at different levels: 365 is three hundreds, plus six tens, plus five ones. Without this insight, the rules for adding digits in the form of a sum, where ten ones are carried over to the tens columns, etc. would have no real basis in understanding. This is also, of course, a type of 'count on' procedure. By the age of elementary addition, children will have had experience with counting, but also with the mixed values of the decimal system like single pennies, ten pence pieces and so on. Krebs et al. (2003) found some children of around 5 or 6 years at a stage in development where they could effectively combine units of different values (pences, five pences and ten pences) in a 'shop' game, but still did not use counting on when given a standard addition problem. As the graph in Panel 16.8 shows, no children who showed advanced counting (counting on or using a number rule like 20 plus 7 is 27) failed the shop task, but there were children who could pass the shop task whilst still showing elementary counting (counting up from zero in the addition task). This suggests that it is specific experience with the decimal system (such as currency) that enables a deeper understanding of additive composition and prompts the insight into why it makes sense to add units on to decades rather counting from scratch.

This is only the beginning of a long journey into calculating with numbers. Addition and subtraction with larger numbers has to become a new skill that no longer employs elementary counting, but new procedures and rules taught at school – even the use of calculators! In fact, in some ways children will have to stop thinking altogether about what the numbers mean and hand over trust to a symbol system with its own rules of combination or what Le Corre and Carey (2007) have described as ' a representational resource ... more powerful than those from which it is constructed'. This becomes especially true when maths goes beyond what can be easily imagined and into the domains of complex multiples, algebraic symbols representing unknown entities, trigonometric functions, and so on.

CHAPTER SUMMARY

Deductive inference and logicomathematical thought refers to the ability to symbolically represent relations and combine them logically, but research with children reveal psychological rather than logical factors at work. Syllogistic reasoning shows difficulty when the stated relations defy real-world knowledge; deontic reasoning is relatively easy due to familiarity with obeying if/then permission rules. Counterfactual reasoning tests the ability to reconstruct different possible antecedent consequence relationships but age of acquisition depends on the complexity of the task. Representation of relational similarity is shown in the ability to detect and use analogies but depends on how well the core relations are themselves understood. Reasoning with quantifiers and continuous dimensions reflects the way the task information is encoded, rather than the acquisition of formal logic and in this regard children show strong similarities with adults. School mathematics requires children to overcome their natural modes of number representation in order to enumerate efficiently and understand the basic principles of addition.

LOOKING AHEAD TO THE CHILD'S FUTURE

In this very last section, we have touched on the beginnings of logicomathematical understanding and how it gets off the ground into something beyond personal discovery and experience. In this sense, we at least started to look into the realm of thought that has led humankind to go as far as the beginnings of time, the most distant reaches of the observable universe and the unobservable possibilities of multiverses and dark matter. Through the language of mathematics and the power of deduction, scientists have revealed the very stuff of which we are made and our place in the cosmos. Whatever the cognitive hurdles they pose for children, the potential to use these tools of science is in every healthy human brain. Mathematics is of course only one of many knowledge domains that require adherence to culture rules and symbol systems; others include music, second languages and the sciences. Of course, human potential is not realised fully or equally in every possible domain for reasons to do with our genes, personal motivation, level of interest and, above all, opportunity to learn. But whatever route a child's education will take, its products and achievements will flower from the all-important seeds of learning sown in the first decade of life. And these are acquired through a natural process of coming to know and understand the physical and human environment in which we all live. This is what we call cognitive development.

REFERENCES

Abravanel, E. (1982). Perceiving subjective contours during early childhood. *Journal of Experimental Child Psychology, 33*, 280–7.

Abravanel, E., & Gingold, H. (1985). Learning via observation during the second year of life. *Developmental Psychology, 21*, 614–23.

Abravanel, E., Levan-Goldschmidt, E., & Stevenson, M. B. (1976). Action imitation: The early phase of infancy. *Child Development, 47*, 1032–44.

Adolph, K. E., Kretch, K. S., & LoBue, V. (2014). Fear of heights in infants? *Current Directions in Psychological Science, 23*, 60–6.

Akhtar, N., & Tomasello, M. (1997). Young children's productivity with word order and verb morphology. *Developmental Psychology, 33*, 952–65.

Alderson-Day, B., & Fernyhough, C. (2015, in press). Inner Speech: Development, cognitive functions, phenomenology and neurobiology. *Psychological Bulletin*.

Aldridge, M. A., Braga, E. S., Walton, G. E., & Bower, T. G. R. (1999). The intermodal perception of speech in newborns. *Developmental Science, 2*, 42–6.

Ames, L. B. (1946). The development of the sense of time in the young child. *Journal of Genetic Psychology, 68*, 97–125.

Ames, L. B., & Learned, J. (1948). The development of verbalized space in the young child. *Journal of Genetic Psychology, 72*, 63–84.

Amsel, E., Robbins, M., Tumarkin, T., Janit, A., & Foulkes, S. (2003). The card not chosen: The development of judgments of regret in self and others. Unpublished manuscript. Weber State University.

Amsterdam, B. (1972). Mirror self-image reactions before the age of two. *Developmental Psychobiology, 5*, 297–305.

Annett, M. (1985). *Left, Right, Hand and Brain: The Right Shift Theory*. Hillsdale, NJ: Lawrence Erlbaum.

Aronson, E., & Rosenbloom, S. (1971). Space perecption in early infancy: Perception within a common auditory-visual space. *Science, 172*, 1161–3.

Atkinson, J. (1998). The 'where and what' or 'who and how' of visual development. In F. Simeon, & G. Butterworth (eds.), *The Development of Sensory, Motor and Cognitive*

Capacities in Early Infancy: From Perception to Cognition. Hove: Psychology Press/Taylor & Francis, pp. 3–24.

Baddeley, A. (1995). Working memory. In *The Cognitive Neurosciences*. Cambridge, MA: MIT Press, pp. 755–64.

Baillargeon, R. (1987). Object permanence in 3½ and 4½ month old infants. *Developmental Psychology*, *23*, 655–64.

Baillargeon, R. (2002). The acquisition of physical knowledge in infancy: A summary in eight lessons. In U. Goswami (ed.), *Blackwell Handbook of Childhood Cognitive Development*. Oxford: Blackwell, pp. 47–83.

Baillargeon, R., Fisher, C., & DeJong, G. F. (2000). Teaching infants about support: What data must they see? Paper presented at the Biennial International Conference on Infant Studies, Brighton, England.

Bahrick, L. E., Lickliter, R., & Castellanos, I. (2013). The development of face perception in infancy: Intersensory interference and unimodal visual facilitation. *Developmental Psychology*, *49*, 1919–30.

Baldwin, D. A., & Markman, E. M. (1989). Establishing word-object relations: A first step. *Child Development*, *60*, 381–98.

Bannard, C., & Tomasello, M. (2012). Can we dissociate contingency learning from social learning in word acquisition by 24-month-olds? *PLoS*, *7*(11), e49881.

Bard, K. A., Todd, B. K., Bernier, C., Love, J., & Leavens, D. A. (2006). Self-awareness in human and chimpanzeeinfants: What is measured and what ismeant by the mark and mirror test? *Infancy*, *9*, 191–219.

Baron-Cohen, S. (1989). The autistic child's theory of mind: A case of specific developmental delay. *Child Psychology & Psychiatry & Allied Disciplines*, *30*, 285–97.

Baron-Cohen, S., Leslie, A. M., & Frith, U. (1985). Does the autistic child have a 'theory of mind'? *Cognition*, *21*, 37–46.

Baron-Cohen, S., Wheelwright, S., Skinner, R., Martin, J., & Clubley, E. (2001). The Autism-Spectrum Quotient (AQ): Evidence from Asperger syndrome/high-functioning autism, males and females, scientists and mathematicians. *Journal of Autism and Developmental Disorders*, *31*, 5–17.

Barrett, M. D. (1978). Lexical development and overextension in child language. *Journal of Child Language*, *5*, 205–19.

Barton, M. E., & Tomasello, M. (1994). The rest of the family: The role of fathers and siblings in early language development. In *Input and Interaction in Language Acquisition*. New York, NY: Cambridge University Press, pp. 109–34.

Bates, E. (1979). Intentions, conventions, and symbols. In E. Bates, L. Benigni, I. Bretherton, L. Camaioni, & V. Volterra (eds.), *The Emergence of Symbols.* New York, NY: Academic Press, pp. 33–42.

Bates, E., Reilly, J., Wulfeck, B., Dronkers, N., Opie, M., Fenson, J., Kriz, S., Jeffries, R., Miller, L., & Herbst, K. (2001). Differential effects of unilateral lesions on language production in children and adults. *Brain and Language, 79*, 223–65.

Bayliss, D. M., Jarrold, C., Baddeley, A. D., Gunn, D. M., & Leigh, E. (2005). Mapping the developmental constraints on working memory span performance. *Developmental Psychology, 41*, 579–97.

Beck, S. R., Robinson, E. J., Carroll, D. J., & Apperly, I. A. (2006). Children's thinking about counterfactuals and future hypotheticals as possibilities. *Child Development, 77*, 413–26.

Behrend, D. A. (1995). Processes involved in the initial mapping of verb meanings. In M. Tomasello & W. Merriman (eds.), *Beyond Names for Things.* Hillsdale, NJ: Lawrence Erlbaum.

Bell, M. A., & Fox, N. A. (1992). The relations between frontal brain electrical activity and cognitive development during infancy. *Child Development, 63*, 1142–63.

Bellos, A. (2010). *Alex's Adventures in Numberland.* London: Bloomsbury.

Benguigui, N., Broderick, M. P., Baures, R., & Amorim, M. A. (2008). Motion prediction and the velocity effect in children. *British Journal of Developmental Psychology, 26*, 389–407.

Benoit, L., Lehalle, H., Molina, M., Tijus, C., & Jouen, F. (2013). Young children's mapping between arrays, number words, and digits. *Cognition, 129,* 95–101

Berko, J., & Brown, R. (1960). Psycholinguistic research methods. In P. Mussen (ed.), *Handbook of Research methods in Child Development.* New York, NY: John Wiley, pp. 517–57.

Bernstein, D. M., Loftus, G. R., & Meltzoff, A. N. (2005). Object identification in preschool children and adults. *Developmental Science, 8*, 151–61.

Blaye, A., Bernard-Peyron, V., Paour, J.-L., & Bonthoux, F. (2006). Categorical flexibility in children: Distinguishing response flexibility from conceptual flexibility; the protracted development of taxonomic representations. *European Journal of Developmental Psychology, 3*, 163–88.

Blaye, A., & Jacques, S. (2009). Categorical flexibility in preschoolers: Contributions of conceptual knowledge and executive control. *Developmental Science, 12*, 863–73.

Blewitt, P. (1994). Understanding categorical hierarchies: The earliest levels of skills. *Child Development, 65*, 1279–98.

Bloom, K., & Lo, E. (1990). Adult perceptions of vocalizing infants. *Infant Behavior & Development, 13*, 209–19.

Bloom, L. (1970). *Language Development: Form and Function in Emerging Grammars.* Cambridge, MA: MIT Press.

Bloom, L. (1991). *Language Development from Two to Three*. Cambridge: Cambridge University Press.

Bloom, L., & Capatides, J. B. (1987). Sources of meaning in the acquisition of complex syntax: The sample case of causality. *Journal of Experimental Child Psychology, 43*, 112–28.

Bloom, L., Tinker, E., & Margulis, C. (1993). The words children learn: Evidence against a noun bias in early vocabularies. *Cognitive Development, 8*, 431–50.

Bluestein, N., & Acredolo, L. P. (1979). Developmental changes in map-reading skills. *Child Development, 50*, 691–7.

Borke, H. (1975). Piaget's mountains revisited: Changes in the egocentric landscape. *Developmental Psychology, 11*, 240–3.

Bornstein, M. H., & Arterberry, M. E. (2003). Recognition, discrimination and categorization of smiling by 5-month-old infants. *Developmental Science, 6*, 585–99.

Bower, T. G. R. (1966). The visual world of infants. *Scientific American, 215*, 80-92

Bower, T. G. R. (1974). *Developmental in Infancy*. San Francisco, CA: W.H. Freeman and Company.

Brace, N. A., Hole, G. J., Kemp, R. I., Pike, G. E., Van Duuren, M., & Norgate, L. (2001). Developmental changes in the effect of inversion: Using a picture book to investigate face recognition. *Perception, 30*, 85–94.

Braten, S. (2008). Intersubjective enactment by virtue of altercentric participation supported by a mirror system in infant and adult. In F. Morganti, A. Carassa, & G. Riva (eds.), *Enacting Intersubjectivity: A Cognitive and Social Perspective on the Study of Interactions*. Amsterdam: IOS Press, pp. 133–47.

Bremner, A., & Bryant, P. E. (2001). The effect of spatial cues on infants' responses in the AB task, with and without a hidden object. *Developmental Science, 4*, 408–15.

Bremner, J. G. (1994). *Infancy*, 2nd edn. Oxford: Blackwell.

Bremner, J. G., & Bryant, P. E. (1977). Place versus response as the basis of spatial errors made by young infants. *Journal of Experimental Child Psychology, 23*, 162–71.

Bremner, J. G., Slater, A. M., Johnson, S. P., Mason, U. C., Spring, J., & Bremner, M. E. (2011). Two- to eight-month-old infants' perception of dynamic auditory-visual spatial co-location. *Child Development, 82*, 1210–23.

Bringuier, J.-C. (1980). *Conversations with Jean Piaget*. Chicago, IL: University of Chicago Press.

Brislin, R. W., & Leibowitz, H. W. (1970). The effect of separation between test and comparison objects on size constancy at various age-levels. *American Journal of Psychology, 83*, 372–6.

Brooks, P. J., & Sekerina, I. (2005). Shortcuts to quantifier interpretation in children and adults. *Language Acquisition: A Journal of Developmental Linguistics, 13*, 177–206.

Brown, R. (1973). *A First Language. The Early Stages*. London: Allen and Unwin.

Brown, R., Cazden, C. B., & Bellugi, U. (1969). The child's grammara from I to III. In J. P. Hill (ed.), *Minnesota Symposium on Child Psychology*. Minneapolis: University of Minnesota Press.

Brubacher, S. P., Glisic, U., Roberts, K. P., & Powell, M. (2011). Children's ability to recall unique aspects of one occurrence of a repeated event. *Applied Cognitive Psychology, 25*, 351–8.

Bruner, J. S. (1957). On perceptual readiness. *Psychological Review, 64*, 123–52.

Bruner, J. S. (1983). *Child's Talk: Learning to Use language*. New York, NY: Norton.

Bryant, P., & Trabasso, T. (1971). Transitive inferences and memory in young children. *Nature, 232*, 456–8.

Bullens, J., Igloi, K., Berthoz, A., Postma, A., & Rondi-Reig, L. (2010). Developmental time course of the acquisition of sequential egocentric and allocentric navigation strategies. *Journal of Experimental Child Psychology, 107*, 337–50.

Busby Grant, J., & Suddendorf, T. (2010). Young children's ability to distinguish past and future changes in physical and mental states. *British Journal of Developmental Psychology, 28*, 853–70.

Busby Grant, J., & Suddendorf, T. (2011). Production of temporal terms by 3-, 4-, and 5-year-old children. *Early Childhood Research Quarterly, 26*, 87–95.

Bushnell, I. (2003). Newborn face recognition. In O. Pascalis, & A. Slater (eds.), *The Development of Face Processing in Infancy and Early Childhood*. Hauppage: Nova Science, pp. 41–53.

Butler, S. C., Caron, A. J., & Brooks, R. (2000). Infant understanding of the referential nature of looking. *Journal of Cognition and Development, 1*, 359–77.

Butterworth, G. (2004). Joint visual attention in infancy. In G. Bremner, & A. Slater (eds.), *Theories of Infant Development*. Malden: Blackwell, pp. 317–54.

Butterworth, G., & Hicks, L. (1977). Visual proprioception and postural stability in infancy: A developmental study. *Perception, 6*, 255–62.

Butterworth, G. E. (1975). Object identity in infancy, the interaction of spatial location codes in determining search errors. *Child Development, 46*, 866–70.

Butterworth, G. E. (1977). Object disappearance and error in Piaget's Stage IV task. *Journal of Experimental Child Psychology, 23*, 391–401.

Butterworth, G. E., & Jarrett, N. L. M. (1991). What minds have in common is space: Spatial mechanisms for perspective taking in infancy. *British Journal of Developmental Psychology, 9*, 55–72.

Bybee, J. L., & Slobin, D. I. (1982). Rules and schemas in the development and use of the English Past Tense. *Language, 58*, 265–89.

Callanan, M. A. & Markman, E. M. (1982). Principles of organization in young children's natural language hierarchies. *Child Development, 56*, 508-23

Campos, J. J., Anderson, D. I., Barbu-Roth, M., Hubbard, E. M., Hertenstein, M. J., & Witherington, D. (2000). Travel broadens the mind. *Infancy, 1*, 149–219.

Campos, J. J., Langer, A., & Krowitz, A. (1970). Cardiac responses on the visual cliff in prelocomotor human infants. *Science, 170*, 196–7.

Canobi, K. H., Reeve, R. A., & Pattison, P. E. (2002). Young children's understanding of addition concepts. *Educational Psychology, 22*, 513–32.

Carey, S., & Diamond, R. (1977). From piecemeal to configurational representation of faces. *Science, 195*, 312–14.

Caron, A. J., Kiel, E. J., Dayton, M., & Butler, S. C. (2002). Comprehension of the referential intent of looking and pointing between 12 and 15 months. *Journal of Cognition and Development, 3*, 445–64.

Carver, L. J., & Bauer, P. J. (2001). The dawning of a past: The emergence of long-term explicit memory in infancy. *Journal of Experimental Psychology: General, 130*, 726–45.

Carver, L. J., Dawson, G., Panagiotides, H., Meltzoff, A. N., McPartland, J., Gray, J., & Munson, J. (2002). Age-related differences in neural correlates of face recognition during the toddler and preschool years. *Developmental Psychobiology, 42*, 148–59.

Chance, J. E., & Goldstein, A. G. (1984). Face-recognition memory: Implications for children's eyewitness testimony. *Journal of Social Issues, 40*, 69–85.

Chen, Z., & Daehler, M. W. (1989). Positive and negative transfer in analogical problem solving by 6-year-old children. *Cognitive Development, 4*, 327–44.

Cheung, C.-N., & Wong, W.-C. (2011). Understanding conceptual development along the implicit-explicit dimension: Looking through the lens of the representational redescription model. *Child Development, 82*, 2037–52.

Chi, M. T. H. (1978). Knowledge structures and memory development. In R. S. Siegler (ed.), *Children's Thinking: What Develops?* Hillsdale, NJ: Lawrence Erlbaum, pp. 73–96.

Chomsky, C. (1969). *The Acquisition of Syntax in Children From 5 to 10.* Cambridge: The MIT Press.

Chomsky, N. (1957). *Syntactic Structures.* The Hague: Mouton and Co.

Christiansen, M. H., & Kirby, S. (2003). *Language Evolution.* Oxford: Oxford University Press.

Clark, E. V. (1971). On the acquisition of the meaning of before and after. *Journal of Verbal Learning & Verbal Behavior, 10*, 266–75.

Clark, E. V. (1973). What's in a word? On the child's acquisition of semantics in his first language. In T. E. Moore (ed.), *Cognitive Development and the Acquisition of Language.* New York, NY: Academic Press.

Clark, E. V. (1987). The principle of contrast: A constraint on language acquisition. In B. MacWhinney (ed.), *The 20th Annual Carnegie Symposium on Cognition*. Hillsdale, NJ: Erlbaum.

Clark, E. V. (2009). *First Language Acquisition*, 2nd edn. Cambridge: Cambridge University Press.

Clark, H. H. (1969). Linguistic processes in deductive reasoning. *Psychological Review, 76*, 387–404.

Clark, H. H. (1970). The primitive nature of children's relational concepts. In J. R. Hayes (ed.), *Cognition and the Development of Language*. New York, NY: Wiley.

Clark, H. H., & Clark, E. V. (1977). *Psychology and Language: An Introduction to Psycholinguistics*. New York, NY: Harcourt Brace Jovanovic.

Clarkson, M. G., & Clifton, R. K. (1991). Acoustic determinants of newborn orienting. In M. J. S. Weiss, & P. R. Zelazo (eds.), *Newborn Attention: Biological Constraints and the Influence of Experience*. Norwood, NJ: Ablex Publishing, pp. 99–119.

Clearfield, M. W. (2004). The role of crawling and walking experience in infant spatial memory. *Journal of Experimental Child Psychology, 89*, 214–41.

Clubb, P. A., Nida, R. E., Merritt, K., & Ornstein, P. A. (1993). Visiting the doctor: Children's knowledge and memory. *Cognitive Development, 8*, 361–72.

Cook, R., Bird, G., Catmur, C., Press, C., & Heyes, C. (2014). Mirror neurons: From origin to function. *Behavioral and Brain Sciences, 37*, 177-192

Cooper, L. A., & Shepard, R. N. (1973). The time required to prepare for a rotated stimulus. *Memory & Cognition, 1*, 246–50.

Corbetta, D., & Bojczyk, K. E. (2002). Infants return to two-handed reaching when they are learning to walk. Infants return to two-handed reaching when they are learning to walk. *Journal of Motor Behavior, 34*, 83–95.

Cox, M. V., & Isard, S. (1990). Children's deictic and nondeictic interpretations of the spatial locatives in front of and behind. *Journal of Child Language, 17*, 481–8.

Craik, F. I., & Lockhart, R. S. (1972). Levels of processing: A framework for memory research. *Journal of Verbal Learning & Verbal Behavior, 11*, 671–84.

Critten, S., Pine, K. J., & Messer, D. J. (2013). Revealing children's implicit spelling representations. *British Journal of Developmental Psychology, 31*, 198–211.

Crookes, K., & McKone, E. (2008). Early maturity of face recognition: No childhood development of holistic processing, novel face encoding, or face-space. *Cognition, 111*, 219–47.

Cuevas, K., & Bell, M. A. (2010). Developmental progression of looking and reaching performance on the A-not-B task. *Developmental Psychology, 46*, 1363–71.

Cummins, D. D. (1996). Evidence of deontic reasoning in 3- and 4-year-old children. *Memory & Cognition, 24*, 823–9.

Curtiss, S., & de Bode, S. (1999). Age and etiology as predictors of language outcome following hemispherectomy. *Developmental Neuroscience, 21*, 174–81.

Dack, L. A., & Astington, J. W. (2011). Deontic and epistemic reasoning in children. *Journal of Experimental Child Psychology, 110*, 94–114.

Dawson, G., & Fischer, K. W. (eds.) (1994). *Human Behavior and the Developing Brain.* New York, NY: The Guilford Press.

de Boysson-Bardies, B., Sagart, L., & Durand, C. (1984). Discernable differences in the babbling of infants according to target language. *Journal of Child Language, 11*, 1–5.

de Haan, M., & Nelson, C. A. (1997). Recognition of the mother's face by six-month-old infants: A neurobehavioral study. *Child Development, 68*, 187–210.

de Heering, A., Turati, C., Rossion, B., Bulf, H., Goffaux, V., & Simion, F. (2008). Newborns' face recognition is based on spatial frequencies below 0.5 cycles per degree. *Cognition, 106*, 444–54.

De Soto, C. B., London, M., & Handel, S. (1965). Social reasoning and spatual paralogic. *Journal of Personality and Social Psychology, 2*, 513–21.

Deak, G., & Bauer, P. J. (1995). The effects of task comprehension on preschoolers' and adults' categorization choices. *Journal of Experimental Child Psychology, 60*, 393–427.

Deak, G., Krasno, A. M., Triesch, J., Lewis, J., & Sepeta, L. (2014). Watch the hands: Infants can learn to follow gaze by seeing adults manipulate objects. *Developmental Science, 17*, 270–81.

DeCasper, A. J., & Fifer, W. P. (1980). Of human bonding: Newborns prefer their mothers' voices. *Science, 208*, 1174–6.

DeCasper, A. J., Lecanuet, J. P., Busnel, M. C., Granier-Deferre, C., & Maugeais, R. (1994). Fetal reactions to recurrent maternal speech. *Infant Behavior and Development, 17*, 159–164

Delack, J. B. (1976). Aspects of infany speech development. *Canadian Journal of Linguistics, 21*, 17–37.

DeLoache, J. S. (1987). Rapid change in the symbolic functioning of very young children. *Science, 238*, 1556–7.

DeLoache, J. S., Miller, K. F., & Rosengren, K. S. (1997). The credible shrinking room: Very young children's performance with symbolic and nonsymbolic relations. *Psychological Science, 8*, 308–13.

Deneault, J., & Ricard, M. (2005). The effect of hierarchical levels of categories on children's deductive inferences about inclusion. *International Journal of Psychology, 40*, 65–79.

Deuchar, M., & Quay, S. (2000). *Bilingual Acquisition: Theoretical Implications of a Case Study*. New York, NY: Oxford University Press.

Deutscher, G. (2005). *The Unfolding of Language: An Evolutionary Tour of Mankind's Greatest Invention*. London: Heinemann.

Diamond, A. (1985). Development of the ability to use recall to guide performance, as indicated by performance on AB. *Child Development, 56*, 868–83.

Diamond, A. (2006). The early development of executive functions. In *Lifespan Cognition: Mechanisms of Change*. New York, NY: Oxford University Press, pp. 70–95.

Diamond, A., & Gilbert, J. (1989). Development as progressive inhibitory control of action: Retrieval of a contiguous object. *Cognitive Development, 4*, 223–49.

Diamond, R., & Carey, S. (1977). Developmental changes in the representation of faces. *Journal of Experimental Child Psychology, 23*, 1–22.

Dias, M., & Harris, P. (1990). The influence of the imagination on reasoning by young children. *British Journal of Developmental Psychology, 8*, 305–18.

Diessel, H. (2004). *The Acquisition of Complex Sentences*. Cambridge: Cambridge University Press.

Diessel, H. (2008). Iconicity of sequence: A corpus-based analysis of the positioning of temporal adverbial clauses in English. *Cognitive Linguistics, 19*, 465–490.

Dodd, B. (1979). Lip-reading in infants: Attention to speech presented in – and out – of synchrony. *Cognitive Psychology, 11*, 478–484.

Donaldson, M., & McGarrigle, J. (1974). Some clues to the nature of semantic development. *Journal of Child Language, 1*, 185–94.

Donaldson, M., & Wales, R. J. (1970). On the acquisition of some relational terms. In J. R. Hayes (ed.), *Cognition and the Development of Language*. New York, NY: Wiley.

Donaldson, M. L. (1986). *Children's Explanations: A Psycholinguistic Study*. Cambridge: Cambridge University Press.

Dore, J. (1975). Holophrases, speech acts and language universals. *Journal of Child Language, 2*, 21–40.

Dore, J. (1978). Conditions for the acquisition of speech acts. In I. Markova (ed.), *The Social Context of Language*. Chichester: Wiley, pp. 87–111.

Dore, J. (1985). Early communication. *PsycCRITIQUES, 30* (8), 613–14.

Dronkers, N. F., & Larsen, J. (2001). Neuroanatomy of the classical syndromes of aphasia. In *Handbook of Neuropsychology*, 2nd edn. *Volume 3: Language and Aphasia*. Amsterdam: Elsevier Science, pp. 19–30.

Duncker, K. (1945). On problem solving. *Psychological Monographs, 58*.

Eimas, P. D., Siqueland, E. R., Jusczyk, P., & Vigorito, J. (1971). Speech perception in infants. *Science, 171*, 303–6.

Eisele, J., & Lust, B. (1996). Knowledge about pronouns: A developmental study using a truth-value judgment task. *Child Development, 67*, 3086–100.

Ervin-Tripp, S. (1970). Discourse agreement: How children answer questions. In J. R. Hayes (ed.), *Cognition and the Development of Language*. New York, NY: Wiley.

Fabricius, W. V., Hodge, M. H., & Quinan, J. R. (1993). Processes of scene recognition memory in young children and adults. *Cognitive Development, 8*, 343–60.

Fajnsztejn-Pollack, G. (1973). A developmental study of decay rate in long-term memory. *Journal of Experimental Child Psychology, 16*, 225–35.

Farrar, M. J., & Boyer-Pennington, M. (1999). Remembering specific episodes of a scripted event. *Journal of Experimental Child Psychology, 73*, 266–88.

Farrar, M. J., & Goodman, G. S. (1992). Developmental changes in event memory. *Child Development, 63*, 173–87.

Fenson, L., Dale, P., Reznick, J., Thal, D., Bates, E., Hartung, J., Pethick, S. , & Reilly, J. (1993). *The Macarthur Communicative Development Inventories: User's Guide and Technical Manual*. San Diego, CA: Singular Publishing.

Fenson, L., Dale, P. S., Reznick, J., Bates, E., Thal, D. J., & Pethick, S. J. (1994). Variability in early communicative development. *Monographs of the Society for Research in Child Development, 59*, v-173.

Ferguson, A. N., & Bowey, J. A. (2005). Global processing speed as a mediator of developmental changes in children's auditory memory span. *Journal of Experimental Child Psychology, 91*, 89–112.

Fernald, A. (1985). Four-month old infants prefer to listen to motherese. *Infant Behavior and Development, 8*, 181–95.

Field, T. M., Cohen, D., Garcia, R., & Greenberg, R. (1984). Mother-stranger face discrimination by the newborn. *Infant Behavior and Development, 7*, 19–25.

Fischer, K. W., & Rose, S. P. (1994). Dynamic development of coordination of components in brain and behavior: A framework for theory and research. In G. Dawson & K. W. Fischer (eds.), *Human Behavior and the Developing Brain*. New York, NY: The Guildford Press, pp. 3–66.

Fishbein, H. D., Lewis, S., & Keiffer, K. (1972). Children's understanding of spatial relations: Coordination of perspectives. *Developmental Psychology, 7*, 21–33.

Fisher, C. (1996). Structural limits on verb mapping: The role of analogy in children's interpretations of sentences. *Cognitive Psychology, 31*, 41–81.

Flynn, E. (2007). The role of inhibitory control in false belief understanding. *Infant and Child Development, 16*, 53–69.

Fodor, J. A. (1983). *Modularity of Mind: An Essay on Faculty Psychology*. Cambridge, MA: MIT Press.

Foreman, N., & Hemmings, R. (1987). The Gollin incomplete figures test: A flexible, computerised version. *Perception, 16*, 543–48. Available at www.Pion.co.uk and www.perceptionweb.com.

Franco, F., & Butterworth, G. (1996). Pointing and social awareness: declaring and requesting in the second year. *Journal of Child Language, 23*, 307–36.

Freedman, D. L. (1992). Locomotor experience and the deployment of attention to near and distant space. Honors thesis, University of California, Berkeley.

Freeman, N. H., Sinha, C. G., & Stedmon, J. A. (1982). All the cars-which cars? From word meaning to discourse processes. In M. Beveridge (ed.), *Children Thinking Through Langnage*. London: Edward Arnold.

Friedman, O., & Leslie, A. M. (2007). The conceptual underpinnings of pretense: Pretending is not 'behaving-as-if'. *Cognition, 105*, 103–24.

Frith, U. (2003). *Autism: Explaining the Enigma*. London: Blackwell

Fuson, K. C. (1988). *Children's Counting and Concepts of Number*. New York Springer-Verlag.

Gallup, G. G. (1970). Chimpanzees: Self-recognition. *Science, 167*, 86–7.

Ganger, J., & Brent, M. R. (2004). Reexamining the vocabulary spurt. *Developmental Psychology, 40*, 621–32.

Garnica, O. K. (1975). How children learn to talk. *Theory Into Practice, 14*, 299–305.

Gathercole, S. E., Adams, A.-M., & Hitch, G. J. (1994). Do young children rehearse? An individual-differences analysis. *Memory & Cognition, 22*, 201–7.

Gelman, R., & Gallistel, C. R. (1986). *The Child's Understanding of Number*. Cambridge, MA: Harvard University Press.

Gelman, S. A., & Markman, E. M. (1986). Categories and induction in young children. *Cognition, 23*, 183–209.

Gelman, S. A., & Tardif, T. (1998). A cross-linguistic comparison of generic noun phrases in English and Mandarin. *Cognition, 66*, 215–48.

Germine, L., Duchaine, B., & Nakayama, K. (2011). Where cognitive development and aging meet: Face learning ability peaks after age 30. *Cognition, 118*, 201–10.

Geschwind, N., & Levitsky, W. (1968). Human brain: Left-right asymmetries in temporal speech region. *Science, 161*, 186–7.

Gibson, E. J. (1991). *An Odyssey in Learning and Perception*. Cambridge, MA: MIT Press.

Gibson, E. J., Gibson, J. J., Pick, A. D., & Osser, H. (1962). A developmental study of the discrimination of letter-like forms. *Journal of Comparative and Physiological Psychology, 55*, 897–906.

Gibson, E. J., & Walk, R. D. (1960). The 'Visual Cliff'. *Scientific American, 202*, 67–71.

Gibson, J. J., & Gibson, E. J. (1955). Perceptual learning: Differentiation or enrichment? *Psychological Review, 62*, 32–41.

Gick, M. L., & Holyoak, K. J. (1980). Analogical problem solving. *Cognitive Psychology, 12*, 306–55.

Gleason, J. B. (2005). *The Development of Language*, 6th edn. London: Pearson Education.

Goldin-Meadow, S., Seligman, M. E. P., & Gelman, R. (1976). Language in the two-year-old. *Cognition, 4*, 189–202.

Golinkoff, R. M. (1983). *The Translation from Relingusitic to Linguistic Communication.* Hillsdale, NJ: Lawrence Erlbaum.

Gollin, E. (1960). Developmental studies of visual recognition of incomplete objects. *Perceptual and Motor Skills, 11*, 289–98.

Gomez, J. C. (2007). Pointing behaviors in apes and humans: A balanced interpretation. *Child Development, 78*, 729–34.

Goodale, M. A., & Milner, A. D. (1992). Separate visual pathways for perception and action. *Trends in Neuroscience, 15*, 20–5.

Goodale, M. A., Milner, A. D., Jakobson, L. S., & Carey, D. P. (1991). Object awareness. *Nature, 352*, 202.

Goodman, G. S., & Reed, R. S. (1986). Age differences in eyewitness testimony. *Law and Human Behavior, 10*, 317–32.

Gopnik, A., & Astington, J. W. (1988). Children's understanding of representational change and its relation to the understanding of false belief and the appearance-reality distinction. *Child Development, 59*, 26–37.

Gopnik, A., & Meltzoff, A. (1987). The development of categorization in the second year and its relations to other cognitive and linguistic developments. *Child Development, 58*, 1523–31.

Goren, C. C., Sarty, M., & Wu, P. (1975). Visual following and pattern discrimination of face-like stimuli by newborn infants. *Pediatrics, 56*, 544–9.

Goswami, U., & Brown, A. L. (1990). Higher-order structure and relational reasoning: Contrasting analogical and thematic relations. *Cognition, 36*, 207–26.

Graf, E.-M. (2010). I'm fed up with Marmite – I'm moving on to Vegemite – What happens to the development of spatial language after the very first years? *Cognitive Linguistics, 21*, 287–314.

Granrud, C. E., & Schmechel, T. T. N. (2006). Development of size constancy in children: A test of the proximal mode sensitivity hypothesis. *Perception and Psychophysics, 68*, 1372–81.

Gregory, S., & Barlow, S. (1989). Interactions between deaf babies and their hearing mothers. In B. Woll (ed.), *Language Development and Sign Language: Monograph 1*. Bristol: International Sign Language Association.

Grezes, J., & Decety, J. (2002). Does visual perception of object afford action? Evidence from a neuroimaging study. *Neuropsychologia*, *40*, 212–22.

Grover, L. (1988). Comprehension of the pointing gesture in human infants. PhD thesis, University of Southampton, Southampton.

Hale, C. M., & Tager-Flusberg, H. (2003). The influence of language on theory of mind: A training study. *Developmental Science*, *6*, 346–59.

Halford, G. S. (1993). *Children's Understanding: the Development of Mental Models*. Hillsdale, NJ: Lawrence Erlbaum.

Hampson, J., & Nelson, K. (1993). The relation of maternal language to variation in rate and style of language acquisition. *Journal of Child Language*, *20*, 313–42.

Happe, F. G. (1995). The role of age and verbal ability in the theory of mind task performance of subjects with autism. *Child Development*, *66*, 843–55.

Harkins, D. A., & Michel, G. F. (1988). Evidence for a maternal effect on infant hand-use preferences. *Developmental Psychobiology*, *21*, 535–41.

Harris, P. L., Brown, E., Marriott, C., Whittall, S., & Harmer, S. (1991). Monsters, ghosts and witches: Testing the limits of the fantasy-reality distinction in young children. *British Journal of Developmental Psychology*, *9*, 105–23.

Harris, P. L., & Nunez, M. (1996). Understanding of permission rules by preschool children. *Child Development*, *67*, 1572–91.

Hauser, M. D., Chomsky, N., & Fitch, W. T. (2002). The faculty of language: What is it, who has it, and how did it evolve? *Science*, *298*, 1569–79.

Hawkins, J., Pea, R., Glick, J., & Scribner, S. (1984). Merds that laugh don't like mushrooms. *Developmental Psychology*, *20*, 584–94.

Hazen, N. L., Lockman, J. L., & Pick, H. L. (1978). The development of children's representations of large-scale environments. *Child Development*, *49*, 623–36.

Heath, S. B. (1983). *Ways with Words: Language, Life and Work in Communities and Classrooms*. Cambridge: Cambridge University Press.

Hespos, S. J., & Baillargeon, R. (2001). Infants' knowledge about occlusion and containment events: A surprising discrepancy. *Psychological Science*, *12*, 141–7.

Hillier, L., Hewitt, K. L., & Morongiello, B. A. (1992). Infants' perception of illusions in sound localization: Reaching to sounds in the dark. *Journal of Experimental Child Psychology*, *53*, 159–79.

Hirschfeld, L. A., & Gelman, S (eds.) (1994). *Mapping the Mind: Domain Specificity in Cognition and Culture.* New York, NY: Cambridge University Press.

Hirsh-Pasek, K., & Golinkoff, R. M. (1996). *The Origins of Grammar: Evidence from Early Language Comprehension.* Cambridge, MA: MIT Press.

Hitch, G. J., Halliday, M., Dodd, A., & Littler, J. E. (1989). Development of rehearsal in short-term memory: Differences between pictorial and spoken stimuli. *British Journal of Developmental Psychology, 7*, 347–62.

Hock, H. S., Romanski, L., Galie, A., & Williams, C. S. (1978). Real-world schemata and scene recognition in adults and children. *Memory and Cognition, 6*, 423–31.

Hoff, E. (2014). Introduction to the special section: Language development in multilingual environments. *International Journal of Behavioral Development, 38*, 307–8.

Holyoak, K. J., Junn, E. N., & Billman, D. O. (1984). Development of analogical problem-solving skill. *Child Development, 55*, 2042–55.

Horobin, K., & Acredelo, L. (1986). The role of attentiveness, mobility history, and separation of hiding sites on Stage IV searching behavior. *Journal of Experimental Child Psychology, 41*, 114–27.

Horowitz, L. M., Lampel, A. K., & Takanashi, R. N. (1969). The child's memory for unitized scenes. *Journal of Experimental Child Psychology, 8*, 375–88.

Howlin, P., & Charman, T. (eds.) (2011). *The SAGE Handbook of Developmental Disorders.* London: SAGE Publications.

Hsu, A. S., Chater, N., & Vitanyi, P. (2013). Language learning from positive evidence, reconsidered: A simplicity-based approach. *Topics in Cognitive Science, 5*, 35–55.

Hulme, C., & Tordoff, V. (1989). Working memory development: The effects of speech rate, word length, and acoustic similarity on serial recall. *Journal of Experimental Child Psychology, 47*, 72–87.

Hunter, I. M. L. (1957). The solving of the three-term series problem. *British Journal of Psychology, 48*, 286–98.

Huttenlocher, J. (1968). Constructing spatial images: A strategy in reasoning. *Psychological Review, 75*, 550–60.

Huttenlocher, J., Smiley, P., & Charney, R. (1983). Emergence of action categories in the child: Evidence from verb meanings. *Psychological Review, 90*, 72–93.

Huttenlocher, P. R. (1994). Synaptogenesis in human cerebral cortex. In G. Dawson & K. W. Fischer (eds.), *Dynamic Development of Coordination of Components in Brain and Behavior: A Framework for Theory and Research*. New York, NY: The Guildford Press.

Inhelder, B. and Piaget, J. (1964). *The Early Growth of Logic in the Child.* London: Routledge and Kegan Paul.

Internicola, R. W., & Weist, R. M. (2003). The acquisition of simple and complex spatial locatives in English: A longitudinal investigation. *First Language, 23*, 239–48.

Itier, R. J., & Taylor, M. J. (2004). Face recognition memory and configural processing: A developmental ERP study using upright, inverted, and contrast-reversed faces. *Journal of Cognitive Neuroscience, 16*, 487–502.

Jackendoff, R., & Pinker, S. (2005). The nature of the language faculty and its implications for evolution of language (Reply to Fitch, Hauser, and Chomsky). *Cognition, 97*, 211–25.

Johnson, M., Dziurawiec, S., Ellis, H., & Morton, J. (1991). Newborns' preferential tracking of face-like stimuli and its subsequent decline. *Cognition, 40*, 1–19.

Johnson, M. H. (1997). *Developmental Cognitive Neuroscience* Malden, MA: Blackwell.

Johnson, M. H. (2002). The development of visual attention: A cognitive neuroscience perspective. In M. H. Johnson, Y. Munakata, & R. O. Gilmore (eds.), *Brain Development and Cognition: A Reader*. Oxford: Blackwell.

Johnson, S. P., & Aslin, R. N. (1995). Perception of object unity in 2-month-old infants. *Developmental Psychology, 31*, 739–45.

Johnson-Laird, P., Legrenzi, P., & Legrenzi, M. S. (1972). Reasoning and a sense of reality. *British Journal of Psychology, 63*, 395–400.

Johnson-Laird, P. N. (1983). *Mental Models: Towards a Cognitive Science of Language, Inference, and Consciousness*. Cambridge, MA: Harvard University Press.

Johnson-Laird, P. N., Oakhill, J., & Bull, D. (1986). Children's syllogistic reasoning. *The Quarterly Journal of Experimental Psychology A: Human Experimental Psychology, 38*, 35–58.

Johnston, J. R. (1988). Children's verbal represenation of spatial location. In J. Stiles-Davis, M. Kritchevsky, & U. Bellugi (eds.), *Spatial Cognition: Brain Bases and Development*. Hillsdale, NJ: Lawrence Erlbaum, pp. 195–206.

Jouen, F. (1990). Early visual vestibular interactions and postural development. In H. Bloch, & B. I. Bertenthal (eds.), *Sensory Motor Organization and Development in Infancy and Early Childhood*. Dordrecht: Kluwer, pp. 199–215.

Jusczyk, P. (1999). How infants begin to extract words from speech. *Trends in Cognitive Sciences, 3*, 323–8.

Kail, R. (1991). Development of processing speed in children and adolescents. In H. W. Reese (ed.), *Advances in Child Develoment and Behavior*, Vol. 23. San Diego, CA: Academic Press, pp. 151–87.

Káldy, Z., & Kovács, I. (2003). Visual context integration is not fully developed in 4-year-old children. *Perception, 32*, 657–66.

Kallio, K. D. (1982). Developmental change on a five-term transitive inference. *Journal of Experimental Child Psychology, 33*, 142–64.

Kamawar, D., LeFevre, J.-A., Bisanz, J., Fast, L., Skwarchuk, S.-L., Smith-Chant, B., & Penner-Wilger, M. (2010). Knowledge of counting principles: How relevant is order irrelevance? *Journal of Experimental Child Psychology, 105*, 386.

Kaplan, P. S., Bachorowski, J., Smoski, M. J., & Hudenko, W. J. (2002). Infants of depressed mothers, although competent learners, fail to learn in response to their own mothers' infant-directed speech. *Psychological Science, 1393*, 268–71.

Karmiloff-Smith, A. (1979). *A Functional Approach to Child Language*. Cambridge: Cambridge University Press.

Karmiloff-Smith, A. (1992). *Beyond Modularity: A Developmental Perspective on Cognitive Science*. Cambridge, MA: MIT Press.

Katz, N., Baker, E., & Macnamara, J. (1974). What's in a name? A study of how children learn common and proper names. *Child Development, 45*, 469–73.

Kellman, P. J., & Spelke, E. S. (1983). Perception of partly occluded objects in infancy. *Cognitive Psychology, 15*, 483–524.

Kendler, T. S. (1995). *Levels of Cognitive Development*. Mahwah, NJ: Lawrence Erlbaum.

Kent, R. (1993). Infants and speech: Seeking patterns. *Journal of Phonetics, 21*, 117–23.

Kermoian, R., & Campos, J. J. (1988). Locomotor experience: A facilitator of spatial-cognitive development. *Child Development, 59*, 908–17.

Kibbe, M. M., & Leslie, A. (2011). What do infants remember when they forget? Location and identity in 6-month olds' memory for objects. *Psychological Science, 22*, 1500–5

Kidd, E., Brandt, S., Lieven, E., & Tomasello, M. (2007). Object relatives made easy: A cross-linguistic comparison of the constraints influencing young children's processing of relative clauses. *Language and Cognitive Processes, 22*, 860–97.

Kidd, E., Lieven, E. V., & Tomasello, M. (2010). Lexical frequency and exemplar-based learning effects in language acquisition: Evidence from sentential complements. *Language Sciences, 32*, 132–42.

Kirasic, K. C., Siegel, A. W., & Allen, G. L. (1980). Developmental changes in recognition-in-context memory. *Child Development, 51*, 302–5.

Klima, E. S., & Bellugi, U. (1966). Syntactic regularities in the speech of children. In J. Lyons & R. J. Wales (eds.), *Psycholinguistic Papers*. Edinburgh: Edinburgh University Press.

Kohler, W. (1925). *The Mentality of Apes* (E. Winter, Trans. 2nd. edn). London: Kegan.

Kornilaki, E. (1994). The understanding of the numeration system among preschool children. MSc dissertation, University of London, London.

Kovács, I., Kozma, P., Fehér, A., & Benedek, G. (1999). Late maturation of visual spatial integration in humans. *PNAS, 96*, 12204–9.

Krebs, G., Squire, S., & Bryant, P. (2003). Children's understanding of the additive composition of number and of the decimal structure: What is the relationship? *International Journal of Educational Research, 39*, 677–94.

Kuczaj, S. A. (1977). The acquisition of regular and irregular past tense forms. *Journal of Verbal Learning & Verbal Behavior, 16*, 589–600.

Kuenne, M. R. (1946). Experimental investigation of the relation of language to transposition behavior in young children. *Experimental Psychology, 46*, 471–90.

Kuglumutzakis, G. (1993). Intersubjective vocal imitation in early mother-infant interaction. In J. Nadel, & L. Camaioni (eds.), *New Perspectives in Early Communicative Development.* London: Routledge, pp. 23–47.

Kuglumutzakis, G. (1999). Genesis and development of early infant mimesis to facial and vocal models. In J. Nadel, & G. Butterworth (eds.), *Imitation in Infancy.* Cambridge: Cambridge University Press, pp. 36–60.

Kuhl, P. K. (1985). Methods in the study of infant speech perception. In G. Gottlieb, & N. A. Krasnegor (eds.), *Measurement of audition and vision in the first year of postnatal life : a methodological overview.* Norwood, NJ: Ablex.

Kuhl, P. K., & Meltzoff, A. N. (1982). The bimodal perception of speech in infancy. *Science, 218*, 1138–41.

Kuhl, P. K., & Meltzoff, A. N. (1996). Infant vocalizations in response to speech: Vocal imitation and developmental change. *Journal of the Acoustical Society of America, 100*, 2425–38.

Lanza, E. (1997). *Language Mixing in Infant Bilingualism: A Sociolinguistic Perspective.* Oxford: Clarendon Press.

Lawrenson, W., & Bryant, P. E. (1972). Absolute and relative codes in young children. *Journal of Child Psychology and Psychiatry, 13*, 25–35.

Le Corre, M., & Carey, S. (2007). One, two, three, four, nothing more: An investigation of the conceptual sources of the verbal counting principles. *Cognition, 105*, 395–438.

Lebedev, M. A., Carmena, J. M., O'Doherty, J. E., Zacksenhouse, M., Henriquez, C. S., Principe, J. C., & Nicolelis, M. A. L. (2005). Cortical ensemble adaptation to represent velocity of an artificial actuator controlled by a brain-machine interface. *The Journal of Neuroscience, 25* (19), 4681–93

Lecanuet, J. P., Gautheron, B., Locatelli, A., Schaal, B., Jacquet, A. Y., & Busnel, M. C. (1989). What sounds reach fetuses: Biological and nonbiological modeling of the transmission of pure tones. *Developmental Psychobiology, 33*, 203–19.

Lee, D. N., & Aronson, E. (1974). Visual proprioceptive control of standing in human infants. *Perception and Psychophysics, 15*, 529–32.

Lee, D. N., & Lishman, J. R. (1975). Visual proprioceptive control of stance. *Journal of Human Movement Studies, 1*, 87–95.

Lee, J. (2011). Size matters: Early vocabulary as a predictor of language and literacy competence. *Applied Psycholinguistics, 32*, 69–92.

LeFevre, J. A., Smith-Chant, B. L., Fast, L., Skwarchuk, S. L., Sargla, E., Arnup, J. S., Penner-Wilger, M., Bisanz, J., & Kamawar, D. (2006). What counts as knowing? The development of conceptual and procedural knowledge of counting from kindergarten through Grade 2. *Journal of Experimental Child Psychology, 93*, 285–303.

Leplow, B., Lehnung, M., Pohl, J., Herzog, A., Ferstl, R., & Mehdorn, M. (2003). Navigational place learning in children and young adults as assessed with a standardized locomotor search task. *British Journal of Psychology, 94*, 299–317.

Leslie, A. (1987). Pretense and representation: The origins of 'Theory of Mind'. *Psychological Review, 94*, 412–26.

Leung, E. H., & Rheingold, H. L. (1981). Development of pointing as a social gesture. *Developmental Psychology, 17*, 215–20.

Lewkowicz, D. J., & Hansen-Tift, A. M. (2012). Infants deploy selective attention to the mouth of a talking face when learning speech. *Proceedings of the National Academy of Sciences USA., 109*, 1431–6.

Lieberman, P. (2002). On the nature and evolution of the neural bases of human language. *American Journal of Physical Anthropology, 119*, 35–62.

Lieven, E. V., Pine, J. M., & Baldwin, G. (1997). Lexically-based learning and early grammatical development. *Journal of Child Language, 24*, 187–219.

Lin, Y., & Zhou, Y. (2005). A multi-level development view of implicit learning. *Psychological Science (China), 28*, 995–97.

Lindsay, R. C. L., Pozzulo, J. D., Craig, W., Lee, K., & Corber, S. (1997). Simultaneous lineups, sequential lineups, and showups: Eyewitness identification decisions of adults and children. *Law and Human Behavior, 21*, 391–404.

Liszkowski, U., Albrecht, K., Carpenter, M., & Tomasello, M. (2008). Twelve-month-olds communicate helpfully and appropriately for knowledgeable and ignorant partners. *Cognition, 108*, 732–9. doi: http://dx.doi.org/10.1016/j.infbeh.2007.10.011

Liszkowski, U., Schäfer, M., Carpenter, M., & Tomasello, M. (2009). Prelinguistic infants, but not chimpanzees, communicate about absent entities. *Psychological Science, 20*, 654–60.

Locke, J. (1983). *Phonological Acquisition and Change*. New York, NY: Academic Press.

Locke, J. (1993). *The Child's Path to Spoken Language*. Cambridge, MA: Harvard University Press.

Locke, J. L., Bekken, K., Wein, D., McMinn-Larson, L., and Ruzecki, V. (1991) Neuropsychology of babbling: Laterality effects in the production of rhythmic manual activity. Paper delivered to the Society for Research in Child Development, Seattle.

Luo, Y., & Baillargeon, R. (2005). When the ordinary seems unexpected: Evidence for incremental physical knowledge in young infants. *Cognition*, *95*, 297–328.

Maas, F. K. (2008). Children's understanding of promising, lying, and false belief. *Journal of General Psychology*, *135*, 301–21.

MacFarlane, A. (1975). Olfaction in the development of social preferences in the human neonate. *Ciba Foundation Symposium*, *33*, 103–17.

MacWhinney, B., & Snow, C. (1985). The child language data exchange system. *Journal of Child Language*, *12*, 271–95.

Mandler, J. M., & Robinson, C. A. (1978). Developmental changes in picture recognition. *Journal of Experimental Child Psychology*, *26*, 122–36.

Maratsos, M. (2000). More overregularizations after all: New data and discussion on Marcus, Pinker, Ullman, Hollander, Rosen & Xu. *Journal of Child Language*, *27*, 183–212.

Marcovitch, S., & Zelazo, P. D. (2003). The A-not-B error: Results from a logistic meta-analysis. *Child Development*, *70*, 1297–313.

Marcus, G. F. (1995). Children's overregularization of English plurals: A quantitative analysis. *Journal of Child Language*, *22*, 447–59.

Marin, B. V., Holmes, D. L., Guth, M., & Kovac, P. (1979). The potential of children as eyewitnesses. *Law and Human Behavior*, *3*, 295–305.

Markman, E. M. (1985). Why superordinate category terms can be mass nouns. *Cognition*, *19*, 31–53.

Markman, E. M. (1989). *Categorization and Naming in Children*. Cambridge, MA: MIT Press

Markman, E. M., & Hutchinson, J. E. (1984). Children's sensitivity to constraints on word meaning: Taxonomic versus thematic relations. *Cognitive Psychology*, *16*, 1–27.

Markman, E. M., & Wachtel, G. F. (1988). Children's use of mutual exclusivity to constrain the meaning of words. *Cognitive Psychology*, *20*, 121–57.

Markman, E. M., Wasow, J. L., & Hansen, M. B. (2003). Use of the mutual exclusivity assumption by young word learners. *Cognitive Psychology*, *47*, 241–75.

Martin, G. B., & Clark, R. D. (1982). Distress crying in neonates: Species and peer specificity. *Developmental Psychology*, *18*, 3–9.

Masur, E. F. (1982a). Mothers' responses to infants' object-related gestures: Influences on lexical development. *Journal of Child Language*, *9*, 23–30.

Masur, E. F. (1982b). Cognitive content of parents' speech to preschoolers. *Merrill-Palmer Quarterly*, *28*, 471–84.

Masur, E. F., & Olson, J. (2008). Mothers' and infants' responses to their partners' spontaneous action and vocal/verbal imitation. *Infant Behavior & Development*, *31*, 704–15.

Maurer, D., & Salapatek, P. (1976). Developmental changes in the scanning of faces by young infants. *Child Development, 47*, 523–7.

Maurer, D., & Young, R. (1983). Newborns' following of natural and distorted arrangements of facial features. *Infant Behavior and Development, 6*, 127–31.

McCabe, A., & Peterson, C. (1985). A naturalistic study of the production of causal connectives by children. *Journal of Child Language, 12*, 145–59.

McColgan, K. L., & McCormack, T. (2008). Searching and planning: Young children's reasoning about past and future event sequences. *Child Development, 79*, 1477–97.

McCormack, T., & Hoerl, C. (2005). Children's reasoning about the causal significance of the temporal order of events. *Developmental Psychology, 41*, 54–63.

McCormack, T., & Hoerl, C. (2008). Temporal decentering and the development of temporal concepts. *Language Learning, 58*, 89–113.

McGarrigle, J., & Donaldson, M. (1974). Conservation accidents. *Cognition: International Journal of Cognitive Psychology, 3*, 341–50.

McGarrigle, J., Grieve, R., & Hughes, M. (1978). Interpreting inclusion: A contribution to the study of the child's cognitive and linguistic development. *Journal of Experimental Child Psychology, 26*, 528–50.

McGonigle, B., & Chalmers, M. (1984). The selective impact of question form and input mode on the Symbolic Distance Effect in children. *Journal of Experimental Child Psychology, 37*, 525–54.

McNeill, D. (1966). Developmental psycholinguistics. In F. Smith & G. A. Miller (eds.), *The Genesis of Language: A Psycholinguistic Approach*. Cambridge, MA: MIT Press.

McShane, J. (1980). *Learning to Talk*. Cambridge: Cambridge University Press.

Meints, K., Plunkett, K., Harris, P. l. L., & Dimmock, D. (2002). What is 'on' and 'under' for 15-, 18- and 24-month-olds? Typicality effects in early comprehension of spatial prepositions. *British Journal of Developmental Psychology, 20*, 113–30.

Meltzoff, A. N. (1988). Infant imitation after a 1-week delay: Long-term memory for novel acts and multiple stimuli. *Developmental Psychology, 24*, 470–6.

Meltzoff, A. N. (1995). Understanding the intentions of others: Re-enactment of intended acts by 18-month-old children. *Developmental Psychology, 31*, 838–50.

Meltzoff, A. N., & Borton, R. W. (1979). Intermodal matching by human neonates. *Nature, 282*, 403–4.

Meltzoff, A. N., & Moore, M. K. (1977). Imitation of facial and manual gestures by human neonates. *Science, 198*, 75–8.

Meltzoff A. N., Moore M. K. (1994) Imitation, memory, and the representation of persons. *Infant Behavior and Development, 17*, 83–99.

Mintz, T. H., & Gleitman, L. R. (2002). Adjectives really do modify nouns: The incremental and restricted nature of early adjective acquisition. *Cognition, 84*, 267–93.

Mix, K. S. (1999). Similarity and numerical equivalence appearances count. *Cognitive Development, 14*, 269–97.

Mondloch, C. J., Geldart, S., Maurer, D., & Le Grand, R. (2003). Developmental changes in face processing skills. *Journal of Experimental Child Psychology, 86*, 67–84.

Montgomery, J. W., Polunenko, A., & Marinellie, S. A. (2009). Role of working memory in children's understanding spoken narrative: A preliminary investigation. *Applied Psycholinguistics, 30*, 485–509.

Moon, C., Bever, T. G., & Fifer, W. P. (1992). Canonical and non-canonical syllable discrimination by two-day-old infants. *Journal of Child Language, 19*, 1–17.

Moon, C., Cooper, R. P., & Fifer, W. P. (1993). Two-day old infants prefer their native language. *Infant Behavior and Development, 16*, 495–500.

Moon, C., & Fifer, W. P. (1990). Syllables as signals for 2-day-old infants. *Infant Behavior and Development, 13*, 377–90.

Moore, M. K., & Meltzoff, A. N. (2008). Factors affecting infants' manual search for occluded objects and the genesis of object permanence. *Infant Behavior and Development, 31*, 168–80.

Morissette, P., Ricard, M., & Gouin-Decarie, T. (1995). Joint visual attention and pointing in infancy: A longitudinal study of comprehension. *British Journal of Developmental Psychology, 13*, 163–77.

Morongellio, B. A., Fenwick, K. D., & Chance, G. (1998). Crossmodal learning in newborn infants: Inferences about properties of auditory-visual events. *Infant Behavior and Development, 21*, 543–53.

Morton, J., & Johnson, M. (1991). CONSPEC and CONLERN: A two-process theory of infant face recognition. *Psychological Review, 98*, 164–81.

Moutier, S., Plagne-Cayeux, S., Melot, A-M., & Houdé, O. (2006). Syllogistic reasoning and belief-bias inhibition in school children: Evidence from a negative priming paradigm. *Developmental Science, 9*, 166–72.

Muir, D., Clifton, R., & Clarkson, M. (1989). The development of a human auditory localization response: A U-shaped function. *Canadian Journal of Psychology, 43*, 199–216.

Muir, D., & Field, J. (1979). Newborn infants orient to sounds. *Child Development, 50*, 431–6.

Mukamel, R., Ekstrom, A. D., Kaplan, J., Iacoboni, M., & Fried, I. (2010). Single-neuron responses in humans during execution and observation of actions. *Current Biology, 20*, 1–7.

Murphy, C. M. (1978). Pointing in the context of a shared activity. *Child Development, 49*, 371–80.

Nelson, K. E., & Kosslyn, S. M. (1976). Recognition of previously labeled or unlabeled pictures by 5-year-olds and adults. *Journal of Experimental Child Psychology, 21*, 40–5.

Newcombe, N., & Fox, N. A. (1994). Infantile amnesia: Through a glass darkly. *Child Development, 65*, 31–40.

Nunes, T., & Bryant, P. (1996). *Children Doing Mathematics*. Oxford: Blackwell.

O'Hearn, K. C., Asato, M., Ordaz, S., & Luna, B. (2008). Neurodevelopment and executive function in autism. *Development and Psychopathology, 20*, 1103–32.

Oller, D., & Eilers, R. E. (1988). The role of ausition in infant babbling. *Child Development, 59*, 441–9.

Oller, D., Eilers, R. E., Bull, D. H., & Carney, A. E. (1985). Prespeech vocalizations of a deaf infant: A comparison with normal metaphonological development. *Journal of Speech & Hearing Research, 28*, 47–63.

Pasnak, R., Brown, K., Kurkjian, M., Mattran, K., & et al. (1987). Cognitive gains through training on classification, seriation, and conservation. *Genetic, Social, and General Psychology Monographs, 113*, 293–321.

Patterson, M. L., & Werker, J. F. (2003). Two-month-old infants match phonetic information in lips and voice. *Developmental Science, 6*, 191–6.

Pennington, B. F., & Ozonoff, S. (1996). Executive functions and developmental psychopathology. *Child Psychology & Psychiatry & Allied Disciplines, 37*, 51–87.

Perner, J., Leekham, S. R., & Wimmer, H. (1987). Three year olds' difficulty with false belief: The case for a conceptual deficit. *British Journal of Developmental Psychology, 5*, 125–37.

Perner, J., & Wimmer, H. (1985). 'John thinks that Mary thinks that': Attribution of second-order beliefs by 5- to 10-year-old children. *Journal of Experimental Child Psychology, 39*, 437–71.

Piaget, J. (1928). *Judgement and Reasoning in the Child*. London: Routledge and Kegan Paul.

Piaget, J. (1962). *Play, Dreams and Imitation in Childhood*. London: Routledge and Kegan Paul.

Piaget , J. (1969). *The Child's Conception of Time*. London: Routledge and Kegan Paul.

Piaget , J. (1971). *Biology and Knowledge*. Edinburgh: Edinburgh University Press.

Piaget , J. (1972). *The Child and Reality*. London: Muller.

Piaget , J. (1973). *The Child's Conception of the World*. London: Granada Publishing.

Piaget, J., & Inhelder, B. (1967). *The Child's Conception of Space*. London: Norton.

Pine, J. M. (1994). Environmental correlates of variation in lexical style: Interactional style and the structure of the input. *Applied Psycholinguistics, 15*, 355–70.

Pine, J. M. (1995). Variation in vocabulary development as a function of birth order. *Child Development, 66*, 272–81.

Pine, J. M., & Lieven, E. V. (1993). Reanalysing rote-learned phrases: Individual differences in the transition to multi-word speech. *Journal of Child Language, 20*, 551–71.

Pine, J. M., Lieven, E. V., & Rowland, C. F. (1997). Stylistic variation at the 'single-word' stage: Relations between maternal speech characteristics and children's vocabulary composition and usage. *Child Development, 68*, 807–19.

Pinker, S. (1994). *The Language Instinct: The New Science of Language and Mind*. London: Allen Lane/The Penguin Press.

Pinker, S. (2011). *Words and Rules: The Ingredients of Language*. London: Harper Collins.

Poeppel, D., & Hickok, G. (2004). Introduction: Towards a new functional anatomy of language. *Cognition, 92*, 1–12.

Povinelli, D. J., Landry, A. M., Theall, L. A., Clark, B. R., & Castille, C. M. (1999). Development of young children's understanding that the recent past is causally bound to the present. *Developmental Psychology, 35*, 1426–39.

Pozzulo, J. D., & Lindsay, R. (1998). Identification accuracy of children versus adults: A meta-analysis. *Law and Human Behavior, 22*, 549–70.

Premack, D., & Woodruff, G. (1978). Does the chimpanzee have a theory of mind? *Behavioral and Brain Sciences, 1*, 515–26.

Provins, K. A. (1992). Early infant motor asymmetries and handedness: A critical evaluation of the evidence. *Developmental Neuropsychology, 8*, 325–65.

Provins, K. A. (1997). Handedness and speech: A critical reappraisal of the role of genetic andenvironmental factors in the cerebral lateralization of function. *Psychological Review, 104*, 554–71.

Pruden, S. M., Levine, S. C., & Huttenlocher, J. (2011). Children's spatial thinking: Does talk about the spatial world matter? *Developmental Science, 14*, 1417–30.

Quon, E., & Atance, C. M. (2010). A comparison of preschoolers' memory, knowledge, and anticipation of events. *Journal of Cognition and Development, 11*, 37–60.

Rafetseder, E., Schwitalla, M., & Perner, J. (2013). Counterfactual reasoning: From childhood to adulthood. *Journal of Experimental Child Psychology, 114*, 389–404.

Redcay, E., Haist, F., & Courchesne, E. (2008). Functional neuroimaging of speech perception during a pivotal period in language acquisition. *Developmental Science*, 11, 237–52.

Reese, H. W. (1968). *The Perception of Stimulus Relations. Discrimination Learning and Transposition*. New York, NY: Academic Press.

Rempel-Clower, N. L. (2007). Role of orbito-frontal cortex connections in emotion. *Annals of the New York Academy of Sciences, 1121*, 72–86.

Ribordy, F., Jabes, A., Banta Lavenex, P., & Lavenex, P. (2013). Development of allocentric spatial memory abilities in children from 18 months to 5 years of age. *Cognitive Psychology, 66*, 1–29.

Richards, B. J., & Robinson, P. (1993). Environmental correlates of child copula verb growth. *Journal of Child Language, 20*, 343–62.

Rigato, S., Menon, E., Johnson, M. H., Faraguna, D., & Farroni, T. (2011). Direct gaze may modulate face recognition in newborns. *Infant and Child Development, 20*, 20–34.

Riley, M., Greeno, J. G., & Heller, J. L. (1983). Development of children's problem solving ability in arithmetic. In H. Ginsberg (ed.), *The Development of Mathemtaical Thinking*. New York, NY: Academic Press, pp. 153–96.

Rizzolatti, G., Fogassi, L., & Gallese, V. (2001). Neurophysiological mechanisms underlying the understanding and imitation of action. *Nature Reviews Neuroscience, 2*, 661–70.

Roodenrys, S., Hulme, C., & Brown, G. (1993). The development of short-term memory span: Separable effects of speech rate and long-term memory. *Journal of Experimental Child Psychology, 56*, 431–42.

Rosch, E. (2002). Principles of categorization. In *Foundations of Cognitive Psychology: Core Readings*. Cambridge, MA: MIT Press, pp. 251–70.

Rose, S. A., & Blank, M. (1974). The potency of context in children's cognition: An illustration through conservation. *Child Development, 45*, 499–502.

Rose, S. A., Gottfried, A. W., & Bridger, W. H. (1983). Infants' cross-modal transfer from solid objects to their graphic representations. *Child Development, 54*, 686–94.

Rosinski, R. R. (1976). Texture gradient effectiveness in the perception of surface slant. *Journal of Experimental Child Psychology, 22*, 261–71.

Routh, D. K. (1967). Conditioning of vocal response differentiation in infants. *Developmental Psychology, 1*, 219–26.

Rovee-Collier, C. K., & Capatides, J. B. (1979). Positive behavioral contrast in 3-month-old infants on multiple conjugate reinforcement schedules. *Journal of the Experimental Analysis of Behavior, 32*, 15–27.

Rowland, C. F. (2007). Explaining errors in children's questions. *Cognition, 104*, 106–34.

Rowland, C. F., Pine, J. M., Lieven, E. V., & Theakston, A. L. (2005). The incidence of error in young children's wh-questions. *Journal of Speech, Language, and Hearing Research, 48*, 384–404.

Russell, J., Mauthner, N., Sharpe, S., & Tidswell, T. (1991). The 'windows task' as a measure of strategic deception in preschoolers and autistic subjects. *British Journal of Developmental Psychology, 9*, 331–49.

Sachs, J., & Devin, J. (1976). Young children's use of age-appropriate speech styles in social interaction and role-playing. *Journal of Child Language, 3*, 81–98.

Samuels, A., & Taylor, M. (1994). Children's ability to distinguish fantasy events from real-life events. *British Journal of Developmental Psychology, 12*, 417–27.

Sandhofer, C., & Smith, L. B. (2007). Learning adjectives in the real world: How learning nouns impedes learning adjectives. *Language Learning and Development, 3*, 233–67.

Sarnecka, B. W., & Carey, S. (2008). How counting represents number: What children must learn and when they learn it. *Cognition, 108*, 662–74.

Schnall, S., & Gattis, M. (1998). Transitive inference by visual reasoning. In M. A. Gernsbacher, & S. J. Derry (eds.), *Proceedings of the Twentieth Annual Conference of the Cognitive Science Society*. Hillsdale, NJ: Lawrence Erlbaum.

Schwarzer, G. (2002). Processing of facial and non-facial visual stimuli in 2–5-year-old children. *Infant and Child Development, 11*, 253–69.

Semenov, L. A., Chernova, N. D., & Bondarko, V. M. (2000). Measurement of visual acuity and crowding effect in 3–9-year-old children. *Human Physiology, 26*, 21–6.

Serkhane, J., Schwartz, J., Boe, L., Davis, B., & Matyear, C. (2007). Infants' vocalizations analyzed with an articulatory model: A preliminary report. *Journal of Phonetics, 35*, 321–40.

Shiffrin, R. M., & Schneider, W. (1977). Controlled and automatic human information processing: II. Perceptual learning, automatic attending and a general theory. *Psychological Review, 84*, 127–90.

Shiller, D. M., & Rochon, M.-L. (2014). Auditory-perceptual learning improves speech motor adaptation in children. *Journal of Experimental Psychology: Human Perception and Performance, 40*, 1308–15.

Shore, D. I., Burack, J. A., Miller, D., Joseph, S., & Enns, J. T. (2006). The development of change detection. *Developmental Science, 9*, 490–7.

Singer-Freeman, K. E., & Goswami, U. (2001). Does half a pizza equal half a box of chocolates? Proportional matching in an analogy task. *Cognitive Development, 16*, 811–29.

Singh, L., Morgan, J. L., & Best, C. T. (2002). Infants' listening preferences: Baby talk or happy talk? *Infancy, 3*, 365–94.

Siqueland, E. R., & DeLucia, C. A. (1969). Visual reinforcement of nonnutritive sucking in human infants. *Science, 165*, 1144–6.

Siqueland, E. R., & Lipsitt, L. P. (1966). Conditioned head-turning in human newborns. *Journal of Experimental Child Psychology, 3*, 356–76.

Slater, A., Mattock, A., & Brown, E. (1990). Size constancy at birth: Newborn infants' response to retinal and real size. *Journal of Experimental Child Psychology, 51*, 395–405.

Slobin, D. I. (1971). *Psycholinguistics*. Glenview, IL: Scott/Foresman.

Slobin, D. I. (1973). Cognitive pre-requisites for the acquisition of grammar. In D. I. Slobin (ed.), *Studies of Child Language Development*. New York, NY: Rinehart and Winston.

Slobin, D. I., & Welsh, C. A. (1973). Elicited imitation as a research tool in developmental psycholinguistics. In C. A. Ferguson, & D. I. Slobin (eds.), *Studies of Child Language*. New York, NY: Holt, Rinehart and Winston.

Smiley, S. S., & Brown, A. L. (1979). Conceptual preference for thematic or taxonomic relations: A nonmonotonic age trend from preschool to old age. *Journal of Experimental Child Psychology*, *28*, 249–57.

Smith, L. B., Thelen, E., Totzer, R., & McLin, D. (1999). Knowing in the context of acting. *Psychological Review*, *106*, 235–60.

Smith, N. V. (1973). *The Acquisition of Phonology*. Cambridge: Cambridge University Press.

Snow, C. E. (1977). The development of conversation between mothers and babies. *Journal of Child Language*, *4*, 1–22.

Sommerville, J. A., Woodward, A. L., & Needham, A. (2005). Action experience alters 3-month-old infants' perception of others' actions. *Cognition*, *96*, B1–11.

Spelke, E. (1976). Infants' intermodal perception of events. *Cognitive Psychology*, *8*, 553–60.

Spence, K. W. (1936). The nature of discrimination learning in animals. *Psychological Review*, *43*, 427–49.

Spinillo, A. G., & Bryant, P. (1991). Children's proportional judgments: The importance of 'half'. *Child Development*, *62*, 427–40.

Stoel-Gammon, C., & Otomo, K. (1986). Babbling development of hearing-impaired and normally hearing subjects. *Journal of Speech & Hearing Disorders*, *51*, 33–41.

Sullivan, R. M., Taborsky-Barba, S., Mendoza, R., Itano, A., Leon, M., Cotman, C. W., Lott, I. (1991). Olfactory classical conditioning in neonates. *Pediatrics*, *87*, 511–18.

Tanz, C. (1980). *Studies in the Acquisition of Deictic terms*. Cambridge: Cambridge University Press.

te Velde, A. F., van der Kamp, J., & Savelsbergh, G. J. (2008). Five- to twelve-year-olds' control of movement velocity in a dynamic collision avoidance task. *British Journal of Developmental Psychology*, *26*, 33–50.

Thatcher, R. W. (1992). Cyclic cortical reorganization during early childhood. *Brain and Cognition*, *20*, 24–50.

Thomson, J. (2007). Promoting the development of pedestrian traffic skills in young children. In G.-J. Pepping, & M. A Grealy (eds). *Closing the Gap: The Scientific Writings of David N. Lee.* Mahwah, NJ: Lawrence Erlbaum.

Thomson, J., & Chapman, R. S. (1977). Who is 'Daddy' revisited: The status of two-year-olds' overextended words in use and comprehension. *Journal of Child Language, 4*, 359–75.

Timmermans, B., Windey, B., & Cleeremans, A. (2010). Experiencing more complexity than we can tell: Commentary on Lamme. *Cognitive Neuroscience*, *1*, 229–30.

Tomasello, M. (1987). Learning to use prepositions: A case study. *Journal of Child Language*, *14*, 79–98.

Tomasello, M., & Akhtar, N. (1995). Two-year-olds use pragmatic cues to differentiate reference to objects and actions. *Cognitive Development, 10*, 201–24.

Tomasello, M., & Farrar, M. J. (1986). Joint attention and early language. *Child Development, 57*, 1454–63.

Tomasello, M., & Kruger, A. C. (1992). Joint attention on actions: Acquiring verbs in ostensive and non-ostensive contexts. *Journal of Child Language, 19*, 311–35.

Tomasello, M., & Mannle, S. (1985). Pragmatics of sibling speech to one-year-olds. *Child Development, 56*, 911–17.

Tomasello, M., & Olguin, R. (1993). Twenty-three-month-old children have a grammatical category of noun. *Cognitive Development, 8*, 451–64.

Tomasello, M., & Todd, J. (1983). Joint attention and lexical acquisition style. *First Language, 4*, 197–211.

Tomonaga, M., & Matsuzawa, T. (2002). Enumeration of briefly presented items by the chimpanzee (*Pan troglodytes*) and humans (*Homo sapiens*). *Animal Learning & Behavior, 30*, 143–57.

Tulving, E. (1972). Episodic and semantic memory. In E. Tulving, & W. Donaldson (eds.), *Organization of Memory*. Oxford: Academic Press, p. xiii.

Turati, C., Simion, F., Milani, I., & Umilta, C. (2002). Newborns' preference for faces: What Is crucial? *Developmental Psychology, 38*, 875–82.

Turner, J. E., Henry, L. A., & Smith, P. T. (2000). The development of the use of long-term knowledge to assist short-term recall. *The Quarterly Journal of Experimental Psychology A: Human Experimental Psychology, 53A*, 457–78.

Uttal, D. H., & Wellman, H. M. (1989). Young children's representation of spatial information acquired from maps. *Developmental Psychology, 25*, 128–38.

Uzgiris, I. C., Benson, J. B., Kruper, J. C., & Vasek, M. E. (1989). Contextual influences on imitative interactions between mothers anmd infants. In J. Lockman, & N. Hazen (eds.), *Action in a Social Context: Perspectives on Early Development.* New York, NY: Plenum.

Uzgiris, I. C., & Lucas, T. C. (1978). Observations and experimental methods in studies of object cioncept development in infancy. In G. P. Sackett (ed.), *Observing Behavior*, Vol. 1. Baltimore, OH: University Park Press.

Volkmar, F. R., & Paul, R. (eds.). (2005). *Handbook of Autism and Pervasive Developmental Disorders.* Hoboken, NJ: John Wiley.

Vurpillot, E. (1968). The development of scanning strategies and their relation to visual differentiation. *Journal of Experimental Child Psychology, 6*, 632–50.

Vurpillot, E. (1976). *The Visual World of the Child.* London: Allen and Unwin

Vygotsky, L. S. (1962). *Thought and Language*. Cambridge, MA: MIT Press.

Wahler, R. G. (1969). Infant social development: Some experimental analyses of an infant-mother interaction during the the first year of life. *Journal of Experimental Child Psychology*, *7*, 101–13.

Walker, R. F., & Murachver, T. (2012). Representation and theory of mind development. *Developmental Psychology*, *48*, 509–20.

Wallace, D. B., Franklin, M. B., & Keegan, R. T. (1994). The observing eye: A century of baby diaries. *Human Development*, *34*, 1–29.

Walton, G. E., Armstrong, E. S., & Bower, T. (1998). Newborns learn to identify a face in eight/tenths of a second? *Developmental Science*, *1*, 79–84.

Wang, S., & Baillargeon, R. (2008). Can infants be 'taught' to attend to a new physical variable in an event category? The case of height in covering events. *Cognitive Psychology*, *56*, 284–326.

Wason, P. C. (1966). Reasoning. In B. M. Foss (ed.), *New Horizons in Psychology*. Harmondsworth: Penguin.

Waterhouse, L. H. (2013). *Rethinking Autism: Variation and Complexity*. London: Academic Press.

Waxman, S. R., & Namy, L. L. (1997). Challenging the notion of a thematic preference in young children. *Developmental Psychology*, *33*, 555–67.

Weigelt, S., Koldewyn, K., Dilks, D. D., Balas, B., McKone, E., & Kanwisher, N. (2014). Domain-specific development of face memory but not face perception. *Developmental Science*, *17*, 47–58.

Weigelt, M., & Schack, T. (2010). The development of end-state comfort planning in preschool children. *Experimental Psychology*, *57*, 476–82.

Weisberg, D. P., & Beck, S. R. (2012). The development of children's regret and relief. *Cognition and Emotion*, *26*, 820–35.

Wellman, H. M., Cross, D., & Watson, J. (2001). Meta-analysis of theory-of-mind development: The truth about false belief. *Child Development*, *72*, 655–84.

Werker, J. F., & Tees, R. C. (2002). Cross-language speech perception: Evidence for perceptual reorganization during the first year of life. *Infant Behavior and Development*, *25*, 121–33.

Werner, H. (1948). *Comparative Psychology of Mental Development*. New York, NY: Harper.

Wertheimer, M. (1961). Psychomotor co-ordination of auditory-visual space at birth. *Science*, *134*, 1692.

White, S. H., & Plum, G. E. (1964). Eye movement photography during children's discrimination learning. *Journal of Experimental Child Psychology*, *1*, 327–38.

Wilcox, T., Woods, R., Tuggy, L., & Napoli, R. (2006). Shake, rattle, and ... one or two objects? Young infants' use of auditory information to individuate objects. *Infancy*, 9, 97–123.

Wilkinson, N., Paikan, A., Gredebäck, G., Rea, F., & Metta, G. (2014). Staring us in the face? An embodied theory of innate face preference. *Developmental Science, 17,* 809–25.

Willatts, P. (1999). Development of means-end behavior in young infants. *Developmental Psychology, 35,* 651–67.

Williams, S. E., & Horst, J. S. (2014). Goodnight book: Sleep consolidation improves word learning via storybooks. *Frontiers in Psychology, 5.* doi: 10.3389/fpsyg.2014.00184

Wimmer, H., & Perner, J. (1983). Beliefs about beliefs: Representation and constraining function of wrong beliefs in young children's understanding of deception. *Cognition, 13,* 103–28.

Wood, C., Kemp, N., & Waldron, S. (2014). Exploring the longitudinal relationships between the use of grammar in text messaging and performance on grammatical tasks. *British Journal of Developmental Psychology, 32* (4), 415–29.

Wohlwill, J. (1965). Texture of the stimulus field and age as variables in the perception of relative distance in photographic slides. *Journal of Experimental Child Psychology 2,* 163–77.

Woll, B., & Kyle, J. G. (1989). Communication and language development in children of deaf parents. In S. von Tetzchner, L. S. Siegel, & L. Smith (eds.), *The Social and Cognitive Aspects of Normal and Atypical Language Development.* Springer Series in Cognitive Development. New York, NY: Springer-Verlag, pp. 129–144.

Wykes, T. (1983). The role of inferences in children's comprehension of pronouns. *Journal of Experimental Child Psychology, 35,* 180–93.

Yates, D. J., & Bemner, G. (1988). Conditions for Piagetian Stage IV search errors in a task using transparent occluders. *Infant Behavior and Development, 11,* 411–17.

Yermolayeva, Y., & Rakison, D. H. (2014). Connectionist modeling of developmental changes in infancy: Approaches, challenges, and contributions. *Psychological Bulletin, 140,* 224–55.

Yingfang, M., & Chunyan, G. (2006). Dissociations between implicit and explicit memory: An ERP study of face recognition. *Acta Psychologica Sinica, 38,* 15–21.

Yonas, A., Arterberry, M. E., & Granrud, C. E. (1987). Four-month-old infants' sensitivity to binocular and kinetic information for three-dimensional-object shape. *Child Development, 58,* 910–17.

Yonas, A., & Hagen, M. (1973). Effects of static and motion parallax depth information on perception of size in children and adults. *Journal of Experimental Child Psychology, 15,* 254–65.

Young, R. M. (1976). *Seriation by Children: An Artificial Intelligence Analysis of a Piagetian Task.* Basel: Birkhauser.

Younger, B. A., & Cohen, L. B. (1983). Infant perception of correlations among attributes. *Child Development, 54,* 858–69.

Younger, B. A., & Cohen, L. B. (1986). Developmental change in infants' perception of correlations among attributes. *Child Development, 57,* 803–15.

Younger, B. A., & Fearing, D. D. (1999). Parsing items into separate categories: Developmental change in infant categorization. *Child Development, 70,* 291–303.

Zaporozhets, A. V. (2002). On the active nature of the visual perception of an object. *Journal of Russian and East European Psychology, 40,* 13–21.

Ziegler, F. V., & Acquah, D. K. (2013). Stepping into someone else's shoes: Children create spatial mental models from the protagonist's point of view. *European Journal of Developmental Psychology, 10,* 546–62.

Zinchenko, V., Chzhi-Tsin, V., & Tarakanov, V. (1962). Formation and development of perceptive activity. *Voprosy Psychologii,* 3, 1–14.

INDEX